T0355133

Rhythm Man

OXFORD CULTURAL BIOGRAPHIES

Gary Giddins, Series Editor

Rhythm Man

Chick Webb and the Beat That
Changed America

STEPHANIE STEIN CREASE

OXFORD
UNIVERSITY PRESS

Oxford University Press is a department of the University of Oxford. It furthers the University's objective of excellence in research, scholarship, and education by publishing worldwide. Oxford is a registered trade mark of Oxford University Press in the UK and certain other countries.

Published in the United States of America by Oxford University Press
198 Madison Avenue, New York, NY 10016, United States of America.

© Oxford University Press 2023

Library of Congress Cataloging-in-Publication Data
Names: Stein Crease, Stephanie, author.
Title: Rhythm man : Chick Webb and the beat that changed America /
Stephanie Stein Crease.
Description: [1.] | New York : Oxford University Press, 2023. |
Series: Cultural biographies series |
Includes bibliographical references and index. |
Identifiers: LCCN 2022053532 (print) | LCCN 2022053533 (ebook) |
ISBN 9780190055691 (hardback) | ISBN 9780190055714 (epub) | ISBN 9780190055721
Subjects: LCSH: Webb, Chick. | Drummers (Musicians)—United States—Biography. |
Jazz musicians—United States—Biography. | Band directors—United States—Biography.
Classification: LCC ML419.W383 S74 2023 (print) | LCC ML419.W383 (ebook) |
DDC 786.9092 [B]—dc23/eng/20221104
LC record available at https://lccn.loc.gov/2022053532
LC ebook record available at https://lccn.loc.gov/2022053533

DOI: 10.1093/oso/9780190055691.001.0001

Printed by Sheridan Books, Inc., United States of America

To Robert, a dancer-writer, who danced through this and much more.

Contents

Foreword

The series of Oxford Cultural Biographies was launched with the specific idea of telling about the lives of artists whose stories had not been told, with particular attention to those whose accomplishments were deeply shadowed by a mythology of apocrypha, uncorroborated tales, and legends too good to be true. From the first, William Henry Webb was high on my list. His brief life was a succession of astonishments, as befits a man who is remembered even today as the King of the Savoy. Unequivocally beloved by fans and peers, this dwarfed hunchback, mangled by spinal tuberculosis, helped to launch the era of big band jazz as its premiere drummer, a matchless discoverer of talent, and a visionary orchestra leader. His impact would be felt long after his death and that of the Swing Era and of Harlem's Savoy Ballroom, where he reigned.

Years ago, in an essay on Chick Webb, I wrote that his story cried out for a novelistic scope and nuance. But I came to suspect that there might be too much of that and not nearly enough in the way of an accurate accounting. I was a kid the first time I heard albums of records he had made for Decca and Columbia, and the rattling excitement of his music overwhelmed me. Those classic performances are now nine decades old, and their elation still shines through, especially the percussion breaks. Elvin Jones once singled out Webb's recording of "Liza" (in a conversation with the writer Chip Stern), calling it "the most fascinating drum solo I'd ever heard, and I don't think there's anything to compare with that."

But who to take on the challenge? Webb died in 1939, and those with living memories of him could be counted on the fingers of one hand. Many people knew that he gave an unknown teenager singer named Ella Fitzgerald her start, or about the time Gene Krupa salaamed to him at the Savoy, or of Webb's influence on swing repertoire, instrumentation, generic crossovers, and every aspect of drumming. Yet even basic elements of his story remained obscure: When was he born? How did the era's racial and economic politics influence the music business? What happened in the controversial battle of bands involving Count Basie? What kind of man was Chick really? And what became of his widow, the mysterious Sally Webb?

In 2002, Stephanie Stein Crease published her superb biography of Gil Evans, *Out of the Cool*. She knew music, big bands, and life-telling, and was obviously a solid writer and a no-stone-unturned researcher. When I approached her, she had another subject in mind, but I asked her to consider Webb. She was instantly taken with the idea, but instead of rushing out a standard proposal, she devoted three years to research, making certain a story was there to tell. She would return from trips to Baltimore and deep dives into African American newspapers with startling details about his early years, not least his birth date, which had been debated by jazz writers for seventy years and is carved incorrectly on his tombstone. Crease reveals the deepest feeling for Webb's humanity I have seen anywhere—with not a little of the novelistic scope and nuance I looked for long ago—but her portrait is always underscored by her staunch and corroborated legwork, accentuating his genuinely heroic stature. She adds telling details to the stories we think we know and takes us into areas that most jazz portraits ignore.

Crease's Chick Webb is inspirational in part because beyond his physical maladies he had to battle for his artistic freedom, not just with detractors, but with ardent, pioneering supporters who believed they knew better than he how to present his music. Her cast of supporting characters brings us into the mechanics of show business: the managerial offices, the biases of publicists and critics, the purity debate of art versus commerce, and the senseless crises that ensued. You'll meet legends of jazz boosterism such as Helen Oakley and John Hammond in ways you haven't before. You might assume that everyone cheered when Chick and Ella (and a hip white arranger named Van Alexander) created one of the best-selling records ever, "A-Tisket, A-Tasket," but that isn't the way it happened.

The lede in the *Baltimore Sun*'s coverage of his funeral rites reads: "The Kingdom of Swing played a dirge yesterday. They buried Chick Webb, the little crippled colored boy from East Baltimore who became—many say—the world's greatest drummer." Twelve hundred people filled the Waters African Methodist Episcopal Church, and an estimated eight to ten thousand more jammed the streets outside. Stephanie Stein Crease tells Chick's story with sensitivity and rigor, in what will surely be greeted as a significant contribution to the literature of American music.

Gary Giddins, Series Editor

Acknowledgments

Many individuals helped me with the research, sources and support needed to complete this biography, including long-time jazz associates and authors, musicians, historians, friends, photographers, archivists, collectors, and the staff of several institutions. My gratitude is endless, and my love of this music and the people who created it over generations is vast. This biography was completed during the COVID-19 pandemic, starting in spring 2020. Luckily, I had conducted substantial research before the pandemic, which disrupted numerous planned visits to contacts, research libraries and special collections in New York, Baltimore, and other places. The only bright side was that, during those early challenging months, I was fortunate to be relatively isolated at home, and able to create my own writer's retreat. During that time, I spoke with people who might have been too busy to talk to me in other circumstances, and who have remained supportive of my telling Webb's story. I hope that I haven't inadvertently omitted anyone in these acknowledgments; if so, please accept this as your acknowledgment, too.

My profound gratitude goes to several Baltimoreans who helped me research the city's rich Black musical history, culture, and communities: to historian and archivist Philip Merrill, and Veronica Carr and Betty Merrill of Nanny Jack & Co., who guided me towards numerous off-the-beaten-path resources; community organizer Ron Miles, founder of the Ralph J. Young-Chick Webb Council, who has worked tirelessly to preserve the importance of the Chick Webb Memorial Recreational Center, soon to be renovated and developed as a multi-purpose center; Professor Alfred Prettyman, philosopher, whose father Edward Prettyman was a prominent orchestra leader in Baltimore from the 1920s to the 1960s; Camay Calloway and Peter Brooks Calloway, close relatives of Cab and Blanche Calloway, whose family's musical legacy, like the Prettyman's and Chick Webb's, owes much to the Black musical heritage of Baltimore as a generative center for early jazz developments.

Very special acknowledgements go to others who shared their insights, knowledge, and resources. Film Director Jeff Kaufman, whose 2012 documentary, *The Savoy King: Chick Webb and the Music that Changed America*, preserved and deepened Chick's story when his legacy was disappearing, gave me access to some of his source material and interviews. Kaufman's research about Webb was among the most extensive conducted in years, and he was fortunate to interview key people who have since passed away. Many thanks as well to Jeff's partner, Executive Producer Marcia Ross. Equally significant for my early work on this project was reading *Go Harlem: Chick Webb and his Dancing Audience during the Great Depression* (2014), the doctoral thesis by musicologist and dance historian Dr. Christi Jay Wells (f/k/a Christopher J. Wells). Well's meticulously researched work explores Webb's music and career, and its impact and relation to the Savoy, the Great Depression, the Harlem community and popular music and dance culture. Wells's subsequent articles and talks about Webb have also been terrific resources for this project.

Judith Tick, author of the new biography *Becoming Ella Fitzgerald: The Jazz Singer Who Transformed American Song*, shared anecdotes, sources and insights about Fitzgerald. We exchanged information about Fitzgerald and Webb and frequently discussed their innovations, their relationship, and their music as they rose to national fame together. Robert O'Meally, who continues to probe the far reaches of the Harlem Renaissance, helped broaden my own scope continually with his wide-ranging lectures and writings about visual artists, writers, and musicians. Chris McKay, researcher and former Schomburg archivist, provided invaluable assistance in uncovering new research about Webb's extended family, particularly about Chick's widow, Sally Webb. Loren Schoenberg, founding scholar of the National Museum of Jazz in Harlem, was an ally for this project from the outset and always patient as, time and again, he generously revisited information about Webb and his peers' activities, music, and legacies.

Several institutions and their staff were vital to this project. The Schomburg Center for Research in Black Culture was one. Brent Edwards, Director of the Schomburg's Scholars-in-Residence Program, and the Schomburg's Division Curators and entire staff did everything possible to open its doors to me and to the Fall 2020 cohort of Scholars-in-Residence in between COVID surges. Very special thanks to the curators and staff who helped us continue our research when the archives were only partially opened: Bridgett Pride, Manuscripts, Archives, and Rare Books Division; Maira Liriano, Jean Blackwell Hutson Research and Reference Division; Michael Mery and Linden Anderson, Photographs and Prints Division; Andrea L. Battleground and Shola Lynch, Moving Images and Recorded Sound Division.

To the New York Library for the Performing Arts: very special thanks to David McMullin, Librarian of the Music and Recorded Sound Division, who assisted me with my research early on; Jessica L. Wood, Assistant Curator, Music and Recorded Sound; Nailah Holmes, Associate Manager, Research Access Services; and Jeremy Megraw, Photograph Librarian, Billy Rose Theatre Division. My sincere appreciation to the Music Division and staff for expanded digital services and continued help during COVID closures and partial closures of 2020–2021.

The Institute of Jazz Studies, at Rutgers University in Newark, New Jersey, was one of my first stops for researching this biography. I was very grateful to receive the Berger-Carter-Berger Fellowship in 2018, which allowed me to dive deeply into Jazz Oral History archives at the IJS, listen to many extensive taped interviews before they were digitized, and explore other materials. Many thanks to Tad Hershorn, archivist (now retired), who helped me with initial resources and contacts, and continued gratitude to archivists Vincent Pelote and Elizabeth Surles.

Many individuals, archivists, and staff at other organizations and musical landmarks were generous with additional material and their time and attention. Very special thanks to Maria Lindley and Francis Dance, daughter and son of Helen Oakley Dance, the pioneering female jazz journalist, record producer and concert promoter; Garvin Bushell, Jr., son of one of Webb's musicians Garvin Bushell; Joyce Hansen, author and daughter of Harlem photographer Austin Hansen; Cliff Malloy, photo archivist; and Michael and Judy Randolph of PoPsie Photos (WIlliam "PoPsie" Randolph, photographer); Jonathan Karp, Binghamton University, SUNY; Brad San Martin, Digital Archivist, Apollo Theater; Phil Gold, another resource about the Apollo's history; Dr. James H. Patterson, Clark Atlanta University, Atlanta, Georgia; Jean-Francois Pitet, early jazz specialist/founder of the Cab Calloway blog; Ricky Riccardi, Director of Research Collections at the Louis Armstrong House Museum; Matthew Rivera, early jazz specialist and founder of the Hot Club of New York; Monk Rowe, Director of the Hamilton College Fillius Jazz Archive. Additional thanks to the devoted staff at WKCR, who are keeping Phil Schaap's treasure trove of interviews and special broadcasts accessible. A very special thanks to Hank O'Neal, photographer, collector, and jazz producer, who reminded me of the magic of early jazz photographs, in which every detail tells part of the story.

Many drummers revered Webb, his virtuosity, and his advanced approach to the drums. I want to extend my heartfelt gratitude to them for explaining and demonstrating their studied knowledge of Webb's technique and musical accomplishments, and of the evolution of jazz drumming: Justin DiCioccio, Chet Falzerano, Jake Goldbas, Ken Kimery, Ulysses Owens, Jr., Bobby Sanabria, Evan Sherman, Hal Smith, and Kenny Washington. Many special thanks to Fred W. Gretsch, fourth generation president of the Gretsch Company, who shared family lore about Webb's association with Gretsch Drums, and to Emi Keffir, Special Assistant, the Gretsch Company.

Special thanks to colleagues and friends for their help, expertise, insight, and support, some of whom read various portions of this book as a work-in-progress. They include Fred Cohn, Linda Dahl, Brent Edwards, David Fletcher, Krin Gabbard, Kristin Booth Glen, David Hajdu, Susan Meigs, Rebecca Reitz, Nick Rossi, and Alyn Shipton.

I am especially grateful to my long-time agent Susan Ramer, of Don Congdon Associates, who helped steer me through this project and others. A huge thanks to her colleague, Katie E. Kotchman, who stepped in when Susan was on leave. Many thanks to Gary Giddins, Series Editor for the Cultural Biography Series of Oxford University Press, who encouraged me to bring this project to Norm Hirschy, Oxford's Executive Editor for Academic and Trade books. Norm was extraordinarily patient as I missed one deadline after another. Additional thanks to OUP's editorial and publication team: Lauralee Yearly, Rachel Ruisard, Gabriel Kachuck, Sean Decker, Kimberly Walker, and Danielle Michaely. Also thanks to Brady McNamara, cover design, and Michael Drakopoulos, author's photo.

Lastly, sincere thanks to my family: India Schneider-Crease, Alex Crease, Debbie Ross Staska, and to my lifelong partner Robert Crease, philosopher, dancer, author, and raconteur. Their support, brilliance, and their own accomplishments kept me afloat. This project would not have to come to pass without their good will, good-hearted irreverence, and love.

Introduction

I don't speak of Chick Webb, the drummer. I speak of Chick Webb, the epitome.

—Jo Jones, drummer

Chick Webb was the boss. That man was touched by God.

—Beverly Peer, bassist

We went to the Savoy in New York. . . . They [Andy Kirk's band] called me in because Chick Webb was really blasting town with all the bands, and they were getting rid of all the bands that came in there. I guess you heard about that era. It was sensational. When Webb came in you just prayed that you'd go over.

—Mary Lou Williams, pianist, composer, arranger

Frankly speaking, Chick's whole life was music, nothing but music. To my knowledge he had no hobbies, no gambling or listening to ballgames or nothing—just music. He talked music from morning 'til night, if you listened to him. That was Webb, he was just wrapped in music, that's all.

—Sandy Williams, trombonist

Chick Webb was the indisputable King of the Drums, and King of the Savoy Ballroom, where he and his band rose to national fame in the 1930s. In the Savoy's thrilling band battles, Webb was fiercely competitive and loved the fight. Trumpet player Roy Eldridge, who also rose to prominence in that decade, said that Webb "ran all the other bands right out of there." Webb's long-time trombonist Sandy Williams vividly recalled how Webb made the band "go into training like we were prizefighters, the brass would be upstairs, the saxes somewhere else. . . . He knew what he wanted and he'd keep after you until he got what he wanted."

This book is the first to tell the complete story of William Henry "Chick" Webb (1905–39), innovative drummer and bandleader in Harlem, who ushered an unknown teenage vocalist named Ella Fitzgerald to stardom, making his band one of the most popular bands in the country. While many people still recognize Fitzgerald's inimitable and beloved voice, Webb's name is not well known today. But his influence still resonates wherever crowds of people dance to a great band playing with power and unity.

Webb's story, like that of Fitzgerald and many other legendary Black musicians, is that of a resilient person whose persistence, creativity, and entrepreneurism enabled him to navigate his way from his family's working-class roots in East Baltimore through the harsh realities of racism and show business. His life was cut short when chronic illness finally overcame him at age thirty-four. He died in June of 1939 in the beginning of an East Coast tour, at the peak of his band's success. By then his dreams as a bandleader—national recognition for him, Ella, and his musicians, most of whom had been with him since leaner times—had been realized.

Before Webb hired Ella Fitzgerald, he reigned at the Savoy Ballroom, the nation's trendsetting crucible of music and dance styles in Harlem, and his band was often heard on live radio broadcasts. He was a forward-thinking virtuoso on drums, and leading drum companies endorsed him and customized their newest equipment for him as his career ascended. His over-sized bass drum was hand-painted with an image of his face with a wide smile that could light up the globe, topped off with a jeweled crown. His last set was a drummer's dream, the Gretsch-Gladstone combination, every detail top of the line down to the lustrous pearl finish, with sparkling chicks. Night after night, seated on his drummer's throne, he made thousands of people dance in the world's most demanding ballroom.

Behind that smile, Webb often hid struggles he had dealt with all his life. His small stature—he was barely four feet tall—and hump on his back were due to spinal tuberculosis, which he had contracted as a child. When the band's performing schedule was nonstop in the late 1930s, he concealed intense physical pain from his bandmates, his closest friends, and even his wife. Periodically, his pain and related ailments would compel him to return to Johns Hopkins Hospital in his hometown of Baltimore, where he'd been treated since childhood.

For years, Webb also struggled to have the best dance band not just in Harlem but on the national stage, as his peers Duke Ellington and Cab Calloway had managed to do. But some of his best musicians, whom he had mentored, were lured by competing band leaders who offered them more money and steadier pay. For Webb, keeping his band going and full of fresh talent in the intense world of big band swing was a battle.

The Chick Webb everyone knew was an optimistic showman and unique musician with a biting sense of humor. Self-pity was completely foreign to him. This four-foot musical powerhouse never viewed himself as diminutive. For those who knew and worked with him, he was a fighter and a giant who took chances on people, notably Ella Fitzgerald.

Webb's achievements were many and varied, deserved and hard-won. He was one of the most influential drummers of the Swing Era, particularly to Gene Krupa, Jo Jones, and younger drummers like Max Roach, Kenny Clarke, and Art Blakey. His virtuosity on drums and his other percussion instruments elevated the drummer to a jazz artist through the bebop years and beyond. Several of his early hires, in addition to Ella Fitzgerald, have had a lasting impact on American jazz and pop music. Saxophonist Johnny Hodges and trumpet player Cootie Williams became two of Duke Ellington's star soloists; Cuban trumpet player Mario Bauza was a force in the development of Afro-Cuban jazz; saxophonist and singer Louis Jordan formed the Tympany Five in the late 1930s, laying the groundwork for rhythm and blues and rock 'n' roll. Edgar Sampson, saxophonist, composer, and arranger, wrote "Stompin' at the Savoy" and other pieces for Webb that became anthems of the Swing Era when covered by bandleaders, Black and white.

This book traces what one could call the Musicians' "Great Migration," which was enfolded in the massive migration of Black Americans from the rural South to northern cities starting in 1910. New York City and Harlem were magnets for performers from the early 1920s into the '30s, and still are. In the 1920s, New York was also a hothouse for the burgeoning radio and recording industries and music publishing. Dance halls, ballrooms, and nightclubs dotted the map. The business of dance bands—Black and white—became an industry in itself as the early dance bands of the 1920s morphed into the great jazz big bands of the Swing Era. Webb's musicianship and growth as a bandleader were in tandem with those developments.

Researching and writing about Chick Webb was challenging. But it was far less daunting and challenging than Webb's own journey when, in late 1924, he left his hometown of Baltimore with his drums, his best friend/guitarist John Trueheart, and a handful of connections to enter the competitive world of Black musicians in Harlem and New York. Again and again, Chick Webb took chances on musicians, advances in musical directions, his own developing virtuosity, and his community.

I took a chance on writing this book, knowing that there was not the huge trove of documentation and footprints—musical and otherwise—that were resources for biographers of other jazz masters. Fortunately, my research took place during an explosion of digital resources. Newly digitized issues of prominent historical Black Newspapers, such as the *Baltimore Afro-American*, the *Chicago Defender*, the *Pittsburgh Courier*, and the *Amsterdam News* were a valuable asset. Their entertainment and cultural reporters covered Webb's entire career, including his first appearances at the Savoy Ballroom, the Lafayette Theater, the Apollo Theater, and radio broadcasts. Their columns and articles appeared a decade before *DownBeat Magazine* came into existence, or its writers paid much attention to Chick Webb.

What I hope has emerged from my research is a group portrait, centered around Webb, that comprises a Webb archive created from many different resources. This encompasses Webb's family life and early years in Baltimore, his lifelong health issues, and his life and career in Harlem, which traversed the high years of the Harlem Renaissance to the creative swing music-and-dance movement of the 1930s that he helped foment. Webb settled in Harlem as it was becoming a beacon for writers, journalists, political activists, artists, and entertainers and musicians of the highest order.

I grew up in New York, a city of music, and I cannot express what a gift this city has provided me, especially a love and appreciation of jazz. None of its jazz soundscapes would have come about without the music of Chick Webb and Ella Fitzgerald. I am indebted to many other musicians, dancers, authors, scholars, and institutions that have helped preserve this legacy and the cultural world of Harlem in the 1920s and 1930s. The late Frankie Manning, Norma Miller, Al Minns, Conrad Gale, Helen Clarke, and other Savoy regulars were friends with my partner Robert Crease, and I learned from the reminiscences and insights that they passed on to him. I also had the unforgettable pleasure of seeing Frankie and Norma dance in person often, and of hearing their stories myself. My research was enriched by many visits to the Schomburg Center for Research in Black Culture, where I was a fall 2020 Scholar-in-Residence; the Institute for Jazz Studies, where I was a Berger-Carter-Berger Research Fellow, 2018–19; and the Library for Performing Arts, Lincoln Center. This book explores the stories of several people involved in the music and entertainment business, such as Moe Gale, owner of the Savoy Ballroom, whose Jewish family emigrated from Eastern

Europe in the late 1800s, as did my family. I hope it sheds light on the racial inequities Webb and others faced off against, while bringing so much excitement and joy to countless people.

Many jazz books and resources mention Chick Webb, his influence, and his intersections with Ella Fitzgerald and other musicians, but they scarcely scratch the surface of his cultural surroundings and his impact. By the end of his short life, Webb was recognized as one of America's most popular musical stars and a cultural hero. Over the past few decades, his story has tragically receded from view. The aim of this biography is to restore Chick Webb's centrality in the development of American jazz and popular music. There he is, in the middle of his band's front line, leading his musicians and thousands of dancers from his drummer's throne.

1

Baltimore Beginnings

Thronged with one of the largest crowds in its history, the internationally known Savoy Ballroom squeaked unmercifully from human weight last Tuesday night. They came from distances far, near and unknown to see and hear those two demons of swing clash in a terrific jam session that kept the entire house spellbound.

—*New York Amsterdam News*, June 1937

On the left platform was Benny Goodman, White King of Swing, on the right was Chick Webb, idol of Harlem, defendant in the great battle of music that was raging the night of May 11. With five policemen on the platform to scare the crowd from rising onto the bandstand, Benny's boys fired the first shot.... It was little Chick's turn when that Webb man opened up on his drums.... It was a torrid battle. Nip and tuck.

—*Metronome*, June 1937

The battlefield was the Savoy Ballroom, which took up most of the entire block from 140th to 141st streets on Lenox Avenue in Harlem, New York City. It was the first ballroom built for Harlem's Black community, but as swing music and dance caught on during the 1930s, the Savoy Ballroom became more than a local destination for great music and the latest dance steps. It was a landmark. Politicians, tourists, stage, screen, radio stars, musicians, and dancers—Black and white—came to be part of the ballroom's high-intensity scene, when bands like Webb's were avant-garde, creating the Kingdom of Swing.

The Savoy Ballroom opened on March 12, 1926, and equaled if not surpassed its whites-only competitors in elegance and size. It could hold four thousand dancers, and its springy maple dance floor was over ten thousand square feet and lit by twinkling colored lights. It had two bandstands along one wall so two bands could alternate sets for continuous music, making it perfect for the ballroom's insatiable dancing audience and for "battle of the bands" contests, which soon became a featured attraction.

On May 11, 1937, almost five thousand people packed the place for a face-off between the bands of Chick Webb and Benny Goodman. Thousands more crowded around the block, kept in line by mounted police. This battle—between Webb, Harlem's own Savoy King, and Goodman, whom the white jazz media had crowned the King of Swing—was polarized by the press, musically and racially, for weeks in advance. Webb led the band from his drummer's throne, sitting in the middle of the band's front row of brass and woodwinds, face to face with dancers and fans crowded up against the bandstand. His powerful and dynamic drumming fired up the audience, obscuring his tiny, four-foot body and the hump on his spine.

By the night's end, with no real voting process except the crowd's applause, Webb was declared the winner. Frankie Manning, one of the Savoy's most innovative dancers among its gravity-defying Lindy Hoppers, remembered: "I saw guys [in Goodman's band] just shake their heads." Goodman's own sensational drummer Gene Krupa physically bowed down to Webb in tribute. "I will never forget that night. Chick Webb cut me to ribbons," said Krupa.

Almost two years after this battle, Webb died on June 16, 1939, at the peak of national fame, his life cut short by the chronic effects of spinal tuberculosis. The jazz world already had plenty of honorific titles—"Duke," "Count," "Pres," and several "Kings." Webb, the "Savoy King," had worked tirelessly for that designation, from his early years as a drummer in the flourishing early jazz scene of his hometown Baltimore to Harlem and beyond. His music set a nation on its feet, crisscrossing limits about popular music, jazz and authenticity, Black and white musical influences, styles and fads. As Webb, Ella Fitzgerald, and the band zig-zagged on tour, they also broke the "color line"—theater by theater, city by city, giving Black artists and entertainers an ever-widening audience.

In the early years of the twentieth century, Chick Webb's parents, William Henry Webb Sr. and Marie Florence Johnson, lived together in one of the two-story row houses lining the streets of a working-class neighborhood in East Baltimore. It was a mile from downtown, and the families who lived there were mostly Black, along with some Jewish and Italian immigrant families. William and Marie rented a floor-through apartment at 308 East Lewis Street, a block that no longer exists. Baltimore's brick row houses were then the predominant housing stock throughout the city, in wealthy, working-class, Black and white neighborhoods.[1] On East Lewis and streets nearby, the houses were narrow, with front steps made of wood. Webb's house had no electricity or indoor plumbing, and people used slop buckets or had outhouses in the back. The city's extensive streetcar lines served East Baltimore's main streets, linking people to downtown and all over the city.

Webb Jr. was born at home on February 10, 1905, when Marie was about twenty years old. He was her second child and was named William Henry for his father. A clerk from Johns Hopkins Hospital filled out Webb's "Record of a Birth" form and filed it with the Baltimore Department of Health. Webb's birth year is correct and is corroborated by the 1910 federal census for Baltimore, which lists his age as five years. The record of his death is not.

Vital statistics and other city records were filled in by hand, and simple errors were sometimes carried forward. Incorrect data or lack of documentation about births, deaths, and health and school records compound the challenges of researching African American family histories like Webb's, whose father's history has been impossible to trace thus far. Another legacy of slavery: the ecology of poverty, racism, and cumulative neglect.

When Webb died in 1939, at the peak of his national fame, his birth year of 1905 was recorded incorrectly on his death certificate, adding to confusion about his age in jazz reference works for decades. The bronze plaque installed over Webb's grave was inscribed as instructed by his widow, Sally Webb, with a crown, a snare drum, and the wrong birth year:

HUSBAND
WILLIAM HENRY (CHICK) WEBB
FEBRUARY 10, 1909
JUNE 16, 1939

This error underscores other stubbornly hazy aspects and trajectories in the arc of Webb's brief life, from birth to death.

The 1910 Baltimore census shows the Webb family still living at East Lewis Street, and that William Sr. was employed as a laborer in a brickyard and Marie as a laundress. By then the children numbered four: Bessie, seven;

William, five; Mabel, three; and Ethel, five months. The Baltimore census, like many US cities, used abbreviations for race: W, M, or B. Marie and young William were each marked "M" for mulatto, and the other family members were marked "B" for Black. Marie gave birth to her first child, Bessie (Mary Jane McGruder), in 1902, followed by Chick three years later. William Sr. and Marie married in 1906, and their two younger daughters were also born at home. Ethel died of pneumonia when she was almost two years old, and William Sr. moved out shortly afterward. The other siblings—Bessie, William Jr., and Mabel—never saw their father again. He died in 1918 when Chick was thirteen. His death certificate, signed by Marie, identifies the cause of death as "catarrh of the liver and self-intoxication."[2]

As a single mother, Marie earned about five dollars a week as a laundress. Marie, her mother Mary (née Fisher), and her sisters created a tight-knit family amid shifting men and circumstances. Mary had three daughters with John L. Johnson, whom she married in 1893: Marie (born in 1884), Emma (c. 1887), and Florence (1892). They remained close through Mary's successive relationships and marriages to Robert Sanders (c. 1899), then to Clarence Jones, who'd been boarding with them. Mary and Jones married in 1919, and they were an anchor for Chick and their extended family for the rest of their lives.[3]

Marie, Chick, and his sisters lived in a couple of different addresses on East Lewis Street, and then joined Mary and Clarence as they moved around the neighborhood, to houses on Ensor Street and Central Avenue. Clarence and Mary Jones eventually moved to 1313 Ashland Avenue in the 1930s. This is where Marie, Bessie, Mabel, and their extended family lived at various times, moving in and out as their circumstances and fortunes changed. The three-story house on Ashland Avenue became the family house. It was home.

Clarence, nicknamed "Coots" (or "Cootzy" by the family), became the steady male presence in young Webb's life, and all the children considered him their grandfather. Clarence worked for many years as a porter and bootblack at Hess Shoes, one of Baltimore's long-established Jewish-owned clothing stores. In Baltimore, as elsewhere, Jewish retailers and their Black employees had complex relationships. As the two most marginalized groups in the city, their relations were both mutually dependent and lopsided, giving rise to some patriarchal yet genuinely caring relationships. Brad Rowe, Bessie's adopted son (born in 1949, ten years after Webb's death), recalled Jones's employer George Hess Sr.: "He loved him [Clarence]. Even after he retired and he was sick for a very long while, Mr. George—we used to call him—would make sure he was taken care of. Cootzy never had to want for anything."[4]

Rowe never knew Chick Webb, but he loved hearing stories about his famous uncle from Bessie, his Aunt Mabel who lived in Harlem, and Clarence, who died in 1961 and outlived many family members. Rowe was born in the Ashland Street house, where Chick's legacy was a palpable presence. Webb's memorabilia "was on the walls, in the closets," Rowe recalled.

> We had some of his 78's. We had a big old portrait of him in the living room. As the house passed down through the family, my niece died and she left all that stuff. And last time I was there it just wasn't there. I can't say what happened to it. But it wasn't there, it was gone.
>
> They really loved him [Chick] and they were really proud of what he had done, so it was a legacy that stayed in the family and we'd always hear about him and his music. And, there was a connection with the recreation center, the church and the family.[5] People would always come up and ask, "You're Bessie Webb, aren't you? You're Chick Webb's sister." When we would go to New York to my Aunt Mabel's house people would say, "You're Mabel Webb, right?" So that was very important to me, and in school the teachers knew of it.

Many of the stories Rowe heard about Chick were from Clarence. "He talked about Chick all the time, that's how I heard stories about him. He would tell us stories until he got up there in age and couldn't remember any more." The family had always been active in the African Methodist Episcopal Waters Church on Aisquith Street, one of the oldest African Methodist Episcopal (AME) churches in Maryland and an anchor in the neighborhood.

> I have to think that Marie [Webb's mother] was as loving as Bessie and Mabel were. We all grew up in that church and that church has a long, long history in Baltimore. . . . I think the whole family at one time or another was an usher in the church. . . . And you probably know that Chick was buried from that church. From what I understand it was so packed that they had people standing outside on the fence and on the roofs of houses and what have you.

After Webb moved to Harlem in the mid-1920s, Webb stayed with the family every time he came to Baltimore, from his early years as a struggling bandleader onward. He was always close to his mother, as Brad Rowe was with Bessie. "I guess you could say he was a pretty big mama's boy," Rowe told an interviewer, laughing. "So he always stayed at the house. That's what I was told. And, well, we were all mama's boys."[6] Webb also helped take care of the family financially when he was finally making money. Rowe said that Webb

> had the caring nature of his mother Marie. He always made sure the family had what they needed. . . . And from what I've been told, the family didn't make a real big deal about Chick being a famous jazz drummer. He was William, he was William to them. That's, that's what they called him, that was his first name. The family didn't call him Chick.
>
> I doubt if success went to his head because of his mother. . . . She made him know who he was and where he came from. Now, I don't remember at any time anybody saying that he got the big head. In fact the only extravagant thing that I've ever heard from the family is that he had his Cadillac, his white Cadillac and his white German shepherd. I guess he was satisfied with that.[7]

During Webb's childhood, Baltimore, the seventh largest city in the US, was racially divided. The advances that Black citizens gained after the Civil War were rolled back, and entrenched racist attitudes among the city's whites hardened. In the early 1900s, Baltimore imposed strictly enforced Jim Crow laws. Shopping, transportation, and use of public buildings like libraries were strictly codified, and basic daily activities for Blacks were curtailed and limited. The city's redlining and restrictive real estate covenants against Blacks and Jews were notorious even at the time.[8]

Even so, Baltimore had long-standing thriving Black communities stemming from the city's geopolitical status as a seaport that was the northernmost southern city and the southernmost northern city. Baltimore and the state of Maryland had the largest population of free Blacks of any southern city and state before and after the Civil War. Washington, DC and Baltimore were the first urban stops up the northern seaboard for the Great Migration, and Baltimore was a city of crossroads. By 1910, the Old West Baltimore neighborhood in particular was economically diverse and culturally rich. Education and a collective spirit of Du Boisian uplift were stressed. It was a desirable place to live and signaled opportunity for many Black families.

But Baltimore lagged behind other major American cities in some fundamental ways. Its lack of a city-wide sewage system resulted in a smelly downtown and unsanitary conditions in congested neighborhoods that contributed to severe public health problems, including a prolonged tuberculosis epidemic. Other deficiencies, such as the lack of standardized fire hydrants, proved disastrous during the Great Baltimore Fire of February 7, 1904, just a year before Webb's birth.

The fire broke out on a Sunday morning in the fourth-floor storage area of a dry goods company. It raged for over forty hours and consumed the entire downtown business area, and "nearly 2000 buildings [were] crushed to ashes. . . . [N]othing remains but a mass of burnt and blistered brick, stone and marble, and a maze of tangled iron, steel and wire."[9] The city's horse-drawn fire trucks, inadequate hydrants and hoses, and unpredictable wind shifts made the fire difficult to control, even with help that swooped in from Annapolis, Philadelphia, Washington, DC, and Delaware. The next day, a strategic effort by Baltimore's fire chief, the militia, and reinforcements from New York City finally contained the blaze and stopped it from spreading to City Hall and across Jones Falls, the estuary running into the east side of the harbor. East Baltimore's main blocks and the neighborhood where Webb grew up were spared. Initially no deaths were reported.

When the extent of the damages was assessed—over 175 million dollars—city government and business elites rallied to issue bonds to rebuild. Downtown Baltimore was remade with stricter building codes, more modern materials, standardized fire hydrants, and, finally, a sewage system. In 1908, the *Baltimore Sun* reported so much improvement and rebuilding in the city's downtown area that many people were misled and confused about the extent of the damages to people's livelihoods, not just property.[10]

In the aftermath, everyone was affected: schools closed, businesses and offices were destroyed or couldn't function, and people lost their homes and means of income. The *Afro American Ledger*, the city's foremost Black newspaper, was the only paper that reported the disastrous impact on Black residents and the inequity in relief efforts afterward. "Notwithstanding there were thousands of colored men and women thrown out of work by the great fire, and notwithstanding the sympathy being extended to the fire sufferers, we notice that all the men engaged in cleaning the streets are white men. This shows to what extent politics has hold of the city. Taxpayers' money is being paid out for this work, and yet, while there are thousands of colored taxpayers in this city, not one colored man is to be benefitted by what work might be obtained just now cleaning the streets."[11]

In 2003 the *Baltimore City Paper* reported the discovery of an article in the *Baltimore Sun* from February 17, 1904: "Body of a Colored Man Pulled from the Basin at Bowley's Wharf." This was the first article that challenged the long-held belief that "not a single life was lost in the great conflagration." The body, severely burned, was found in the harbor by patrols from the Naval Reserves. The man's only means of escape was to jump into the harbor.[12]

Webb's neighborhood survived intact, but East Baltimore did not benefit from the city's extensive rebuilding and reinvestment effort. West Baltimore was also largely spared from the fire's destruction but had better infrastructure in the first place. With its wide tree-lined streets, three-story row houses with marble steps, and nearby Druid Hill Park, it was one of the most self-sufficient and attractive Black communities in the country.[13] By 1915, the area, spread over 175 square blocks, was a haven. Some Baltimoreans would say it was "Harlem before Harlem," with excellent schools, devoted educators, many church denominations, benevolent societies, Black-owned businesses, and cultural groups. Pennsylvania Avenue and nearby blocks were the site of Baltimore's Black entertainment district, a hive of small clubs and dance halls, and the Royal Theater (originally called the Douglass Theater) an incubator of talent as well as a tour stop for bands and famous acts coming and going from New York, Philadelphia, and Washington, DC.

When Chick was three or four he was afflicted with the rare strain of bacteria that causes spinal tuberculosis, which is different from the highly infectious strain of pulmonary tuberculosis that resulted in epidemics in Baltimore and many big cities (one hard-hit area near downtown Baltimore was called "Lungo").

Webb's illness and spinal deformity came to be surrounded by as much error, confusion, and myth as other aspects of his short life. According to Rowe and other family members, he fell down the steps rushing to greet his grandparents who were coming down the street and injured his back, and as a result he got tuberculosis of the spine. There is no medical evidence for that, but Webb was diagnosed with spinal tuberculosis, a chronic disease that affects spine development in children. He grew to be only four feet tall with a deformed spine and a hump on his back, and he could barely walk until he had surgery a few years later. The surgery improved Webb's mobility, though he had an impaired gait and other serious health complications as an adult.[14] In his book *Jazz and Death*, Dr. Frederick J. Spencer, Associate Dean Emeritus of the Medical College of Virginia, examined Webb's medical history and criticized false or implausible claims about Webb's disease.

> It is wrong to write that he was "Born w. [*sic*] a physical deformity described as TB of the spine," or that he was "born crippled." Nor did he have "congenital tuberculosis of the spine." Unlike syphilis, tuberculosis is not transmitted in the womb. But Webb did develop tuberculosis as a young child.... Another account says, "A normal child at birth, young Webb suffered an accidental fall during infancy which shattered several vertebrae, leaving him deformed and crippled." If several of Chick Webb's vertebrae had been smashed or shattered, he would probably have experienced permanent muscle weakness, even paralysis, from damage to his spinal cord or nerve roots.... Webb may have had an injury, but his tuberculosis vertebrae caused his typical gibbous spine.... Chick Webb must first have had tuberculosis in a lung or the intestine. Blood-borne, it spread to his spine and led to a permanent deformity.[15]

Webb's family was fortunate to have Dr. Ralph J. Young as their doctor. Young, a pioneering Black physician who graduated from Howard Medical School in 1916, practiced at a clinic in East Baltimore and was one of few Black physicians to be certified by Maryland's Department of Health and to have privileges with Johns Hopkins Hospital.[16] Young first cared for Webb at home or at the clinic. Johns Hopkins Hospital was founded in 1893 with innovative policies and vision. According to its uniquely egalitarian charter, any one of any race, sex, or age could get treatment, as could anyone unable to pay. In practice, that was not the case, and Hopkins has had a long and troubled relationship with the Black community.[17] Webb was incredibly lucky in his experiences there. Years later, as a successful entertainer, he returned to Hopkins whenever he had serious health problems, and he and Dr. Young became close friends.

As a child, Webb's disability may have held him back from attending school regularly. His unusual gait and hump on his back caused plenty of teasing and bullying, and neighborhood kids started calling him "Chick." "The name [Chick] was actually a slur because of the condition of his back," said Rowe. "He had to be a really strong person to deal with his deformity and probably took a lot of guff being called Chick, Chicken, Chick."[18]

Webb's physical limitations did not stop him from other things. He sold newspapers in downtown Baltimore to help earn money for the family when he was around nine years old. Neighbors remembered seeing him pulling around a little red wagon with his newspapers at a busy corner near downtown.[19]

Webb had competition; selling newspapers was a way for boys to earn some money, but they had to attract steady customers. Rowe's impression was that Webb liked being on the streets and was a "great little hustler." Seeing him hauling his wagon around must have been "a unique sight. I would suspect that it took a lot of 'can-do-it-ness.' . . . Growing up with Bessie, she always told me there was no such words as 'I can't.' She got that from her mother and Marie instilled it in Chick, too."[20] Cab Calloway, born in late 1907 and another future star from Baltimore, climbed on and off streetcars selling papers during rush hours—something Chick could not do as easily. For Chick and Cab, earning money and the adventure of the streets were more exciting than grade school, which neither attended regularly.

Many of Baltimore's public schools for Black children were housed in substandard buildings and supplied with leftover textbooks and equipment from white schools. Yet in oral histories and interviews, older Black residents said that their education before school desegregation was superior.[21] The city's Black teachers were often graduates of prominent Black colleges and universities such as Fisk, Howard, Hampton Institute, and Morgan College who could not get jobs teaching in white schools. Frederick Douglass High School, founded in 1883 and the jewel of the Black school system, was the second Black public high school in the country. One of its acclaimed teachers was W. Llewellyn Wilson, the first African American music teacher hired by the all-white Department of Education. Wilson taught piano, theory, and composition, led countless ensembles for over forty years, and was involved in every corner of Black musical life in Baltimore.[22] Many musicians and entertainers, including Anne Wiggins Brown, who debuted the role of Bess in the first production of *Porgy and Bess*; classical prodigy turned-jazz pianist Ellis Larkins; and Blanche and Cab Calloway (who was more attentive as a high school student at Douglass), studied with Wilson.[23]

The excellent musical education at Douglas High School was an inadvertently beneficial side of segregation, which re-enforced what Alfred Prettyman called the "duplicate administrative structure" in education and other city offices that fortified rather than damaged Black middle-class life. Eventually, desegregation would destroy this, with Black administrators

losing their authority—which, says Prettyman, is "one of the aspects of desegregation that is not paid attention to very much."[24]

Webb did not attend Douglass, and it is unknown how many years of
school he completed. Rowe's impression was that school was not high on
Webb's agenda, due to either lack of interest or his reaction to students'
teasing. Webb's musical education came from everywhere except school.

Music and sound sparked Webb's interest from early childhood. He
"dodged Sunday school to learn drums from a parade band."[25] Neighbors
couldn't help noticing his constant percussion-making on fence posts and
garbage cans. Again, according to family lore, Dr. Young suggested that
Webb learn to play drums as a form of physical therapy and to strengthen his
spine. Webb didn't need encouraging; he loved drums and drumming. By age
eleven, he'd saved enough money selling newspapers to buy a used drum set.
He imitated the style of drummers he'd heard in parades or in park bands. He
also started practicing tricks: rapid-fire drum rolls and tossing drum sticks
high in the air and catching them.

When Webb's name popped up regularly in entertainment columns in the
1930s, journalists never succeeded in getting him to talk about his family or
childhood, nor his illness or disability. But he couldn't escape other people's
descriptions. Words like "hunchback," "midget," "dwarf," "cripple," and "half-
pint" followed him the rest of his life.

2

Baltimoreans in the Music World

It is doubtful if there is another city in the United States as musical, that is to say, more rich in musical history and tradition, and where a greater number of practitioners of the art have always been found and are to be found today, speaking strictly from a Negroe standpoint, than is Baltimore.

—*Baltimore Afro*[1]

In Baltimore, there was good jazz in just about every cabaret, no matter how low or cheap. Baltimore musicians had more technique than the New York players.... They were very fly, smart, creative improvisers. But they didn't play the blues the way the musicians from the South did. Their jazz was based on ragtime piano practices, and piano ragtime influenced the way they played their horns.

—Garvin Bushell[2]

Ragtime shaped Webb's sound world. As he was growing up, it was already a catch-all term for songs or styles performed with a syncopated rhythm, stemming from its origins as piano music. Baltimore was a major center for ragtime on the East Coast, and its pianists advanced the style by competing with each other in piano and organ "duels" in nightspots near Pennsylvania Avenue, a storied central hub of Baltimore's Black entertainment scene. One of the major contenders was Eubie Blake, who would trailblaze the way to Harlem for other Baltimore musicians.

Ragtime went hand in hand with the craze for popular dancing that began in American cities around 1910, fueling a frenzy for places to go dancing and for bands that could play the music. The dance craze was a piece of the expanding mosaic of American urban life, with multiple streams of people relocating from rural areas during the Great Migration, and from immigration. Dancing was not just for rich people in their ballrooms, but for everyone. Vernon and Irene Castle, a white exhibition ballroom dance couple, helped spread this craze when they returned to New York in 1912 after a successful few years among wealthy patrons across Europe. Back in New York, they updated their style with ragtime music and turned dances like the cakewalk and turkey trot—rooted in Black culture—into trendy, de-eroticized dances, democratizing social dancing and lending it respectability.

The Castles soon had wealthy clients among elite circles in New York, and well-to-do enclaves in the United States. But they also toured all over the country, performing for working class audiences and blurring the line between professional and amateur dancers by getting out on the dance floor with their fans.[3] The Castles chose James Reese Europe, the pioneering Black conductor, bandleader, and musical activist, as their music director. Europe's ensembles were already in demand among white elite clients. Still, it was a progressive choice when public performances by white and Black artists together were rare, if not unacceptable, and even illegal in some parts of the country.

Europe had moved to New York in 1904 and was part of a circle of artists, musicians, actors, and writers—including Bert Williams, James Weldon Johnson, and his brother John Rosamund—instigating a "new" Black theater movement to counter what passed for popular entertainment: racist Blackface minstrel/vaudeville shows. In 1910 Europe founded the Clef Club, a union and support network for Black musicians. The club's contracts for performances stipulated fair pay and ensured that a Black musician could show up for a job and not be expected to wash dishes or mop floors afterward. As Eubie Blake put it, Europe did for Black musicians what Martin Luther King did for the rest of Black people.[4]

Europe's drummer Buddy Gilmore was an influence himself as one of the first "trap" drummers to convert the sounds of a three-person percussion section to one person on drums. His earliest (1913) recordings with Europe's Society Orchestra show off his upbeat lift on two-step ragtime marches and brisk foxtrots, punctuated with bright bells, whistles, and chimes.[5]

Baltimore's ragtime and early jazz ensembles played music similar to the sound of Europe's small groups: syncopated cakewalks and marches, and "ragged" versions of popular songs for dancing. Webb probably heard Eubie Blake with theater bands, and popular local bands like Professor Joe Rochester's Drexel Ragtime Syncopators and Ike Dixon's Jazz Demons, among others. Rochester and Ernest Purviance, Baltimore's "Dance King," frequently produced special events such as the Darktown Strutters May Ball, which drew hundreds of people from nearby counties and from Annapolis and Washington, DC. A few years later, Ike Dixon's band played at the newly opened local "electric" amusement parks, and in the 1920s engaged in "Battles of Music" in Philadelphia and DC. Weekly dances sponsored by Black benevolent societies in large venues like the Richmond Market Armory, the Old Fifth Regiment Armory, and Pythian Castle Hall were part of Baltimore's musical soundscape. The Masons in Baltimore and on the Eastern Shore, in particular, had many accomplished musicians among their members, and their women's association, Sisters of the Eastern Star.[6]

One can view the range of Baltimore's Black musicians in Coleman's Colored Business Directories, whose first edition in 1913–14 predates the "Negro Motorist Green Book" by over twenty years. Coleman's directories included listings for classical musicians, music schools, instructors, dance band leaders, dancing instructors, piano tuners, etc.[7] Among them were the city's prominent orchestra leaders, including A. Jack Thomas, founder of the Aeolian Music Institute; Charles Harris and Edward Prettyman, who led the municipally funded segregated park bands, the Commonwealth Park Band and City Colored Band; and T. Henderson Kerr, who made a point of advertising that his group played no jazz. Many park band musicians were classically trained and also played "hot" jazz in small clubs in East Baltimore and along Pennsylvania Avenue. Just about every musician, even the Black orchestra leaders, had other jobs to make enough money for their families to live on. Baltimore's musical offerings—church music, brass bands, parade bands, ragtime, and early jazz groups—gave Webb his sound world, a rich diversity of music in a city sharply divided into Black and white.

> The Jazz music and the Jazz dance have been with us for nearly a year. Everybody has been so busy doing it and watching it, that the more thoughtful have just begun to wonder what it means and where it comes from. . . . You simply listen to the music and find yourself going through the right motions. . . . [T]he popular music of the day is several centuries old. . . . [A]t bottom it is nothing more than the wild syncopated boom-pa of a drum of the African wild man. The Jazz is the newest contribution of a civilization that is so often said to "have left absolutely no traces."
>
> —*Baltimore Afro*[8]

Chick Webb was self-taught on drums and learned by copying other drummers around town and by working things out on the bandstand as a young teenager. According to his grandfather Clarence Jones, Webb's first professional jobs were with small bands at the dance halls and basement clubs around Pennsylvania Avenue. His spinal condition was not a handicap to his growing musicianship, but getting around with a drum set on his own was difficult, then and ever after. Jones told a reporter that he'd "tote the little fellow on his back up the rickety staircase to the Lafayette Dance Hall on Pennsylvania Avenue. . . . I used to tote Chick on my back many a night. I'd come back for him about two in the morning and carry him home, carrying his drums with me."[9]

In the early 1920s Webb joined the Jazzeola Orchestra, led by clarinetist Percy Glascoe. The group had typical small dance band instrumentation—trumpet, trombone, clarinet, violin, piano, banjo, and drums—and could expand or contract depending on the pay and venue. Newspaper ads usually listed bandleaders' names, not sidemen's, so exact dates when Webb performed with that band and others are not documented. Fox and Glascoe's Jazzeola Orchestra played at popular Pennsylvania Avenue–area spots, such as Galilean Fisherman's Hall and the Richmond Market Armory.

Percy Glascoe, born in Baltimore in 1895, first worked as a circus musician, considered the low end of the profession, even by other musicians. "People felt that members of the circus, particularly musicians and roustabouts, were a low element of people," said Garvin Bushell, a clarinetist and saxophonist who got his start in circus bands and later had a remarkably long career in New York, including stints with Chick Webb. Bushell described awful traveling conditions and also "great black clarinet players with circuses in those days. Percy Glascoe from Baltimore was one."[10]

By 1920, Glascoe had moved into a more respectable role as a dance band leader. Besides the Jazzeola Orchestra, he led the Kit Kat Orchestra and other dance bands, which might have had some of the same personnel. In the late 1920s, Glascoe became president of the Black branch of the Baltimore Musicians' Union, Local 543, and led the Plantation Orchestra, a popular local dance band.[11] A genial showman, Glascoe was known as the "laughing clarionetist," adept at producing comic novelty sounds. On stage, Glascoe, like all the top-tier Baltimore musicians, dressed in tie and tails. He was a great ragtime practitioner and an expressive musician who could play the blues, Tin Pan Alley songs, dance numbers, and novelty tunes. Chick learned a lot from him about showmanship and versatility—crucial skills for landing steady gigs as a sideman.

The Jazzeola Orchestra had another teenage member besides Webb, banjoist-guitarist John Trueheart, who had moved to Baltimore from Virginia in 1921. He and Chick were sixteen years old, though Trueheart lived on his own, while Chick was then living with his mother, Marie, as boarders. As things turned out, Webb and Trueheart became best friends for life.

Years later, Webb often mentioned playing with the Jazzeola band on excursion boats on Chesapeake Bay. The particular boat he worked on, Captain George Brown's steamboat, the *Starlight*, has its own story and working on it was an enviable gig in the summer.

An engineer by profession who became a successful Black businessman in Baltimore, Brown bought the *Starlight* in 1909, and later a beachfront property he named Brown's Grove, where he built an amusement park. Brown's ventures gave Baltimore's Black residents a beautiful summer day on the Chesapeake, away from the city's intense heat. He also created many jobs: ship's pilots and crew, musicians, stewards, and vendors running amusement rides and concessions at Brown's Grove. Brown's ads in the *Afro* proudly exclaimed that the *Starlight* "is the only steamer and Brown's Grove the only park in the State of Maryland run exclusively for Colored People and by Colored People."[12]

Everything about the *Starlight* and Brown's Grove was first class, including the caliber of the musical groups. In the early 1920s the Jazzeola Band, A. Jack Thomas's band, and Ernest Purviance's dances onboard were weekly attractions. Sometimes Brown's trips involved many of the city's best musicians:

DON'T FORGET, THERE WILL NOT BE ANY MUSIC IN
BALTIMORE ON JUNE 4TH. WHY?
LOCAL 543, A.F. of M.
Baltimore's Whole Family of Colored Musicians, Including A. Jack Thomas
Band, are Going to
BROWN'S GROVE ON THE STEAMER STARLIGHT
On Sunday, June 4, 1922[13]

A. (Alfred) Jack Thomas was a musical entrepreneur and activist, educator, conductor, and composer. He'd settled in Baltimore in 1919 after his regiment band, the 368th, returned from France during World War I. Thomas's band was not as well known as James Reese Europe's 369th (the regiment band of the Harlem Hell-Fighters). But Thomas, like Europe had in New York, elevated the status of the city's Black musicians, and of the "Colored" Local 543, founded in 1918. Thomas convinced city officials to fund one of his ensembles, and his "Colored Park Band" was paid the same as the white municipal bands: fifty dollars a week to the leader, and twenty-five dollars a week to the members.[14,15]

Webb did not perform with the Colored Park Band, but Cy St. Clair, a tuba player who also migrated to Harlem in the 1920s, claimed that Webb occasionally played with the Merry Concert Band, based in Cambridge, Maryland, just south of Baltimore on the Eastern Shore. "If there was a baseball game, we played for that," said St. Clair. "They had a parade, we played for that. . . . Some of the men in the band were young and had ideas like I had. We wanted to play hot, only in those days we didn't call it that. The older men wanted to follow the music exactly." St. Clair's recollections add weight to situating Baltimore as an incubator for early jazz: "Baltimore was a center for music for as long as I can remember. . . . The Sho' fed Washington, Philadelphia and later some New York bands. . . . Eastern jazz was not as lusty as what came out of New Orleans," said St. Clair. "It was more in the piano roll style and rife with melody. It was probably not a great deal different from the jazz that Duke Ellington and Claude Hopkins were later to bring to New York."[16]

The *Afro* boasted about the city's Black musicians—classical, ragtime, and early jazz—in two articles in September 1921, which J. A. Jackson, *Billboard's* first Black music journalist, summarized in his next column: "Baltimoreans in the Music World."[17] These articles mention A. Jack Thomas; soprano Abbie Mitchell, who toured with vaudeville stars Bert Williams and George Walker; educator W. Llewellyn Wilson; and ragtime pianists and composers Eubie Blake and Edgar Dowell. One article highlights Thomas's ambitious projects: he was "establishing the most completely equipped conservatory ever organized in this city. . . . He also wanted to bring in famous white artists . . . whom the race-prejudiced attitude of white promoters prohibit the colored music-lover and student from ever hearing," notably Fritz Kreisler, the Austrian-born violin virtuoso.[18]

In 1921, Eubie Blake and his co-writer Noble Sissle had phenomenal success with their runaway Broadway hit in 1921, *Shuffle Along*. The publicity the show generated and news about other Baltimoreans gave the *Afro* plenty to brag about: "We cannot but fail to bask in the sunshine of our fellow townsmen who have placed us on the artistic map. What an array: Eubie Blake . . . Elmer Snowden, Blanche Calloway are all carrying on superbly."[19]

Unfortunately, no recordings of early Baltimore jazz ensembles have surfaced. The closest one can come to imagining their music is by listening to recordings of these musicians after they had moved on. Glascoe made several records in New York City in the mid-1920s. "Stomp 'Em Down," a duet with pianist Lem Fowler, shows Glascoe's impressive range on clarinet as he riffs playfully and freely on a simple blues. Eubie Blake's "Baltimore Buzz," a 1921 record with his Shuffle Along Orchestra, is a "foxtrot in honeysuckle time," a lightly orchestrated piano rag. It is embellished with a few "hot" phrases from various instruments floating behind the scored passages, with violin filigrees and cymbal splash accents, polished but not fussy, meant for showing off and dancing.[20]

By the time Webb was a teenager, many of Baltimore's best musicians had moved to New York and Harlem (or, in Blanche Calloway's case, Chicago). They joined what one might call the "musicians' migration," a substream of the African American diaspora to northern cities in the first decades of the twentieth century. Hundreds of thousands of Blacks moved north, fleeing conditions long shadowed by enslavement, violence, poverty, and Jim Crow laws. The influx to Harlem peaked in the mid-1920s and continued through the 1940s, with people surging up the Eastern Seaboard, and from the West Indies and Caribbean. Among them were musicians and entertainers, from optimistic amateurs to experienced professionals. Rumors of jobs and dreams of better opportunities than menial work were powerful incentives. Whether they were well educated and from middle-class families like Fletcher Henderson, then one New York's most prominent Black bandleaders, or from working-class backgrounds, musicians, dancers, singers, and actors headed for Harlem and New York City.

New York City in the 1920s was the nexus of emerging mass media: a thriving music publishing center, an expanding recording industry, and a scattering of rogue radio stations that were realigned by a consolidated industry a decade later. These arms of music production made for an entrepreneur's paradise and grew in tandem with entertainment venues sprouting all over the city. Theaters, movie palaces, nightclubs, dance halls, and ballrooms for all budgets beckoned to a native and newly transplanted young population—white, African American, and immigrants—trying to find their way in an urban environment enthralled with its own sense of modernism. New York offered an open invitation for musicians and songwriters to hustle onboard with the new technologies. Many of Baltimore's top musicians accepted it and went to Harlem, temporarily or permanently.

Percy Glascoe was one of them. In 1924, Glascoe performed with Mamie Smith and her Jazz Hounds, who were in Baltimore on an East Coast tour. Smith, the first Black female star blues singer, was a breakthrough artist of her time. Her career-launching hit "Crazy Blues," recorded in 1920, spawned a niche market in "race records," targeted for Black audiences, that revolutionized pop music production by Black artists and introduced it to white audiences. Author and cultural historian Daphne Brooks synthesized this breakthrough: Smith and her ambitious producer-songwriter Perry Bradford "upended the soundtrack of American life. Record labels now believed in the (monetary) value of Black mass cultural art, and they provided Black artists with access—though still heavily mediated by white executives—to recording their own music."[21]

The Jazz Hounds invited Glascoe to play with them on their way back to New York City, their home base. Glascoe stayed in New York for almost two years, working with various bands, including an engagement with other Baltimoreans in Wilbur De Paris's Orchestra at the Cinderella Ballroom, in the theater district. Glascoe also teamed up with pianist Lem Fowler, and between 1925 and 1926 they pumped out twelve to fourteen records. Some of them are prime examples of the instrumental ragtime-inspired small band jazz of those years, but none really caught on.[22]

Baltimorean pianist/songwriter Edgar Dowell, born in 1892, played the resort circuit in Atlantic City and Asbury Park before settling in New York around 1919, where he occasionally worked with Eubie Blake. Dowell quickly connected with other Black songwriters and early recording artists and became manager of Clarence Williams Publishing in 1922, with an office in Tin Pan Alley.[23] One of Dowell's tunes, "That Da Da Strain," covered by Black and white bands, became an anthem of the Jazz Age. Dowell co-wrote several topical tunes about Harlem's large Caribbean community with Clarence and Spencer Williams. One of the most popular was "West Indies Blues," though the song's publication and first recording was delayed by Marcus Garvey's arrest and release from prison, between 1921 and 1923.[24] Dowell also collaborated with lyricist Andy Razaf (who became far more famous for his work with Fats Waller); they co-wrote a string of songs together and had their own biweekly half-hour radio show on WHN, one of the city's "rogue" radio wires. An occasional bandleader and frequent behind-the-scenes contributor to several Black revues throughout the 1920s, Dowell died in 1938, never achieving the legacy of Razaf or Eubie Blake, a jazz icon who lived to be almost a hundred years old.

Eubie Blake had a blazing career in New York by the time Webb arrived there. Born in Baltimore in 1883, Blake honed his prodigious skills on piano as a nine-year-old, playing ragtime, popular songs, and light classics at Aggie Sheldon's, one of Baltimore's most famous brothels. Blake recalled an organ dueling contest with Dowell as a teenager: "He cut me so bad. He played more notes in his left hand than I did and wiped me right off the place. Then he took my girl!"[25] In summer 1915, Blake and a singer named Noble Sissle from Indiana were hired to work with Joe Porter's Serenaders in Riverview Park in Baltimore, a whites-only amusement park considered the "Coney Island of the South." A few months later they went to New York, where Blake was soon hired by James Reese Europe as an assistant for his many projects and ensembles; Blake then convinced Europe to hire Sissle too.[26]

Blake and Sissle's *Shuffle Along* was the first Broadway show created and performed solely by African Americans. It was produced on a shoe-string budget, but the production level—costumes, choreography, and musicianship—were first-rate wholly unique creations, the epitome of Black culture and style that mirrored trends in Harlem. "What the show lacked in glitz, it made up for in talent," wrote Caseen Gaines.[27] In September of 1924, Sissle and Blake scored another hit with their next show, *Chocolate Dandies.*

Blake's success in New York generated an exodus of younger Baltimore musicians and entertainers. Chick Webb, Blanche and Cab Calloway, and, a few years later, Billie Holiday would become the city's most notable musical and entertainment emigres. In 1934 the *Afro* elevated its boast: "There Would Be No Harlem if There Wasn't Baltimore."

The Calloways personified Baltimore's multifaceted musical life, from church soloists to the stage. Their mother was a church organist and educator, and both siblings sang and studied music under the watchful eye of W. Llewellyn Wilson at Douglass High School. Cab, more streetwise, was a paper boy (like Chick), groomed horses at Pimlico racetrack as a teenager, and did "a million odd jobs for money." Blanche, a star soloist in church and school productions, joined one of the touring companies for *Shuffle Along* in 1921 (initially upsetting her mother) and then *Plantation Days*, bringing her to Chicago, where she was soon a star in revues at the Sunset Cafe, the city's name-dropping jazz hub. Blanche paved the way for Cab, who followed her to Chicago in 1926, where she helped get him his first high-visibility job. Cab learned his show-stealing moves from Blanche. She was a dynamo who never

stopped moving on stage and introduced an intimate call-and-response connection with her audience. A few years later, they both were sensations in
Harlem. Peter Brooks, Cab Calloway's grandson, painted a lively picture of
Baltimore's intertwined musical lives: "There was an extraordinary kind of
mentorship-environment. Eubie Blake would bring in this person and that
person, and young musicians like Blanche and Chick were getting training
and professional experience in front of an audience. It was the happening
thing to do at that time, to have live music, and have kids kind of making it
happen for you."[28]

Other Baltimoreans-turned-Harlemites were the banjoists/guitarists
Elmer Snowden and Clarence Holiday. Their journey to Harlem predated
Webb's by three years, and eventually they worked in similar circles.
Snowden, born in 1900, befriended Holiday in school, and Eubie Blake once
hired Snowden over his friend because Holiday couldn't read music yet.
They both still lived with their parents in 1917, when Holiday announced to
Snowden that he was the father of a newborn baby girl, Eleanor Fagan—the
future Billie Holiday.[29]

Around 1920, Snowden worked a circuit between Baltimore and
Washington, DC, playing with Gertie Wells, a popular pianist/bandleader
from DC whom Ellington cited as an influence. In 1923, Snowden moved
to New York for a job he'd snagged as bandleader at the Hollywood Club,
a speakeasy in midtown Manhattan. He called the group he assembled the
Washingtonians—later led by Ellington—with Ellington on piano, saxophonist Otto Hardwick, and drummer Sonny Greer. A few months later,
Snowden got bumped out of the band when the others found out he was
siphoning off some of their pay. Ellington was already getting attention for
the band's sound and style, and for some original tunes.

These musicians stuck it out in New York, as Webb would. Making it professionally in New York and Harlem wasn't easy. Newcomers faced competition with each other and from New York City natives, who often had a
jump on an ever-shifting scene. Opportunities existed—for the persistent,
talented, entrepreneurial, and those able to make good connections or who
had them already. A musician had to be able to play Tin Pan Alley songs,
foxtrots, ragtime dances, and most of all the Charleston, the dance craze that
lit up New York's nightlife and put a spotlight on drummers, who had to set a
hyped-up tempo and keep it razor-sharp.

Webb's professional beginnings took place in Baltimore's smaller musical hothouse, a great training ground. There was stiff competition to get

the best gigs, and perform with Baltimore's best bandleaders. Even so, some Baltimore-Harlem transplanted talent—influential musicians like Edgar Dowell and Elmer Snowden, and unique exotic dancer Earl "Snakehips" Tucker—have been forgotten. They have been "blacked out," as Andy Razaf wrote decades later, by the sins of omission or commission of music historians.[30] Webb aimed high and—as his cousin Brad Rowe pointed out—had to have a lot of "can-do-it-ness." Soon, Webb and Trueheart would make their move to Harlem. A few Baltimoreans were already there to help them out.

3

Scuffling in Heaven

In 1924, Webb turned nineteen. He had been performing since he was ten years old on Baltimore's streets, in its dance halls and clubs, and on Chesapeake Bay's excursion boats. He memorized music quickly, was a great timekeeper, and was adept at crowd-pleasing drummers' tricks and drum rolls. He had already proved himself as a reliable sideman with Baltimore bandleaders such as Percy Glascoe. Webb and John Truehart started talking about moving to New York.

Webb's grandfather Clarence Jones had always encouraged Webb as a musician and found ways to help him out. A friendly man, Jones became acquainted with some of the bandleaders and musicians his grandson worked with, and had his own connections from working at Hess's Shoe Store. These included Joe Gans, the first Black world-champion boxer, who had pumped his earnings into his Goldfield Hotel, where Eubie Blake dazzled listeners with his piano playing.[1] In fall 1924, Jones contacted a pianist he knew in Harlem, Hughie Woolford, an old Baltimore friend of Blake's. Woolford, one of the founding members of James Reese Europe's Clef Club, was a pianist and bandleader on the white society circuit.[2] Woolford invited Clarence and his family to visit. The *Afro* mentioned this in its weekly "Society" column.

Mr. and Mrs. Clarence Jones and Mr. William Webb spent the week-end as the guest of Mr. and Mrs. Hughie Wolford [sic], of 528 Lenox Avenue, also as the guest of Mr. and Mrs. Eubie Blake of the *Chocolate Dandies* show now playing at the Colonial Theater and Mrs. Edith Johnstone, of New York City.[3]

Hearing Blake and Woolford talk about New York's theater and music world made a huge impression on Webb. Baltimore had a far smaller scale of opportunities. Thanks largely to Eubie Blake, Baltimore musicians had a good reputation in Harlem. Blake's success was legendary. *Shuffle Along*, cowritten with Noble Sissle, had generated several hit songs and the careers of Florence Mills, Valaida Snow, and Josephine Baker, all of whom would become stage sensations in Paris and other European capitals. In October 1924, when Webb made his first visit to New York, people were buzzing about *Chocolate Dandies*, Sissle and Blake's latest hit show. Their theatrical productions inspired a succession of revues by other Black composers and writers, who in turn became influencers in New York's entertainment landscape. These shows also created a high bar for Black musicians, singers, and dancers trying to make it in New York.

Trueheart made the first move and left Baltimore to join a small band in upstate New York. The job only lasted a couple of weeks, and he returned and told Chick that "work was rather scarce around New York." Undaunted, in 1925 Trueheart and Webb left together for New York City, supposedly "without telling their folks," carrying little more than their instruments, clothes, and train fare.[4] Their arrival coincided with Harlem's cultural hustle and flow: people stepping out dancing and club hopping, the sounds of early jazz pouring out of basement clubs, theaters, and hallways at rent parties. There was a growing demand for Black musicians and entertainers against the shady backdrop of Prohibition's gangsters, bootleggers, and racketeers who had a heavy hand in the club scene and underground economy. Webb stepped into Black Harlem's self-aware, alluring world, teeming with energy and first-rate performers. Said drummer Sonny Greer, who'd come to New York with Duke Ellington in 1923, "Harlem was heaven. That was the name of Harlem then—it was heaven."[5]

The reality for most people was different. Central Harlem was a congested area twenty blocks long and five avenues wide where apartments were scarce and rents high. Until the 1920s, "Harlem wasn't really Harlem then," recalled saxophonist Russell Procope, born in 1908, whose family moved to the neighborhood when he was a teenager. They'd been living in San Juan Hill neighborhood in the West Sixties, then a mixed neighborhood bordering Hell's Kitchen and what is now Lincoln Center for the Performing Arts. "Black people lived all over the City—33rd Street, 23rd Street, down in the Village, up and down Broadway, Third Avenue, the West 60s. Then people in Harlem began renting to the colored people, so naturally there was a status symbol to live in Harlem. All the people down where I lived, they'd say, 'Oh, yeah, we're moving up to Harlem.'"[6]

The area grew quickly with the influx of Black New Yorkers moving uptown and of people of color migrating to Harlem from America's Deep South, the Caribbean, and Africa. Frank Byrd, a Harlem writer employed by the Federal Writers' Project in the 1930s, wrote that by the mid-1920s over two hundred thousand people lived in Central Harlem. Some buildings and blocks overflowed with boarders sharing carved-out spaces, resulting in tenement conditions and risks to people's safety and health.

> In many instances, two entire families occupied space intended for only one family. When bedtime came, there was the feverish activity of moving furniture about, taking down cots, or preparing floor space as sleeping quarters.... Large rooms were converted into two or three small ones by the simple process of strategically placing beaver board partitions. These same cubby holes were rented at the price of full-sized rooms. In many houses, dining and living rooms were transformed into bedrooms soon after, if not before, midnight. Even "shift-sleeping" was not unknown in many places. During the night, a day worker used the room and soon after dawn a night worker moved in. Seldom did the bed have an opportunity to get cold.... In spite of this, blacks continued to pour in until there was a solid mass of color in every direction.[7]

Newcomers and New York natives were at the mercy of price-gouging landlords, and many people had trouble covering expenses. Employment for most Black residents was largely limited to menial work, and white-owned businesses on the commercial hub of 125th Street did not hire Blacks. New York City had its own uncodified Jim Crow system.

Through the musicians' grapevine, Webb and Trueheart found rooms and hangouts. They moved into a rooming house on 131st Street that catered to entertainers and musicians. Bardu Ali, who worked with Webb starting in 1934 as "front man" and conductor, remembered seeing Webb there for the first time, and knew the landlady. "Her name was Mrs. Foots. And you know, performers and musicians get behind in their rent. These old ladies, real old ladies, they would let you slide by."[8]

Webb and Trueheart's next discovery was the Rhythm Club, on Lenox Avenue and 132nd Street. The "unofficial" union for Black musicians, it was a great place to meet people and possibly get work. Webb and Trueheart found out that there was work for musicians, but Harlem's talent pool was deep. Ginger Young, also from Baltimore, helped run the club along with Bert Hall, giving tips, guidance, and encouragement to many young musicians.[9] Young wanted to help Webb and Trueheart out, knowing how tough it was for newcomers who didn't have any kind of reputation yet. Jobs were posted on a bulletin board, and theater managers and club and dance hall owners called for specific musicians. Calls also came in from people looking for musicians for private parties, dances, and luncheons. At night, the club hosted jam sessions where Webb and Trueheart heard the best musicians on the scene. The environment was friendly, but the "cutting contests" were fiercely competitive.

Webb was soon a familiar figure outside the Rhythm Club, where musicians hung out day and night, trading stories and passionately extolling the latest musical trends. He was hard to miss: an outgoing, loquacious, extremely short person with a handsome face and hump on his spine, eager to make a good impression and find a gig.

The Rhythm Club was on the same block as the Lafayette Theatre, which presented premiere Black entertainment: revues; celebrities such as Bill "Bojangles" Robinson, Johnny Hudgins, and Florence Mills; chorus dancers; and comedians—the "new" Black vaudeville for Black audiences. It was the first theater in the entire city that had an open seating policy: no "nigger heaven" here, unless the upper balcony seats were all you could afford. The original Tree of Hope, a literal touchstone for good luck, stood right near the theater in the wide meridian on Lenox Avenue, a "Boulevard of Dreams" for musicians and entertainers stretching over four blocks.

Over time Webb became friends with other young musicians, all looking for work: saxophonists Johnny Hodges and Elmer Williams, trumpet player Bobby Stark, pianist Don Kirkpatrick, and bassist/tuba player Elmer James among them. They spent their nights running around to jam sessions and many afternoons at the Rhythm Club, shooting pool, playing cards, or rehearsing together for occasional jobs for dances or parties.

Heaven or not, Webb and Trueheart were now struggling financially. Webb's family in Baltimore did not have much money, but his life there was stable, thanks to his mother and tight-knit extended family. He and Trueheart had worked fairly steadily in Baltimore, even though pay for Baltimore's dance band musicians was lower than New York's, about seven to ten dollars a week (with tips in some places).[10] New York City and Harlem had a loose "pecking order" for musicians to get noticed and hired. Jam sessions were the first rung.

Harlem's jam sessions created the stuff of legend; Ralph Ellison described them as arenas of "antagonistic cooperation," fierce competition among friends in a creative space.[11] Guitarist Danny Barker, who moved to Harlem in 1930 via New Orleans and then Chicago, recalled his first trip to the Rhythm Club: "The corner and street were crowded with musicians with their instruments and horns.... What I saw and heard I will never forget. A wild cutting contest was in progress, and sitting and standing around the piano were twenty or thirty musicians, all with their instruments out waiting for a signal to play choruses of Gershwin's 'Liza.'"[12]

Harlem's jam session scene had its own protocol, hierarchies, and surprises. They were key to improving musical skills, picking up on new trends and tunes, hearing the competition, getting noticed, and—hopefully—lining up work. "The colored musicians, we had just millions of them, fabulous," said drummer Sonny Greer. "You could go next door and hear the damnedest horn blowing things you ever heard in your life.... All them guys were sharks—they had to be because it was a jungle. Everybody was waiting for you to make a mistake and they got you."[13] Sessions usually took place at small clubs after hours; a few clubs, like Small's, had sessions on Sunday afternoons. Some places paid for a house pianist or duo to accompany soloists (imagine jamming to Willie "the Lion" Smith), but most jam sessions were not paying situations. Clubs had different jam session nights for specific instruments. At Mexico's, Monday was trumpet night, Tuesday saxophone night, and so on. The Bandbox hosted jam sessions primarily for newcomers; at the Rhythm Club and other spots, the best musicians in the city would show up, but there were unspoken rules about who got on the bandstand first. Saxophonist Teddy McRae, who started working with Webb in 1936, recalled, "You could go to the Rhythm Club and the musicians there gave you an idea of how you were progressing—the way they cut with each other, then you'd get in and blow something with them. You'd stand behind them 'til it was your turn. We could rub elbows with the top men. You could walk into a place and there's Coleman Hawkins, there's Louis over there, Fats Waller, all those boys sitting around. J.P. Johnson sitting there playing the piano."[14]

Webb often went from one club to another, and sought out drummers' nights. A couple of more experienced drummers heard him and tried to help him out. One was Tommy Benford, one of the first modern-sounding drummers working in Harlem. Benford often accompanied Wille "the Lion" Smith at jam sessions at the Rhythm Club. Ginger Young introduced Webb to him and asked Benford if Webb could play at some parties with him or sit in. This did not work out too well. Benford said that Willie "the Lion" couldn't stand Webb ("he didn't have it together yet") and, for a few months, wouldn't let him play at these jam sessions. "He'd work different jobs, but no name bands picked Chick then, he just did 'pick-up' jobs. And there weren't that many really organized bands yet."[15]

Rent parties were the next rung up, and a good source of money for some musicians. Music from rent parties spilled out of windows and doorways on Saturday nights, attracting people from off the streets, as well as many neighbors. Rent party scenes were vividly depicted by several upstart writers of the Harlem Renaissance, including Langston Hughes, Claude McKay, Zora Neale Hurston, and Wallace Thurman, and in essays by Black writers of the Federal Writers' Project. Frank Byrd wrote:

> It cost each individual very little, probably much less than he would have spent in some public amusement place. It became a cheap way to help a friend in need. It was such a good, easy way out of one's difficulties that others decided to make use of it. The Harlem rent-party was born.[16]

Admission was generally twenty-five cents, and guests could buy bootleg liquor and southern food. Drummer Sonny Greer claimed to be big on the rent party circuit with Fats Waller, one of Harlem's favorite stride pianists, even before Duke Ellington. Waller, James P. Johnson, and Willie "the Lion" Smith were in high demand and sometimes played four or five parties on a Saturday night. If space allowed, there might be a horn player or two. These parties took place in crowded parlors and more spacious ones in the upscale brownstones on Harlem's Sugar Hill. A room was cleared for dancing, with a piano or small combo crammed into a corner.

Greer knew how to take advantage of these situations. "We had the New York parlor socials sewed up. . . . Give me a dollar, all the food and drinks you want. . . . Everybody comes, they'd pass out invitations like handbills. . . . I'd take a hat, then get some chicken, potato salad, go home and that would carry me three days. That's how we saved, put it in a little drawer in the living room. We lived that way. Only open the drawer if a close friend came by. . . . I had a drawer full of turkey and ham and potato salad, and never opened that drawer to someone that wasn't a good friend of mine."[17]

Willie "the Lion" Smith loved the social mash-up. In his memoir he recalled "formally dressed society folks from downtown, policemen, painters, carpenters, mechanics, truck men in their workingmen's clothes, gamblers, lesbians and entertainers of all kinds."[18] The maids, laundresses, and workmen would part with their hard-earned rent money to help pay their neighbors' rent.

Langston Hughes romanticized these parties in his autobiography, *The Big Sea*:

> The Saturday night rent parties that I attended were often more amusing than any nightclub, in small apartments where God knows who lived— because the guests seldom did—but where the piano would often be augmented by a guitar, or an odd cornet, or somebody with a pair of drums walking in off the street. And where awful bootleg whiskey and good fried fish or steaming chitterling were sold at very low prices.... I can still hear their laughter in my ears, hear the soft slow music, and feel the floor shaking as the dancers danced.[19]

Rent parties were a great social leveler and community builder. They provided entertainment for the people who couldn't afford Harlem clubs, which were increasingly expensive and exclusive and catered increasingly to white tourists during the late 1920s. Some parties became such a mainstay of Harlem's underground economy that outsiders inevitably got in on the action, and specific parties were advertised on a white tourist circuit. Others—innocently called "buffet flats"—were covers for gambling rings, racketeering, and prostitution; some of these operations got taken over by white mobsters seeking a quick profit and using extortion to "protect" the hosts.

In the 1920s, "the 'Negro' was in vogue," Hughes wrote. Black art, music, and dance entered New York City's mainstream culture, attracting white admirers and imitators. One result was an updated source of employment in Harlem—dancing schools—which supported two vocations: instructors to teach the dances and musicians to play for them. (Ten years earlier, several dancing schools in the Tenderloin district were shut down as centers of prostitution.) Social dance scholar Danielle Robinson traces the "fertile conditions for professional black dance teaching" to the "superficial but overt embracing of blackness that occurred during the Jazz Age.... The black associations of jazz dancing and music did not need to be as veiled as they had been with ragtime; rather they were celebrated—the more *authentic* the better.... Black dances, not black dancers were the real stars of the Jazz Age." Black dance teachers were sought out by Broadway stars and "wannabees" to learn the shimmy, the Black Bottom, and the Charleston, as well as by regular people, Black and white, trying to emulate them.[20] Dance academies and classes popped up in lofts and spare studios in Harlem and all over the city. The employees of dancing schools had a new respectability: Black dance "professors" and female instructresses had more prestige and pay as dance teachers than at menial jobs, and musicians could get steady work at decent hours. Schools that couldn't afford live bands used a Victrola, while those that could hired a pianist or small combo (five to six pieces).

"The bands in those schools had top-notch guys," said Teddy McRae, whose first steady job in New York was at a dancing school. "They were clean places. Men would come like they were dressed for work. A lot of men came to learn so when they got out someplace, they could dance.... The girls would teach them how to dance, waltz, fox trot. We'd play all the latest pop music. That's what gave the band a good name—if you could play all the show tunes, all the pop music, the waltzes, Gershwin songs, tango. Let me tell you, those schools were good schools for young musicians that were coming up that really wanted to learn how to play."[21]

Russell Procope's first steady job as a musician was at a dancing school. Then eighteen, he was getting occasional gigs when a booking agent called him about a spot in a band at the Parody, a dancing school on 116th Street. "I'd never had a job where you go to work every night.... The dances were very short. You played a chorus, a chorus and a half, and every time the music stopped they [the customers] had to give another ticket. That's the way it was." The tunes were kept short to make the customers buy more tickets. The bands used stock arrangements, and no one played solos. Hundreds of dime-a-dances a night were the product. "You played so much music," said Procope. "You played 50 minutes, then would rest ten minutes, or 55 minutes and rest five 5. If you had to get off the bandstand you just got off, or got off to get a sandwich. But the music was continuous."

One night Procope got lucky. Still living with his family, and not a big club goer at that time, he walked into the Bamboo Inn out of curiosity. He had come right from his job at the Parody and was carrying his saxophone case. It turned out that the house band needed a saxophonist, and after a brief audition on the spot, he was hired.[22]

"The Bamboo Inn is the place to see 'high Harlem,'" Wallace Thurman wrote in *A Negro's Life in New York's Harlem*. As he described it, the Bamboo Inn was nothing like most Chinese restaurants around Harlem. It was an elegant space with a balcony, and a jazz dance band playing nightly for dancers, under a huge gyroflector throwing off colored lights, the 1920s version of a disco ball. Well-off Harlem matrons had luncheons or charity events there, or hosted dances for their daughters' debuts. It offered "the allure of the Orient combined with the comfort of the best that can be offered in American and Chinese foods and snappy entertainment. No cover charge!"[23]

The Bamboo Inn was just one pinpoint on the "Nightclub Map of Harlem"—the patchwork of clubs in Harlem in the late 1920s to early 1930s. Many were Black owned but during Prohibition were bought by white mobsters and managed by their former owners. Clubs like the Sugar Cane at 135th and Fifth Ave were typical: damp, dimly lit cellar clubs, with about twenty tables around a tiny dance floor, and just enough room for a piano and small combo. Procope remembers Pod & Jerry's as the best place to hang out: "Everybody in Harlem, and the people from downtown, used to frequent these places. In those days, nobody was afraid to go anywhere. You'd see people from downtown in high silk hats and the ladies in diamond and furs strolling down the street at 3 or 4 o'clock in the morning."[24]

In *Jazzmen*, one of the first anthologies about jazz musicians (published in 1939), early jazz historian Charles Edward Smith wrote that one of Webb's first jobs in New York was at Healey's Balconnades, "the dance hall at the end of the Great White Way" on West Sixty-Sixth Street, where name bands like the Original Memphis Five played in the early 1920s.[25] Jobs in dance halls and small clubs, whether basement dives or exclusive Black-and-tan cabarets, could supply steady employment for a few weeks or months if—like Duke Ellington and His Washingtonians—one got along well with the dance hall operators or gangster club owners. Musicians had to prove themselves constantly.[26]

The top trendsetting Black band in New York was the Fletcher Henderson Orchestra, one of the house bands at the Roseland Ballroom starting in 1924.[27] Henderson, born in 1897, grew up in a middle-class Black family in Cuthbert, Georgia; his parents were strict about their children's education, including music studies. Henderson was already an accomplished pianist when he moved to New York City in the early 1920s to study chemistry at Columbia University. He earned money demonstrating songs in a music store and left school after he was recruited by Harry Pace for his trail-blazing new venture, Black Swan Records, the first Black-owned record company. Henderson was hired as an accompanist and soon became the label's recording manager, which led to landmark recordings of early jazz and the formation of his recording bands, the nucleus of the future Fletcher Henderson Orchestra.[28]

Roseland was then the premiere fashionable dance emporium in midtown Manhattan, and Henderson's band alternated with white dance bands like Sam Lanin's for a whites-only audience. Through Don Redman's clever and innovative arrangements, the band's irrepressible jazz spirit, and forward-reaching soloists Louis Armstrong and Coleman Hawkins, the Henderson Orchestra became a forceful influence in large ensemble playing and represented the epitome of Black New York style and musicianship. In 1928, Henderson's musicians were also among the best paid: seventy-five dollars a week for most of the sidemen, and more for soloists.[29]

Guitarist Danny Barker recalls being awestruck the first time he heard Henderson's musicians jamming at the Rhythm Club. "His band was the greatest in the world. He knew it because he was being copied by everybody. His sidemen were the best and he paid the highest salaries. Every colored musician knew and read about his famous sidemen."[30]

Working for elite Black bandleaders like Fletcher Henderson, Sam Wooding, and Billy Fowler at the Roseland Ballroom and Club Alabam was a top-rung gig. These leaders could afford to keep stable personnel and hire their pick of musicians. Their orchestra's sounds and styles evolved to accompany the Charleston, the Black Bottom, and other trending Black dances, as well as elaborate floor shows. There was a fluidity of influence between Black and white musicians, but New York City's dance bands and theater bands were segregated in the 1920s. This was the professional milieu, though Local 802 was one of the first integrated musicians' unions in the country and recruited Black members through Harlem delegates like Henry Minton and Bert Hall.

The landscape of dance places in Harlem changed radically on March 12, 1926, when the Savoy Ballroom opened its doors for the first time. High-end cabarets with dancing and elaborate floor shows like the Cotton Club and Connie's Inn were for whites only, but the Savoy was intended and built for Black audiences. It soon became the crown of Harlem's musical scene, even though it did not pay as well as other spots, a source of resentment among musicians for years. Harlem residents proudly claimed it as their own. It took Webb more time than he'd hoped or envisioned, but in a few years, no band was more synonymous with the Savoy Ballroom than Chick Webb's.

Webb's spinal condition did not seem to be an issue in his early years as bandleader. None of his friends or colleagues from this time recalled that Webb was impaired or suffering then. If anything, he was energetic and persistent about getting work. Nonetheless, there were obstacles. Webb did not have the suave looks of Duke Ellington or other elegant young musicians and performers. Some bandleaders took one look at Webb and his deformed spine and didn't even want to hear him.

Webb kept going, meeting people and networking. After the Balconnades job ended, Bobby Stark started working with Edgar Dowell, the composer and ragtime pianist from Baltimore, who led his own dance bands occasionally. Dowell was active on several fronts: as songwriter for the hit revue "How Come," music publishing insider, and recording artist. Stark convinced Dowell to let Webb come to a few rehearsals. Dowell didn't want Webb to play or even sit in with his band. For one thing, he already had a drummer, and Webb may have seemed pretty "green" to him, compared to New York musicians.

According to an unsigned three-part profile of Webb in *DownBeat*, December 1937–February 1938 (the first lengthy feature articles about Webb in a music publication or any white publication), Stark invited Webb to tag along when Dowell's band had an audition for a club called the Palace Gardens. Dowell's drummer had gotten lost and never showed up. Impatient, the club owner told Dowell that the band had to audition or leave, and Dowell let Webb play. Webb impressed the manager so much that he gave Dowell the gig on condition that Webb be the drummer.[31] A couple of weeks later, Webb was able to get Dowell to hire Trueheart too. This was exactly what the two friends needed: exposure, steady work, and money. Webb and Trueheart reportedly made sixty dollars a week for a few months, an incredible sum for them, most of which Webb sent home to his family. When that gig ended, Dowell went on to other jobs without them, and Webb and Trueheart were back at the Rhythm Club.

After a few months in Harlem, Webb was a familiar figure yet still on the outskirts, workwise. The job with Edgar Dowell did help Webb's "stock go up"—his reputation on the street. For Webb and other newcomers, every jam session or occasional gig was an audition; every chance encounter could lead to possibilities. Webb knew it was a matter of survival to develop flair, musically and otherwise. To get and keep good jobs, dance band musicians also had to look really sharp and wore matching black dress suits or tuxedos, matching ties, and shiny patent leather shoes, complete with spats.

Webb and his friends kept crossing paths with Duke Ellington and Sonny Greer at the Rhythm Club and around the neighborhood. Ellington's

Washingtonians all lived in Harlem, and after they were done with their nightly gig at the Kentucky Club in midtown, they joined the round of jam sessions and club hopping. In the fall of 1926, on an ordinary afternoon at the Rhythm Club, everything turned around for Webb. Ellington casually offered him what turned out to be a life-changing opportunity—the chance to become a bandleader.

4

A Bandleader's Beginnings

The average musician hated to go home in those days. He was always seeking someplace where somebody was playing something he ought to hear. Ten o'clock in the morning someone would come by and say, "Man, they're jamming at so-and so's and over he'd go. If you went home before nine in the morning you were an amateur.

—Sonny Greer[1]

Webb was now part of a roving group of young musicians, going out almost every night to the basement clubs in the brownstones that lined West 132nd and 133rd Street. These blocks were a meeting point of the "two Harlems." As John Gennari and others noted: one was where "Harlemites lived, worked, and entertained themselves. . . . [T]he other was a 'leisure zone' for white cultural dippers and treasure hunters."[2] On 133rd Street—called "Jungle Alley" by white tourists—"everyone rubbed shoulders," wrote Cary D. Wintz, "gay and straight, whites from across the city, working class Blacks as well as intellectuals, writers, musicians, artists, businessmen, criminals, and prostitutes."[3] These clubs had a different atmosphere than Connie's Inn or the Cotton Club, where the "whites-only" audience was situated away from the entertainers at a safe remove—what Sonny Greer later called the "Cotton Curtain."

Webb and his friends went to jam sessions every night—at Mexico's, the Nest, the Bandbox, and other places all within couple of blocks. Guitarist Danny Barker said: "133rd Street in Harlem had a raft of joints. . . . You 'dived in and dived out'—enjoying music, having fun." Mexico's, a long narrow basement room at 154 West 133rd Street, was Duke Ellington's favorite, a jam session hub that Webb regularly attended. Trumpet player Rex Stewart wrote that Webb and Duke palled around a lot in the years before Ellington and his orchestra got established at the Cotton Club. They had a close friendship that was apparent to musicians at the time but isn't talked about in jazz reference works.

From 1925 to early 1927, Ellington and the Washingtonians were the house band at the Kentucky Club (formerly the Hollywood Club), a tiny basement speakeasy not far from Times Square. The band was popular with the club's audience, which included small-time mobsters and club owners who sometimes asked Ellington and Greer to find musicians who sounded like them. Bootlegged booze and generous tips were part of the picture, as were potential raids and shutdowns. It was here that Duke tried out his original tunes, and the band edged toward an identifiable sound with Bubber Miley on trumpet and "Tricky" Sam Nanton on trombone using plungers and wah-wah effects. Someone offered Duke a booking at a nearby club called the Black Bottom, named for the dance that had recently overtaken the Charleston in popularity. Professor Brenda Gottschild, a cultural historian and dance scholar, called the Black Bottom more overtly sexual, the "ur-buttocks dance of the early twentieth century."[4]

Ellington and Greer went to the Rhythm Club to find some musicians for the job. Webb, Trueheart, Hodges, and a couple of other friends were hanging around and playing pool. On the spot, Ellington, six years Webb's senior, asked him if he wanted to be a bandleader, knowing that Webb and his friends worked together occasionally.

Years later, Ellington proudly took ownership of his prescient decision. "I made Chick a bandleader when I was working at the Kentucky Club. When some of the boys around downtown decided to open up a new joint they'd stop by and tell Sonny Greer and me." According to Ellington, Webb asked what he had to do to be a bandleader. "All you do is collect the money and bring me mine." Ellington had been a contractor during his early years as a bandleader in Washington, DC and took a 10 percent cut. In Ellington's apocryphal account, Webb replied, "Is that all I have to do? . . . Okay, I'm a bandleader."[5]

Hodges, who was hired by Ellington in 1928 and became one of the most idolized jazz soloists, told his own version of the story. Duke had asked him first, but Hodges didn't want the responsibility. None of this group really knew what it took to lead a band. "We were hungry and Chick had to make the grade, or we wouldn't have stood to listen to him again that season."[6]

Ellington had moved from Washington, DC to New York in 1923, ambitious and interested in New York's wider range of opportunities. He was hustling in several modes: as a bandleader, as a composer and songwriter, and as a pianist, trying to get a nod of approval from the great Harlem stride pianists. He was strikingly handsome, dressed impeccably, and carried a briefcase on his song-selling rounds. Trumpet player Rex Stewart, another on-the-scene Harlem musician, wrote: Duke's "first line of strategy was to always present an immaculate appearance, both for himself and for his organization, which he accomplished with great care."[7]

When Ellington met Webb in the mid-1920s, he and the Washingtonians were getting noticed at the Kentucky Club. The band got a good write-up in *Variety*, and acclaimed white bandleaders and musicians working nearby like Paul Whiteman, already called the "King of Jazz," started coming to hear them. So did a young songwriter and song plugger named Irving Mills, who heard potential in Ellington's early compositions. Mills asked Ellington if he could be Duke's manager. That was a new role for Mills, and one that he shrewdly developed into a multifaceted career for himself and Duke Ellington, who had to navigate Mills's opportunistic strategies carefully as he forged his extraordinary career.[8]

Webb didn't have a manager when Ellington made his offer; nor did he have Ellington's polished demeanor. But Webb had the nucleus of a good ensemble for his first bandleading job: Trueheart, Hodges, Stark, and pianist Don Kirkpatrick, who was Hodges's brother-in-law. As a group, they felt confident; this was the chance they'd been hoping for.

Webb discovered that as a bandleader he would have a lot more responsibilities than giving Ellington his "cut." He had to make sure the group had enough material to play from 10 p.m. until 3 or 4 in the morning and please the audience. He had to make sure everyone was well dressed and alert. The Black Bottom was an illegal speakeasy and could get raided and closed down at any moment, so Webb also had to make sure the band got paid in cash every night. Ellington's band was already popular with the speakeasy set, so Webb and his musicians emulated their sound and basically jazzed up danceable pop songs of the day, such as "I've Found a New Baby" and "Bye, Bye Blackbird."[9]

Working for gangsters had some advantages. They could be generous with tips; if they liked what the musicians played, they literally threw cash at them. Saxophonist Charlie Holmes, who worked with Webb and in other top Harlem bands, described what happened at many uptown clubs: "Around three o'clock in the morning all the other places would be closed, and then the gangsters would start falling into this place. They'd come in with their chicks and start throwin' money all over. All you had to do was play something that they liked, and boy, they'd throw a hundred dollar bill up there in a minute. . . . I didn't mind working for gangsters."[10]

Webb and saxophonist Johnny Hodges were now close friends and spent so much time together that people thought they were cousins. Both of them enjoyed playing jokes and never let on that they weren't related. They both were really serious about music, analyzed what other jazz musicians were doing, tried to advance their skills, and debated musical fine points about what they heard at clubs or on records. Rex Stewart was a terrific observer of his musician friends and the Harlem scene: "It was a sight to see and hear him [Webb] and young Johnny arguing about how a saxophone riff should be played. . . . Verbally they would square off at each other like a pair of bantam cocks."[11]

Hodges had an easier time financially in New York than some of his peers. He still performed with several bands in Boston, his hometown, and went back and forth. He would work in Boston and save enough money "to come back [to New York], probably three or four weeks later, join another band, get some new ideas, and go back to Boston."[12] When Webb and his band started to get steadier work, Hodges dropped other things to join him.

According to the 1937 profile of Webb in *DownBeat*, "this band was very terrific" at the Black Bottom, was paid two hundred dollars a week, and that Webb paid Duke thirty dollars for his fee. They played at the Black Bottom for five months—a lengthy residency for those uncertain times. During the Jazz Age, work was actually scarce for most musicians; long engagements at clubs or ballrooms were elusive for novice bandleaders like Webb. After a long dry spell, Ellington reportedly helped Webb get another job at the Paddock Club, one of many speakeasies in midtown. Webb was able to add three musicians: tenor saxophonist Elmer Williams, trombonist Wilbur de Paris ("Slats"), and Leon England or Elmer James on tuba or bass (both played with Webb frequently in the mid-1920s). The author wrote that the band was "sensational" at the Paddock, and their arrangements were "so marvelous that Fletcher Henderson wanted to buy their scores, but none of their original things were written out." This job ended after a few months when the Paddock burned down.[13]

Despite these setbacks, Chick enjoyed the status that being a bandleader conferred on him. More than anything he wanted to get more work for him and his friends, and have the band known as an entity. In 1927, his personnel were usually the same as they had been for the Paddock Club, an octet. Like other bands of that period, they used different names for different purposes: the name that stuck was Chick Webb and His Harlem Stompers.

In early February 1927, Chick Webb and His Harlem Stompers were hired to play at the Savoy Ballroom for the first time. The week before, their name appeared in print—also for the first time—in an ad for the Savoy in the *Amsterdam News*. The headliner was Fess Williams and His Royal Flush Orchestra.

HEAR THE KING OF ALL JAZZ KINGS
FESS WILLIAMS AND HIS NEW ROYAL FLUSH ORCHESTRA
Alternating with CHICK WEBB and His Harlem Stompers
A THOUSAND NEW FEATURES WITH MANY ALLURING SURPRISES
WILL TICKLE YOU SILLY
OH! MY YES! BE SURE AND PAY US A VISIT THIS WEEK[14]

Fess Williams and His Royal Flush Orchestra had been the Savoy's leading resident band since the Savoy Ballroom opened. Born in rural Kentucky and the grandson of slaves, Williams had come to the Savoy with his group via a circuitous route whose last stop had been a roadhouse in Albany. Williams played clarinet and alto sax and was the band's leader and featured vocalist; he was a sparkling showman, who often wore a white top hat and white rhinestone-studded tuxedo. He and the Royal Flush quickly became a Savoy audience favorite.[15]

The Savoy Ballroom was an enviable place for bandleaders and musicians to work from the moment it opened, March 12, 1926. It was also one of the most demanding—bandleaders and their musicians had to meet the dancers' nonstop expectations. The Savoy Bearcats, another Savoy favorite, often played opposite Williams's band during the ballroom's first year. These were preswing years, when the size and instrumentation of dance bands were still in flux, and there was no sound amplification. Williams's Royal Flush now had ten musicians (up from eight): two trumpets; one trombone; three saxophones/clarinets, including Williams; and a rhythm section of piano, banjo, tuba, and drums. The Bearcats had ten or eleven pieces, including leader Leon Abbey on violin, and gifted pianist Joe Steele, who moved to

New York from his native Boston after graduating from the New England Conservatory in 1924.[16]

For Webb and his band, this first date at the Savoy was the most prestigious job they'd had. For weeks before the event, he insisted that the band rehearse every day and try not to get overshadowed by Williams. The Stompers must have put on a good show; Charlie Buchanan, the Savoy's manager, hired them again for the Savoy's first anniversary celebration coming up in March.

Hodges told his friends in Boston about the Stompers' upcoming Savoy appearance, and several of them made a plan to come to New York and hear them. They were teenagers, still in high school and living at home, earning a few dollars playing dances or odd jobs. Two of them, Harry Carney and Charlie Holmes, were saxophonists from a Black neighborhood in Cambridge, Massachusetts, where almost everyone grew up learning an instrument. Holmes was given an oboe so he could play in the school orchestra, and later on acquired a clarinet and alto saxophone. As a teenager, he "lived for music, that's how inspired I was. I just imagined that the oboe was a saxophone."

As the date approached, everyone chickened out except Holmes and Carney. Holmes said: "I told my Mama I was going to stay with some friends of Harry's mother, and he told his Mama the same thing. Well, as it happened, we did go to a friend of his mother's, she knew that he was coming. . . . [S]he had a room, and we stayed there that night."[17] They brought their instruments; even as teenagers these two never went anywhere without them. Hodges told them to come right to the Savoy: "It [the Savoy] was the most gorgeous thing I'd ever seen in my life," Holmes recalled, his voice brightening when he told this story decades later. "I'd seen nice-looking ballrooms, but nothing like that. We walked right in, and went right in front of the bandstand, and started talking to Johnny while the band was still setting up. 'Hey, yeah, Johnny, blah-blah-blah.' And here come the bouncers and ran us right off to the side. I said, 'Look, that's my friend, that's my friend!' "

Hodges came right over and introduced his friends to Webb. "Chick was crazy about Johnny, and made us feel good, right at home."[18] Holmes and Carney were starstruck and couldn't believe how Fess Williams's band and the Stompers kept the thousand-plus dancers going strong for hours.

The night did not end at the Savoy. After the dance was over, Hodges took his friends to Mexico's for the jam session. The place was packed when they walked in at 1:30 a.m. Holmes was stupefied when Coleman Hawkins, then twenty-three years old, made his way to the bandstand. Hawkins, now the star soloist in Fletcher Henderson's Orchestra, was stretching the expressive and technical limits of the tenor saxophone, which he helped transform from a novelty instrument into a dominant voice in jazz instrumentation. Holmes remembered every minute of the night: "Well, he [Hawkins] was the master, you know—there was something different when he blowed, too. Nobody else would play any more tenor that night. They wouldn't play it. Couldn't get 'em to play it." Hodges had a good reputation with the older musicians. After Hawkins's solo he announced that it was time to "hear the alto players." Hodges took a solo and then passed the spot to his Boston friends, Harry Carney and Charlie Holmes.

"I was scared to death just being there with all those sharks, they were big men to me," Holmes remembered. "I said, 'No, I'm not gonna do no playin'.' Well, they begged me to play, so I did—what little I knew. And I got to rockin' and carryin' on. So damn, they applauded! Somebody said to Chick Webb, 'He's out-swinging your man Johnny Hodges!'"

The next day, Webb ran into Hodges and his friends on the street. "Here he comes now," Webb said when he saw Holmes. "This is the man who out-swung Johnny Hodges in the cuttin' contest last night."[19] Thanks to Webb's bragging, Holmes and Carney ended up getting hired to play in the alternate band at the Savoy for a few nights, right next to Webb's Harlem Stompers. They could not believe their luck.

Holmes decided to stay in New York City, alarming his parents, especially when he told them that he wanted to leave high school. Carney decided to stay too, and his mother's friend let them stay at her place. After a few weeks Holmes was hired by Billy Fowler for his band at the Club Alabam on Broadway, a big-time cabaret with a full floor show. Holmes played alongside some top Harlem musicians, including saxophonist Edgar Sampson, trumpet player Ward Pinkett, and trombonist Ed Cuffee.

Holmes was thrilled. "I was getting $65 a week! . . . I was 17 years old, and making three or four times as much money as my daddy was making. The average working man made $15–18 a week. And I damn near sent all of my money back home, trying to prove how good I was doing in New York, because I didn't want my parents to worry."

After a few weeks, guitarist/banjoist Freddy Guy, one of Ellington's Washingtonians, invited them to rent a room in his apartment. Guy was married and lived a floor above Ellington, who used to come by all the time. Holmes and Carney paid four dollars a week for their room.

Holmes's parents were worried. They thought that New York City was a terrible place, even though their son was well paid and was looked after by the older musicians. They warned him, "'When you go there, don't look up in the air!' I guess somebody was supposed to knock me in the head or something when you look up in the air," said Holmes. "There were so many tales out about New York, and I didn't find it nothin' like I was told. I was having a ball over here, believe me. And I was meeting so many fine people, and going to all of these different places and things. As long you got a pocket-full of money, which is what I had."[20]

The Harlem Stompers were gaining a foothold, literally, among the Savoy's irrepressible dancers. Savoy manager Charlie Buchanan hired them again for another high-profile event coming up in May of 1927: the Savoy's first high-pitched "battle of the bands." Musicologist and dance scholar Christi Jay Wells describes the history and character of the early "Battles of Music." The idea, Wells writes, came from the early twentieth-century New Orleans musical scene, where rival musical groups promoted themselves through informal contests. Ballrooms in the North began to stage similar battles in the 1920s to advertise themselves, using the language of military combat to amplify excitement. These events—examples of what Ralph Ellison called "antagonistic collaboration"—pitted bands against each other regionally, stylistically, and even racially. Band battles became a regular Savoy attraction, a marketing ploy that worked. As the smaller jazz dance bands of the 1920s morphed into the seventeen-piece swing dance bands of the 1930s, these battles were contested ferociously among fans and the entertainment press, who turned some of them into the stuff of jazz legend. Chick Webb would become one of the leading contenders.[21]

The Savoy's first battle took place on May 15, 1927, and Savoy owner Moe Gale and Buchanan promoted it with a blitz of advertising and word of mouth. The orchestras of Fletcher Henderson and Fess Williams were booked to compete against jazz pioneer King Oliver and his Dixie Syncopators, who were coming from Chicago to play at the Savoy for a few weeks. All three bands had star status, and Fess Williams's Royal Flush Orchestra now had a big radio following. The fourth band, Chick Webb's Harlem Stompers, an octet, was the dark horse, familiar to Harlem musicians and some local followers. No prizes were offered to the winning band—just tons of publicity and the adulation of the audience. When the doors opened at 10 p.m., a capacity crowd of four thousand entered and hundreds of people were turned away. It was the Savoy's biggest night since its opening. This event got a rave review in both the *New York Herald Tribune*—a major white New York City daily, in what was perhaps the paper's first review of Black dance bands—and the *Amsterdam News*, the most prominent Black newspaper in New York. Both papers gave Chick Webb and His Harlem Stompers the band's biggest affirmation to date. Both reviewers also invoked what would become a steady drumbeat of "battle" rhetoric and laid out different historic examples. The battle theme would underscore scads of reviews in the following decade, when the Swing Era's big band battles were fought in ballrooms across the country.

The *Amsterdam News* reporter enlists Civil War generals to paint the scene:

> Not since Grant took Richmond, nor ever since Sherman said war was what he said it was has such a gripping, stirring sensation swept the nation as this remarkable battle of "Jazz Warfare."... Who can remember the time when such personalities as Fletcher Henderson with his soul stirring army of blue blowers; King Oliver, the big man ... who told his boys to go east and conquer; Fess Williams ... who has more than 100,000 music lovers eating out of the hollow of his hand; and last but not least that great big-little fellow Chick Webb, who stands 3'2" in his stocking feet and weighs 75 pounds soaking wet.

That last bit was not true; Webb was four feet tall. It's rare for a journalist to exaggerate someone's shortness to capture the dramatic effect, but it worked.

> These four bands raised the roof.... The building shook with applause, the throngs went wild with enthusiasm.... It is difficult to determine who won this historic battle of music. In the humble opinion of this writer, the people were the winners.

The reviewer left no doubt as to his pride for the place, the event, the music, and in particular the leader of the last of the four bands.

> Chick and his Harlem Stompers, the least famous of these bands, were up last.... [O]ur little friend Chick Webb stepped right up and proceeded to knock them cold, just as he's been doing all along. Those who attended that battle of music will never forget it.[22]

The *New York Herald Tribune* reporter applauded all four bandleaders, using the embedded racist expressions of the time. "Although no one sang a 'mammy' song last night ... Harlem did some strutting as it has never strutted before. Five thousand swains and dark-hued flappers danced everything from a comparatively sedate two-step to an agitated Tampico trot." The writer then set the battle scene in the American Revolution, with the three New York bands "standing ground" in Harlem, where "jazz is aesthetic and appreciated."

Like the Concord farmers three of Harlem's finest exponents of syncopated sonata stood embattled against an invasion that reversed Horace Greeley's adage and came East. Chicago sent King Oliver.... He laid siege to New York, but principally to Harlem.... Arrayed against him were Fletcher Henderson, who nightly sets Broadway on its ears; Chick Webb, who yields to no-one in punishing a drum and Fess Williams, Harlem's own prophet of those who worship at the feet of a Twentieth Century Pan. Each orchestra let go with all it had ... while dance-mad youth gouged themselves in the feats of a certain brand of noise that won't let anybody stay still.[23]

Webb's musical circle and former bandleaders in Baltimore kept up with the good news about him. Shortly after his triumph in the Savoy's first band battle, Webb's band was booked to be the headliner in Baltimore at New Albert Hall, with his former bandleaders getting second billing. For the first time in the *Baltimore Afro-American*, Webb's name and photo were front and center:

LITTLE CHICK WEBB

And his New York Harlem Stompers, Direct from the Savoy Ballroom, N. Y. City

TUESDAY, MAY 17	WEDNESDAY, May 18
With Ike Dixon's Orchestra	With Percy Glascoe's Orchestra

The caption under the photo of the band finally gives the two formerly anonymous sidemen recognition in their hometown: "John Trueheart, a well known Baltimore boy, and CHICK WEBB, leader are Baltimore's two well known musicians ... Come Out! They are Red Hot! Don't miss hearing them!"[24]

In the summer of 1927, Webb made some progress as a bandleader. He joined Local 802, the largest musicians' union in the world. Local 802 replaced New York's Local 301 in 1921 after conflicts had arisen between leadership and members involving contentious theater practices, overly liberal policies toward transfers from other locals, and scabbing.[25]

Local 802's new leaders created incentives for joining and tried to make its members feel supported. By the mid-1920s, Local 802 had an influx of Black members from the Clef Club and New Amsterdam Musical Association (NAMA). A slowly increasing number of Black jazz bandleaders, recording artists, and musicians joined, including Fletcher Henderson, Coleman Hawkins, Clarence Williams, Sam Wooding, and Duke Ellington. The union finally recognized the fact that Black dance band and club musicians had a huge impact on the entire city's musical employment. In September 1926, tenor sax player Henry Minton (who founded Minton's Playhouse in 1938) became the first Black delegate. He encouraged other Black musicians to join and looked out for their interests, even though as a contractor he too evaded contracts for casual gigs. Applicants had to prove that they were working professional-level jobs and had been New York City residents for at least six months, and perform a brief live audition. Union reps from Local 802 were likely to stop by high-profile places like the Savoy and Lafayette Theater, where Webb started leading his band more frequently in 1927 and 1928, to check for violations.

Then as now, musicians' jobs were hard to come by, and Local 802 musicians sometimes took noncontract jobs. Local 802 was zealous about overseeing contracts and frequently brought up members on charges when rules were violated.

When Webb joined Local 802 in 1927, the union had close to fifteen thousand members who could be heard in symphony and opera houses, theaters, musicals, cabarets, movie palaces, honky-tonks, ballrooms, amusement parks, and more. Joining the union was a necessary step, and Webb's musicians became members. For a while Local 802 was known as the Two-Dollar Union for its two-dollar membership fee (thirty-one dollars today), which ate into the slim earnings of Webb and his musicians. A few months after he joined the union, Webb and his sidemen's names, addresses, and phone numbers appeared in the Local 802 Directory for the first time. A great resource for musicians, the directory listed Webb's address as 158 West 131st Street, where he shared rooms with his best friend and bandmate from Baltimore, guitarist/banjoist John Trueheart. They remained roommates for several years.[26]

Webb was soon called out by Local 802's Governing Board for failing to file weekly reports. So were Fletcher Henderson and Duke Ellington; they were all fined five dollars. In Webb's case, this was steep; he and his bandmates were still scuffling for every dollar, while Henderson's was one of the best-paid Black bands in New York City.

In summer and fall of 1927, Chick Webb and His Harlem Stompers were a hit whenever they appeared at the Savoy. They also performed as part of a revue at the Lafayette Theater, another famous uptown entertainment hotspot. That July, Webb got a shout-out from the *Afro* by Eva Jessye, who had recently moved from Baltimore to Harlem and wrote an entertainment column, "Around New York," for the paper: "Chick Webb, now featured at the Savoy, has the hottest eight-piece band in the country, according to those who know bandeology." Jessye had joined the musicians' migration herself, leaving her post as choral music director at Baltimore's Morgan College to further her own career as a choral director and composer in New York City.[27]

Jessye's column noted that Fess Williams was leaving the Savoy for the summer, and that Arthur Gibbs's band would have the job while the Royal Flush were on tour. Webb now understood that Charlie Buchanan's hiring practices for bands were subjective and could be mercurial. The Savoy only paid Local 802 minimum scale for ballrooms—approximately thirty dollars a week, which was far less than what Fletcher Henderson was getting for his men at Roseland, about seventy-five dollars per man, per week. Buchanan and Gale got away with it then and for years to come due to the ballroom's centrality in Harlem. For all its seeming success, the Savoy barely broke even every week.

The *Afro* reported other news about Webb too, in the paper's society pages. His grandparents visited New York City for a week in September 1927. Webb's younger sister Mabel had gotten married and moved to Harlem with her husband, Wilbur Porter. Mabel and Chick both hosted dinners to celebrate the visit: "Mr. and Mrs. Wilbur Porter gave a dinner in honor of Mr. and Mrs. Jones of Baltimore. . . . A dinner was given by Mr. William (Chick Webb) in honor of his grandmother and grandfather."[28] Despite his growing bandleader status, Webb had nowhere near the volume of work as more prominent and experienced bandleaders. Even with the proliferation of new places to dance, there were still relatively few dance bands that had steady jobs. The top-tier Black bands—Fletcher Henderson's and Duke Ellington's—could only employ so many musicians. The fifteen- and seventeen-piece swing dance bands would not become standard for another few years.

Ellington wrote about this period in 1940, for an article in *Swing: The Guide to Modern Music*: "There wasn't near enough work for everybody that could blow horns, and what musicians didn't have steady jobs would spend their days standing out on the street gabbing, always arguing about the respective merits of somebody else. It was still too early for the fellows to get real big-time about money, and all the musicians who weren't working steadily played gigs around town and didn't bother about reputation."[29]

5

Savoy

"The World's Finest Ballroom"

Walking into the building at the Savoy was like walking up the stairway to heaven. As you came up, your back was to the band, then you'd turn around and face this floor filled with people dancing. You could feel the floor bouncing and the bands burning. It was a hell of a feeling.

—Frankie Manning[1]

"Stomp" bands were the rage during the late 1920s, when Chick Webb's band pounded out up-tempo Charlestons and two-steps for dancers at the Savoy Ballroom and a few other spots. The band's popularity there—holding their own alongside the best jazz orchestras in the city—didn't guarantee frequent or future bookings. The Savoy's first few years of existence were an experiment that no one expected to succeed. Fortunately, the Savoy's detractors were soon proved wrong.

The founding of the Savoy, "The World's Finest Ballroom," is, among other things, the story of intersecting migrations in Harlem: of Afro-Americans, Afro-Caribbeans, and Eastern European Jews. This was not unusual in the entertainment business, a conduit for migrants from different trajectories to interact. In the Savoy's case, the intersection involved Black musicians, dancers, and entertainers and Jewish entrepreneurs, in a complicated marriage of opportunity of people largely sidelined from mainstream professions.

The money to build the ballroom came from the Galewskis, a family of Jewish immigrants who started a leather business in the early 1900s. A listing in the January 1921 issue of *Trunks, Leather Goods and Umbrellas, A Journal of Information for the Trade* notes that S. Galewski & Sons Inc., a bag and suitcase company, had been incorporated with 125,000 dollars in stock, with

> Sigmund Galewski as President, and Moses Galewski as secretary and treasurer. Sigmund will continue in charge of the office and buying, and Moses will have charge of the factory as before. The new concern will extend the line to include a greater assortment of styles in the higher grades, and attractive offerings in kits, coat cases and overnight bags.[2]

Sigmund Galewski, an affable businessman, and his wife, Anna (née Schwarz), had each been part of the massive migration of Jews from Eastern Europe and met and married in New York City in 1897. Within a few years Sigmund had his own suitcase manufacturing company with a showroom on the Lower East Side, near where they lived, and he later started a millinery business. By 1910 the Galewskis and their three sons—Moses ("Moe"), Joseph ("Tim"), and Conrad—moved to the southern part of Harlem, and in the early 1920s to a large apartment on Riverside Drive, their most upwardly mobile move. That neighborhood was a mix of brownstones and large apartment buildings, with views of the Hudson River and leafy tree-lined streets. Their sons began using the assimilated surname Gale.

Sixty years later, Conrad, the youngest brother, recalled what happened: "The Roseland Ballroom's manager [Isadore Jay Faggen] had suggested to an uncle of mine [Charles Galewski], who was in real estate, the possibility of building a colored ballroom in Harlem. But suddenly he went broke, and then they approached my father. My father knew nothing about running ballrooms, and gave the job to my brother Moe, who was out of a job."[3]

Faggen (known as I. Jay Faggen) had a good reputation as a ballroom manager and entrepreneur. Originally from Philadelphia, he moved to New York in 1920 to manage the Rosemont Ballroom in downtown Brooklyn; then, with other partners, he built and managed Manhattan's Roseland Ballroom in 1923, and the Arcadia a year later. These were the most capacious and ornate ballrooms in the city, built to accommodate over three thousand dancers. In February 1925, *Variety* published an item, perhaps prematurely, that Faggen was "personally supervising the erection of a new spacious ballroom for colored patronage.... Faggen has Negro capital interested and is in control of a sizable block of the enterprise in exchange for his services."[4]

Faggen, also from an Eastern European Jewish family, found his first partner for this venture in Sigmund Galewski. Sigmund was initially dubious about investing in a Harlem ballroom, but he was convinced by his wife, Anna, who supplied most of the money. Conrad Gale described his mother as a "striking beauty" with a big heart. "She had a feeling for an act of human kinship. My mother always felt a sympathy for the Negro—in terms of discrimination, of lack of opportunity. . . . My father did, too, but nothing like my mother. He was a businessman. . . . He was the front for money. The other Charlie had real estate—but they [Faggen] needed hard cash. It came from my mother, who supplied most of the cash."[5]

Sigmund was also looking to launch his eldest son, Moe, in a career and viewed the ballroom as a possibility. Moe had jumped around in several small enterprises, but couldn't seem to stick to any of them. One was illegal. In early February 1922, Moe was arrested along with twenty-seven other men by federal marshals who uncovered an interstate auto insurance scam in which car owners arranged to have their cars stolen. No record exists of Gale's conviction, and this incident never appeared in the many glowing press reports about the Savoy Ballroom's early years.[6]

Sigmund's idea was not for Moe to be the ballroom's manager—he and Faggen planned to hire a Black manager. Moe would learn the business while looking after the family's financial interests in the place.

Faggen and Moe Gale agreed on a few basic ideas: Harlem's Black community would have its own neighborhood Roseland, with high-quality music and entertainment and no bootleg liquor, gangsters, or vices. The ballroom would be a safe, welcoming place for Black Harlemites as its principal audience. "The idea was, this was going to be a Black ballroom for Black people run by Black people, and not be exploited," said Conrad Gale.[7] Faggen and Gale also envisioned it as a space that could be used for community and political events, including those of Harlem's numerous social clubs. The ballroom would be constructed and designed to be as elegant and upscale as Roseland and the Arcadia but affordable for Harlemites. They named it after the Savoy Hotel in London, to evoke European grandeur.

They leased an empty lot on Lenox Avenue between 140th and 141st Streets from the Third Avenue Railroad System (TARS), which had operated horsecar lines, streetcars, and eventually buses extending throughout upper Manhattan. The company had been using this lot as a dumping ground for obsolete equipment, including remnants of horse carriages.[8] They formed a corporation, Associated Ballrooms, Inc. Sigmund Galewski, Moe's father, secured a lease for the TARS property but took no part in decision making.

Construction began in the fall of 1925, around the same time that Chick Webb moved to Harlem.

Gale and Faggen posted a job for a manager to start planning the ballroom's opening and operation, aiming to open in early 1926; the job would pay 150 dollars per week, an excellent salary in those years. Hiring Charles Buchanan, then twenty-seven years old, turned out to be one of their best decisions. Born in the British West Indies, Buchanan moved to Harlem with his family when he was six years old. A tall, striking, confident man, Buchanan was starting to make a living as a realtor in Harlem and really knew the community.[9] Buchanan was immediately involved in major decisions about logistics, policies, decorating, and assembling a staff. He proved to be an excellent manager, though he had never done anything like it before. Neither had Moe Gale. Neither had anybody.

The Savoy Ballroom took seven months to build and ended up costing over five hundred thousand dollars for a two-story building that took up most of the block and housed other businesses on the street level. The entrance was on the ground floor in the middle of Lenox Avenue, and at night its marquee lit up the block, a glowing electric sign with dancing music notes surrounding the ballroom's name. On the inside, cascading chandeliers hung over two curved marble staircases leading up to the ballroom, which took up the entire second story. The spring-loaded maple dance floor—soon called "The Track"—was over ten thousand square feet, with multicolor spotlights creating a dancing play of lights on the dancers. Along the far wall were two bandstands, near each other so that two bands could alternate sets in a continuous flow of music.[10] The ballroom was built to accommodate two thousand dancers "without anyone ever kicking anyone," recalled Frankie Manning, one of the Savoy's legendary dancers. For special events crowds of over four thousand jammed the place, with lines of people around the block trying to get in.

In its early years, the Savoy Ballroom was not a Jazz Age tourist destination for white tourists looking for a good time in Harlem. It was meant for Harlemites, which made it completely unlike exclusive, whites-only or "Black-and-tan" expensive cabarets or taxi dance halls. But it is misleading to say that the Savoy Ballroom was "integrated." Initially, the ballroom didn't encourage white visitors. "You could go to the Savoy for years and years and never know that there was any white involvement there at all," said Conrad. "They couldn't keep whites out but they did not want a white trade up there. . . . It had no white feeling whatsoever."

Still, a few white visitors came, including artists and scholars, such as British aesthete Harold Acton, who had been encouraged to visit by his friend, the choreographer Sergei Diaghilev. Another visitor was the innovative female photographer Berenice Abbott, who wound up taking one of the most famous photographs of the Savoy Ballroom.

Abbott had been living in Paris, where she was an assistant to surrealist artist and photographer Man Ray (born Emmanuel Radnitsky) and became a successful portrait photographer herself. She resettled in New York in the late 1920s, moving into the Hotel des Artists and setting up her new studio. A'Lelia Walker, one of the most written-about salon hostesses in Harlem Renaissance circles, invited Abbott to go dancing in Harlem and to go to the Savoy. Abbott, who had a keen interest in dance, immediately knew she wanted to photograph the dancers there. On her second trip she brought along a special camera and secured permission—probably from Buchanan. Knowing that the ballroom's lighting was inadequate, she used a magnesium flash. The explosion of light from the flash caused so much chaos that she was asked to leave and was only able to take that one photo.

According to Hank O'Neal, Abbott's former mentee and long-time assistant, the camera she used was smaller than most box cameras of the time and more mobile, and the negatives were produced on glass plates. Only one contact print of the photo surfaced in her archives fifty years later. The band playing that night happened to be Chick Webb and His Harlem Stompers. It's a remarkable photograph, and Abbott's focus is clearly on the dancers, all of whom are immaculately dressed, men in suits and ties, women in elegant dresses—unlike the looser clothes Lindy Hoppers wore a few years later. Webb and his musicians are in the background, also immaculately dressed. Their instruments and equipment offer a snapshot of jazz history; bassist Elmer James has a tuba in tow; John Trueheart has a banjo and guitar; the singers (probably trumpet players) use megaphones since the ballroom wasn't amplified yet. Webb is caught with one arm raised, like he's in midbeat. Most jazz band photos of that time were posed, with band members and their instruments neatly lined up in a row. This is most likely the first indoor photo of a jazz band in action.[11]

Starting in the mid-1930s, with the combined popular explosion of big band swing and swing dance, white college kids, jazz lovers, and jazz musicians started coming to the Savoy regularly, as did celebrities such as Orson Welles and Marlene Dietrich. During those years "The World's Most Famous Ballroom" became even more "world famous."

Richard Gale, Moe's son, spoke about his father Moe's role at the ballroom, and how he changed: "It wasn't as if my father initially entered into this venture to promote interracial understanding and relationships. He wanted to make a buck. But as things progressed, he began to appreciate what the Savoy could do, the crucial role it played in helping overcome a great deal of the prejudice and hatred that separated Black and white people." Frankie Manning said, "People came to the Savoy and they forgot about racism."[12]

Faggen, Moe Gale, and Buchanan knew that the Savoy's open "democracy on the dance floor" policy would make it a target for the authorities and took daily precautions against any whiff of a scandal or illegal activity. Bouncers and staff were on the lookout for snuck-in booze, fights, and rowdy behavior, knowing that the police would pounce given any pretext.

Buchanan also wanted women to be able to come to the ballroom alone or with friends and feel safe, and not get hassled or harassed. He hired a team of ex-prize fighters and football players as bouncers. Those bouncers were "the most severe bouncers that ever graced a ballroom," recalled Buck Clayton, a trumpeter who played briefly with Duke Ellington, then for decades with Count Basie. "If you did something wrong they would throw you out of the Savoy twice. First . . . they would throw you down the steps, then they would come down the steps themselves and finish by throwing you out the door."[13]

In the months before the Savoy opened, Buchanan hired a staff of over eighty people—office helpers, porters, bouncers, cooks, waiters, dishwashers, stage hands, and hostesses—all of whom were Harlem residents. In February, Faggen launched what was at the time an innovative ad campaign, running weekly newspaper ads about the new ballroom. The ads promised the dance-loving public and "every member of the family" that:

— a large dance floor, unobstructed by pillars, will give ample room for dining in comfort
— the most skillful orchestra will produce the most rhythmic dance music . . .
— headliner vaudeville entertainment will be introduced
— good taste and good manners will prevail
— a scientific ventilation system will keep the temperature comfortable and the air fresh and clean

The ad promised that the Savoy Ballroom will be "recognized instantly as the greatest and best in New York."[14]

The Savoy's inaugural ball on Friday, March 12, 1926, was extensively promoted, and Faggen, Moe Gale, and Buchanan shrewdly invited politicians and prominent city officials: New York City Mayor James J. Walker, the Police Commissioner, and Harlem church dignitaries and celebrities.[15]

More than anything, the Savoy's founders did not want officials or potential patrons to confuse the Savoy with the numerous clubs, cabarets, or dance halls that sold illegal liquor. Admission was affordable: fifty cents on weeknights and seventy-five cents on weekends (sixty cents if you arrived before 6 p.m.). There were weekly free nights and "specials": raffles, Charleston competitions, beauty contests, bathing beauty contests, fashion shows, giveaways, and vaudeville acts for holidays and special events.[16] The management's' goal was to provide "clean, high-class entertainment where anyone can come and dance as long as he or she may wish."[17] In July, the Savoy opened its "Chinese kitchen," attracting two thousand people in the middle of a hot Sunday afternoon. The big crowd came to enjoy "dancing and chop suey. . . . The addition of the Chinese kitchen makes it one of the finest dining rooms in Harlem. Electric fans and other cooling devices make the Savoy a desirable place for recreation during the summer."[18]

The featured bands for the Savoy's inaugural ball were Fess Williams and His Royal Flush Orchestra, and Duncan Mayer and the Charleston Bearcats (soon known as the Savoy Bearcats), but the "name" attraction was Fletcher Henderson's Orchestra, who did not appear until 1 a.m., after their Roseland job. The band gave a thrilling performance, responding to the Savoy audience's wild enthusiasm. Henderson's musicians soon started making impromptu appearances at the Savoy, and the orchestra performed there for special events. Its appearances helped make the Savoy not only the premier spot to dance but also the place to hear the best jazz musicians in the city. Both the Royal Flush and the Bearcats were so popular at the Savoy that they became the regular house bands until 1928 (though not exclusively).

Fess Williams, a Tuskegee graduate, had worked his way with his small band from his native Kentucky to Chicago, then to a roadhouse job near Albany in the summer of 1925, before coming to New York. Williams's Royal Flush Orchestra had broadcast live from station WGY in Schenectady, New York, which then had one of the most powerful radio transmitters in the country. Faggen heard the band on the radio and drove up to Albany to check them out. He immediately signed them to perform at the Rosemont in Brooklyn, which he still managed. With Fess's bluesy half-spoken-word vocalizing and the band's good-time flourishes, they were a hit and stayed on in Brooklyn for a few months. Faggen thought that Williams and his band would be perfect for the Savoy.

The Charleston Bearcats were already well known in Harlem. Their personnel included stand-out musicians such as pianist Joe Steele, violinist Leon Abbey, and drummer Willie Lynch. They had been a featured band at the Nest Club when they were offered the opportunity to open at the Savoy, and then became one of the ballroom's first "house" bands. The Bearcats, a cooperative, soon replaced their nominal leader Duncan Mayers with Leon Abbey and changed its name to the Savoy Bearcats.[19]

Both bands blossomed at the Savoy, giving them opportunities and media exposure. Helen Armstead-Johnson, theater historian and friend of Williams in his later years, described Williams's role in the Savoy story, one usually overshadowed by bandleaders with more lasting footprints: "The air was full of talk about a ballroom that was being built in Harlem. Needless to say, every Black musician who had anything to offer was after the job. But when the owners heard Fess, they signed him immediately for the opening. . . . Fess says his band was just above average musically. The qualities which made it outstanding was the unique tempos plus entertaining features. It was a rare treat to see Fess in his high hat and diamond studded suit. . . . [O]ther nights he would be bedecked in his white suit with the gold lapels."[20]

During the Savoy's first few months, it promoted its resident bands' mounting accomplishments. June 16, 1926, was declared "Fess Williams's Night of Happiness," with giveaways to the audience: six phonographs and 2,500 copies of "My Mama's in Town/Make Me Know It," the band's first record for the Harmony label. This record shows that Fess was not being overly modest. Except for Williams's expressive vocalizing, the Royal Flush sounded "just above average" on "Make Me Know It," a slow drag with New Orleans–inspired polyphonic wailing. You can imagine Williams, though, sparkling and suited up, mesmerizing an audience with this kind of number. (The band's biggest hit records were for Victor, after it left the Savoy.)

In mid-August, a Savoy ad in the *Amsterdam News* announced:

The Savoy Bearcats, Direction of Leon Abbey, are the first colored orchestra that has ever been signed exclusively to record for the Victor Phonograph Company.

Do you know what that means? It means that the Savoy Bearcats are
THE WORLD'S GREATEST COLORED ORCHESTRA
Hear them every night and Sunday afternoon at the Savoy Ballroom[21]

A few days later, the paper printed a letter by Jerome Bourke clarifying the Savoy's claim. Bourke wrote that in 1923 he "had the privilege of playing with a colored orchestra *having an exclusive contract with the Victor Company*," namely "Arthur Gibbs and His Gang." He was not writing this letter "in an antagonistic spirit but as a matter of enlightenment to the Savoy Management and the public. More power to the Savoy Bearcats."[22]

The Bearcats' early recordings show an identifiable "New York" dance band sound largely influenced by the Henderson Orchestra's performance style and Don Redman's arrangements. Their first Victor recording was a brilliant cover of Henderson's "Stampede," an up-tempo romp through tight ensemble passages with call and response—a literal stampede of color and rhythm. Joe Steele, who worked with Webb later on, was a virtuosic pianist who played with flair and panache, yet still provided an anchor in the rhythm section.

The Savoy's immediate success provoked resentment among other Harlem nightlife stakeholders and plenty of rumors. Two weeks after it opened, Faggen placed an ad that offered a "$1000 REWARD" for information about a "malicious report . . . that we are charging extra for every dance in addition to the regular admission price and that it is quite expensive to come here for an evening's pleasure. SUCH A REPORT IS ABSOLUTELY FALSE!" The ad reiterated the ballroom's prices and reminded the public that "The Savoy is your ballroom, by far the most beautiful in the world, with two orchestras playing for you . . . and its entire personnel composed of colored people who are trained to serve and amuse you at a cost that is ridiculously small. Come and see for yourself!"[23]

The Savoy became an economic engine for Harlem, and some employees stayed on for decades. Savoy hostesses were an attraction themselves. The Savoy followed the ballroom practice of the time by offering lessons by its "dancing instructresses"—twenty-five cents for three dances—to men shy or insecure about dancing. The hostesses had to be beautiful, intelligent, educated, poised, and had to dance skillfully. They also had to be quick to cue the bouncers if any customers were out of line. Here again, the Savoy's hiring policy was selective, and atypical of other Harlem night spots. Savoy hostesses could be dark-skinned. At the Cotton Club and other whites-only venues, hostesses and chorus girls had to be light-skinned and pass what was called the "brown paper bag" test; their skin tone had to be lighter than the color of a brown paper bag.[24]

By most accounts, Savoy employees were glad to have a decent job in Harlem and excited about this unusual enterprise. Faggen, Gale, and Buchanan were thrilled that opening night was a huge success, as was the first month of operation. In April, they gave the entire staff a raise in recognition of their teamwork and efforts to get the Savoy open and running smoothly.[25]

Buchanan was attentive to every detail; nothing escaped him or betrayed his vision. He started a "School of Courtesy," which employees were required to attend twice a week. The purpose was to teach staff "the most intelligent means of handling the public"—to keep cool, be polite, and know when to summon a bouncer. He also started a merit system and gave monthly bonuses to outstanding employees.[26] Vigilant about whom he hired, Buchanan kept a close watch on the hostesses and bouncers so the ballroom would not get shut down (which it did not—amazingly—until 1943). Buchanan proudly claimed that the Savoy management paid its employees well especially compared to other jobs in Harlem. "It paid each married employee no less than $40 per week ... roughly three times the average salary for men in Harlem."[27]

Norma Miller, whose family lived around the corner from the ballroom, became one of the Savoy's elite Lindy Hoppers in the mid-1930s. She started sneaking into the ballroom at age twelve (the minimum age was sixteen): "Buchanan was brilliant—he worked for Moe Gale, but everybody else worked for him." Her comment was not entirely a compliment. As time went on, Buchanan took advantage of his powerful position; not everything he did was straight up. He took cuts from number runners who frequented the ballroom and Harlem contractors, and he and Gale were notoriously cheap when it came to paying musicians. They hardly ever paid more than Local 802's minimum, thirty-three dollars per man per week, and more for the leader. Nonetheless, in his early years as manager Buchanan had an impeccable reputation and had the respect of the entire Savoy staff. He was a pillar of Harlem's business community for decades.

Helen Clarke, one of the hostesses, recalled: "To be hired, Mr. Buchanan would check your background, family, schooling everything. He kept an eagle eye on you. . . . We had rules and regulations. A wardrobe mistress always checked our dresses to see if we looked all right. There was a ticket seller in a booth when you entered. . . . Buchanan would stand by the door. If you were five minutes late you'd be sent home. No fraternizing with musicians. No leaving the place with anyone."[28]

A few days after Chick Webb and His Harlem Stompers' triumph at the Savoy's first "Battle of Music", another event became the name of a new dance. On May 20, 1927, a twenty-five-year-old US air-mail pilot named Charles Lindbergh took off from Flushing Meadows on Long Island and landed in Paris the next day. Bells tolled across the country and radio broadcasts, newspapers, and newsreels celebrated this first solo flight across the Atlantic. The pilot's name migrated to the Black dance that was evolving at the time— the "Lindbergh Hop." Over the next few years, this dance style—better known as the Lindy Hop—took off, propelled by a swing beat. Music and dance would evolve together, especially at the Savoy Ballroom. Webb himself was one of the avant-garde drummers and stylistic innovators of this forward-moving jazz rhythm that dancers loved—swing.

The dance and rhythmic emphasis of the Lindy Hop shifted from the one-step and two-step dances identified with the Jazz Age, like the Charleston and medium-tempo foxtrots. Swing rhythm didn't accent the second and fourth beats but moved across all four beats, anticipating the next measure or musical phrase. The dancers used lower, more grounded hip movements, with a loose-limbed feel. The basic dance phrase was stretched out over two measures—an eight-count rather than four—allowing the two partners to "swing out" from each other and improvise, an innovation in social dance at that time. Partners did not have to mirror each other's step patterns but kept to the beat, and rejoined their partner along with musicians' phrasing.

Initially, the Lindy was considered too wild to be performed alongside conventional dancers. At the Savoy, dancers trying out this new style were cordoned off in a corner of the ballroom. During the 1930s, this corner became a hallowed spot itself, where dancer Frankie Manning took off with the jaw-dropping acrobatic moves he invented called air-steps, in which one partner flipped another in sync with the music. Dancers and on-lookers were swept up by the power and propulsion of Webb's band's music. In that decade, Webb—as bandleader and drummer—would be indelibly identified as the King of the Savoy.

But Webb's ascendancy to the crown was never a straight shot. During the summer of 1927, he and the Harlem Stompers only played at the Savoy a few times, for private dances hosted by the Neighborhood Frolic Club or the Interstate *Tattler*, Harlem's social and entertainment weekly paper.

Other opportunities came along, prompting Webb and his bandmates to rehearse often and stay optimistic about their prospects. Chick Webb and the Harlem Stompers had their first recording date on August 25, 1927, for the Vocalion label's "race records" series. The band recorded a blues number, "Low-Levee-High Water," a common flood-themed blues in the wake of the catastrophic spring 1927 Mississippi flood.[29] Most of the core Stompers were on the date: Bobby Stark, Johnny Hodges, Elmer Williams, Don Kirkpatrick, Benny James, and Leon England (Webb's main banjoist/guitarist John Trueheart was not on this date). Vocalion never released "Low-Levee-High Water," and a "B" side was never recorded. One can only guess that the band didn't sound good enough to release the record or they couldn't finish in the allotted studio time of two hours—not uncommon for bands making their first records.

In mid-October of 1927, Chick Webb and His Harlem Stompers finally landed a steady engagement at Rose Danceland, a small dance hall on the second floor of a building on 125th Street and Lenox Avenue. The building is still there, its painted art deco cornices and other elements of the original structure intact. As of 2022, there is a Starbucks and smoke shop on the street level, and Harlem United, a non-profit services organization, is housed upstairs in the former ballroom.

In the 1920s and early '30s, Rose Danceland was a dime-a-dance place that catered to a white clientele, especially single men. It didn't have the cachet of the Cotton Club or Connie's Inn or other uptown cabarets. But Rose Danceland still offered white tourists from downtown an uptown experience, where they could hear the hippest dance music and dance with Black hostesses for ten cents a dance. Like other Harlem nightspots, the venue offered white patrons the pretense of mixed-race socializing and dancing without integrating the venue.

For Webb and his band, the Rose Danceland engagement offered the relief of steady employment. Rose Danceland also had a radio wire, and starting on October 23, 1927, the band could be heard on WHN two or three times a week; the *Daily News*, *Herald Tribune*, and other New York City dailies printed broadcast times for "Chick Webb and His Orchestra." On December 9, 1927, Webb's band got its first extensive review in *Variety*, by Abel Green, the writer who had been the first to single out the music of Duke Ellington and the Washingtonians at the Kentucky Club. At the time Green was one of the few white entertainment columnists who kept up with musical developments by New York's Black jazz orchestras.

> Rose Danceland is the wooziest of creep joints and does not rate classification or identification of a night club, except that it might serve as an appetizer for an excursion in the Harlem joints.... Situated on the spade-ofay deadline, the place compromises by catering to whites with a colored band dispensing. It was the dark jazzists that prompted the visit on the "rave" of an enthusiast that the best colored dance band in New York was hiding its light behind the prosaic bushel of a common dance hall.... Chick Webb and His Harlem Stompers are the aggregation, playing colored man's jazz az iz. It's the Caucasian element that knows its jazz az iz that converted an impossible loft into a heavy money-maker.

Green knew his readers and thought that the right business person could make more of Webb and his ensemble in this place or anywhere.

> Shrewd exploitation could make this place a rubber-neck stop off and a smart tourists' novelty.... The ultra type of jazz that Webb purveys is just too bad. What a smart room of sizable accommodations, catering to collegiates could do with Webb! He'd have the kids hungry for his conceptions of the standard blues or even the "Rhapsodie in Blue" blued like Gershwin never dreamed of.[30]

Green wrote through the proprietary lens of a white entertainment reviewer of his time. But he could envision Webb's potential for a broader audience years before the Swing Era became an era. The Savoy management, though, was not as prescient as Green and did not pick up on Webb's magic just then. What were Gale and Buchanan thinking? Did they really think that the Bearcats were that much better than the Stompers? Was Chick's octet not big enough to power up the thousand or so dancers who came to the Savoy most nights? Did the Savoy job require a handsome charismatic leader like Fess Williams?

During the Savoy Ballroom's first eighteen months, Gale and Buchanan's choice of bands exceeded their expectations. Neither Fess Williams nor the Savoy Bearcats had much of a fan base until nightly adoration at the ballroom attracted radio and recording interest. Gale and Buchanan knew that Harlem's musical talent pool was huge. They took advantage of local talent and bands on tour; they knew they could book bands at the last minute for minimum pay. They also started taking advantage of other situations that meant more money for them.

Fess Williams recalled: "The band became so popular that the Savoy management felt it imperative for us to play there every night. However, social clubs in ... Jersey and Brooklyn paid exorbitant prices to have us from 1 A.M. to 3 A.M. These engagements are what opened Moe Gale's eyes and started him in the booking business."[31]

The main thing was that at the Savoy, dancers ruled. If a band didn't excite the dancers, it wasn't asked to return. Guitarist Lawrence Lucie remembers one of his first visits: "I'll never forget going up those stairs and hearing that rhythm and seeing those dancers; the battle that night was between Fess Williams and Lockwood Lewis. The whole floor was shaking."[32]

Large ballrooms like Roseland and the Savoy attracted 1,000 to 1,500 dancers on an average night, and over 4,000 for band battles or other events. Between 1928 and 1929, Fletcher Henderson expanded his band to twelve musicians to project over the crowds. The larger bands required more fully orchestrated parts that made the brass and saxophone sections play powerfully together. Arrangers played an increasingly important role in molding a band's sound. The top Black arrangers in those years—Don Redman and Benny Carter—skillfully featured Henderson's best soloists, notably tenor saxophonist Coleman Hawkins. Redman and Carter also wrote inventively for brass and woodwind sections, whether call-and-response style or as an interesting textural mix using clarinet and other doubles. Sophisticated dance music with inspired "hot" solos was the prevailing trend among New York's Black dance bands.

Webb's steady gig at Rose Danceland allowed him to expand the Stompers to ten musicians: two trumpets; one trombone; three saxophones; piano; guitar or banjo; tuba or bass; and drums. Although Webb could follow a score and memorize music almost instantaneously, he did not read or write notation. Thus far pianist Don Kirkpatrick did most of the band's arrangements or the band worked out arrangements together. Now Webb needed a bigger "book," a larger collection of arrangements. The Cuban trumpet player Mario Bauza, who joined Webb's band in 1933, said, "Chick used to pay five dollars a week for the room in Harlem, and sometimes at the end of the week he might not have the five dollars because he would pay

$100 or $75 for the best arrangement. Every nickel he could get went to buy good arrangements."[33]

Webb's name started to pop up more regularly in Black and white enter-tainment pages. In December 1927, *Billboard* reported that Johnny Hyde, a booking agent, had engaged Chick Webb and His Entertainers for the Loew's theater chain for a vaudeville tour, starting in Manhattan on January 5, 1928.[34] On January 14, 1928, "Chick Webb and His Creole Orchestra" got a thumbs up in the "Listening In" column in the *Afro* for their hour-long broadcast over WPAP of "real blues, through the courtesy of Loew's Theatres. In this outfit, Chick plays a 'doggie drum,' Elmer Williams is the tenor saxophonist; Bobby Stark the cornetist, and Johnny Hodges the feature saxophone soloist. All of the members of this group are vocalists of no mean ability, as well." After this broadcast, the band members dashed back to Loew's Lincoln Square Theater, where they were to begin their tour.[35]

A few days later *Variety* reported that the William Morris office had booked Webb's band for this tour.[36] The Morris agency had its roots in vaude-ville and branched out into booking bands in movie theaters, ballrooms, and radio stations as those businesses increasingly overlapped. White booking agents and media entrepreneurs like Moe Gale (who started his own booking agency in 1932) were the gatekeepers, controlling access to both Black and white audiences. Webb was ready for some help getting bookings, though the Morris office took a standard 10 percent booking fee.

William Morris's bookings for a largely unknown Black band like Webb's were not ideal. The Harlem Stompers were on a bill with Dewey Brown, a comedian and dancer, and Marion Bradford, a "soubrette," in a small show. Booked for three weeks in Boston and small cities in New England, they ended up stuck without pay in places without much winter business. This was the occupational hazard that Black entertainers faced on the road, even with a reputable booking office. The band returned to New York with no money and had lost their steady spot at Rose Danceland. Webb and Trueheart were back in their shared rooms, sharing whatever food they had.

6

Harlem Stompers

Our own Little "Chick" Webb himself, in person, is appearing this week at the Lafayette with his versatile orchestra. Chick and his boys have recently returned from Boston and vicinity, where they filled some good dates for two weeks.

—*Pittsburgh Courier*, March 1928[1]

In early 1928, several major Black newspapers printed entertainment items about Chick Webb and His Harlem Stompers: the *Amsterdam News*, *New York Age*, *Pittsburgh Courier*, *Baltimore Afro*, and Harlem's own gossip and society paper, the *Interstate-Tattler*. One would think this exposure would have helped Webb get more work. In March, the band was back in New York, jobless, after their ill-fated tour to Boston and small towns in Massachusetts. They never heard from Johnny Hyde or the Morris office again. Gigs came one by one.

Rose Danceland's manager had filled the Stompers' spot and hired drummer Tommy Benford to put together a dance band. Benford gathered several experienced out-of-work musicians, including clarinetist Barney Bigard, saxophonist Russell Procope, trumpet player Ward Pinkett, and pianist Luis Russell. Procope, one of this band's younger members, remembers it being a great ensemble and learning opportunity, despite some turnover as musicians got better opportunities.

Before Webb's vaudeville tour, he and the Stompers had helped improve Rose Danceland's reputation. The hall had installed a radio wire, and "Chick Webb's Orchestra" could be heard two or three times a week in the tristate area. Now, the Stompers had lost both their steady job and their radio exposure.

Fortunately, the band's dry spell didn't last long. They were hired for the week of March 18, 1928, at Harlem's Lafayette Theater, on a bill with producer Irwin C. Miller's new revue, *Let's Dance*. It was the Harlem Stompers' debut at the theater, and their first time with a big stage show. Over the next few years, the Lafayette would be as crucial to Webb's performing career as the Savoy and, a few years later, the Harlem Opera House and the Apollo Theater.

The show's producer and the theater both have fascinating backstories. Irwin C. Miller was one of the most successful Black theater producers of the 1920s, and was known as the Black Ziegfeld. Born in Tennessee in 1884, Irwin was the older brother of Flournoy Miller, cowriter and costar of Eubie Blake and Noble Sissle's hit show *Shuffle Along*. Irwin began his career in vaudeville, but got tired of getting burned by white booking agents and producers. He decided to produce and book his own shows. In 1925 he staged the first version of *Brown Skin Models*, a revue featuring dazzling Black female singers and dancers in ensemble numbers, along with comedians and other acts.[2] Eleanor Hicks, a friend of Webb's and John Trueheart's from Baltimore, was chosen for one of the tours, then decided she didn't want to leave home.[3] Miller's new show, *Let's Dance*, used his winning format and featured several of his star performers and comedians and over forty chorus dancers.

The 1,500-seat Lafayette was considered "American's Leading Colored Theater," from its opening in 1912 through the early 1930s. It was a sumptuously decorated venue on Lenox Avenue between 132nd and 133rd. Shortly after opening it instituted an open seating policy; Black patrons could sit in the orchestra and were not relegated to the "nigger heaven" upper balcony that most other theaters had. The theater's new manager, Lester Walton, an influential Black journalist and activist, initiated this with help from the newly formed NAACP. As a result, New York City enacted the first no-segregation laws in public theaters in the country. Other white theater owners in Harlem and midtown Manhattan managed to find ways to avoid this with exclusionary pricing and reservation systems that continued for years. As Ted Vincent wrote in *Keep Cool*, "The struggle for artistic freedom and the right to be heard was paralleled by the struggle of African-American audiences to obtain a seat at a performance."[4]

In 1925, the Lafayette had a new manager, Frank Schiffman.[5] Schiffman's cost-cutting methods—not running ads in Harlem's Black weeklies and hiring subpar talent—infuriated Harlem activists and patrons. Schiffman relented, and the Lafayette soon regained its status as a premier platform for Black performers, stage shows, and jazz orchestras.[6]

The theater's ads for *Let's Dance* billed Webb's band as "Chick Webb and His Roseland Orchestra." Webb's band had not yet played at the Roseland Ballroom, but for marketing purposes it made sense to appropriate the name of the well-known Roseland Ballroom instead of Rose Danceland. Webb and his musicians had to elevate their visual showmanship for the Lafayette's tough audience and cultivate a rapport that reached beyond their dancing fan base.

Let's Dance received a couple of terrific reviews from the Black press; so did Webb's band. The *Amsterdam News* wrote: "Chick Webb's Roseland Orchestra was received in a manner rivaled only by the reception of Fletcher Henderson at his recent appearance at the Lafayette." The *Tattler's* review was mixed but had interesting things to say about Louise Cooke's solo dance act: she "thrills with a dance that some would call naughty and others art. . . . Folks from the Village would call it art, I suspect. . . . But then there are some erstwhile and goodly folks here in our Ebony Kingdom who would be oh so terribly shocked at the way Louise twists and wriggles to the enlivening strains of Chick Webb's musicians."[7]

After *Let's Dance* closed at the Lafayette, Miller split his cast and crew into two smaller groups and sent them on two different tours. That was Miller's strategy—to develop a show and launch it on the road. Webb's band was not part of the tour; it performed its own set and only accompanied a couple of acts. Miller could be as cavalier about stiffing talent as white managers were. His touring show did not include a pit band, only one or two regular musicians. For the Lafayette, Miller sent his musical director to Buffalo to hire a band and then left them stranded afterward. "The show worked one week at the Lafayette, and then the men found themselves far from home and jobless."[8]

For now, Webb was back to hustling one-nighters and holding frequent rehearsals, knowing that his musicians would take whatever other jobs they could get.

Webb continued to hone his skills as a forward-thinking drummer and bandleader. He sought musicians—friends and bandmates—who were on his wavelength, able to play dance music that was starting to swing, and improvise "hot" solos in the manner of Ellington's band. Duke Ellington was not yet *Ellington*, the "beyond category" bandleader who composed everything from timeless dance tunes and hit songs to suites and extended works. He was getting attention at the Cotton Club from its nightly broadcasts, and from gangsters who loved his band's sound. But even Ellington had to navigate a competitive musical environment.

In the late 1920s, Webb, Ellington, and Charlie Johnson were among the younger bandleaders nudging jazz styles forward with more arranged dance music; Don Redman and Benny Carter had planted the seeds for this with Fletcher Henderson's Orchestra. The differences between emerging jazz styles in Harlem and elsewhere were dramatized in the spring of 1928, when the self-professed "inventor of jazz" blew in from Chicago. Ferdinand Joseph LaMothe, a skinny man with an outsized personality and an endless supply of flashy suits, was better known as Jelly Roll Morton.

Then almost forty years old, Morton had been a polymath as a youth in his native New Orleans: an innovative composer, arranger, pianist, and band-leader. His New Orleans–bred style of stomps, slow drags, blues, and del-icately crafted arrangements were crowd-pleasers in Chicago clubs in the mid-1920s, and his recordings with his Red Hot Peppers were big sellers for the Victor label. When he arrived in New York, Morton expected a trium-phant reception, but much to his amazement it took him awhile to get estab-lished and find work. Young Harlem musicians knew Morton's reputation but not his music. In the spring of 1928, Tommy Benford asked Morton to take over as leader at Rose Danceland.

Initially Morton had a hard time keeping this band together. Guitarist Danny Barker recalled:

> Jelly was constantly preaching that if he could get a band to rehearse his music and listen to him, he could keep a band working. . . . Most of the time musicians would arrive at the last minute, or send a substitute. . . . I learned later they were angry with him because he was always boasting about how great New Orleans musicians were. Jelly's songs and arrangements had a deep feeling that lots of musicians could not feel and improvise on, so they would not work with Jelly—just couldn't grasp the roots, soul, feeling. At that time most working musicians were arrangement-conscious, following the pattern of Henderson, Redman, Carter and Chick Webb. Jelly's music was considered corny and dated.[9]

Morton did find a ready audience outside the Rhythm Club. He loved to argue and Webb loved to argue with him. Clarinetist Barney Bigard, who played with Morton in the Rose Danceland band along with Ward Pinkett, Russell Procope, Benford, and others and recorded with him in the late 1920s, remembered:

> Jelly was kicks. . . .[H]e always loved to fuss and argue with somebody. He knew it all. He and Chick Webb would stand on a street corner and argue so

bad you could've become rich selling tickets. Chick would just rile him up to get him going. Jelly would tell Chick he was the greatest and Chick would tell him, "Yeah! Well, come around to see my band tonight. We just got a new arrangement on so and so, and Chick would hum the whole thing out of his head, top to bottom. Jelly would say, 'That ain't shit. Listen to this one.' . . . It was a show between those two guys. Chick with his poor little crooked back and Jelly with that great big diamond stuck in his teeth. I guess ordinary people had never seen nothing like that before.[10]

On May 6, 1928, Webb and His Harlem Stompers returned to the Savoy Ballroom for another "Battle of Jazz," this time billed as a "Mammoth Melody Massacre." In its first two years, the Savoy had only occasionally hosted advertised battles; it was expensive to hire name bands, or three or four bands for the same night. But these special events drew bigger audiences and created a band-sized cutting context, prompting the bands to double down on their crowd-pleasing efforts. For this event, the Savoy management went all out. The ad pictured a gladiator and promised "12 hours of musical bombardment . . . no advance in prices."

The *Amsterdam News* noted:

We do not believe that so many musicians have been gathered together under one roof for a special entertainment since the first night James Reese Europe led an augmented orchestra of the famous Clef Club at Manhattan Casino. Among the well-known leaders appearing at the head of the various jazz bands will be Lloyd Scott, Chick Webb, Alex Jackson, Charlie Johnson, Fess Williams and Fletcher Henderson. . . . To the credit of the management be it said that they have always tried to please and hold their large patronage by offering things not to be found at any other place of its kind in the city catering to Negroes.[11]

The *Interstate Tattler* loaded its preview of the event with hyperbole and invented quotes:

In years to come historians will record the day when six of the world's most famous orchestras met on a common battlefield and jazzed their way into the hearts of thousands of enthusiastic dancers, each leader confident that he will receive the public's favor as expressed in the following interview that makes us feel assured that the brand of music has never been equalled in the history of the ballroom.

Fess Williams: . . . between you and me these other bands play sweet music, but when it comes to saturating sheiks and shebas with salubrious spasms of syncopated sonatas, you have to hand us the applause. . . .

Chick Webb: Henderson, Johnson, Jackson and Scott, sure they play good music, but if you're asking me, I can blindfold the boys in my band and let 'em play from memory, and they'll come down the line a winner like a trombone slide. . . . I'm not conceited or anything like that, but when I stomp 'em, they stay stomped.

Fess Williams didn't show up for the "jazz war" on May 6. He had been in Chicago since February 1928, working as the master of ceremonies (M.C.) for the newly built Regal Theater there, a luxury venue for Black audiences that was the first of its kind in the city's South Side Bronzeville neighborhood. The Regal's representatives had come to New York the previous fall to persuade Williams to take the job, and he had signed a six-month option.

"That night, I told the Savoy owners of this fabulous offer, but I didn't mention that I had already signed the contract," Williams said years later. Buchanan and Gale were not happy about Williams taking a leave but after a few days of wrangling agreed to it. Buchanan hired Lockwood Lewis, Williams's former mentor from Kentucky, as leader of the Royal Flush until after July. He would send the band out for summer dates, with the understanding that Williams would return for the fall 1928 season.

That never happened either. Williams was treated more royally by the Regal's management than at the Savoy. Williams and the Royal Flush had been very happy at the Savoy, but Williams now felt mistreated and forced out.[12]

A typewritten letter from Williams to Buchanan in April 1928 about the matter reveals that Williams was as tough as Buchanan, and did not intend to return from Chicago. The Royal Flush would join him a few months later.

Dear Charlie:
Yours of the 3rd inst. [installment], received and in answer I will say, I was more than glad to hear from you; although why did you take your own sweet time answering; why the neglect? . . . Why do you think I am becoming a member of the 100% Wrong Club? . . .

I did not know your battle of music was going to be so early in May and the way things look now, it is very doubtful whether or not I will be able to make it there so soon. If you use all of the Bands which you mentioned in your letter, I am sure you can get along fairly well without me. Has Chick Webb got his band back together?[13]

Word quickly got out that Fess Williams was leaving the Savoy. Several Harlem bandleaders began jockeying for the job, including Webb. Alex Jackson's band, from Cincinnati, stayed on through the July 4 weekend. The *Tattler's* occasional "Savoy Topics" column of July 6 reported: "Well, folks, after July 6th, Chick Webb and His Harlem Stompers will be back with us again.... Chick and his boys are big favorites with SAVOYITES and while everybody will regret the loss of Alex, on the other hand we'll rejoice at having reclaimed Chick."[14]

Bit by bit, gig by gig, Webb tried to keep the band together. His determination and optimism, along with his musical direction, continued to inspire friendship and loyalty. The band's mainstays had been with him for over a year: Johnny Hodges, Don Kirkpatrick, Leon England, Elmer Williams, Bobby Stark, and John Trueheart, his banjoist/guitarist and Webb's roommate and steadfast friend.[15] Webb sometimes took the band out for dinner, though he could hardly spare the cash.

During the summer of 1928 there were a couple of personnel changes. Johnny Hodges joined Duke Ellington's orchestra, which was touring while the Cotton Club was closed for the season. Ellington had been trying to recruit Hodges for months, and Hodges finally agreed to leave Webb—reluctantly, since they were such tight friends. Hodges was replacing Duke's alto player and fellow-Washingtonian Otto Hardwick, who had a drinking problem and didn't show up on time at the Cotton Club or for recording sessions. Hodges was supporting a wife and baby back in Boston and now needed the steady income. Webb generously let Hodges go. This was a milestone in Hodges's life and career. Hodges, whose melodious sound was recognizable even then, became one of the most idolized jazz soloists with the Ellington Orchestra. Hodges's tenure with Duke lasted for decades, with a few periods on his own as a bandleader, recording artist and featured soloist.

Another gifted young musician soon entered Webb's orbit: Charles "Cootie" Melvin Williams, a seventeen-year-old trumpet player from Mobile, Alabama. Williams's migration to Harlem was crazily circuitous. He learned to play trumpet with his school band, and by age eleven, older musicians took notice. Bands from New Orleans and Florida came to Mobile to play dances and would "ballyhoo"—go around neighborhoods on a truck, shouting and playing music—to advertise their dances, and Cootie would jump on the truck and "sit in." When he was fifteen, a band came through led by Calvin "Eagle Eye" Shields, a pianist/bandleader from Jacksonville, Florida, whose best soloist was clarinetist Edmond Hall. Ten years older than Williams, Hall convinced Shields to hire Williams. Hall said years later: "As he was still in his teens, his father made me take care of him. I hope I did. We were together a long while."[16]

A few months later, Hall joined Miami-based bandleader Alonzo Ross and brought Cootie with him. Ross's Deluxe Syncopators were the house band at a Black nightclub near Miami Beach. The band broadcast live weekly on WIOD, from the station's studio right by the beach.[17] Cootie recalled, "No colored were allowed on the beach then. They used to sneak us over to the radio station and back."[18]

A talent scout from Victor Records heard them and paid for the band to get to Savannah, Georgia, where the company had a mobile recording unit. None of the band members had been north of Florida. Hall remembered this vividly: "When the records came out, the manager of the Roseland heard them and sent for us." That manager was I. Jay Faggen, co-owner of the Savoy, who still was involved with the Rosemont in Brooklyn. Hall continued: "We played at the Rosemont. That's how I came to New York. I'll never forget the day I arrived, March 15, 1928. It was the first time I saw snow."[19]

Williams never forgot either. The band traveled by freighter and docked in Brooklyn. They were whisked off to a boarding house near the Rosemont, in downtown Brooklyn. When the band finished its two-week run, Ross and most of his musicians headed back to Miami, where they made excellent money, 150 dollars a week per man. Williams and Hall had no intention of returning. "When I used to say my prayers at night," Williams told an interviewer years later, "I used to say, 'Dear Lord, please hurry up and let me grow up so I can get to New York!' I didn't care how I got there, I was coming. This is the place I wanted to be all my life. I'm not thinking about going back to Florida."[20]

Williams and Hall rented a room above a bakery in Brooklyn where they could get a roll and coffee for a dime, and soup and bread for dinner for fifteen cents. They spent a lot of time sitting on the stoop, and passersby asked them what they were doing. "We said we need some work, we're musicians. They said, 'Why don't you go over to New York?' We said we *are* in New York!"[21]

Finally, someone advised them to take the subway to Harlem and go to jam sessions. They got uptown and ended up at the Bandbox. Williams took his turn on trumpet. "I start blowing, and someone says, 'Somebody get Chick Webb!'" Webb, always on the lookout for talent, came right over. After the session, Webb asked Williams where he was from and Williams told his story. "I didn't know who I was talking to." Webb took him to Brooklyn in a taxicab and paid the landlady, and they picked up Cootie's bags and went back to Harlem. Cootie moved into Webb's place that night.

Webb and Trueheart were still renting rooms on West 131st Street, right off of Lenox Avenue in central Harlem. With Cootie, the three of them shared two rooms. Cootie got into the Harlem scene quickly, including going to the Bandbox every morning for the free musicians' breakfast—rolls and coffee. Hall, meanwhile, landed a job with the Claude Hopkins band, who had just returned from Europe, had an established reputation, and was standing in for Fletcher Henderson's Orchestra at Roseland, on tour for the summer. Williams said, "Now, he [Hall] was all straight. Before that, what little money I had from Chick, I'd help him out when I was working. Now he sometimes helped me."[22]

Webb now had a new friend and roommate, and a new Harlem Stomper. In mid-August 1928, the band was gearing up to return to the Savoy. They would be broadcasting twice a week from the ballroom via remote wire from station WMCA, located at the Hotel McAlpin. "The two bands now playing and broadcasting are 'Chick Webb and His Harlem Stompers' and 'Willie Lynch and His Rhythm Aces.'"[23]

Webb's bravado with his peers didn't translate to being assertive with the Savoy's managers or other ballroom and theater managers. Lillian Johnson's five-part profile of Webb in the *Afro* (written after his death) describes a meeting with Webb, Hodges, and I. Jay Faggen, which probably took place in 1927 or '28. Faggen was about to offer Webb a contract, but Webb was hesitant: "I don't think I want to be the leader of a band right now." Hodges stepped right up and said, "Oh, yes, he does!"

Johnson's story continues:

The man who hired them said he would pay each of the band boys $67.50 per week, and $75 for Chick, the leader. This surprised the little Webb boy very much as he and the boys had been making equal money up to that time. . . . Another of the Savoy's officials [probably Buchanan] was present at the time, and when he saw how surprised Chick was at the higher rate of pay, he took him aside and told him not to be a "wise guy," and not try to get more than he was entitled to. He also told Chick that he might as well be satisfied. "Make up your mind to be content with what you are given and don't try to be smart," he told the little maestro. Chick, who was very green, and who had the Southern flair for being extra polite, apologized very profusely to this man, and agreed to be satisfied.[24]

The pay Johnson mentioned is hard to document. Alto saxophonist Hilton Jefferson, who joined Webb's band after Hodges left, said the salary at the Savoy then was thirty-three dollars a week. "Buchanan who was running the Savoy said that no musician is worth more than that. . . . At first we all chipped in to buy our own uniforms." Fess Williams and his band were probably paid more, since Williams was a tougher businessman than Webb, and had a bigger following.

In a subsequent segment, Lillian Johnson wrote that Webb signed the contract and "was such a huge success that his contract was renewed at the end of the year, and he was allowed to add two more men."[25] Johnson's series, along with Webb's three-part profile in *DownBeat* in the winter of 1937–38, are among the few sources of information about Webb's early career; some details that kept resurfacing in articles by other writers are difficult to verify. Thus far, no surviving contracts between Webb and Moe Gale or Charles Buchanan have turned up, and Local 802 does not have any of Webb's contracts in its archives. Richard Gale, Moe's son, once said his father did everything with Webb "on a handshake."

In any case, Webb didn't have much leverage. He didn't have Ellington's bandleading experience or glamorous looks nor Fess Williams's sparkling tuxedos, nor was he a cutthroat negotiator. His band was not yet in demand. In the late 1920s, for all the hype about the Jazz Age in New York and Harlem's busy club scene, bandleaders and their ensembles were easily replaceable.

Charles Buchanan, whose myriad roles at the Savoy included hiring bands, was now in a position of power: the Savoy's success in its first two years was largely due to his managerial skills and community ties. "Charles Percival Buchanan . . . the young chap for whom many predicted failure," wrote Floyd Calvin, the influential editor of the *Pittsburgh Courier,* in a front-page profile, "fooled them all." In 1927, Calvin reported, the Savoy grossed a million dollars a year, paid "$200,000 per year back to the race in salaries," and spent 150,000 dollars a year in advertising, mostly in Harlem newspapers.[26]

Moe Gale trusted Buchanan's vision for the Savoy, to give "our people the best of everything. This place can't be beat for an evening of enjoyment.... The strict discipline of our employees, the charm of our interior, the good music, the spacious dance floor, the courtesy of the hostesses, all contribute to make one relax and enjoy himself." Calvin, the *Courier's* founder, was a "race" man and found a kindred spirit in Buchanan: a "staunch believer in the Negro business man, he [Buchanan] believes great things will be accomplished in Harlem by the Negro as soon as he learns how to pull together a little better."[27]

Webb at this point was a terrible businessman, but he was a great talent scout, fiercely competitive musically, and totally dedicated to his band. Not everyone could make do during his frequent "dry" spells. Saxophonist Charlie Holmes (Johnny Hodges's friend from Boston) briefly joined Webb's band in late 1927. Holmes observed the loose loyalty of Harlem musicians when it came to paid engagements and left Webb for a steadier job with the house band at the Nest Club. Holmes said that he always had his horn under his arm, carrying his clarinet and soprano sax

in a raggedy little bag. Always ready for the occasion, you know. Some of us used to wear tuxedos all day long. If we had a gig coming, we'd be all dressed! ... Chick would get a kick out of hearing the band rehearse. He liked to hear it rehearse so much he didn't create any work for it! So everyone was working in someone else's band, too. I don't know what they [managers, club owners, etc.] had against Chick. He didn't get work, or he'd get on a job and didn't work that long. He had a great band and great arrangements, but I can't pay the rent talkin' about "I work in Chick Webb's band!"[28]

Webb, Cootie Williams, Trueheart, Kirkpatrick, and Elmer Williams made a pact: they would work together as a unit, no matter what. Webb's promise was even more emphatic: he would not change the band's personnel for anyone, except to add additional horn and brass players when he could afford it.

That changed when Webb and Williams were involved in an incident in October 1928 at the newly redecorated Alhambra Dance Hall on Lenox between 126th and 127th, above the Alhambra Theater.

The Alhambra Dance Hall had reopened in early October 1928 after lying empty for over a decade. Up a steep staircase from street level, it had been elegantly renovated in an attempt to position it as a smaller Savoy, catering to a Black audience. One night Webb, Williams, and a few other Stompers visited the Alhambra to check out the competition. They started hooting at the band on stage, whom they thought was second-rate. The bandleader told Webb to stop harassing them. Webb then tried to convince the Alhambra's manager to hire his band, saying that "a good orchestra was in the street and a ham fat bunch working."[29]

H. G. DeLeon, the bandleader, filed charges against Webb with Local 802. Webb was summoned before the union's trial board and ordered to pay a thousand-dollar fine, which he could not begin to do. Webb panicked and asked DeLeon to withdraw the charge. DeLeon was willing, but Local 802 kept the charge on record despite Webb's inability to pay. He was reprimanded and told never to malign union musicians ever again or discourage them from working, which was against union rules. This episode damaged Webb's standing both among potential employers and at the Alhambra Dance Hall. A few weeks later, the ballroom's manager cut costs by letting go of one band—DeLeon's—who then asked Local 802 to sue the Alhambra for non-payment. Local 802 was about to take legal measures to recover the money owed, then discovered that "Keith Theatrical Enterprises [the 'owner'] took out all the fittings and decorations and locked the door on the place."[30]

Webb soon had other issues with Local 802 back at the Savoy. A delegate came by the ballroom and discovered that Cootie Williams didn't have a Local 802 card and hadn't put in for a transfer.

Williams recalled: "I didn't belong to 802. So the delegate talked to Chick, and Chick got mad at him, and they got in a big argument." The delegate took Williams aside and said, "I'll tell you what I'm going to do, boy, for you. I'm going to let you put in your transfer. Now, I give you the privilege to work with anybody else in New York except Chick Webb."[31]

Former Baltimore Newspaper Boy

After the blowup with Local 802 about the incident at the Alhambra, Webb had even more trouble finding work. He returned home to Baltimore for Thanksgiving week, which was noted in the *Afro*'s "Society" column. "Chick Webb, of New York City, spent a week with his grand-parents, Mr. and Mrs. Clarence Jones, of this city. While here he was entertained by his friends."[1]

The *Afro*'s "Society" page kept up with Webb and his family, who maintained close ties though Chick and his younger sister Mabel Porter were settled in Harlem. Bessie was often mentioned in this column, since she was active in several clubs connected with AME Waters, the family's neighborhood church. Chick's visits and his family's were "Society" items, too; he was an important New York musician and bandleader whether he had work or not. In early 1929, the *Afro* reported that Bessie visited Harlem and stayed with Mabel. They went to see Lew Leslie's latest hit revue, *Blackbirds of 1928*, still on Broadway, and other top Black shows. Mabel then went to visit the family in Baltimore.

For Webb, this holiday season was bleak, workwise. After the Alhambra incident, Buchanan was reluctant to hire Webb's band at the Savoy. Buchanan had had other run-ins with Local 802 delegates, who dropped by the ballroom unannounced to make sure that union bands were performing, and that newly arrived musicians had their transfer cards in order, as Cootie Williams had not. "The delegate didn't let me work with Chick Webb," Williams recalled. "And Chick Webb said, 'Well, I ain't going to let him work with anybody else. I'll just keep him out here.' Like that." Chick took care of Cootie, and "he'd give me a few bucks," hoping the six-month transfer period would pass with no further incident.[2] Added to that mishap, the Savoy was staging another multiband "battle of music" on December 12, without Chick Webb and His Harlem Stompers. The contenders were the bands of Duke Ellington, Charlie Johnson, Arthur Gibbs, Lockwood Lewis, Lloyd Scott, and Ike Dixon. Webb knew Dixon from Baltimore, and had even worked with him. He must have been stung that Dixon's band was invited and not his own.

The same unnamed reporter who'd covered the Savoy's first big battle, which included Webb, in May 1927 for the *Amsterdam News* recycled the title—"Battle of Jazz Stirs Vast Crowd"—and the Civil War rhetoric when covering this one for the *Pittsburgh Courier*. Dixon's band got noticed for "that Baltimore rhythm which seems to make your feet step around like on air."[3]

Ellington was now becoming more of a celebrity. His band's broadcasts from the Cotton Club were heard across the country, and his hit records for Victor—"Diga Diga Doo" (from *Blackbirds*), "Jubilee Stomp," and "I Must Have That Man"—were from his shows there. Harlemites were thrilled to hear Ellington's orchestra at the Savoy because the Cotton Club didn't admit Black patrons. For the Savoy event, crowds of people "had to be turned away, the consensus of opinion being that the contest had ended in a multiple tie"— as did most of the Savoy's band battles.[4]

The Harlem community regarded the Savoy as its own. The entire management of the place was Black. Buchanan handled all the day-to-day finances: he dealt with the cashiers, and he or his assistant, Harold Parker, collected the rent from the downstairs storekeepers. "He [Buchanan] handled the money first. That was the original concept," said Conrad Gale, Moe Gale's brother. For the most part the Galewski family and Moe Gale were inconspicuous at the ballroom.

"You never saw them," Conrad Gale continued. "This was a Black business, a Black-run entity for Blacks—their ballroom. In the early years there was no desire for white patronage. You never saw white help or white management. . . . Buchanan was an efficient, stern manager. No joking around with Charlie Buchanan. He had an air of being important. He wasn't one to be too friendly with."[5]

Sigmund Galewski managed the family's financial interests in the Savoy, interactions with banks and the Third Avenue Railroad Company, and taxes. He was not involved with daily business matters or music and dance trends. "My dad wouldn't know who the band was playing this week." Sigmund did deal with some other problems. "The Savoy bouncers would throw some unruly person out, they'd sue, and Sigmund would hire the lawyers."[6]

In the Savoy's early years, Buchanan built up patronage from Harlem's networks of social clubs, fraternal organizations, church groups, etc. Again, in keeping with the owners' and Buchanan's initial vision, the Savoy became a kind of community center and hosted club-sponsored dances and balls, many of which were fundraisers. The Harlem's Women's Auxiliary held bridge parties on Saturday afternoons, followed by dinner and dancing. The proceeds went to the Auxiliary's usual charities, a list that grew longer during the economic depression of the 1930s. Other nights could be reserved for club-sponsored dances and events. The Savoy also hosted events for a different audience. Themed masked balls such as Arabian Nights or the South Sea Isles Ball were highly anticipated semiannual events with awards given out by Broadway stars at the end of a grand midnight promenade. These balls, where people went all out in elaborate cross-dressing drag and gender-fluid splendor, were in vogue in Black communities in Washington, DC, Chicago, Harlem, and other urban centers. Dance scholar Marya Annette McQuirter notes that though the balls attracted a wide cross-section of guests—from celebrities, artists, and writers to society matrons—"tensions around identity were often resolved in these spaces, if only momentarily.... [B]lack participants ... bonded across lines of sexuality and gender to protest the inordinate presence of whites at these balls."[7]

The *Afro's* "NEW YORK" column described one, in late 1929: "Like all Harlem fancy dress balls, the gentlemen from the downtown choruses who thrill over the donning of feminine attire were by far in the majority. But after all, one has to admit that they know how to wear clothes and certainly give the best shows." *Variety* described another: "The useless sex made merry last week at a black-and-tan drag at the Savoy Ballroom in Harlem. The wise mob goes for this one regularly. It's an Arabian Nights' masque ball, rivaled only by a drag at Renaissance hall annually."[8] The *Asbury Park Press* (from the New Jersey resort town) reported:

> Whenever Harlem society arranges a ball, they try to keep it a secret in order to avoid being pushed off their own floor by white visitors. The other evening at the long awaited South Sea Isles Night in the great Savoy Ballroom ... there were almost as many white as black dancers.... In describing it, use of the term riot of color is certainly appropriate.... With 3,000 in the crowd, there was no trouble. This seemed to me to be extraordinary, considering the fact that a lot of the whites, many of them notables, seemed looking for trouble.[9]

The Savoy's weekly beauty contests and fashion shows celebrated Black pride and beauty. These were for Black audiences, Harlem on display for itself. These events differed dramatically from stage shows at the Cotton Club and similar venues that featured only light-skinned exotic dancers and chorus girls for white audiences.[10]

More than anything else, the Savoy's "regular" crowd in the late 1920s and onward were people who loved to dance to cutting-edge bands that played for them, and nondancing fans who loved the music and wanted to be part of the scene. Webb and his peers paid close attention to which bands got hired, for how long, and who was getting the most attention. Buchanan and Gale hired bands for the Savoy that were not known nationally, like Fess Williams's Royal Flush and Leon Abbey's Savoy Bearcats, and kept them on if the bands proved popular. For special occasions, they hired name bands like Fletcher Henderson's, Duke Ellington's, and, in the early 1930s, top white bands like Guy Lombardo and His Royal Canadians and the Paul Whiteman Orchestra which broke attendance records and drew tons of publicity. Musicians frequently came to the Savoy to check out other musicians, just like they did at jam sessions.

By early 1929, Fess Williams, Leon Abbey, and their bands had moved on, their success at the Savoy prompting other opportunities. Abbey's band had been in Europe since late 1927, where they were well received in theaters and salons and were slated for a three-month run in Paris.

Fess Williams and the Royal Flush had been at Chicago's Regal Theater for about a year and got high praise—"Just too bad"—from the *Chicago Defender*. But Williams's initially good rapport with the Regal's owners was fraying. "Fess came here as director and master of ceremonies and met very trying circumstances. Seemingly, for one to get a break here, he must be in the ring or a local product. Fess came here on his own hook, introduced the acts, tooted his saxophone, and "carried on" until he made them like it. . . . Now comes the news that Fess will soon be headed for Harlem."[11]

In the first few months of 1929, Buchanan hired everybody but Chick Webb, and even looked at other bandleaders from Baltimore. The *Afro* reported that Irvin Hughes, leader of Baltimore's Royal Theater Symphony, was offered a contract at the Savoy and turned it down. Webb must have felt betrayed when he found out about this—, not by his hometown peers, but by Charles Buchanan.

Even so, Webb had a generous spirit, especially for his musicians. He always had an ear out for what was going on in other bands, and didn't stand in the way if one of his men got a better job, as Johnny Hodges had. In Cootie Williams's case Webb even helped the young trumpet player get a much better job, first with Fletcher Henderson, and a few months later with Duke Ellington.

Webb heard that Henderson needed another trumpet player to go on the road with his orchestra for a couple of weeks when Rex Stewart had left the band. "Fletcher had to get permission from Chick for me to go with him," Williams recalled. "And I went out with Fletcher. Then we came back to New York. We were supposed to go to Roseland for a Sunday matinee. I thought I was supposed to go right back to Webb."

Williams was upset; a couple of Fletcher's musicians pressured him about the matinee, but he didn't feel obligated to go. "The arrangement was that I was only to go on the road with him [Henderson] until the band comes back. That was the agreement between him and Chick. So I don't go and make the matinee. So they can't start playing nothing. They got somebody to come up and get me." Henderson's musicians didn't know about this agreement, and Fletcher might have forgotten it himself. Williams relented and went downtown to Roseland.

When Williams arrived at the ballroom, "Big Green"—trombonist Charlie Green, who'd once scared trumpet player Rex Stewart out of Henderson's band—was sitting behind Williams. Stewart's description of Big Green was not exaggerated. "Now Big Green was 6 foot plus, his manner was rough and loud, and he was always ready for a fight. . . . He became even more frightening when he'd brandish his six-shooter, which kept company with his gin in his trombone case."[12]

That day on the Roseland bandstand, Green threatened Williams: "'I'm going to kill you when you get off there. When you get off this bandstand, you little so and so, I'm going to kill you.' I was shaking like a leaf. So we kept on playing and kept on playing, and Bobby Stark says, 'Hey, you leave that boy alone. Don't you bother that boy. Shut up and leave that boy alone!' And he [Green] shut up!"

Cootie was stunned. Stark, a small man himself, was unfazed by Green and had stood up to him before. Williams stopped being afraid. "I got the fear out of me, and went on playing. And I wasn't afraid of him anymore."

After the Roseland matinee, Fletcher called Webb, asking him to let Williams stay in his orchestra, and Webb agreed. Now Williams gave Chick money, since he wasn't getting much work.

Williams stayed with Fletcher Henderson's band for a few months in 1929. The band had incredibly talented soloists, particularly tenor saxophonist

Coleman Hawkins, the superstar of the orchestra. But the person Williams listened to most was trumpet player Bobby Stark, who'd helped out Webb in his first few months in New York and played with Webb's band various times in the 1920s and 1930s.

A few months later, Webb found out that Ellington had fired trumpet player Bubber Miley, whose "wah-wah" sound was the centerpiece of Duke's band at the Cotton Club. Miley had stopped being reliable. Cootie recalled: "Every time some big shot come up to listen to the band, there wasn't no Bubber Miley! And he [Duke] had the whole band built around Bubber Miley!"[13]

Webb told Duke to "go get Cootie." In his memoir, Ellington recounts: "Chick Webb came running up to me one night at the Rhythm Club, and he said, 'Hey man, I got a hell of a trumpet player. He was with me for awhile, but he's too much for me. Fletcher heard him and hired him, but that style don't fit Fletcher's band. . . . Fletcher doesn't give him any solos. So, if you want him, he wants to come with you.'"[14]

Johnny Hodges and Cootie Williams were Chick's closest friends besides John Trueheart. Webb's generosity in letting them join Duke Ellington's band led to career-making changes for them, but they were both reluctant to leave his band. Clarinetist Barney Bigard, who joined Ellington around the time that Hodges did, said that "those two loved Chick so much that Duke . . . practically had to get on his knees to get them to leave. . . . Finally, Chick told them to take the job because he was able to see that it would be better [for] them in the long run. He was just that kind of guy and he liked Duke a whole lot."[15] Fletcher Henderson, another generous leader in dealing with his musicians, let Webb be the mediator, and Cootie Williams then joined Ellington's band. Williams said that Webb used to tell Duke, "I'm going to get my two men back from you one day!"[16]

Hodges had been with Duke for several months when Cootie Williams came in, and the two also became good friends. Up until then, Williams had heard Ellington's band on the radio and hadn't witnessed Miley and trombonist Tricky Sam Nanton using plunger mutes in person. "I thought that was comedy music," said Williams, "and I used to laugh when Tricky would start blowin'. . . . [I]t sounded funny to me. Tricky didn't say nothing. Then he comes up to me, sitting up there playing, and said, 'Well, this man hired me to play like that.' So I kept listening to Tricky, and one night I had the plunger, and I went, 'Wah, wah.' And I woke up everybody! They said, 'That's it, that's it! Keep on, that's it!'" No one had mentioned to Williams that the "wah-wah" sound was exactly what Duke wanted, and let him make that realization himself.[17]

> Little Chick Webb, former Baltimore newspaper boy, now head of Chick Webb's Harlem Stompers, one of New York's ace dance orchestras ... is being complimented by the Seventh Avenue gang for landing the biggest talkie contract ever issued a color dance orchestra.
>
> —*Baltimore Afro*[18]

Webb and His Harlem Stompers had a reputation as a terrific "stomp band"—one with a fast tempo and clean rhythm—even without the visibility that comes with a steady engagement. In March 1929, Webb landed a fantastic opportunity when his band was hired for the nightclub scene of *After Seben*, a thirteen-minute, two-reel "talking picture" comedy starring James Barton, a white vaudeville comedian and dancer who in his day was compared with Al Jolson and Bill "Bojangles" Robinson.[19] Sound films were still new; the first feature-length synchronized sound movie, *The Jazz Singer*, starring Jolson, had been released only two years earlier, in October 1927.

Filming took place at the Paramount Studio in Long Island City in March and April. The movie is essentially an elongated, vaudeville-type skit with a flimsy plot line. Barton is in blackface, and the rest of the cast is Black. The nightclub scene takes up Reel 2, beginning with Barton playing the nightclub's janitor; he is also the club's M.C., and is featured singing a jail-house blues, and later on performing an extended dance solo.

Cultural historian Krin Gabbard, who writes extensively about jazz and film, identifies the film's minstrel underpinnings, which is essential to any understanding of *After Seben*. The film, which viewers today would find troubling and racist, carries the minstrel and vaudeville traditions into this new media—talking pictures. Gabbard explains:

> Sporting a tall top hat, Webb is barely visible at the top of the screen. Like the distinguished jazz violinist Stuff Smith, Webb surely wore the hat as a nod toward black minstrelsy. Although most admirers of jazz artists would rather not acknowledge the fact, much of jazz history is rooted in minstrelsy and blackface performance.[20]

Appearing in blackface throughout the film, Barton pretends to be African American. All the other performers in the film, however, are Black [and not "blacked up"]. . . . Barton was clearly inspired by Al Jolson. . . . In 1927, when he starred in *The Jazz Singer* Jolson played a white singer who appears on stage in blackface. But in his many Broadway shows in the late 1910s and 1920s, and like Barton in *After Seben*, Jolson performed *as* an African American. Throughout the film Barton imitates Black people, but he regularly makes room for Black performers, some of them extremely talented.[21]

In the last four minutes of *After Seben,* you can view music and dance history unfold. Webb's band plays "Sweet Sue" for three couples competing in a dance contest. The first two couples improvise Charleston-like steps, and the partners occasionally break apart at arm's length, mirroring each other's moves. The third couple—"Shorty Stump" (Shorty Snowden) and "Liza Underdunk" (Maddie Purnell)—move a little differently. They break apart at arm's length much more freely, and she twirls and dips with moves that don't mirror her partner's, before the two Cakewalk off the floor. Their mode of dancing—breaking apart at arm's length but able to improvise individually—is the germ of what would soon grow into the Lindy Hop.

The focus is more on the dancers than the musicians; still, it is a beautiful scene of a great dance band doing its job. Webb's band provides a spirited, up-tempo rhythm that lifts and carries the dancers. The rhythm section—banjo, piano, drums, tuba—keeps the tempo precise and steady for all three couples. The brass players vary the lead for each couple, with clarinet and saxes playing short obbligatos. "Tiger Rag" is a tour de force for Barton, dancing with an imaginary partner: he's a poignant charmer—an elastic Charlie Chaplin with "Snake Hips" Tucker moves. The band plays this standard tune at a breakneck clip, with clarinet leading, and the rest of the horns playing a New Orleans–inspired romp behind him. You can clearly see a few band members: John Trueheart on banjo, Elmer Williams on saxophone, and Edwin "King" Swayzee on trumpet. Unfortunately, Webb is mostly out of view. You can just barely see his lopsided smile for a few seconds.[22]

The film was supposed to include a scene with Webb's band playing "Kidney Feet," a song-and-dance step "sweeping the country," according to the *Courier*. "Chick's boys will record this number for one of the big record companies very shortly. The number is featured by Duke Ellington, Charlie Johnson, Elmer Snowden orchestras and is the talk of New York."[23] "Kidney Feet" did not make the final cut, nor did Webb's band ever record it.

After Seben was released May 18, 1929, and shown in theaters around the country for months as an added attraction. It was one of several jazz-themed "talkies" that came out in 1929, two of which are acclaimed classics of early jazz in film: *Black and Tan*, starring Duke Ellington, and *St. Louis Blues*, Bessie Smith's only appearance on film. A review in *Motion Picture News* calls *After Seben* a "well stocked laugh maker.... It could really be placed in the same class with *St. Louis Blue*, except that its story is not very strong and it has not the motivating power of a famous song.... *After Seben* is a high class piece of goods.... There are some dancing scenes in which negro energy just overflows.... This one is good for first run showings and all the way down the line. It may be it hasn't been 'dumbed down' enough for the stick audiences.... [T]he flaws are negligible."[24]

Webb's and his band's involvement in this film was a milestone, and the only film in which he is featured. Its uniqueness has attracted the attention of jazz film scholars and jazz dance historians, despite Barton's stereotypic racist depictions, typical of that time. Publicity about the film worked to Webb's advantage. An ad for an upcoming date in Philadelphia makes the most of that: "JUST LOOK, the most Sensational Dance Band in America: CHICK WEBB AND HIS HARLEM STOMPERS, direct from the famous Players-Paramount Studios—Hear them in the Talkies and Dance to their Marvelous Music."[25]

In the summer of 1929, Webb subbed for Duke Ellington's Orchestra at the Cotton Club. The club, like Connie's Inn and other expensive, exclusive, white-audience performance spaces, was far different than the Savoy Ballroom. These clubs did not serve Harlemites but were New York City's Jazz Age spaces for cultural transactions, serving, as dance scholar Danielle Robinson writes, the "overt embracing of 'blackness'" by enthusiastic white patrons at revues, cabarets, and dance emporiums.[26]

At Roseland, it was a stretch for Webb's band (now named Chick Webb and His Roseland Orchestra) to fill in for the nationally famous Fletcher Henderson Orchestra, who'd been performing at Roseland for four years and was far more experienced, bigger, and had fabulous arrangements. But pleasing dancing audiences was what Webb and the Stompers did well, and Webb's band performed at Roseland for short periods over the next couple of years.

The Cotton Club was another story. Webb's band was substituting there for Ellington's, who—in another first for Black bandleaders and their musicians—was performing on Broadway in *Ziegfield Follies*. The Cotton Club was owned by the organized crime leader Owen (known as "Owney" or "The Killer") Madden. The Cotton Club and its midtown counterparts like Club Alabam traded in slave plantation names and decor to "sell" the best offerings in New York–style Black music and dance in a byzantine set of cultural exchanges and appropriation. The Cotton Club seated about seven hundred people and was off-limits to Harlem's Black residents, except for those who worked there or celebrities like dancer Bill Robinson. The stage set was a replica of a Southern plantation porch, with a painted backdrop of willow trees and slave cabins. The floor shows were extravaganzas of jungle-themed choreography, hot music, and spectacular exotic dancers and dance ensembles. Performers and bands worked three ninety-minute shows a night, after which the band played for dancing.

Everything had to run like clockwork. "A lot of people worked hard to put those shows together.... [T]hat was the Cotton Club spirit," said Calloway, whose band took over from Ellington at the Cotton Club in 1931. "Work, work, work. Rehearse, rehearse, rehearse.... Get it down fine. If the chorus line wasn't rehearsing the bands was. If the band wasn't rehearsing, the act was.... We knew we couldn't miss a lick."[27]

While Webb and his band could play their own music for dancing, they had to play the show's book for the floor shows and acts, and emulate Ellington band's sound and style as well. Musicologist and dance scholar Christi Jay Wells explains: "Webb stepped into the same role through which Ellington had launched his career with colorful, exotic compositions to accompany the club's salacious floor shows. The style ... took on the moniker 'jungle music.' "[28]

Ellington, who had never set foot on a plantation or in a jungle, had tailored his band's music for the Cotton Club's revues with a heavy tom-tom beat and dramatic growls and wah-wahs from the horns. The percussion accents and expressive sounds from the horns were woven into Ellington's compositions and style during these years, his emergence as a composer. Other Harlem bands quickly picked it up.

"Jungle music" was presumably what the Brunswick producer wanted for Webb's first recording sessions for the label, on June 14 and June 27, 1929. Brunswick released Webb's first 78-rpm records "Dog Bottom" and "Jungle Mama" under the name "The Jungle Band," without Webb's name attached as leader. "The Jungle Band" was a Brunswick pseudonym also applied to Ellington's Brunswick recordings made while he was under contract with

RCA Victor. The same name was used for Brunswick's other double-dealing instances, wanting to capitalize on the "jungle" trend that Ellington, in effect, set in motion, without ever endorsing that as a "brand" for his music.

Ten musicians played on these sides: Ward Pinkett and Edwin Swayzee, trumpets; Robert Horton, trombone; Hilton Jefferson and Joe Garland, alto saxophone and clarinet; Elmer Williams, tenor saxophone; Don Kirkpatrick, piano; John Trueheart, banjo or guitar; Elmer James, tuba; and Webb, drums.[29] Webb's pianist and chief arranger Don Kirkpatrick wrote a Don Redman–style score for "Dog Bottom," with a Charleston beat headed toward swing. The introduction hurtles into a whirling melody played by a trio of clarinets, followed by a series of short, hot, improvised solos showing off Webb's musicians. Side B, "Jungle Mama," is a bluesy foxtrot played at a midtempo crawl, with growls by trumpet and trombone, similar to many of Ellington's recordings from this time. These records, like Ellington's 1920s 78-rpm recordings and those of other Harlem bands, are a sonic landscape of Jungle Alley, the central Harlem blocks around West 132nd and 133rd Streets that were lined with small basement clubs and cafes, with crowded walk-up apartments above. These are the brownstone blocks where Webb had lived since he first arrived in Harlem. It was a vibrant, crowded, middle-class and working-class neighborhood, where people actually got up early to go to work and came home at night to sleep.

In November 1929 a *Pittsburgh Courier* review, under the subheading "Chick Webb Clicks," gave the "two hot records" a brief thumbs up and singled out trumpet player King Swazey (Edwin Swayzee): "Rumor has it that Webb's gang will shortly replace Duke Ellington's bunch at the Cotton Club."[30]

Then came Black Tuesday, October 29, 1929, when the Wall Street stock market crashed stupendously after weeks of wildly roiling world markets and years of a speculative bubble. This precipitated a decade-long economic depression that would grow deeper and grimmer through the 1930s. Superficially at any rate, people in Harlem appeared to be making do. Duke Ellington's and Fletcher Henderson's bands still had long residencies, and some of the best young musicians had their pick of jobs. "Work came fast and furious," said saxophonist Russell Procope. "The business was good at that time. You could leave one job and go on another job or just freelance with different people."[31] Things might have been easier for top sidemen like Procope than for talented bandleaders who couldn't quite sustain a steady gig.

8

Ol' Man Depression

In the months leading up to Black Tuesday, as effects of the October 1929 stock market crash spread, Webb's band had a string of temporary but prestigious jobs—in *After Seben*, at the Cotton Club, and back at the Lafayette Theater. These high-profile engagements and the radio and press exposure positioned Webb and His Harlem Stompers in the top tier of New York's Black dance bands. Webb was able to expand his band to fourteen pieces for the big fall revue at the Lafayette Theater, "Halloween Fantasy," which got immediate raves.[1]

But Webb still couldn't land a steady "house band" engagement. In Aubrey Brooks's column for the *Tattler*, "About the Musicians," Brooks broadcast Webb's dilemma: "Poor Chick Webb. We often wonder if Chick was born under an unlucky star. He really tried hard to put over his band. He obtains capable men, but bad management seems to almost ruin Chick. We have often advised him as to what he should do, and we feel confident if he will do that he will come out all right—that's all."[2]

One wonders what kind of advice Brooks gave Webb. If you compare Webb's recordings—"Jungle Mama" and "Dog Bottom"—with those of other dance bands of the time, the Stompers hold up admirably. But Harlem's musical environment was unpredictable, and audiences were always looking for the next sensation. Some newcomers seemed to fly right to the top. That fall, Webb ran into two of them, fellow Baltimoreans Blanche Calloway and her younger brother Cab. They would soon be friends and fellow performers, all circling in the same orbit.

In fall 1929, Blanche Calloway, now twenty-seven years old, was a far bigger star than Cab. She had first come to New York in 1926 to perform at Ciro's, an elegant club in midtown Manhattan, and at the Lafayette Theater. Stunningly beautiful, Blanche did song-and-dance routines in a cabaret style that was more European than American. Blanche also cultivated call-and-response vocal numbers that Cab would make his signature a few years later.

Blanche was a featured star in Chicago, at the famed Sunset Cafe and other clubs, when federal agents cracked down on the city's mob rule and speakeasies in the late 1920s. The city's top musicians—including Jelly Roll Morton, King Oliver, and Louis Armstrong (who returned to Chicago in 1926)—came to New York, which offered a bigger playing field. Blanche was gregarious and charming and reached out to her entertainment contacts. According to Peter Brooks, one of Cab Calloway's grandsons and Blanche's great-nephew, "Aunt Blanche was the type of person—and all the people from Baltimore were like that—that the first thing she would have done when she got to New York was to look up Chick Webb. She knew he'd tell her the truth about the music scene."[3]

In September 1929, Cab was touring with the Alabamians, the band he'd started fronting just a few months earlier at the Sunset Cafe. The band, nominally led by its popular bandleader Marion Hardy, was touring on the way to New York and was a hit in clubs and ballrooms along the way. Cab had picked up crucial elements of performing style from Blanche: he was constantly in motion, interacting with the audience and his musicians. A reviewer from the *Kansas City Star* raved about him: "a loose-jointed young man named Cab Calloway goes into acrobatic frenzies as he leads them."[4]

The Alabamians' last tour stop—and most important—was at the Savoy Ballroom for the fall season opening, September 20, 1929.

SAVOY'S GRANDEST GRAND FALL OPENING . . .
HEAR! That new kind of music
HEAR! The sensation of the West
HEAR! For the first time in New York
Marion G. Hardy's ALABAMIANS with Cab Calloway
CECIL SCOTT, The Saxappealer with a bagful of new tricks, new songs, new tunes and WOW, what a new brand of stomp.[5]

Buchanan had booked the Alabamians for two weeks at the Savoy, in keeping with his practice of trying out bands from out of town, which were generally cheaper to hire than top New York bands. He'd then invite crowd-pleasers for longer stays or for return visits.

Marion Hardy and the Alabamians did not get an invitation and returned to Chicago. Cab Calloway, like Webb, was ambitious and decided to stay in New York. He thought he could find work as a singer, dancer, or M.C. and could wait out the six-month transfer period to join Local 802 as a bandleader.

Cab got lucky almost immediately. The *Philadelphia Tribune* reported: "Cab Calloway, Baltimorean and brother of the famous Blanche Calloway, has replaced Paul Bass as juvenile in the current Broadway hit, 'Hot Chocolates' at the Hudson Theater. Cab is featured in the song 'Ain't Misbehavin', the Fats Waller song that Armstrong debuted in the show when it opened a few months earlier." Cab probably got the part through Armstrong, who was a friend of Blanche's from Chicago.[6]

Hot Chocolates was playing on Broadway at the Hudson Theater and uptown at Connie's Inn. Cab made the most of Waller's new song, whose double-entendre lyrics and catchy melody were perfect for his melismatic voice and mobile facial expressions.

Peter Calloway Brooks said that in the first decades of the twentieth century young Black Baltimoreans—like Cab, Blanche, and Chick Webb—were raised to be polite, friendly, and confident. They were "the first generation that could exhale" and could use their talents to find and create opportunities. Brooks surmised that Webb and the Calloways were friends in those years in New York, though they would be competing with each other for the same jobs. "Cab revered Chick Webb because Chick had come from Baltimore, just like he did and Chick had already made it at the Savoy. That provided for Cab a real platform—because Cab must have felt—well, if Chick can do it, I can do it too. Chick was definitely a trailblazer for Cab, and for Blanche."[7] Still, for all the camaraderie, Webb may have felt professionally threatened by Cab, who was a sensation in Harlem with his outrageous dance moves, powerful voice, and amazing good looks. Meanwhile, the Calloways thought Webb was a big success in New York, leading his own band of talented jazz musicians at the Savoy, the Lafayette, and other top venues.

In September 1929, a flurry of nightclub and ballroom openings kicked off the season in Harlem. With several bands returning from tours, there was a lot of bouncing around among musicians and bandleaders. Russell Procope was among them. "There was a guy named Peekaboo Jimmy, and he'd see you and say, 'I've got some gigs for you!' And he'd take out your book and write all these jobs down. And the next job I think I got was with Chick Webb."[8]

After Black Tuesday, many musicians in Harlem didn't feel the immediate impact, and for a short time life seemed to go on as usual. Like other Black communities, people had chugged along for years with high unemployment, low wages, and were underemployed and undervalued as professionals. Many Harlemites saved whatever they could to dance at the Savoy once a week or see a show at the Lafayette. These were their neighborhood shrines, as solid as church, and helped sustain Harlem's entertainment world.

Webb was scraping by again after the band's engagement at the Lafayette Theater ended. "Chick was trying to get his thing together," said Teddy McRae, a saxophonist and arranger who joined Webb in 1936. "I used to go out and watch them rehearse. I loved Chick. After rehearsal, he used to take the band over to this place on Lenox Avenue. This lady would cook cheap dinners—a southern dinner—like collard greens, yams, some kind of ribs. He would take the whole band over and buy everybody dinner. And this was like 15 cents, or 25 cents apiece. Collard greens and corn bread. We'd all sit around and eat, find out when the next job was coming up. Or try to go out and find a gig."[9]

As the Depression bit deeper, the orchestras of Duke Ellington, Fletcher Henderson, and, from 1931 onward, Cab Calloway and a few others not only kept working but also became more well known, thanks to their increasingly broad exposure on remote radio broadcasts, which were picked up across the country. Chick Webb would be part of a fortunate set of Black bandleaders whose bands worked all the way through the Depression.

Webb and his band expanded their repertoire for all possible tastes. Teddy McRae recalled that Webb had at least 150 dance arrangements even then, for every conceivable style and rhythm. It was during these early years of bandleading that Webb knew the band's key to survival was versatility. They performed anything a particular audience wanted, and aimed for an authentic sound and rhythm, whether it was a Viennese waltz, a tango, a fox trot, a slow drag, or a hot stomp.

This versatility was particularly important at the Alhambra Ballroom, where Webb's band started performing almost every weekend in early spring 1930. It had been closed since Webb's incident there with Local 802 in fall 1928. Moe Gale and Buchanan decided to lease the space; they had it redecorated and used it for dances for social clubs and business organizations. The Pittsburgh Courier predicted success for the venture: "The new dance space will run on the same high order of the Savoy itself, according to Charles P. Buchanan, the crack Savoy manager who is one of the sharpest and most able executives of the race."[10]

The Alhambra was much smaller than the Savoy, with a five-hundred-person capacity. Today, it still functions as an elegant venue for weddings, banquets, private dances, and the like, though you still have to climb two steep flights of stairs or wait for the slow antiquated elevators. Its elegant details have been beautifully maintained: ornate plaster moldings, curlicued hardwood railings, a curtained bandstand, a sizable dance floor surrounded by round tables, and a balcony with curved box seating. Buchanan deputized Harold Parker, his assistant manager, to run it.

Webb's band played at the Alhambra for formal balls for clubs like the all-male Alwyns Club, which brought in a fashionable decorator from Chicago, who transformed the ballroom into a "veritable fairy garden ... built around a beautiful fountain with a marble faun.... Chick Webb's Alhambra Orchestra furnished the music." The Alwyns Club's activities, like those of other exclusive clubs aligned with Alain Locke's philosophy of racial uplift, promoted a cultural life defined by formality and elegance, often leaning on European models. "High culture was a universal ideal to which all striving peoples could have access to and strive towards."[11] Instead of the Charleston, stomps, or the Lindy Hop, these clubs' young members enjoyed dancing to Viennese waltzes and moved with erect balletic posture. As Christi Jay Wells describes, these balls often included dance presentations that emphasized "poise, grace and beauty," and displays of neo-Grecian discipline, and study of high "physical culture."[12]

Other social clubs and fraternities might not have been so aspirational. Their members and guests just wanted to dress up, show off, dance, and have a good time. Jerry Major's "New York Social Whirl" column describes a dance hosted by the Phi Beta Sigma Fraternity:

> Chick Webb and His Chickens furnished the best music ever.... The doors closed promptly at 12:30 [a.m.]. But even before then the room was filled. We jammed the boxes and all.... We danced and danced and danced—and sipped and sipped.... We danced some more til three. Scrambling for coats and hats ... waiting turns to be taken down the elevator.... The Alhambra Ballroom is way up.... [Y]ou hate to climb downwards.... [W]e did not want to go home, so we all went to divers places. My crowd took in Tillie's where we had chicken, fried potatoes, spaghetti and all.[13]

Jerry Major (aka Gerri Major, née Geraldyn Hodges) had been writing about cultural events in Harlem in her "Society" columns for top Black

newspapers since her arrival there from Chicago in the mid-1920s. A powerhouse of talent and energy, Jerry chronicled Harlem's cultural activities
and kept tabs on art exhibits, fashion shows, and literary and political salons
that flowered during the Harlem Renaissance and kept going—though less
lavishly—through the Depression.[14] She covered the latest music and theater
events too—from soprano Abbie Mitchell's recitals and classical concerts to
"Music Week in Harlem" at the West 135th Street YMCA, which had a different lecture theme and concert each night. At one dance at the Rockland
Palace, the hosts suddenly announced a vote for the most popular Harlem orchestra: "Duke Ellington had the votes completely sewn up, by a wide margin."
The competition included Charlie Johnson; Louis Armstrong (then leading
Carroll Dickerson's orchestra); the Missourians, now led by Cab Calloway;
and Chick Webb. "Snake Hips seemed to be having the time of fifty men."
In another column Jerry confessed her one big Depression expenditure—
she called it her "dissipation"—buying an orchestra seat to "hear, see and
gloat over Maurice Chevalier and Duke Ellington at the Fulton Theater
(downtown)." She topped off that week with a VIP event in honor of singer
Taylor Gordon: "All the Theater Guild big shots who promoted *Porgy* were
there: Muriel Draper, the Green Pastureites, Carl Van Vechten . . . Langston
Hughes, more charming than ever."[15]

Major's columns were written with the sensitivity of a trustworthy, knowl-
edgeable insider, embracing the spectrum of Harlem's struggling but vibrant
cultural life in the early 1930s. She wrote:

> No one in America was closer to the pulse of colored life than the society
> editors of the black press. Through their columns and news items about
> the most intimate phases of black life, they did more to interpret the so-
> cial patterns of the community than the sociologists or psychologists. They
> also did more to dignify colored womanhood than all of the other media
> specialists put together.[16]

By the end of March 1930 Cab Calloway had gotten his transfer to Local 802
and, needing a band, Charlie Buchanan paired him with the Missourians,
who'd worked at the Cotton Club under a different name. Soon, the
Missourians were playing at the Savoy, and were also in rotation with
Webb at the Alhambra for private dances. Gale and Buchanan recognized
that Cab could be the next big thing. On May 14, 1930, Calloway and the
Missourians were in their first "Battle of Music," a "Million Dollar Affair in

Musical Talent," with Webb's band as one of the contenders along with Duke Ellington's, Fletcher Henderson's, Cecil Scott's, and Lockwood Lewis's. The Savoy's ad used its perennial boast: "The event will make the first time in history that six orchestras of the scope and reputation of the above named groups have ever met and the carnival is expected to draw one of the greatest crowds New York has ever seen." Two weeks later, Harold Parker staged a smaller "Battle of Music" at the Alhambra, which also featured Webb and Calloway.[17] Musically, Webb's band was far superior to the Missourians, but Cab himself stole the show.

Calloway's energy and charisma were so impressive that Moe Gale offered him a long-term contract to become his booking agent and would pay Calloway a hundred dollars per week. Cab was featured at big events at both the Savoy and the newly redecorated Alhambra, which now had "luxurious, futuristic and ultra modern decorations and lighting effects—floating clouds behind the orchestra, revolving lights, flickering squares of light fountain trellis, a wonder palace." One night the Alhambra staged a full show, headed by Cab, with other acts by his sister Blanche, Lindy Hoppers, and tap dancers. Blanche was starting to make more frequent New York appearances herself.[18]

Cab Calloway was invited to perform at some of New York's biggest events of the 1930 holiday season. One of the them was the *New York American*'s Radio Ball at the Roseland Ballroom, a benefit for Christmas charities: "The 22 largest and most popular bands of New York will appear. Among the list are Duke Ellington, Cab Calloway, Luis Russell, Charles Johnson, Fletcher Henderson and Chick Webb. Rudy Vallee is the master of ceremonies."[19]

The Savoy's plans for Christmas Eve 1930 were still lavish, despite the worsening economy. The management wished their patrons "a Merry Christmas with Fletcher Henderson and Chick Webb at the head of their two orchestras.... [T]he celebration will not end until the Savoyans bid all hands a Happy New Year."[20] The ballroom served sundaes named for Cab Calloway and Chick Webb and gave its patrons party hats, noisemakers, and so forth for Harlem's annual postmidnight parade on Lenox Avenue.

In spring 1931, the Cotton Club's gangster owners decided that Calloway and the Missourians would succeed Duke Ellington at the club. Ellington and his orchestra were leaving the club after their successful four-year run, punctuated by many hit recordings. Calloway was a different kind of bandleader and performer than Duke Ellington. *Variety* reported: "Calloway is a superlatively aggressive and talented leader as compared with Ellington's

extreme modesty. The 11-man band is about 100 degrees hotter and its ca-
cophony of rhythm more enticing. If real lowdown blues is what is wanted
Calloway is the boy to serve it up." The reviewer also singled out Blanche
Calloway, "a dusky belle with great coon-shouting pipes."[21] Ellington's
manager, Irving Mills, helped smooth the way for Cab Calloway's hiring at
the Cotton Club, after Ellington announced that he was moving on. Mills
recognized Calloway's tremendous potential—as a performer, bandleader,
and recording artist—and signed Calloway on as a client.[22] Cab's recording of
"Minnie the Moocher" in March 1931 sold hundreds of thousands of copies
after its release and has been iconic ever since.

Cab on stage was everything that Chick Webb could not possibly be. Cab
danced, he sang, he ran from the audience to his musicians, hair falling into
his eyes, his coattails flying. Webb was a virtuoso drummer, who skillfully
led the band from his drummer's throne. He was totally attentive to musical
details, the fine points, as well as advances in swing rhythm and the most
up-to-date inventive dance arrangements. His sheer energy at the drum set
and occasional tricks—tossing up drumsticks or playing big cymbal crashes
for effect—were mesmerizing. Mainly, Webb loved his band and the music
they were making. He was all about musicianship and achieving a unique
ensemble sound.

Trombonist Sandy Williams, who played with Fletcher Henderson's band
before joining Webb's band in 1932, said: "We used to rehearse quite often.
Even back then Chick had several arrangers come to rehearse tunes, and he
would spend his last nickel on an arrangement."[23]

By the end of 1931, the economic downturn was clearly not temporary and
conditions for many people were devastating. The glamor of white scene-
seekers "slumming" in Harlem was fading, though the Cotton Club and
other whites-only Jazz Age clubs hadn't closed their doors yet.

The most lucrative musical work in New York City during the early years
of the Depression was locked up by a clique of young white musicians who
emerged from the ranks of top white dance bands led by Paul Whiteman, Red
Nichols, and Jean Goldkette, the Detroit-based bandleader. Radio and studio
ensembles and most Broadway pit orchestras were exclusively segregated in
the 1920s and 1930s, and would be for decades. Black musicians complained
about this discrimination, but Local 802 did nothing to address it, nor did the
International American Federation of Musicians. The racial divide in studio

work was also due to the virtual monopoly held by two of the biggest studio contractors who would not hire Black musicians.[24] Their "pool," all excellent sight-readers, included Tommy and Jimmy Dorsey, Jack Teagarden, Glenn Miller, Gene Krupa, and Benny Goodman. In 1931, clarinetist Goodman reportedly earned as much as four hundred dollars a week for radio and recording sessions and working six nights a week in Red Nichols's orchestra for the Gershwin's latest Broadway hit show *Girl Crazy*.

Remarkably, Webb and his band were also busy with bookings. They played for several weeks at the Roseland Ballroom in fall 1930 when Fletcher Henderson was persuaded to bring his band to headline at Connie's Inn.[25] In early winter 1931, Chick Webb and His Roseland Orchestra was booked for "Roseland Revels," a new revue at the Lafayette Theater, directed by the acclaimed Harlem producer/director/choreographer Leonard Harper. After the show's run at the Lafayette, the *New York Age* reported that Webb's Roseland Orchestra and the show's comedians Joyner and Foster would stay on at the theater: "The first is undoubtedly one of the finest orchestras in the city. . . . Webb has just completed a long run at Roseland where they have not only been a hit, they have also became one of the leading orchestras over the radio. The band is composed of all local boys and predictions are made freely that they are second in merit only to Duke Ellington's marvelous aggregation of musicians."[26]

Russell Procope moved between Fletcher Henderson's Orchestra and Webb's frequently from 1929 to 1931. He was with Webb's band when it expanded to twelve pieces: three trumpets, two trombones, three saxes, and the rhythm section.

> He [Webb] was very, very ambitious. He wanted to get to the top—every move he made, every tune he played, he wanted it better. When he got in the position to, he bought uniforms for the band. When we [Webb's band] were down at Roseland and bands were battling up at the Savoy, we came up after Roseland. These five bands had been making a lot of noise all night, and we played and romped and stomped and whatever. When Fletcher Henderson went on tours and when Duke Ellington was out of town, we used to stick our chests out and say, "Now *we are* the best band in New York."

Procope admired Webb as a person and as a leader. "Chick would never sit on the side or stand up with a baton. He'd only let someone else sit in on his drums when he was absent. He had an uncanny ability about running the band, picking the arrangements, playing them in the right manner. A lot of times in rehearsals, he'd go off in a corner and listen to see if we were playing it [the arrangement] right."[27]

Webb and other Harlem bandleaders still raided each other's bands, even during these unstable economic times. This was a common practice among dance bands, both Black and white. One instance got so much attention among Harlem musicians that it was dubbed "The Big Trade," an incident referred to later on in several books about the Swing Era. Webb's band acquired alto saxophonist Benny Carter and trombonist Jimmy Harrison from Henderson's band in exchange for alto saxophonist Russell Procope and trombonist Benny Morton.

Percival Outram reported the "trade" in his "Activities among Musicians" column for the *New York Age*:

> Here is a peculiar coincidence, happening to two bands of the first class caliber. Fletcher Henderson released his first sax and trombone player; Chick Webb, at the identical time, released his first sax and trombone player. Fletcher hired the two men from Chick's band, and Chick took Fletcher's two men. None of the musicians lost a day's work, and both principals are satisfied and think their orchestra is strengthened by this unprecedented incident. Henderson was at Connie's Inn, in Harlem, and Chick Webb is and has been for months playing at Roseland on Broadway, where Fletcher for very many years was an attraction.[28]

For Webb, this trade was only possible because his band was working more steadily. Even so, for Russell Procope, who rejoined Henderson: "It was a very good trade because I doubled my salary.... Of course, Fletcher was known all over and at that time Chick's was a local band and wasn't doing much broadcasting." Procope recalled one night before the trade when Webb's band battled Henderson's at the Savoy: "I have a vivid memory because Benny Carter was playing with Fletcher then. We didn't think of it as a battle, 'cause Fletcher Henderson was the tops, he was the greatest. But that night Benny Carter didn't show up, and I bounced from one band to the other. I had a great time."[29]

Webb and Henderson had previously swapped musicians, but Webb also wanted Henderson's arrangements. Benny Carter, a top arranger as well as saxophonist, offered to adapt some charts he'd written for Henderson for Webb's band and write some new ones. During his brief tenure with Webb

between 1931 and 1932, Carter was a huge influence. His writing and musicianship helped push Webb's band toward a more sophisticated New York
dance band style.

On March 31, 1931, Webb's band recorded three tunes, all arranged by
Benny Carter for Vocalion, Brunswick's race records label, shortly after the
"Great Trade." The personnel included Webb's mainstays: Don Kirkpatrick,
piano; John Trueheart, banjo and guitar; and Elmer James, tuba and bass.
Tenor saxophonist Elmer Williams is rejoined in the sax section by Hilton
Jefferson, alto saxophone, and the addition of Carter to the reed section
makes these recordings particularly fabulous. The three trumpet players,
Shelton (Scad) Hemphill, Louis Hunt, and Louis Bacon, had probably been
performing with Webb that winter. Procope, who worked with this ensemble
before rejoining Henderson, recalled that Webb heard Louis Bacon and
Louis Hunt working at a dancing school and hired the two of them together
because they'd already been playing together.

All three sides—"Heebie Jeebies," "Blues in My Heart," and "Soft and
Sweet"—show a well-rehearsed ensemble, revealing Webb's high standards
in the details and orchestral approach, yet have a loose, sensual feel. The
highlight of this session is the stunning rendition of "Heebie Jeebies," an
Armstrong hit from 1926. The band is clearly headed towards a modern-
sounding fluid swing, far ahead of what most other bands of the time were
playing, which was still two-step-oriented Charlestons and foxtrots. Jazz
historian Gunther Schuller rightly singles out the sax section, "tinged with
Benny Carter's luminous lead alto." Elmer Williams's forward-thinking solo
deftly crosses over bar lines with rangy, wide-angled melodies. There are also
notable solos by the great trombonist Jimmy Harrison, who soars on his brief
tuneful solos, and whose open-throated generous sound gives the brass section a lushness. "Heebie Jeebies" ends with Webb on celesta, a delectable kiss
of an ending.[30]

The abundant coverage by the Black entertainment press of the variety of
musical activity in Harlem obscures how deep the Depression's effects were
getting. Outram reminded Local 802 members to apply for the union's own
"relief checks" and mentioned upcoming benefits, events, and the latest Local
802 infractions. Moe Gale and Charles Buchanan strategized ways to keep
the Savoy going. "The Savoy, with its big investment involved, is striving with
might and main to worst 'Old Man Depression.' Gale and Buchanan have

offered "attraction after attraction to stimulate and focus attention on their ballroom."[31]

The Savoy broke all its attendance records in April 1931 when Guy Lombardo and His Royal Canadians played at the ballroom, "thus giving patrons the opportunity not only to hear but see this famous organization of white musicians." Lombardo's orchestra's phenomenal success at the Savoy has baffled jazz critics of the last twenty or thirty years, who still take issue with "sweet" versus "hot" jazz—looking though the reverse end of a musical telescope. But Savoy dancers loved romantic music, not to mention the chance to dance to a world-famous radio orchestra playing just for them. Lombardo's was the first top white orchestra to perform at the Savoy, and it would not be the last.

During the Depression, Sigmund Galewski and Moe Gale wanted to protect the family's financial investment in the Savoy Ballroom. But they also wanted to protect their staff and keep people working. Scores of musicians earned at least some of their income at the Savoy during these dark economic times. The Kansas City outfit, Bennie Moten and his thirteen-piece orchestra (now recording for Victor), was a big hit at the ballroom in April 1931, and was again that October. At that time, Moten's band included guitarist/arranger Eddie Durham and pianist Bill Basie—the future Count Basie.[32] The Savoy's dancing crowds loved the Moten band's riff-and-blues-based early swing style, in contrast to the intricately arranged dance music in vogue in Harlem. That fall, the Savoy also presented an old favorite, Fess Williams, who was back in Harlem with a revamped band.

The Savoy Ballroom hosted or cosponsored frequent raffles, giveaways, and celebrity-filled benefits at the ballroom and at other Harlem venues. Buchanan helped plan a huge benefit at the Lafayette Theater for unemployment relief, and Webb's was among several top bands slated to appear. On November 11, 1931 (Armistice Night), the Savoy hosted a "Hard Times Ball (Depression Dance) admission 50 Cents; free beer and pretzels; wear your oldest clothes; hats, dresses, suits, etc., given free to poorest dressed." With these constant efforts, the "Savoy Ballroom refuses to allow Harlemites to forget or ignore its spacious and handsome ballroom."[33]

Gale and Buchanan kept reassessing what strategies would help the Savoy stay open, including adjusting ticket prices, as Harlem theaters did. They pulled out of the lease of the Alhambra Ballroom in just less than a year, and it closed in December 1931. Soon after, they reserved one or two nights a week at the Savoy for private dances and social clubs.

Webb and Blanche and Cab Calloway kept overlapping at the Savoy and other gigs in Harlem. In October 1931, Webb's band and Blanche Calloway and Her Joy Boys went on tour together for an unprecedented five-band roving "Battle of Music." The other bands were Benny Moten's, Zack Whyte's Beau Brummels, and Roy Johnson's Happy Pals, all of whom were crowd-pleasers at the Savoy Ballroom.

Blanche Calloway was one of a handful of female bandleaders at that time, along with pianist Lil Hardin and cornetist Valaida Snow. Calloway had been encouraged to start her own orchestra in March 1931 by Sam Steiffle, owner of Philadelphia's Pearl Theater. She had been the featured headliner at the Pearl in spring 1931 and for a few weeks was accompanied by members of Andy Kirk's Clouds of Joy, who'd been stranded on tour without Kirk.[34] Once Kirk reunited his band for new bookings, Blanche assembled her own band, which included Cozy Cole on drums (his first big band job), Edgar Battle on trumpet and arranger, and Ben Webster on tenor saxophone.

The five-band "veritable caravan of music" moved out of New York in early October. The tour—composed of all one-nighters—was organized by the Associated Colored Orchestra leadership, assisted by Moe Gale, who was trying to break into the band booking business and had contacts with a few theater owners. The tour's first dates were in Philadelphia, Baltimore, Richmond, Virginia, and Washington, DC, followed by a swing in Pennsylvania to York, Harrisburg, and Pittsburgh. From there they played theaters in Ohio, finishing up in Cincinnati.[35]

Blanche Calloway and Her Joy Boys were the crowd's favorite at almost every date. In mid-October the "Battle" was held at Washington, DC's Masonic Auditorium, and the *Pittsburgh Courier* called it "the most sensational dance and music spectacle yet to be seen here." The article mentions Calloway's new records for RCA Victor and a renewal of her contract at "a fabulous increase in salary.... Devotees of Terpsichore will be given the opportunity of dancing to torrid arrangements and renditions of her 'Jazz-Boys.' ... Peppy, fiery, vivacious, Blanche will show the reasons why she is at the top of the ladder of musical fame.... She will be playing opposite four other nationally famous bands ... who will strive to outplay her in a battle of music supremacy." This may be the first time that a reviewer rooted for the female bandleader to win![36]

Other press previews and reviews were equally hyperbolic; local reporters clearly wanted to attract audiences for this unusual five-way band battle. Presenting a five-band package for only one night was expensive, and an ad from York, Pennsylvania, lists one-dollar admission, higher than usual for that area. In Pittsburgh, the event was at the Pythian Temple: a "super-musical extravaganza . . . for one night only. The forthcoming music battle is reputed to be the most costly, most elaborate, most spectacular and the most entertaining novelty dance attraction yet to be presented in Pittsburgh . . . a veritable war of music, loaded with the most celebrated dance band headliners and entertaining orchestras."[37] One wonders about the Associated Colored Orchestra's strategy in mapping this tour, and what each band was paid.

That October, the *Chicago Defender* ran an article entitled "Depression Does Not Worry Orchestra Men":

> This thing Depression which has moved into every country and all lines of promotion and work evidently has spared the traveling orchestras. Last week Andy Anderson, writing for ANP [Associated Negro Press] asked ten leaders of bands how they felt about the thing and to a man they denied feeling its effect.[38]

Oddly, Anderson did not mention in his introduction that one of the "men" was a female bandleader, a rarity at the time. He interviewed Blanche Calloway and the other four leaders from the "Battle of Music" tour—Webb, Bennie Moten, Zack Whyte, and Roy Johnson, as well as Noble Sissle and Duke Ellington.

Webb was typically optimistic and upbeat: "The young musical hounds who constitute the Chicks are not at all frightened by the tenseness of the situation, especially in the orchestra field, and we are confident in our ability to weather the storm with perfect ease. That is a characteristic of ours, and we are by no means intending to be different now. We will blow our way to the top!"[39]

9

On the Road with Louis

Hobo, You Can't Ride This Train

My my my my, listen to that rhythm train, boys
I bet there's a lotta hoboes, lord, settin' on them rails
Even A-number one and all
'em cats, yeah man

All aboard for Pittsburg, Harrisburg, oh all the burgs
Hobo you can't ride this train
Now I'm the brakeman and I'm a tough man
I ain't jokin', you can't ride this train
[Instrumental interlude]
Now listen here boys—
Boys, you ain't so bad
After all, you all right with me
I think I will let you ride with me.

—Louis Armstrong[1]

The winter of 1932–33 was the worst yet for the country and Harlem. Hardship was visible everywhere. Heartbreaking photos and newsreel footage show long unemployment lines, breadlines, tent camps, and the hardscrabble existence of thousands of people—mostly men—young and old, jumping onto freight trains and railroad cars. They were hitching a ride to anywhere to find work or dubious shelter in train yards and stock cars. "Riding the rails" was commonplace and dangerous. People were frequently hurt or even killed by accidents, railroad guards, and train workers.

Louis Armstrong, the famed "Modern Angel Gabriel," recorded "Hobo" with Chick Webb and his band on December 8, 1932, one of the trumpet star's first recordings for RCA Victor. The song, which Armstrong wrote, is as much an anthem of the Great Depression as Yip Harburg's iconic "Brother, Can You Spare a Dime?," a top hit of 1932 sung by Bing Crosby. Louis turns the tables racially and takes ownership. He's the boss—the train's engineer—who catches the hobos on his train but decides they are "all right" and lets them stay. Armstrong's spoken-word vocalizing, witty and sly, and Webb's perfect drum work, steady and chugging, capture the humanity of the scene as Louis gives these men a break. A ride with him would chase anyone's hard-luck blues away.

Norma Miller grew up around the block from the Savoy Ballroom and became one of its best young Lindy Hoppers, and one of most outspoken and long-lived. She often said: "In Harlem, we had the Depression *before* the Depression."[2] Still, the impact on Harlem was now widespread, even if it did not hit all at once, or all places equally.

George Schuyler, Harlem Renaissance editor, author, and satirist, summarized a report from the National Urban League in his "Views & Reviews" column of January 1932: "We learn that in 106 urban centers, which include the largest Black Belts in the country, the unemployment rate among Negroes is greater than among the whites, but the Negroes get less of the available jobs than the whites, being dependent largely on charity. This condition practically forces them back to the days of chattel slavery. . . . [E]ven when 'prosperity' returns there will be a large army of jobless, and the majority of its members will be gentlemen and ladies of color." In 1931, more than 25 percent of Harlem's adult population was unemployed. Household income fell 43 percent from 1928. The Depression caused increased competition with whites for even the worst jobs. "Every job became a white man's job."[3]

In Webb's circles, employment for Harlem's musicians, dancers, and entertainers dwindled from the fizzy roving nightlife scene of the late 1920s. Between 1931 and 1934, the worst years of the Depression, a handful of Harlem musicians and bands kept working, though there were dramatic differences in pay, prestige, and fields of influence. Ellington's and Calloway's success throughout the Depression was largely due to the efforts of manager Irving Mills. Ellington and Calloway were Mills's top artists, and he helped them produce multiple revenue streams as recording artists, performers, and songwriters, and took a healthy percentage of their earnings. They knew who they were working with and stayed vigilant in their white manager–Black client partnerships, what Jewish studies scholar Jonathan Karp calls "the marriage of Jewish entrepreneurship to the black mystique." Mills also did everything to present Ellington and Calloway and their orchestras in a high-class manner to the media. Ellington's clarinetist Barney Bigard said, "We worked clean through the Depression without knowing that there even was one."[4]

Moe Gale did not have Mills's music publishing experience—the linchpin of the music industry—and was not as prominent in the music industry yet. He was not as flamboyant, either. Though he was a friendly man, he didn't exert a "front-of-house presence" at the Savoy Ballroom and was largely inconspicuous there. The Savoy never made a profit, so Gale started some sidelines. "Nobody made money," said Conrad Gale, Moe's brother. "It was the spinoffs. It was only when Moe went into the agent business, that he made a name for himself." In 1931, Gale formed Gale Enterprises Inc., a management and booking agency that helped book the five-band "Battle of Music" tour in October 1931, featuring Webb's band with Blanche Calloway's and others (see chapter 8). Gale hoped his agency would open up a "new and lucrative field for orchestras and entertainment. By thus doing we will stimulate employment among musicians to aid the quick return of 'good times.' . . . Our next road trip, starting in early January will travel through 11 states. Chick Webb and his orchestra with the world champion 'Lindy Hop' dancers are the attraction."[5] By the mid-1930s, Gale became a well-known "gatekeeper" himself as he secured radio, recording contracts, and—eventually—top bookings for Webb and his popular clients.

In 1932 Webb's band still had dry spells, but they didn't last as long. They appeared in stage shows at the Lafayette and other top Black eastern theaters: the Howard in DC, the Royal in Baltimore, and the Pearl and Strand Theaters in Philadelphia. In February 1932, "Chick Webb and His 12 Little Chicks" were part of a new sixty-member revue at the Lafayette, headlined by Buck and Bubbles, vaudeville tap dancers and comedians who were now stars in their own right after appearing on Broadway in *Ziegfeld Follies* in 1931.

In June 1932, Webb's band was back at the Roseland Ballroom, filling in for Claude Hopkins and His Orchestra while it was on tour. In Aileen Eckstine's "Wave Lengths" radio column for the *Pittsburgh Courier*, Eckstine raved about Webb's band after catching their live Roseland broadcast: "Chick Webb broadcasts some very torrid tempos over station WABC at the magic hour of 1 o'clock in the morn."[6] Eckstein's opinion didn't help; this season, Webb's band didn't go over so well at Roseland. So for a few weeks Roseland did not have a Black orchestra alternating with a white one for the first time since 1924, when Fletcher Henderson's Orchestra started playing there. Outram of the *New York Age* chastised Webb: "Maybe Chick's orchestra failed to keep the grade. And now we see the unusual sight of two white orchestras playing Roseland, Webb and his orchestra being relieved of their obligations. Too bad. Good orchestras of today have to rehearse under competent direction before exhibiting their wares on the air, and free-for-all playing is taboo."[7]

What did Outram mean by "free-for-all"? Were Webb's best sidemen taking overly long solos? Was the band under-rehearsed on tricky arrangements or were there new sidemen who didn't know Webb's book? Since there are no other source reports, it's hard to know just what went wrong.

Fortunately, Webb had other things lined up. In mid-June, the band was featured with three other top Black orchestras—Fletcher Henderson's, Luis Russell's, and Teddy Hill's—for the Savoy Ballroom's annual employees' breakfast dance. In late summer 1932, "Chick Webb and His Roseland Orchestra"—as local ads called it—toured white resorts and dance halls along the Susquehanna River, in Pennsylvania, from Wilkes Barre to Harrisburg, preceded by glowing little listings in local papers. Webb's band had played in some of these spots in summer 1930, and it's unclear if this tour came through Moe Gale's efforts to book the band or Webb's.

The tour's final stop was on Reist's Dance Boat in Harrisburg. George K. Reist, a local avid boatsman, started his first "dance boat" in 1930, a small houseboat with an open roof, and expanded to a "former coal barge outfitted with a band shell at one end, a night club at the other and a dance floor in the middle." During the summer it carried "thousands of dancers up and down the Susquehanna River." Reist's Dance Boat drew audiences from a hundred miles away, and smaller boats would caravan alongside to hear the music.[8] Most of the bands that played on the boat were local white bands. Tickets for local bands were thirty-five cents, but for Webb's band, now heard weekly on radio, they were fifty cents. As the Swing Era took hold, Reist's barge hosted several name bands, including those led by Andy Kirk and Gene Krupa.

Webb's "Colored Orchestra" was popular on this tour and returned to Reist's Dance Boat and other resorts through Labor Day weekend. Clarinetist Garvin Bushell described this trip at length in his memoir and in interviews. He joined Webb's band that summer along with trumpet player Bobby Stark, both of whom were top-notch sidemen who were out of work. Bushell recalled:

We went out on the road, but we weren't getting paid. . . . In Harrisburg we stayed with a woman named Caroline, who had a large boarding house. Nobody had any money. But Caroline was nice to us, because Chick had been through before. Caroline served liquor and had women there; you could go upstairs with a chick anytime you wanted. So Caroline let us sleep on the floor of her living room, all sixteen of us.

The next morning the valet woke us up and said we had to leave, since we were supposed to be on Long Island that night. Caroline said, "You got any money, boys?" I don't think there was two dollars between the whole sixteen of us. But she gave us bacon and eggs and coffee, and sent us on our way.

When the band finally got to the dance on Long Island, the musicians demanded to get paid that evening or they would not work. Webb said he'd do what he could, but he didn't pay them that night either. Bushell continued:

So we were heading back to New York in our two Cadillacs, and the chauffeurs hadn't been paid, either. One of them pulled over to the side of the road, and said: "Webb, you've got some money, and you're going to pay me. I don't care about the damn band, but give me some money for gas."

Chick said, "I ain't got it."

The chauffeur opened up the car and started pulling out all the music and the stands and books. We got out to help him. There was Chick with his drums and books and stands way out on Long Island, at four o'clock in the morning. We left him sitting there in the woods by himself.

He just said, "It's all right. I don't give a damn."

We figured he might come through with some money, but he didn't. He called our bluff!

The musicians started to drive off, but an oncoming thunderstorm made them feel guilty. They turned around to get him. "'Y'all didn't have to come back, it don't make no difference to me. I ain't got no money. That's it.' We told him to get back in the car, and took him back to New York."[9] Webb had a stubborn streak, but it's hard to say just why he was unable to pay them—if he'd gotten stiffed along the way or used the money to cover road expenses, other band debts, or pay for new arrangements. Webb's sidemen knew he was generous; he wouldn't have pocketed the money for himself.

Back in New York, Webb's band could be heard on WMCA four times a week and played for "breakfast dances" at the Savoy, another strategy to help the ballroom maintain its Depression-era audience. On October 1, 1932, the Savoy hosted "one of the greatest lineups of musical talent assembled for any dance . . . the nationally famous Cab Calloway and his Cotton Club Orchestra." Fletcher Henderson got second billing and "Chick Webb and His Chicks" were number three. The ad announced, "They [Webb's band] will continue to play indefinitely at the Savoy."[10] This was big news for Webb—he finally got the hard-won Savoy residency he'd been after for five years. Chick Webb's Chicks and Gus Dorival's San Domingans played nightly at the ballroom for most of the fall. Gale was now Webb's manager and booking agent, though his "contract" was still a handshake. The Savoy would be Webb's main base for the next eight years.

The San Domingans are a link to New York's Afro-Caribbean musical stream that had been flowing to the US since before World War I, when James Reese Europe hired several Caribbean musicians, many of them Black, for his Clef Club Orchestra. After Europe's death, Noble Sissle carried this forward and he and his wife took in musicians from Puerto Rico, the Dominican Republic, and Cuba when they first came to New York. Trumpet player Mario Bauza, whom Webb would hire in 1933, was the Sissles' houseguest for over a year. The San Domingans was formed in 1929 and co-led by cousins Enrique Duran and Gus Dorival. They were a jazz-oriented band whose personnel were mostly Dominicans but also included Cubans, Panamanians, African Americans, and West Indians. Their key to longevity at the Savoy (they played there frequently between 1932 and 1934) was versatility in playing updated ballroom styles—jazz-oriented early swing, foxtrots, waltzes, and the rhumba, then catching on with New York dancers.[11]

The landscape of performance venues in Harlem kept shifting. Small clubs were doubly hit by the Depression and by the repeal of Prohibition in 1933. Black-owned speakeasies closed, but then some reopened with a new name and a white owner who often retained the former Black owner as manager. The closures included a landmark, Pod & Jerry's. "Once the capital for all merry-makers, it is closed now, no more does Willie 'the Lion' [Smith] play the piano with a cigar tucked behind his mouth." According to Smith, "Legal liquor did what scarcer tips and shuttered warehouse of the Depression had failed to do." The color bar in elite Harlem clubs and cabarets dropped along with attendance. By the fall of 1933, Connie's Inn closed and reopened as the Harlem Club, with a scaled-down floor show, open to all. The Cotton Club closed its doors in 1935.[12] Jazz Age Jim Crow was no longer viable when club owners needed more patrons.

Meanwhile, the Lafayette Theater, the Harlem Opera House, and, starting in January 1934, the Apollo Theater—under new ownership—were all trying to keep their doors open. Their survival involved a financial and class struggle between the Black community and Harlem's predominantly Jewish theater owners, looking to cut expenses. Splashy revues with big casts and lots of acts were too expensive to stage. At the end of 1932, the Lafayette was "the only theater in Harlem where race musicians are employed now using an orchestra, the other theaters only using talking pictures."[13]

At the Savoy, Gale and Buchanan kept shifting priorities. The Savoy was more generous to its patrons than to the musicians, who were generally paid minimum Local 802 scale for ballrooms, thirty-three dollars per sideman per week. For the audience there was free admission almost every night for various occupations or "specials," all of which benefited Harlemites. Panama Francis, a drummer who played frequently at the Savoy Ballroom in the late 1930s to 1940s, explained: "Monday night was Ladies Night, Tuesday was for the 400 Club. Thursday Night was 'KM' Night-—kitchen mechanic night— for the sleep-in maids; women packed the ballroom, and the guys followed them. Saturday was like salt and pepper, with as many white kids as black."

In the early 1930s, Broadway theaters did not all go dark, but by 1932 the record industry plummeted: sales of 78-rpm records dropped to two million in 1933 from over one hundred million in 1929, a loss of over seventy million dollars in profits.[14] The Depression wiped out the small innovative labels, such as Okeh, Vocalion, and Gennett, that had helped popularize both blues and jazz recording artists. By 1932, only two major record companies survived: Victor (which was bought by the Radio Corporation of America [RCA] in 1932) and Columbia (acquired by CBS in 1938).[15] Radio—cheaper entertainment in most households—became the dominant medium. But the Depression also hit New York's indie radio stations of the 1920s, which introduced live broadcasts via remote wire from the Savoy, the Cotton Club, and other nightspots; these were driven under in the 1930s by the consolidation of major radio networks.

In 1932, Louis Armstrong was a national celebrity, and his band was advertised as the "highest paid colored band in the world." Armstrong's 1931

Okeh recordings as a vocalist—"Sleepy Time Down South" and "You Rascal, You"—had made him a huge crossover star with white audiences and sold one hundred thousand records between 1931 and 1932.[16] In those same years, Armstrong got caught between two managers, both connected with different mobsters. Tommy Rockwell, Armstrong's Artist and Repertoire (A&R) Director at Okeh and his manager at the time, steered him to record popular songs featuring his singing. Armstrong, like Ellington and Calloway, knew he was being fleeced for performance fees and royalties. But he was not prepared when Rockwell and the owners of Connie's Inn in Harlem sent thugs threatening him at gunpoint for an alleged breach of contract in Chicago, where Johnny Collins, Rockwell's former errand boy, had arranged a gig for him. Collins immediately hired bodyguards for Armstrong, booked a tour out of town, and declared himself Armstrong's manager.

In July 1932, Armstrong left for a three-month music hall tour of Great Britain, for which Collins botched most of the logistics. Armstrong's fame had preceded him, and his presence as a Black artist and virtuoso confounded white critics and audiences. British trumpet players insisted on examining his instrument to see if it had some special valve that allowed him to play the way he did. Hannen Swaffer, critic for the *Daily World* of London, insulted Armstrong's looks in vitriolic racist terms, then wrote that Armstrong's "trumpet playing was as revolutionary as Richard Strauss's opera Elektra had been in 1909."[17]

Webb first met Armstrong in New York in early March 1929, when the trumpeter made his debut at the Savoy Ballroom accompanied by Luis Russell's band. Armstrong packed the ballroom for two nights, and hundreds of people could not get in the door. Armstrong was honored with a banquet, with Fletcher Henderson as M.C., and speeches from Tommy Rockwell, Chick Webb, and Benny Carter. Over the next two years, Armstrong came to New York for other gigs, and Webb saw him at various Harlem hangouts.

When Armstrong's ship docked in New York on November 9, 1932, after his first tour of Great Britain, he "made a beeline to Harlem," and ended up at Big John's bar, where he was "penned in his corner by a crowd of friends about six feet thick."[18] Armstrong was booked to star in the revue *Hot Chocolates of 1932* in late November, coproduced by Collins and Connie's Inn's owners, who'd reconciled with Collins for this show, a potential hit. Collins also finalized a pending contract with RCA Victor, and a recording session was scheduled for December 8, 1932.

The 1932 version of the *Hot Chocolates* revue was scheduled to open at Connie's Inn on November 26, 1932. Louis didn't have a regular band in New York and didn't have time to put one together. Gunther Schuller, who devotes a chapter to Armstrong's big bands in his comprehensive history of the Swing Era, wrote: "In his never ending search for an orchestra, he now chose Chick Webb's 11-piece band." Schuller didn't think they were the best accompanists for Armstrong but were a "considerable improvement over the [Zinn] Randolph band," with whom Armstrong had been working until recently. "Webb's band had at least a modern conception which was related to and was in fact an offspring of Armstrong's earlier stylistic revolution."[19] Collins hired Webb's band for the show and the upcoming recording session for Victor.

Though Webb's band was now on a more regular rotation at the Savoy, performing with Armstrong was an incredible opportunity. *Hot Chocolates* tryout runs took place at Connie's Inn, and at the Lafayette and the Pearl Theaters in late November. A month later, the show played to packed houses at the Royal and Howard, in Baltimore and DC, including a Christmas Eve show. In January 1933, *Hot Chocolates* was back in New York for a longer run at the Lafayette and at Connie's Inn. The pace was insane but typical for that era: five shows a day.

Music critic Irving Kolodin, whose specialty was classical music and opera, reviewed the show for *Americana Magazine*.

> Some night when you have endured the gilded banalities of a Broadway show, drop your program into the nearest ashcan and take yourself to a midnight performance at the Lafayette. . . . If you want to observe the festivities at their giddiest, wait for Maestro Chick Webb and his orchestra, but more particularly watch for an occasion when the unapproached, unapproachable Louis Armstrong is socking it out. . . . A blast out of the Webb outfit and from the wings trots out a little brown man, gleaming like a new pair of shoes. . . . [A]s a vocalist what he does with words and rhythm is audible joy. . . . [T]hen he raises the trumpet to his lips and goes to town. . . . His trumpeting virtuosity is endless . . . triplets, chromatic, eerie counterpoints that turn the tune inside out. . . . [T]he effect is electrifying.[20]

Except for Kolodin's review and a few other press mentions, Webb and his band were in Armstrong's shadow for *Hot Chocolates*. The Washington, DC *Afro-American* raved about Louis, praised Webb's drumming, but wrote that this edition of the show "proved to be a fizz.... Carroll Dickerson [Armstrong's former bandmate from Chicago] directed Chick Webb's band, with Chick at his usual masterful post on the drums.... [T]he orchestra has improved greatly since that tour taken last year."[21] Whatever the critics thought, the November and December shows prepared Webb's band to accompany Armstrong for his first RCA Victor recording session.

The fact that the recording session took place at all, during that uncertain time for the industry, testified to Armstrong's selling power. The session was scheduled to start at 2 a.m. at RCA Victor's Camden Studio, a church that the company bought and converted years earlier to record the Philadelphia Symphony. The Church Studio, as it was called, was right across the Delaware River from Philadelphia and renowned for its acoustics and its pipe organ, which Fats Waller swung out on for his own recordings. Armstrong and Webb's band came directly from the Pearl Theater in Philadelphia, where they had just finished the midnight show, their fifth that day, and had played for two live radio broadcasts.

Armstrong biographer Ricky Riccardi offers the most complete details to date about this recording session, which has been largely overlooked by Armstrong scholars and avid followers. Armstrong's recordings with Webb and his band were Eli Oberstein's first for RCA Victor as a producer. Oberstein was anxious to get going with Victor's new star artist, the first of other top Black artists who signed with the label at that time.[22]

The musicians arrived at the Church after 1:30 a.m., and Armstrong had a painful swollen lip and was exhausted. "I didn't see how poor old Pops was going to blow note one," recalled clarinetist Mezz Mezzrow, who was along for the ride that night. "They [the recording engineers] wouldn't let Chick Webb use his bass drum on this date, mainly because Louis's lip was in such bad shape and without the bass, he wouldn't be pushed so hard."[23]

Some of Webb's long-time sidemen accompanied Armstrong on these recordings: Don Kirkpatrick, piano; John Trueheart, guitar; Elmer James, bass and tuba; Elmer Williams, tenor sax. Trumpet players Louis Bacon and Louis Hunt had been with Webb's band on and off for the previous year, and trombonist Charlie Green played with the band in the summer and fall of 1932. New members were Pete Clark, clarinet and alto sax, who became a solid member of the reed section, and alto saxophonist Edgar Sampson, who would help crystallize Webb's band's sound as its main composer/arranger.

The session went until 5 a.m. In spite of Armstrong's serious lip problem (which was chronic) and the nonstop performances of the previous day, Armstrong's extraordinary stamina kicked back in. He slowly builds the drama as vocalist and on trumpet on the first song, "That's My Home," a follow-up to his big hit of 1931, "When It's Sleepy Time Down South," both written by the René Brothers. "That's My Home" displays Armstrong's singular blend of faux southern comfort, signifying yearning and affection for his New Orleans roots despite the region's brutal racial history. "Sleepy Time" and similar sentimental songs became lifelong staples in Armstrong's repertoire.

Webb's drums can barely be heard during Armstrong's vocals in the song's first chorus. But as Louis's trumpet solo builds on the second round, Webb's brushwork is solid and emphatic. He and the ensemble provide a solid, lightly swinging rhythm as the sighing reed ensemble accompanies Armstrong as he soars to his final high note.

Webb kicks it up on "Hobo," the B-side of "That's My Home." His accelerating snare drumming is captured clearly by Victor's engineers, and Mezzrow on train bells and whistles gets the train moving. En route Louis calls: "All Aboard . . . for Pittsburgh, Harrisburg, oh, all them burgs." Webb expertly picks up the speed to a steady chugging swing. During the first chorus, Armstrong—half-singing, half-speaking—cheerfully deliberates the fate of the hobos. Brief solos by Elmer Williams, tenor sax, and then Charlie Green, trombone, greet Louis's vocalizing before he takes his solo, rising quickly and brilliantly to a signature high Bb. The band replies with a joyous hoot when Armstrong finally decides to let the hobos ride, just before Webb puts on the brakes.

The foxtrot "I Hate to Leave You Now" was composed by Armstrong's good friend Fats Waller, with lyrics by Harry and Dorothy Link; this was the song's debut. It was the third song recorded at the session, probably at 3:30 a.m. Mezzrow was worried about Armstrong's lip, already taxed by performances of the day before, his brilliant high notes on the previous two recordings, plus two additional takes for each song. Armstrong soulfully states the melody with a singing muted trumpet, accompanied by Webb's sweet and slow sax section, before launching into the lyrics, giving the song the pitch-perfect "Satch Meets Fats" vibe—sexy, playful, and sweetly romantic. Kirkpatrick slightly flubs the transition to the modulation, making Webb's cymbal crash announcing Louis's final trumpet solo sound a little clumsy. Then Louis takes the last chorus on trumpet and pulls out all his high-note reserves and climbs valiantly to the final high C.

At 4:30 a.m., Webb's band stomps it out on the last song, "You'll Wish You'd Never Been Born," a clone of Armstrong's big hit for Okeh in 1932, "I'll Be Glad When You're Dead, You Rascal, You." Webb's strong brushwork on snare pushes the beat forward, but Elmer James's tuba reins it in. Webb still gets the band swinging to Louis's sly vocals, and Elmer Williams's tenor solo is his perfect complement. In one twelve-bar chorus Williams's melodic yet modern phrasing is mesmerizing. Armstrong scolds Mr. "So-and-so" between the next two solos, Charlie Green's on trombone, then Pete Clark's on clarinet, swirling prettily before the trumpet star's own final chorus. Armstrong wastes no time getting to his full-out high-note bravura performance. He's a dervish in a flash of blues, with the band's brass slurring and reed's wailing in a contrary motion call and response. This last song of the session was recorded twice: the first take and the alternate (Take 2) cap off Armstrong's and the band's marathon thirty-six hours—from their shows in Philadelphia the previous day to these recordings.

"That's My Home" and "Hobo, You Can't Ride That Train" may not have sold as many copies as other Armstrong records, but they were on the "Hit Parade" in early 1933 for several weeks, peaking at positions seventeen and ten, respectively. Walter Winchell, the era's famous syndicated gossip columnist, wrote: "An orchid to 'I Love Every Little Star,' from 'Music in the Air.' Ditto to Louis Armstrong's version of 'That's My Home,' a hot plate!"[24] "That's My Home" received renewed interest during the COVID pandemic of 2020, when a blog called "That's My Home" by Armstrong biographer Ricky Riccardi went viral and helped reintroduce these recordings.[25]

After the December 8, 1932, session and a few more *Hot Chocolates* shows, Armstrong returned to the Pearl Theater, this time accompanied by Charlie Gaines's pit band, which included alto saxophonist Louis Jordan (Jordan would play with Webb a few years later, then hit stardom himself with his pioneering R&B group the Tympany Five). Gaines's band accompanied Armstrong on his next Victor session, on December 21, 1932.[26]

Webb and Armstrong reunited for the tour back at the Howard Theater in DC the week before Christmas, then performed at the Royal in Baltimore for Christmas week, and played a midnight dance at Lehmann Hall on Christmas night.

The *Pittsburgh Courier* raved about *Hot Chocolates* at the Howard: "Supported by Chick Webb and his band, the one and only Louis

Armstrong has been playing to packed houses at every performance. . . . One of his outstanding numbers was 'On the Sunny Side of the Street.' " This song was another example of Armstrong's debut of a song that quickly became an American pop and jazz standard, written by the Cotton Club hit songwriting team, Jimmy McHugh and Dorothy Fields.[27] Performing pop material with Louis Armstrong and seeing how he left audiences spellbound had a generative influence on Webb. Armstrong was a star—a master virtuoso on his instrument and unique interpreter of popular songs, making him a huge success with white audiences. This experience would provide a model for Webb with his own band and his future star vocalist, Ella Fitzgerald.

Mezzrow, still traveling with the band, witnessed what he thought was one of the most dramatic moments in Louis's career on Christmas Eve 1932, when Armstrong and Webb's band played for a white audience at Lehmann Hall in Baltimore, Webb's hometown. Lehmann Hall was a far cry from the Royal, the Howard, or other Black theaters or ballrooms, familiar territory for Armstrong and Webb. It was a small three-story building built by Baltimore's sizable German community and housed a German movie theater, a ratskeller, bowling alleys, and a dance floor. It was the site of numerous concerts of traditional German music and a Kinderchor (children's choir).[28]

Clearly, Armstrong was so famous that manager Collins could book him anywhere. Mezzrow's recollection of this night revolved around Armstrong's worsening lower lip. Before the show, Louis lanced the infected area with a needle to try to relieve the swelling and pain.

"This was the real drama of Louis life, taking place before all those people who thought they were just seeing another good show. . . .[T]he tones that came vibrating out of those poor agonized lips of his sounded like a weary soul plodding down the lonesome road, the weight of the world's woe on his bent shoulders, crying for relief to all his people. . . . There were tears in all the eyes . . . for wonderful, overworked, sick and suffering Louis himself, the hero of his race."

Mezzrow wrote that Webb's entire band was sobbing as Armstrong started his final chorus, heading for his high-note finale. "Chick Webb used all the masterful tactics he knew on the drums, trying to roll and punch out his feelings for Louis, giving him all the foundation he could. . . . The lights came down . . . because the manager didn't want the audience to see how everybody was sobbing." As the house went wild, Armstrong's lip was oozing blood as he "managed to smile and bow and smile again, making pretty for the people."[29] At this time, Webb was a healthy twenty-seven-year-old, with seemingly infinite energy and stamina. In a few years, Webb's touring schedule would become almost as nonstop as Armstrong's. This personal drama—performing through intense physical pain to keep the show going, keep the band working, and keep the audience happy—would be Webb's own.

Armstrong and Webb's band were due back at the Royal for a midnight show of *Hot Chocolates* on New Year's Eve, then double-booked at the Renaissance Ballroom back in Harlem for a gala twelve-hour "breakfast dance" with several other bands. Armstrong was completely spent and left the tour before New Year's Eve for his home in Chicago, determined to take time off and rest. For the moment, Webb and his band remained, as did the rest of the *Hot Chocolates* cast, to soldier on with the last few dates.

10
A Bandleader's Rise

JEFF KAUFMAN: Talk about when your dad [Moe Gale] signed up Chick.

DR. RICHARD GALE: Well my father told me that he never had a formal contract with Chick. It was done on a handshake. And that is the background of the photo that appears in the Ella Fitzgerald book; where my father is handing Chick Webb a dollar and shaking hands. And between them is the press agent with a jeweler's eyeglass peering at that dollar bill to see if it's a fake. Now somebody who's not in the know wouldn't understand it. But it's because they never had a formal contract. So he's giving him a dollar to close the deal.

JEFF KAUFMAN: Talk about that again.

GALE: My father told me that he never had a formal contract with Chick Webb; that it was done on a handshake.

JEFF KAUFMAN: And why was that?

GALE: I don't know.

JEFF KAUFMAN: There are a lot of sharks and snakes.

DR. RICHARD GALE: I just don't know the reason why.[1]

"He [Webb] was ambitious to have an orchestra," wrote *Pittsburgh Courier* reporter Chappy Gardner in 1933.

He collected eight or ten young school boys who could play instruments fairly well. But he had no place for them to play—and no pay for them, even should they get an engagement. They all slept in a big ground-floor room at 131st Street and 7th Ave with their leader. They were loyal, though, going days without anything regular in the food line better than hot dogs. After begging theatrical managers and dance hall magnates for a trial, one day Chick Webb got a break. I could not help thinking of this boy's hard luck in starting as I sat in the Lafayette Sunday night and heard his very tuneful band receive rounds of applause. "Chick's" rise is the answer to pluck, hustle and "guts" to those who keep constantly at it, believing in himself.[2]

Chappy Gardner was one of Webb's long-time admirers in the Black press. That particular Lafayette revue, late January 1933, exemplifies the theater's programs during these deep years of the Depression. The show was "a delightful combination of stage and screen entertainment." The stage presentation was Chick Webb's Orchestra, and dancers and comedians who were well known to Harlem audiences from revues such as Lew Leslie's *Blackbirds* or *Rhapsody in Black*. The casts of these revues were scaled down to ten to fifteen entertainers. Shows before the Depression had casts of fifty and more and star headliners like Ethel Waters or Florence Mills.

Like Gale and Buchanan at the Savoy, Frank Schiffman, the Lafayette's manager, did everything he could to keep the theater open and present live performers. By this time, other Harlem theaters cut their stage shows completely and just showed movies. "The Lafayette Theater announced a reduction in its already low admission price.... [A]dmission prices now range from 15 to 40 cents during the week, with a slight increase on Sunday."[3]

Interestingly, Webb's band's fee for his week at the Lafayette, January 28, 1933, was twelve hundred dollars, up from nine hundred dollars the previous fall. The band's raise may have been because of Webb's recent work with Louis Armstrong, which gave him more status. This leverage did not last long, especially when Schiffman was trying to cut expenses. For Webb's next engagements at the theater, in June and August 1933, the band was paid eight hundred and nine hundred dollars, respectively.[4] Webb's engagement at the Lafayette was followed that month by two star attractions from Chicago: pianist Earl Hines and His Grand Terrace Orchestra, and trumpet player/conductor Valaida Snow, who would appear with Webb a few months later. Snow, like Blanche Calloway, was a stunning multi-talented entertainer and accomplished musician. In addition to being a singer, dancer, and excellent conductor, she was a jazz trumpet player championed by both Earl Hines and Louis Armstrong.

Snow and Calloway were both musically trained bandleaders who knew how to conduct an ensemble; they weren't like some "front-of-band" M.C.s who waved batons around. Their sparkling stage personas, glittery dresses, and glamour bring to mind what people said about tap dance star Ginger Rogers: Rogers could do everything her partner Fred Astaire did, in high heels and backward. The fact that Snow and Calloway were Black female bandleaders in a male-dominated role, said Margo Jefferson, author and cultural historian, "de-masculinized their skills and accomplishments as schooled musicians and bandleaders. They didn't have to compete with Duke or Cab—they were in a league of their own."[5]

That June, both Webb and Valaida Snow were back at the Lafayette, together. The Lafayette was showing the film adaptation of Eugene O'Neill's novel *The Constant Woman*, and the stage show featured Snow conducting Webb's band and as trumpet soloist. Snow was "playing on her silver cornet, demonstrating her versatility," wrote the *Amsterdam News*, while "Chick Webb's orchestra is heard at its best."[6] It's doubtful that Webb viewed Snow's conducting his band as demeaning to him, as some other Black bandleaders might have. This may not have been a feminist gesture on his part, either. Webb was generally good-willed toward other musicians, and pairing his band with Snow was good showpersonship for both of them, with Snow as conductor and soloist for a top Harlem band.

It's tempting to glorify the experience of going to the Lafayette Theater, a magnet for the neighborhood for seeing a movie and live entertainment, even if the shows were now scaled back. Some people had a different view. Trumpeter Roy Eldridge remembered that "you could sit in the show and get high, you know what I mean. And I lit up, too, because it was always a sad picture at the Lafayette during those days. So, I'd sit through that, and I got high and stayed 'til the show came on again."[7]

Webb had loyal advocates among Black entertainment reporters, such as Chappy Gardner and Billy Rowe, who was soon to become a *Pittsburgh Courier* columnist. Other writers were lukewarm and even insulting, like gossipy curmudgeon Ted Yates, a six-foot-four-inch-tall, well-dressed man about Harlem whose peers called him "the sepia Walter Winchell" and was Winchell's Harlem "informant." Yates occasionally gave Webb a rambling, ambivalent plug:

> Chick Webb is but two and a half feet in height, he weighs 110 pounds. . . .
> To look at him you'll agree that he's puh'lenty "security" complex. . . .
> To hear him tell it, there isn't a better drummer in the United States. . . .
> Chick is a swell guy, I like his style of drumming. When he takes his band
> into Connie's Inn next week I'll be rooting for him but—he isn't the best
> drummer in the land. Not for me!!! Bulging his neck back and forth, Chick
> conducts in masterful style, he has rhythm in his sticks when he beats a
> drum. . . . Recorded last month for Louis Armstrong. . . . Louis thinks

Chick's band is swell! . . . Chick Webb will be billed at Connie's Inn as the "King of Them All." . . . As I said, he's a wail of a drummer but there are some more boys who can beat it out. . . . Sonny Greer of Duke Ellington's band; Manzie Johnson of Don Redman's Orchestra and LeRoy Maxey of Cab Calloway's Cotton Club Band are a few. . . . This was written by request. . . . Less prating, Chick, let me see you go at Connie's Inn. Have I been a nice feller or no?[8]

A couple of weeks later, Yates claimed he'd been manipulated:

It seems that you [Yates referring to himself] got Chick Webb's goat. . . . [L]isten Ted, he told Roosevelt Jones (so R.J. says) that he didn't know you, and that you never interviewed him. . . . Boy, call in the witnesses. . . . We'll see what we shall see. . . . Who cares whether Chick's at Connie's Inn or not? He wanted to be mentioned! You solidly "sent" him! That's all that matters, unless the "King of all Drummers" wants to continue it from here![9]

In early 1933, some wisps of Depression clouds seemed to be lifting in the entertainment world. Maurice Dancer reported: "The return of Harlem nightlife was very much in evidence over the weekend, with all clubs and after yawning places turning them away . . . and that certainly doesn't look very much like the old depression. . . . A week ago Sunday night was Duke Ellington's formal reopening at the Cotton Club. . . . It seemed the stage, screen, and radio as well as society and the fourth estate sent their biggest names to welcome Duke back home . . . back where he first created musical history just six years ago."

Earlier on Webb had lost two of his best musicians to Ellington's orchestra, Johnny Hodges and Cootie Williams, though the two bandleaders remained friends. Webb's chronic problem, even with more steady work, was the Savoy's low pay scale.

Still, talented young musicians found their way to Webb. In 1933, thirty-three dollars a week went a long way, and Webb was considered one of the top bandleaders in Harlem. Between 1931 and 1934, Webb hired key musicians, some of whom would make a lasting impact on American jazz and pop music. Trumpet player Mario Bauza became a force in the development of Afro-Cuban jazz in the 1940s. Benny Carter, a formative arranger and saxophonist for Fletcher Henderson and others, was with Webb's band briefly between 1931 and 1932. During that time, Carter helped push Webb's band toward a more sophisticated style with his arrangements of "Heebie Jeebies," "Soft and Sweet," and others.[10] Edgar Sampson, like Carter, was a multi-talented saxophonist and composer/arranger, and wrote signature pieces for Webb—"Let's Get Together," "Stompin' at the Savoy," "Don't Be That Way"—that are enduring anthems of the Swing Era. In this same period, Webb hired sidemen with unique musical styles: Taft Jordan and Bobby Stark, trumpet; Sandy Williams, trombone; John Kirby, bass; and Joe Steele, piano. All of them were excellent section players and soloists who helped define the band's ensemble sound. Over the next three years, jazz author/historian Gary Giddins wrote, "Webb stubbornly refined his band and found an orchestral style all his own."[11]

Of all Webb's hires in these years, Edgar Sampson had the biggest impact on the sound of Webb's band. To Gunther Schuller, "Sampson was to Webb's band what [Sy] Oliver was to Jimmie Lunceford and [Jimmy] Mundy to [Earl] Hines."[12] Sampson's compositions and arrangements, tailored for Webb's musicians, firmly solidified the band's sound as a unit, driven by Webb's forward-leaning swing.

Sampson, born in New York in 1907, was prodigiously musical from childhood. He started on violin at age six, then taught himself to play clarinet and alto sax as a teenager when his interests turned to jazz. Sampson's first public performances were on violin in 1925, at the 135th Street Harlem YMCA, a cultural hub during the Harlem Renaissance and through the 1930s. The building still stands today, a solid brick edifice, its tiered upper stories climbing to a clock tower that stands tall, guarding the surrounding blocks of central Harlem's brownstones.

In the mid-1920s, still a teenager, Sampson worked with various top Black ensembles, including Duke Ellington's.[13] During his tenure with Fletcher Henderson's orchestra from 1931 to 1932 at Connie's Inn, he was immersed in the band's intricate arrangements by Carter and Redman. Other notable players were with Henderson then, too: Bobby Stark, Russell Procope, and Sandy Williams, some of whom went back and forth between Henderson's band and Webb's without any "Great Trade" fanfare in the press.[14] In the fall of 1932, Henderson's band took off for an RKO theater tour, but Sampson didn't go, and Webb talked him into joining his band in time to tour and record with Louis Armstrong. Webb's orchestra recorded Sampson's "Let's Get Together" in January 1934, but the band was already performing it and other tunes and arrangements by Sampson before he joined Webb in 1933.

Webb was obsessive about amassing a huge library of arrangements, building on Don Kirkpatrick's early arrangements for the band, and Sampson's and Benny Carter's. Benny Carter wrote "specials" for Webb while he was in the band (1931–32) but also adapted arrangements he'd written for Fletcher Henderson and other leaders. For this service Carter usually charged five dollars a score. Horace Henderson, Fletcher's younger brother, also customized some of Fletcher's arrangements for Webb's band—infuriating his older brother when Webb would pull these out unannounced during "battles of music" with the Fletcher Henderson Orchestra at the Savoy.[15]

Over the years Webb collected hundreds of arrangements and sorted them into different "books" for different purposes: dance styles and rhythms, set lists for radio programs, stage shows, or fierce band battles. Among musicians, Webb's attention to arrangements was legendary. According to trombonist Quentin Jackson, "Chick couldn't read a note. But you would play an arrangement and Chick could phrase that arrangement like you had just played it, the last time you ran it down. He would phrase the arrangement, too. He knew how to do the crescendos and decrescendos. . . . You could play a solo and he'd come over to you and hum every note you played."[16]

Bassist Milt Hinton recalled:

He liked to trade arrangements, you know. His only concern was for that band. He could sing the whole arrangement, everybody's part—and you couldn't get away from him! You know, you'd get a little bored sometimes when he got into his second or third arrangement. He's telling you, "And Bobby's going to play this here" and then he'd go " . . . da de-de, do do-do-da-do." He'd be standing there waiting for Chu Berry because Chu promised him that he was going to give him two Cab Calloway arrangements for one of his Benny Carter arrangements.[17]

Webb could follow a score and had an unerring musical memory. If he heard a wrong note from a section, he would find the source immediately and correct the player. After a performance Webb would compliment his sidemen's best solos by singing them, note for note. Webb's melodic skills on drums shaped the phrases and dynamics of the arrangements, and he led the band from the drums as skillfully as any first-rate conductor. Bauza said that Webb had "the best guys arranging for him . . . he had to pay the arrangers, but that was his idea. He'd say, 'I want the best band, I want the best arrangements. I got to go to the top, and I'm going to be there, and I've got to get there!' "[18]

One can hear all this come together on several records Webb's band made between December 1933 and July 1934, for Columbia and Okeh, and for the new Decca label in fall 1934. Swing-era specialists and jazz historians have perennially grumbled about the inadequacy of Webb's recordings, in terms of quality and musicality. But remembering Webb's performance context— in the ballroom, playing for dancers—is crucial; imagine hearing this great band up close while dancing.

These sides—snapshots of Webb's band developing during that time—are a joy to hear. Edgar Sampson's arrangements were a fundamental part of that process, as was the synergy that musicians such as Joe Steele, Sandy Williams, Bauza, and Taft Jordan brought to the ensemble sound. The main ingredient is rhythm. By this time, the band was clearly swinging. As Gunther Schuller noted, Webb, guitarist John Trueheart, and the addition of bassist John Kirby formed a rhythm section that could "outswing any other.... Most of the credit must go to the incomparable Webb himself, but during Kirby's tenure it was a truly invincible section." They are aided by the brilliant pianist Joe Steele, a solid accompanist and fabulously flighty soloist who breaks into gorgeous Harlem stride passages on some of these records.[19]

These 78-rpm recordings include a range of material, starting with the December 1933 covers of the Armstrong hits "On the Sunny Side of the Street," featuring Taft Jordan on trumpet and vocals, and a madly swinging "Darktown Strutters Ball," arranged by Benny Carter. There are several original titles and arrangements by Edgar Sampson: "Stompin' at the Savoy," "Don't Be That Way," and "Blue Minor," a fabulous minor romp with great solos by Sampson, Sandy Williams on muted trombone, and trumpet player Bobby Stark, who had rejoined Webb.

Webb was now completely identified with the Savoy Ballroom, and the band's name is labeled "Chick Webb and His Savoy Orchestra" for the twelve sides recorded for Columbia and Okeh between December 1933 and July 1934. These recordings were produced by John Hammond, a fact that is remarkable for its omission in the heaps of material written by and about Hammond. Then twenty-three years old, Hammond was omnipresent at Harlem clubs and at the Savoy as jazz enthusiast turned music journalist, and novice radio and record producer. Hammond's legacy has been both celebrated and demonized for his outsized influence as a wealthy white opinionated gatekeeper and know-it-all. But 1934 was one of Hammond's best years in his early career as a record producer. His interactions with Webb and other Black musicians were frequent as he ran around trying to establish his niche in the jazz scene. His role as a producer for Webb was probably more supervisory than hands-on at that time, as he rushed to get the music he liked the best (at any given time) out to the public.

Amazingly, Webb's recordings for Columbia and Okeh were sandwiched between Hammond's outstanding early work as a producer for these labels from 1933 to 1935—from Bessie Smith's last records to Billy Holiday's first—with Benny Goodman and a mixed band, and with Teddy Wilson in his debut recordings as leader. In terms of Webb's legacy on records, some of the Columbia recordings are among his band's greatest instrumental sides. The sax section sounds lush and gorgeous on "Let's Get Together," and Webb swings powerfully on the band's first recording of "Stompin' at the Savoy."

In 1934, Webb's recording career took off in tandem with his exploding radio exposure. By this time Moe Gale, thirty-six years old, was well connected in the music industry. He had established relationships at NBC, one of the three major radio networks, and with Jack Kapp, who founded US Decca Records that summer. Gale milked his leverage with both companies and finally did important work for Webb's career. The Gale agency announced that Webb's band "has been signed by NBC for three weekly blasts as an exclusive sustaining feature on a coast-to-coast hook-up. Moe Gale, radio manager and artist representative, negotiated the deal for the Webb organization, and this marks the first time that a Harlem orchestra has ever been signed for a network studio sustaining program."[20]

That summer, Webb was also the first Black bandleader to sign on with Decca Records, an independent spin-off of British Decca. Kapp capitalized on hidden opportunities amid the crashing of the recording industry to launch the label in the US. Kapp had an impressive track record. He'd been an influential producer for Brunswick (Columbia) when its US branch floundered during the early 1930s. Brunswick's top white recording stars—Bing Crosby, Tommy and Jimmy Dorsey, the Boswell Sisters, and others—followed Kapp and signed on with Decca. Kapp probably made offers to Duke Ellington and Cab Calloway, but they kept making records for Brunswick and Okeh at manager Irving Mills's insistence until both artists signed with RCA Victor in 1933.[21]

Kapp was undaunted. "After nearly sucking Brunswick's old roster completely dry," wrote jazz historian John McDonagh, "Kapp turned to the future, he reached out to the next four important Black bands." Earl Hines and

Fletcher Henderson were with Decca only briefly, but "Jimmie Lunceford and Chick Webb would come on for the long haul."[22]

Webb's first sessions for Decca were in September and November of 1934, and three of the tunes and all the arrangements were by Edgar Sampson. Webb hired saxophonist Wayman Carver as fourth reed player, adding more heft to the sound of the reed section and overall power of the band. On "Don't Be That Way" and "Blue Lou," the four-person saxophone section resonates on Sampson's signature trilling reeds and ensemble passages. On "Don't Be That Way," Webb takes one of his first full solos on his records and plays punchy clean breaks, outlining every phrase of Sampson's perfect arrangement. This debut recording of the tune sparkles at Webb's brisk tempo, with call-and-response riffs between saxes and brass, and brief bursts by the brass.

Webb now had a trifecta: a regular platform at the Savoy, steady exposure on radio, and a recording contract with Decca, one of the most promising new record labels of the 1930s. Gale was not as shrewd and cutthroat as Irving Mills, but he too built his career on the backs of Black talented artists—Webb was his first—and his dealings were hardly transparent. There is no paper trail to Webb's success.

Radio and records now brought Webb and the band a wider audience and entry into the arena of popular music. Along with that came a tangled set of issues involving appropriation, authenticity, and the power of white "gatekeepers" like Gale, Mills, and others who kept altering the rules of the music business—to both benefit and exploit their Black clients, all of whom were literally changing the "color" of American entertainment.

Webb's expanded radio presence gave him a tangible change in status. Fan letters poured in, and the press was everywhere. From the *Chicago Defender*:

Although Chick has been playing music for more years than he cares to remember, it is only recently that he has entered the "big-money" class [hyperbole, obviously]. Right now he is riding high on the crest of a national popularity wave. Directly responsible for his fame are his almost daily broadcasts on the NBC coast-to-coast network, in addition to his nightly programs heard on the new American Broadcasting System chain. . . . [I]n theatrical parlance, Webb's band is known as a "show-stopper," his stage appearances being greeted with wild acclaim. Only recently he was forced to do 23 encores of one number, holding the show for 40 minutes overtime. His recordings have leaped into the "best-seller class." His newest discs,

"Let's Get Together" and "Free Love" have been widely acclaimed by music critics.... These tunes were written by Chick in collaboration with Edgar Sampson, his first sax player.[23]

Between 1933 and 1934, Webb made three other important additions to his band. One was Cuban trumpet player Mario Bauza, who came to New York because he wanted to learn to play American jazz. He'd followed the path of other Cuban and Caribbean musicians who had settled in East Harlem, some of whom helped generate the "Latin tinge" in popular dance music in New York.[24] Bauza was born in 1911, in Havana, Cuba, where he'd been a clarinet prodigy as a youth. In 1930, he came to New York after playing professionally with the Havana Symphony and with dance bands in nightclubs. One of his first stops was at the Lafayette Theater to see Ellington and his orchestra. "I got into the theater when it opened at 9 o'clock the morning. And I stayed there until they finished up that night." Bauza soon joined the stream of newcomers at the nightly jam sessions at the Rhythm Club. At first he played saxophone, but after being told he should play with more volume, he started bringing his trumpet.

"The guys that were hanging around there were ... all the big musicians in those days—Benny Carter, Russell Procope, Johnny Hodges, Fletcher Henderson ... !" Bauza recalled. "I used to hang around there all day, and before I knew it I was speaking English. There weren't any Spanish-speaking musicians around there then, so I had to either speak English or die."[25]

In fall 1932, Bauza started playing with the Santo Domingo Serenaders (also called the San Domingans), who were playing opposite Webb's band at the Savoy. After a few weeks, he found out that Webb had an opening for a trumpet player. "I never had any idea that I was going to play with him [Webb], because he was the best in the business," Bauza recalled. "To me, 'til today, I don't think that there has been anybody with a better idea of how to form an orchestra, how to play, than him. He was a hell of a musician.... He had a conception about rhythm and the arrangement, how to play it. For me, there was nothing like it."

Bauza first stayed with Noble Sissle, who'd returned to New York in 1930 after playing in elite circles in France for three years. His reassembled band was quickly a favorite with Black and white audiences and found plenty of work on the wealthy white society circuit. Mario usually played in Sissle's small ensemble (quartet or quintet) for these events. Sissle's groups were multiracial, similar to the personnel of James Reese Europe's Clef Club

Orchestras, and included Black Cubans, light-skinned Afro-Caribbeans, and Afro-Americans. Bauza admired Sissle tremendously: "He was an aristocratic man, very refined. He was catering to all the rich white people. He'd just come back from Paris, but he took me in and loved me, and everything I did was wonderful."

One of the Serenaders heard that Webb had an opening for a trumpet player and encouraged Bauza to audition. That meant performing live with the band at the Savoy. Bauza recalled: "I'm nervous, but I play, play, play all night. Then Webb says, 'We're going to have rehearsal right after the job. You got a half hour to go buy yourself a sandwich, then come back for the rehearsal.' When I got back, I look for the guys. Webb said, 'Never mind the guys—this rehearsal is for you!' I said I'd never seen a rehearsal for one man. And he said, 'That's the way I'm going to do it with you. Take such and such a number out.'"

After Bauza started playing Webb said, "Don't phrase like that," and hummed the way he wanted Bauza to phrase the music. They got through this "rehearsal" at about 5 o'clock in the morning. Bauza told him, "I don't think I'm the man you want. You need a man here with experience."

Webb said, "If you listen to me, you're the man I want." He told Bauza to come play with the band again the next night and stay for "rehearsal." Bauza did and felt that he was in over his head. He said, "Chick, I don't think I'm the man you need. I appreciate your giving me this opportunity."

Webb's reply was emphatic: "No, no, no, no—you just listen to me, you'll be fine."

Bauza took the chance, joined Webb's band, and took his advice. "I kept listening to the guy. About six months later, there was one day I'll never forget.... After work he says, 'Fellas, I want to announce something. Starting today, the man in charge to call the shots is Mario.' That was the biggest thing that ever happened in my life! I didn't know what to say! So, I started calling numbers myself, got the rehearsing going all right—everything went beautifully!"[26]

Webb was never a great businessman, even with his elevated exposure and status. In 1934, competition was still fierce among bandleaders and the venues themselves. Saxophonist Teddy McRae said: "This was really the Depression. Things were really bad. Everybody—Teddy Hill—everybody was just gigging around. Scuffling and really scuffling." Competition to get into a band that had any steady work at all was tough, and the talent pool was as big as ever. McRae recalled:

> To get in a band like Fletcher Henderson's or Chick Webb's or Teddy Hill's, or a young guy with a great band . . . not only do you have to be a great musician, but you had to be a gentleman. You had to live clean. They didn't just take you in there. You had to live up to them. . . . Duke never changed musicians much—his band was set. When he brought somebody in it was because of something he wanted from a top musician. . . . He didn't just hire someone to fill a chair—no.[27]

Neither did Chick, but he couldn't always hang on to the best person for the chair. That changed in the fall of 1934, when Webb began having more radio spots and the Decca contract. Webb had grown into his leadership.

Bauza, who worked with Calloway later on, pinpointed a few differences in their leadership styles:

> Calloway was a very strict man—everything about him was business. But no matter how much he wanted to be a musician, he always had a tendency to relate more to show business. He was looking for a way to sell the thing. It's what they see—that's what they buy from Calloway, they'd get all the singing and dancing and jumping. That's what people wanted to see and he wanted to give them a performance. Chick was the musician bandleader, not a public bandleader. That's a different approach. He had a physical problem—yeah, he was a hunch. It would've been difficult for him to do what Calloway did. He was strictly a hell of a drummer. When the music was ideal it was unbelievable, but he didn't care much about the public. He cared more about how he thought the music should be played. And that was a hell of a thing to relate to in those days, especially a colored band to the white people.[28]

Gale and Buchanan wanted to keep boosting Webb's popularity. They thought an out-front conductor or singer would enliven the band's stage presence. In spring 1934, they hired Bardu Ali as M.C. and conductor, and Charles Linton, a suave, handsome vocalist who fit beautifully in the smooth male "crooner" mode of current hit makers like Rudy Vallee and Bing Crosby. Reporter Ted Yates was all in favor: "Shy for the present, Linton will be recognized as the sepia Bing Crosby, he has that kind of voice—only it is a golden one."[29]

Ali had several different vaudeville acts going in Harlem and also worked as a freelance M.C. In March 1934, Ali was M.C. for a week at the Harlem Opera House, where he was anointed "Harlem's newest sensation." A few weeks later, Gale hired him to front Webb's band, and the Black press took notice: Ali was "suave of manner and possessed of an easy flow of stage vernacular, [he] is appearing not only as master of ceremonies, but also as director of Chick Webb's Orchestra, and he does plenty."[30] Ali did everything expected of a showman in Harlem; he was an exuberant host and comic who performed acrobatic moves and led the band with a baton, though Webb actually led the band from the drum throne. Gale hoped that Ali would attract as much attention as Cab Calloway did.

Ali's life and career, like others in Webb's band, had a striking, winding trajectory. He was the son of Moksad Bardu, a Bengali Muslim peddler who settled in the late 1800s with a few fellow peddlers in New Orleans. They married Creole or African American women there, started families, formed a tight-knit community, and were among the first merchants of ornate Bengalese handicrafts and Indian silks in the US. Ali's wife, Ella, joined the Great Migration northward in 1918, after Moksad died due to a brief bout of tuberculosis. She and five of their eight children traveled north and moved in with her sister in the Bronx.

A few years later, Bardu and his brothers moved to central Harlem to seek work. Bardu had shown business ambitions and started a dance team, "Baby and Ali." One of his brothers was their drummer. Bardu also booked himself in clubs and theaters as the "King of Jesters" and eventually got work as an M.C.[31]

Ali was an immediate attraction with Webb's band and a few months later was lured by producer Lew Leslie to go to London with the new iteration of *Blackbirds* He returned to New York in early winter and Gale rehired him right away. "Maestro Ali expressed himself as being very, very happy to be in the States again. He is also quoted on the fact that it is hard for American actors to save any money from their European engagements because of the 25% tax extraction demanded by the King."[32]

Charles Linton moved to Harlem in 1932 from Miami, where he "sang all his way through school, made his own spending money from his warbling since the age of seven." He'd won several amateur contests at small Harlem clubs, which is how Buchanan discovered him. Webb tried him out at the Savoy, and he quickly won over the Savoy audience and the entertainment press. Linton is "slender, weighs 150 pounds, has straight Black hair, dreamy eyes.... He stops the dancers nightly with his renditions of 'Solitude' and 'Trees.' Makes even the 'Continental' sound 'pash ... crooning over WMCA with Chick Webb's band, at the Savoy Ballroom. He has really made a hit. A thousand paragraphs for your success."[33] Linton had the perfect voice for the "soft and sweet" music that Webb himself loved to play and that romantic dancing couples wanted to hear. This is a side of Webb's music that jazz critics later on couldn't reconcile with the powerful swing drummer who rocked the Savoy.

"The return of Harlem nightlife" that columnist Maurice Dancer wrote about didn't erase the Depression's effects, and his column's frothy tone makes it easy to overlook items like this: "Among the interesting reopening during the week was that of the Morocco Club.... Among those present was Chick Webb, who had just finished at the New Dixie Ballroom because of no pay.... The popular dance act Meeres and Meeres terminated their Connie's Inn engagement because of no pay."[34] The Depression was not over yet.

The entertainment world was never a steady financial proposition, and nonpayment to artists, an occupational hazard, was worse now. One dramatic example was the short-lived "new" Dixie Ballroom, which opened on 125th Street in March 1933, in the space that was formerly Rose Danceland, the whites-only/Black entertainment taxi dance hall where Webb's band had their first long residency in 1928. The Dixie Ballroom, according to the *New York Age*, was now owned by the "genial Marx Brothers, C. and A., who elegantly redecorated the 'dancing Mecca as far south as 125th Street.'" They rebranded the ballroom and modeled it on the Savoy with similar events—band battles, breakfast dances, etc.—and hired Harold Parker away from the Savoy as manager, who in turn lured Webb with promises of a long-term residency. This venture was widely discussed in the Black press, and not just as a fabulous new dance venue that would rival the Savoy at lower ticket prices. The fact that the renamed Dixie Ballroom "will go colored," announced the *New York Age*, "marked the entering wedge of the Negro on the most important business street north of the midtown sector."[35] Harlem's 125th Street corridor was still a bastion of white business interests. The Dixie was held up as a hopeful model for ending segregation on 125th Street, something Harlem activists had been fighting for.

After its packed opening night, the Dixie Ballroom did not get a steady crowd despite its low ticket prices (twenty-five cents for ladies and thirty-five

cents for gentlemen). Two months later it closed, and Webb's band was soon
back at the Savoy. Musicologist and dance scholar Christi Jay Wells points
out that this episode revealed "the social, economic, and racial dynamics
of Harlem's nightlife that had far-reaching impacts throughout the 1930s
on Webb's career and on Harlem's cultural and political life more broadly."
One significant impact was the loosening of the exclusionary racial divide of
Harlem clubs and cabarets that went back to the Jazz Age of the 1920s.

Starting in the mid-1930s, the Savoy had a larger racially mixed audience
than in its founding years, though it was the Savoy's Black audience who
danced their way through the Depression. Dancer Frankie Manning went
to the ballroom almost every night: "These were the depression years . . . and
dancing was an outlet for people because there wasn't much else to do."[36]
Buchanan's and Gale's flexible maneuvers enabled the Savoy to survive during
the Depression. Though the Savoy did not officially lower its admissions fee
(fifty cents before 6 p.m., eighty-five cents starting at 8 p.m.), its weeknight
specials offered free admission to some group (Mondays were Ladies Nights,
etc.), so plenty of dancers came every night of the week. Charles Buchanan's
view echoed Manning's experience: "To a certain group of young people the
Savoy was their life. That's all they had. We used to see the same kids come
there every day. Some of them had holes in their shoes."[37]

Another growing impact was the Savoy's community relief efforts;
government-sponsored programs failed to reach a broad spectrum of Harlem
residents. Webb and other Black bands and entertainers donated their services for dances and benefits sponsored by the Urban League, the NAACP, fraternal organizations, fraternities, sororities, and social clubs for Christmas
food and gift giveaways, children's hospital funds, and unemployment and
hunger relief. Sponsoring organizations and causes became more overtly political as national and international events unfolded. In May 1933, Pullman
Porters, one of the strongest Black labor unions, held benefits at the Lafayette
to support workers who had been laid off. The Savoy hosted events for anti-
lynching campaigns, Republicans of the Spanish Civil War, the Writer's
Guild, and other labor unions. The Savoy also sponsored "Scottsboro Balls"
for the Scottsboro Boys Legal Fund almost every year from 1932 to 1938.
This was no coincidence. Black civil rights and social justice organizations
had established a presence in Harlem, starting in the early 1900s, as the dual
forces of the Great Migration and, later, the Harlem Renaissance generated
a diverse range of voices, publications, organizations, boycotts, and media
attention.

Buchanan was the liaison for the events at the Savoy. He was a progressive leftist, aligned with prominent Harlem politicians—a good man to know. In the early 1940s, he collaborated with Adam Clayton Powell Jr. on Powell's new venture, the *People's Voice*, an activist newspaper featuring works by an array of Black writers including novelist Anne Petry. Buchanan ensured that the ballroom was central to Harlem's community life. Gale gave Buchanan free reign and supported these events and activities, even as he became more successful as a white show business gatekeeper/manager. Gale's son Richard explained, "My father entered this just as a business man, a young hustler. [H]e came out of it a very transformed person who cared very deeply."[38]

Webb himself came from the robust helping tradition in Black communities, nurtured in his family by his mother, Marie, and sister Bessie. Webb was an active participant for many Harlem benefits and volunteered his and his band's services.[39] Webb was also an active figure in the Rhythm Club, which became more proactive under Bert Hall's leadership.[40] Managers Bert Hall and Ginger Young, with the help of Webb, Teddy Hill, and other musicians, passed along networking opportunities and spread the word about jobs. Webb always looked out for his musicians' best interests and openings for other colleagues. His life and outlook had expanded tremendously with his growing success. Webb was generous—with his family, friends, and colleagues, and for Harlem's social justice and relief causes—with no pretensions.

On November 3, 1934, the *Chicago Defender* broadcast to the country what everyone in Harlem already knew: "Harlem Raves Over the Music of Chick Webb."

> In every field of endeavor and in every generation there are but a few names that gain prominence as the creators of vogues and trends which domi-nate a country. In the world of dance music, Chick Webb is acclaimed as one of the outstanding ultra-modern rhythm stylists, originator of a de-finitive brand of syncopation, characterized by a "swing" rhythm. His in-dividualistic style is aped and copied by other bandleaders throughout the country.... [R]ight now he is riding high on the crest of a national popu-larity wave. Directly responsible for his fame are his almost daily broadcasts on the NBC coast-to-coast network, in addition to his nightly programs on the new American Broadcast System chain.[41]

"Little Chick Webb" was no longer little. His band had grown to fourteen pieces with full brass and woodwind sections; it was a tight ensemble that played with finesse and an irresistible dance groove.

That fall, a seventeen-year-old girl who made a few dollars dancing and singing on the streets got her first big break. On November 21, 1934, Ella Fitzgerald won the Apollo Theater's Amateur Night contest, Harlem's most popular and well-attended amateur contest. In existence just a few months, the Apollo's Amateur Nights gave the theater, its shows, and the finalists a boost, whether they won or not. The Apollo's owners had signed a deal with NBC earlier that fall, and the contest was now broadcast live. This was not Fitzgerald's first contest, nor the first time she won first place.

But Fitzgerald's win put the young singer on the map in Harlem, even though her "prize" didn't materialize until she won another amateur contest a few months later, at the Harlem Opera House. That was the catalyst for Ella Fitzgerald's entry into Webb's circle.

11

Showtime in the Theater Wars

Ella Fitzgerald, after she won that contest at the Apollo, we [Tiny Bradshaw's band] had come back into Harlem at the Harlem Opera House.... That's when they were giving Amateur Contests every week—and the Apollo was controlled by the same people, so they put Ella with us.

You see, at that gig with us at the Harlem Opera House, she broke up the show, she tied the show up. They put her on last because of her being an amateur. We had so many big stars from the Cotton Club on that show, they wouldn't put her in front of them. And she just wrapped that thing up, body and soul. They had to bring the curtains back up. She took about three or four encores after every show.

And you know, they put her way in the dressing room way up at the top—what we'd call the Crow's Nest. I wouldn't put my dog up there. I told the guys, "Hey, let's go up there and give her some encouragement.... [S]he didn't have adequate clothes to wear, you know, she was just an amateur then.

—Happy Caldwell[1]

Happy Caldwell, Tiny Bradshaw's music director and saxophonist, first heard Ella Fitzgerald the week of February 15, 1935, when Bradshaw's band swung back into Harlem after a two-month tour, Bradshaw's first as a band-leader.[2] The Harlem Opera House was just half a block east of the Apollo Theater, and had recently started its own Amateur Night. There are no letters or papers that document Fitzgerald's competing in the Harlem Opera House's contest. More likely, her week with Bradshaw was her overdue prize for her winning Amateur Night at the Apollo. For a brief time both theaters were co-managed by the same people. Fitzgerald's name appeared in small print in the Harlem Opera House's weekly ad in the *Amsterdam News*, along with other Cotton Club stars whose names are now clouded over in Harlem entertainment history. During that week, Fitzgerald repeatedly sang her three well-rehearsed songs, "Judy," "Believe It Beloved," and "Object of My Affection," all radio hits by the Boswell Sisters, the close-harmony style vocal trio, whose tightly arranged vocals and early scat singing were influential to Ella and many others.[3] Several musicians on the bandstand and in the house were impressed by Fitzgerald's pitch-perfect voice, lyrical phrasing—directed right at you—and playful spirit of swing. Wearing a new dress, paid for by Caldwell and his friends, Ella would soon become the object of everybody's affection.

Benny Carter and his newly formed band performed often at the Apollo in fall 1934, including the night that Ella won the amateur contest. Carter sang Ella's praises to Fletcher Henderson and other bandleaders, including Chick Webb. Apparently, Henderson was put off by her poor clothes and appearance and wouldn't listen to her sing. Neither did Webb, even after some prodding by Carter and Charles Linton and, a few months later, Bardu Ali. In early winter 1935, Webb and the band were booked every day and night, did a couple of short tours, and were getting new offers for bookings. Webb knew he had to play out his current stardom carefully so his band wouldn't just be a fading "latest sensation."

Chick Webb's band was booked at the Harlem Opera House in early March 1935. It was a few weeks after Ella's triumph there, in the midst of intensifying conflicts between the owners and managers of the Harlem Opera House and the Apollo Theater dubbed "the Harlem Theater Wars." The two theaters were within half a block of each other on 125th Street, and the "wars" were between the theaters' managers, Frank Schiffman of the Harlem Opera House (HOH) and Morris Sussman of the Apollo Theater. Ella's emergence in Harlem's amateur contests was part of this picture.[4]

The Apollo Theater, with a capacity of 1,506, opened in 1914, as Hurtig & Seamon's New Burlesque Theater, a whites-only variety house. Comedian Fannie Brice had performed there in its early glory days. By the early 1930s it was a tacky burlesque house featuring striptease acts for white men; it was shut down in 1933 during an anti-vice campaign. Sidney S. Cohen, who owned other theaters in midtown, bought the building at a Depression-era bargain price, though starting a new theatrical venture in Harlem was a financial risk at that time. He hired Morris Sussman, a real estate colleague, as manager. Sussman, whose German Jewish family first immigrated to London, had no business experience in Harlem, nor in entertainment. But he was a willing agent for change and never lost his British accent, polite manners, sense of fairness, or his cool. At the suggestion of Romeo Dougherty, activist editor of the *Amsterdam News*, Sussman convened a round table of Harlem editors and journalists, including Dougherty, Bessye Bearden, Jack Trotter, Floyd Calvin, and Chappy Gardner, for advice.[5]

Starting on opening night, January 26, 1934, the New 125th Street Apollo Theater became the hotspot for Harlem audiences and entertainers. Sussman, like I. J. Faggen and Moe Gale did while planning the Savoy Ballroom, sought input from the Black community from the outset. He hired an all-Black staff "from the front ticket-taker to the last brick-bat."[6] With the exception of the short-lived Dixie Ballroom, this hiring policy was rare among the all-white-owned stores and businesses along 125th Street in Harlem, and the Apollo Theater was a bright spot. Daily picketing and ongoing "Don't Buy Where You Can't Work" boycotts finally gained traction on 125th Street as Harlem's Black residential area expanded southward. Frankie Manning, one of the Savoy's elite Lindy Hoppers, remembers: "On 125th Street, a person couldn't get a job at Woolworth's. You could go in and buy whatever you wanted, but it had all white employees, and you could not go to the soda fountain and sit down and eat with the rest of the people."[7] Doll Thomas, who worked at the Apollo for many years as stage manager and technician, said it was all "Jim Crow" without the "Colored" signs.

Sussman brought in first-rate talent despite extra costs, advertised in the Black press, and kept ticket prices low for the still-strapped community. Ticket prices for Webb's band as headliner at the New 125th St. Apollo Theater were ten to fifteen cents from 9:30 a.m. to 12:00 p.m., fifteen to twenty cents from noon to 5 p.m., and then twenty to thirty-five cents from 5 p.m. on.[8] Sussman hired Clarence Robinson, veteran Cotton Club revue producer, and Ralph Cooper, a favorite neighborhood M.C. and entertainer. Like the Savoy, the Apollo offered special weeknight incentives with prizes, raffles, and giveaways; beauty contests; and Lindy Hop and Shim Sham contests.

The biggest draw, which packed the place and became a star-launching platform, was the Apollo's Amateur Night contest on Wednesdays, between 11 p.m. and midnight. Wednesday night was the best night of the week for the finals: most of the theater's stage shows ran from Friday to Thursday, so by Wednesday, audiences were ready for something new. Monday nights were for auditions. Cooper, previously employed by Frank Schiffman at the Lafayette, jumped at his new role at the Apollo, especially on Amateur Nights. The contests started being broadcast nationally in mid-November 1934:

HARLEM AMATEUR NIGHT IS WINNING RADIO PLAUDITS

The midnight radio riot from the heart of New York's Aframerican city-within-a city, "Harlem Amateur Night" is causing greater numbers of listeners to turn to the channels of the American Broadcasting System net-work stations every Wednesday night.... One of the fastest and probably the noisiest programs on the air, this hour is bedlam from start to finish.... [W]ithin a few seconds the quivering amateur knows the verdict of the au-dience. If he's good, he'll get through the number. If he isn't he never gets the chance to finish, because the audience is very definite in reactions. A pistol shot signifies ignominious defeat.[9]

The Apollo's Amateur Nights helped launch the careers of many legendary Black artists over the decades: Ella Fitzgerald (the first), Sara Vaughan, Dionne Warwick, Gladys Knight, James Brown, and others. The winners were chosen by the audience's applause. For contenders, entering the contest was a survival strategy, and winning could open the door to new opportunities. The Apollo's Amateur Nights were unforgettable spectacles that involved everyone on stage and backstage, and the audience from the orchestra to the upper balcony. Oversize personalities were born and ruled the proceedings, including Ralph Cooper, a handsome song-and-dance man and now M.C., and Porto Rico, whose given name was Norman Miller, a stagehand who created the role of Executioner.

The "midnight radio riot" broadcast not just emerging talent but the Apollo itself. The theater quickly radiated interest, locally and nationally. These broadcasts also made Schiffman and his boss Leo Brecher worried about their 125th Street property, the Harlem Opera House. The Theater Wars had heated up all through the fall of 1934. This was not a fair fight. It was a sustained series of attacks on Morris Sussman by Schiffman and theater owner Brecher, who'd monopolized several Harlem theaters, most of which were now movie houses without live entertainment. The Schiffman/Brecher team was determined to get controlling interest of the newly revamped Apollo Theater. At one point they sent armed thugs to rob Sussman of the daily cash take at gunpoint. Schiffman hired the same or similar acts and big bands for the Harlem Opera House, literally down the block. He started Tuesday Amateur Nights, dance contests, and other "specials," and paid for his own radio wire deal on WNEW. Other tactics caused the Apollo's stage manager to have a nervous breakdown.[10]

A few months later, Sussman's hands-off boss, Sidney S. Cohen, died of a heart attack in his midtown office.[11] Sussman then had to defend his interests in the Apollo by himself, along with the progressive policies and programming he'd initiated.

"The difference between Morris Sussman and Frank Schiffman was simple: Sussman was a wonderful person," Cooper wrote in his memoir. "He was not acquainted with show business at all; but he had the absolute willingness to learn and do things that were right for the people.... Sussman was smart and he was fair, and when he put the word out that he wanted to make the Apollo a stage for entertainment, all the theater people hailed it as a breakthrough and a progressive step in the history of Harlem show business."[12]

The war was resolved by spring 1935 when Schiffman and Sussman nominally agreed to co-run both houses together. The main victors, before and during the truce, were entertainers and musicians, most of whom were based in Harlem. They got more weeks of employment, more visibility, and more radio exposure. The bands were typically now thirteen- or fourteen-piece jazz big bands and had top billing almost every week. At the Harlem Opera House, Tiny Bradshaw's week was sandwiched between Earl Hines's Grand Terrace Orchestra (from Chicago) and Cab Calloway's Cotton Club Orchestra. Webb's band was booked twice at the Harlem Opera House in fall 1934, then followed Calloway's week there in early March 1935; his fee for himself and the band went from 700 to 950 dollars. Webb's band debuted at the Apollo in July 1935, with their new singer—Ella Fitzgerald. A "world series" of big band talent performed on these rival stages.[13]

Even so, there wasn't enough audience to sustain both venues. By the end of 1935, Schiffman and Brecher closed the Harlem Opera House and pressured Sussman to sell his interest in the Apollo. Cohen was dead; Sussman had lost his main backer and couldn't outbid them. In most references to Apollo history, Morris Sussman has been erased.[14] Schiffman, who then ran the Apollo for decades, was among several white Jewish theater manager/owners who, Janus-like, both promoted and exploited Black talent, first at the Lafayette, then at the Apollo. Schiffman often stiffed or underpaid artists and acts and colluded with other theater and club owners and booking agents in egregious deals. His son Jack admitted, "There wasn't any rhyme or reason to band salaries in the 1930s." While Webb's band was paid 950 dollars, Jimmie Lunceford's band earned 1,750 dollars for the same intense schedule: five shows a day, six days a week.

Yet not everyone hated Frank Schiffman. Over the years, he supported and donated to numerous causes and organizations in Harlem. And he ventured into the margins by featuring and promoting Black entertainers— comedians, dancers, blues singers, and jazz bands—when Jews and Blacks expanded these margins into wide avenues.

Chick Webb benefited from the Harlem Theater Wars during all its phases. His band had regular bookings at the Lafayette and at the Harlem Opera House, and would be a big attraction at the Apollo. He'd learned to be more shrewd himself in navigating the circle of white gatekeepers. Even so, there were cruel surprises. In late fall 1933, Webb became a moving target in an intercity theater war that also involved Schiffman and Brecher. Their rivals in Philadelphia sought to cut down their influence and bring down the Lafayette Theater by threatening talent on tour: "Things came to a head last week in Philadelphia when Chick Webb was stopped by a number of gangsters in an attempt to make him gorge up moneys which the gunmen suspected he had received to pay off some of his musicians. It is further claimed that they hoped by this move to prevent Webb's entire band from moving into the Lafayette Theater, where they were billed."[15]

This probably wasn't the first or last time that Webb had to give up his cash take to thugs. But unlike Louis Armstrong, Webb had no bodyguard or road manager yet and handled his band's cash payments after gigs.

Still, Webb's career was on an upswing, thanks to his triweekly NBC national radio slots that started in November 1934. His increased visibility in the Black press emboldened reporters to focus on subjects other than Webb's band and music.

Floyd J. Calvin, senior editor of the *Pittsburgh Courier,* wrote:

Now that Chick is "in front and on top," broadcasting a half hour three times a week over WEAF and WJZ to millions of radio fans throughout the world—the new hounds are flocking around to get the lowdown on this new celebrity's personal likes and dislikes. With the smiling and popular Chick they are all "likes"—there are no dislikes. . . . He is an ardent Broadway item making the rounds of good shows, and especially those with good band music. Being the "new man from Harlem," he is given the right of way in the White Way section as such. . . .

[T]there is only one possible cloud that might arise on the now crystal clear horizon of the baton-waving Chick. He might go intellectual. Reason: Chick has been meeting some people from Columbia University lately—that hotbed of brain trusters that coughed up the New Deal. Now Chick is going around pondering absentmindedly such poly-syllabic words as "regimentation," "politico-economic," etc. They're dangerous for a mere bandmaster—these Columbia philosophers. But Chick's friends say rather facetiously that they aren't worried about the "intellectual" bug because these newly found friends of his from the brain trust factory are ladies, and Chick is noted for emerging master of any situation where the fairer sex is involved, it making little difference whether they are classified as flappers or psychiatrists.

Calvin went on to note that Webb's "is one of the only four colored bands making records now," and that "Paul Whiteman, Isham Jones and other leading bandmasters from downtown and NBC officials and announcers and production men come to Harlem frequently to be in the circle of good cheer dispensed by the famous Chick Webb and his friends."[16]

Webb's band went on a short eastern tour in December 1934, ending at Pittsburgh's Savoy Ballroom for New Year's Day, then headed back to New York.[17] They were due to leave for a second tour in February, which was delayed by a blizzard. Buchanan took advantage of this and sprang a surprise "battle of music" with Webb's band and Willie Bryant's, who also had a big radio audience. Webb revised his repertoire, "adding a number of new tunes that will hit the rhythm spot that makes everybody wiggle when the right notes are sounded."[18]

Webb's finances improved enough to rent an apartment at 226 West 139th Street, a beautiful two-block stretch of Harlem aptly named Strivers Row. The building still stands, and the whole block is still one of the prettiest blocks in central Harlem, with hidden gardens and plenty of trees and greenery. It was a major move for Webb, and the first time that he and his best friend/guitarist John Trueheart did not share living quarters since they had settled in Harlem ten years earlier. In really tough times, they'd shared their rooming-house rooms with seven or eight bandmates and friends.

Webb's image caught up with his status as a top bandleader. Dancer Norma Miller said: "Even with that hump on his back, he was a sharp cat and a sharp dresser. He always had a good-looking girl on his arm." Webb was outgoing and charming and had no trouble attracting women. Miller remembers him strutting about the Savoy with an elegant Savoy hostess on each arm, escorting him to his throne on the band stand. Chorus girls, hostesses, musicians—everybody now wanted to be seen with him.

That winter Webb started dating a woman named Sally Hart (née Martha Loretta Ferguson), who had moved to Harlem from the Pittsburgh area. Hart and Webb soon were seen everywhere together, and she went to the Savoy every night that Webb's band was playing. Webb's sidemen and others on the scene all thought she was a great conversationalist, intelligent, and beautiful. Chick and Sally soon started living together at his Strivers Row apartment, and before long people assumed they were married.

Like many young women during the Depression, Sally Hart was looking for better opportunities. She was born in 1913 in Pittsburgh but grew up in nearby McKeesport. The area's steel mills drew many thousands of Black people north for jobs during the Great Migration. Hart viewed herself as a glamorous modern young woman and hooked her dreams on entertainment circles. At age sixteen, Martha Loretta lived on her own in Homestead, also close to Pittsburgh, and worked as a hostess at a Black-and-tan night club, where she met Martin Hart, a technician in a steel mill.[19] In 1929 the couple eloped to a border town in West Virginia in 1929, where marriage ages were not scrutinized and she passed for eighteen. The marriage did not last long. Hart sued for divorce: Sally had refused to give up her nightclub job, which caused a rift between the couple because Hart didn't approve of her working there. Martha Loretta did not appear at their divorce hearing, and Hart told the court that he'd heard that she'd moved to Detroit to become a singer. It is unclear exactly when Sally Hart moved to Harlem, if she had friends there, or where she lived before she met Webb. Once she moved in with Chick, she was completely devoted to him. Whether or not Chick and Sally were ever legally married is still unconfirmed; no marriage certificate has been found despite thorough research. But society columns later on called her "Mrs. Chick Webb," and photos show a stunning light-skinned woman at various events and on trips with her Harlem women friends.[20]

> Ali saw me, and he told Chick about me. He had me sneak into Chick's room and had me sing. And they gave me my first chance, they were going to play at a Yale prom. And Chick told me if they liked me there then I had a job. So the kids liked me there and that's how I started my singing career.
>
> —Ella Fitzgerald[21]

The first three months of 1935 were the best yet for Webb's career, and he was welcomed back to the Savoy like a conquering hero. During the band's short winter tour, he'd attracted record crowds to Detroit's famous Greystone Ballroom, to Pittsburgh's Savoy Ballroom and to the Mirador Nightclub in nearby Homestead. In early March, Webb's band was scheduled to play again at the Harlem Opera House, now an important venue—thanks in part to the Theater Wars.

Jazz historians often overlook the importance of the Harlem theater shows as performance spaces for the emerging great Black swing bands. Tours often started with a run at the Apollo or the Harlem Opera House (and the Lafayette, until 1933), then headed out on the Black theater circuit. Harlem's stage shows had a familiar format, rooted in Black minstrelsy, vaudeville and the hit revues of the 1920s: comedians, a chorus line, dazzling tap dancers, and now a fourteen or fifteen-piece jazz big band. Former stars from the Lafayette like Pigmeat Markham, Buck and Bubbles, and the brilliant mime and dancer Johnny Hudgins were still audience favorites at the Harlem Opera House and the Apollo. But Harlem's audiences were always hungry for new talent. In 1935, the sensational Nicholas Brothers were on their way up, as was comedian Jackie Mabley, later known as "Moms."

At the Apollo, big bands started to perform on stage after Earl Hines refused to have his famous Chicago-based Grand Terrace Orchestra perform in the pit; it was too crowded and he had just bought his musicians new white uniforms. For added visual appeal, the Apollo had elaborate embroidered or painted backdrops. Some bands broke down into smaller groupings to accompany the acts. The schedule was crazy for performers: shows ran from Friday to Wednesday and played five or six times a day on weekends, including the wildly popular midnight shows.

Happy Caldwell, Tiny Bradshaw's music director, said: "Ella was unknown then." Caldwell thought Fitzgerald was influenced by the Earl Hines Orchestra's version of "Object of My Affection," a radio hit before the Boswell Sisters' recording. Webb had added this song to his set list the previous year, so it was "in the air." "Earl Hines used to broadcast it from Chicago all the time from the Grand Terrace—that's where she [Ella] got the knack for wanting to sing it. . . . She'd come down to the Rhythm Club and sit there and plunk on the piano and sing. . . . The boys, you know, we all encouraged her. . . . That was just the beginning. She locked it up."[22] Fitzgerald was then going on eighteen years old, homeless, and living by the grace of her wits and a few acquaintances who helped her out. For money, she occasionally ran numbers and busked on the street. She was simultaneously shy and ambitious, taking a chance on her talents after a rough couple of years.

Born in Virginia in 1917, Fitzgerald grew up with her mother Tempie, half-sister Frances, and Portuguese stepfather in a diverse working-class part of Yonkers. As a young teen, she loved dancing and singing, imitating what she heard on the radio and records with friends. Encouraged by her mother, she won a few local talent shows sponsored by Westchester's Black social clubs as a tap dancer. She and a friend made enough spare change dancing on the street to go to Harlem to see a movie or go to the Savoy. She also started skipping school and got caught for truancy. In April 1933, Ella, then almost sixteen, was sent to the New York State Training School for Girls, a reform school in Hudson, New York. On the intake log, her offense was that she was "ungovernable and will not obey the just and lawful commands of her mother—adjudged delinquent." Unruly behavior by girls was cause for being judged incorrigible and unjustly incarcerated. Black girls at the school were treated more harshly than whites; they were placed in solitary confinement for small transgressions, and most likely suffered physical abuse. All of this was a cruel penalty for missing school.[23]

Fitzgerald ran away from the Hudson school and went home to her family in Yonkers. Her mother still encouraged her to sign up for amateur contests (which often had cash prizes) and helped her sign up for the brand-new Apollo contest in fall 1934. Tragically, Tempie died in a car accident in October 1934, and Ella soon left home for Harlem. A month later, on November 21, Fitzgerald appeared at the Apollo as a finalist. Wearing her well-worn flowered dress, a thin sweater with a fake fur collar, and work boots that she often wore to hide her thin legs, she was nudged on stage by the M.C. Ralph Cooper.

Forty years later, Fitzgerald described what happened: "I really went on stage to try to be a dancer. In Yonkers I was known as one of the great little tap dancers. But when I got on the stage [at the Apollo] I lost my nerve. And the man said, 'Well, you've got to do something. So I tried to sing like Connee Boswell, and I sang 'Judy' and 'Object of My Affection,' and that's how I won first prize."

Fitzgerald's act followed a pair of semipro tap dancing sisters, whose costumes glittered and sparkled as they tapped out their synchronized moves: "Those two sisters, they were the stars of the show at the Apollo," Fitzgerald recalled, "and I was the first amateur that came out behind them, and that is that why I think I lost my nerve! 'Cause these girls, they stopped that show tap dancing—there was nothing that could make me go out on that stage! So, yes, we really should thank those sisters, 'cause I've got news for you. For my hometown I was all right, but if I tried to be a dancer, I'd have starved."[24]

In February 1935, Bardu Ali heard Fitzgerald at the Harlem Opera House, singing a few numbers with Tiny Bradshaw's band. Ali had recently rejoined Webb's band after being in London for a few months with *Blackbirds*. He often went to other theaters and clubs to check out the shows. "[S]he [Ella] had won first prize at the other theater, which was the Apollo Theater down the street, owned by the same people. And if you win a prize they give you a week's work. So they gave Ella a week there with Tiny Bradshaw. . . . I heard her there."

Ali was impressed by the young singer and kept urging Webb to go hear her, but Webb ignored him.[25] He may not have cared about having a female singer, which was not a trend yet for jazz big bands. Plus, Webb already had two singers, Charles Linton, who handled all the foxtrots and romantic ballads, and trumpet player Taft Jordan, who sang blues vocals and songs that Louis Armstrong popularized.

Mainly, Webb was busy. The band traveled a lot that winter and was getting offers to appear in places they'd never been. He'd been working persistently for over eight years for his band to get this kind of recognition; now they were working steadily, making records, and were all over the airwaves. Teddy McRae said, "Chick knew where he wanted to be this year and the next year and the next year." During the first week of March 1935, Webb's band packed the Harlem Opera House, like fellow Baltimorean Cab Calloway had the previous week.

In addition to Bardu Ali, other musicians also thought Fitzgerald had special talent and tried to connect her with bandleaders that could offer her work. Charles Linton, who'd heard Ella early on, said that Moe Gale wanted to add a girl singer as another attraction for Webb's band. Linton claims he forced the issue by threatening to quit if Webb didn't at least give her a hearing.[26]

Fitzgerald herself said that it was Ali who finally got Webb to listen to her sing. Ali took her to Webb's dressing room at the Harlem Opera House. He remembered that the other sidemen teased him about this. "[S]he wasn't a fine-lookin' chick, so they all said, 'Hey, look at old Bardu and this chick.'

I said, 'No man, this is the girl who can sing!' " Fitzgerald may have been more worried about meeting Webb than the sidemen's sexist teasing, but issues of lookism, sexism, and racism in entertainment circles trailed her throughout her career.

Ali told John Trueheart to get his guitar out to accompany her. "[W]hen she sang about eight bars of 'Object of My Affection,' then you could hear a pin drop in the room, because she sings just like a horn." That was the ultimate compliment to a jazz vocalist from a jazz musician.

Author and cultural critic Margo Jefferson suggested other reasons that might have contributed to Webb's hesitance: "Was he afraid that the sight of two plain people on stage, one malformed, the other dowdy and gawky, presumed too much on the good will of the audience?"[27] Webb decided to let her try out with the band two days later, on Friday, March 8, 1935, at St. Elmo Hall, the residence of the seniors-only division of the Delta Phi fraternity at Yale University. Ali said that before their trip Webb and the band all pulled together for Ella. "Chick sent home and got a dress of his wife's. She [Ella] wore a size 10 then. You could see how small she was on this picture. . . . [S]omeone went out and bought some shoes for her."

St. Elmo Hall, built in the 1880s, stands on the edge of Yale's gracefully laid-out campus, a different universe than the neighborhood around the Savoy Ballroom. Yale's prestigious fraternities were supported by old money, enough for the students to hire famous musicians and bands. Paul Whiteman's orchestra was booked for the junior prom, one of the university's biggest social events of the year. Webb's band was among several others booked for after-prom dances that night, from 1 a.m. to 7 a.m. The St. Elmo dance was open to all students, as were the other after-prom dances, featuring Isham Jones's Orchestra, a Whiteman small group, and Fats Waller and His Rhythm. Webb's band and the others were booked for Saturday night too. This would be an all-out party weekend.

According to a couple of alumni, Webb and the band performed at the end of a long wood-paneled room in St. Elmo Hall. The students flipped over Ella. "We saw a nervous youngster wearing a gingham dress with a flower in her hair," said a St. Elmo-Yale alumni. "We went nuts for her. We all loved her. . . . [S]he sang with all that freedom and all that excitement."

Ali recalled: "We only had those three songs, 'Believe It, Beloved,' 'Object of My Affection,' and 'Judy.' " The band had lead sheets and "faked" some parts for an orchestrated sound. "She sang those three numbers, but then the kids kept on asking for the girl to sing again. We didn't have nothing else for her to sing!" Ali continued. "So one year from that day we came back to play that same fraternity dance at Yale University, and I just stopped directing the band, and just watched thousands of kids sitting on the floor. She had made it, and at one year."[28]

After that weekend, Webb gave Fitzgerald a longer tryout with the band back at the Savoy Ballroom. Webb slowly introduced Fitzgerald to the Savoy audience, and initially she only sang one or two numbers at the end of each set. Like Webb, she was a striver and ambitious. She knew that she was getting her big break and respected his leadership. He was the King of the Savoy—Harlem royalty.

Though female singers weren't typically featured with jazz dance bands, there were notable exceptions. Mildred Bailey started appearing with Paul Whiteman's Orchestra in 1929, then with the Casa Loma Orchestra and others. In the early 1930s, Blanche Calloway was a star attraction with her Joy Boys, and Ivie Anderson joined Duke Ellington's Orchestra in late 1931.

Fitzgerald was younger than any of them. Musically, she was a quick study. Though her teenage voice was light and airy, her pitch, sense of swing rhythm, and phrasing were spot-on. Like Webb, she had a phenomenal musical memory and memorized music rapidly. She could also sight-read. After her two-week tryout at the Savoy, Webb agreed to keep her on. Sally Webb and the Savoy hostesses helped Fitzgerald with new dresses, shoes, and accessories, getting her hair styled, and developing a stage presence.

This was a pivotal period for the band, and for the young Ella Fitzgerald. The band was getting lots of radio play, in and out of the Savoy, and performed at many East Coast one-nighters. The Savoy audience warmed up to Webb's new hire, and he simultaneously encouraged and cautioned her. Years later she recalled his warning her about the temptations of stardom: "You never want to be someone who goes up too fast because you'll come down the same way, and you'll meet the same people coming down as you did going up."[29]

Webb, Sally, and others kept close watch on Ella. Rumors soon surfaced that Webb had adopted her. "Chick had a small apartment," Linton recalled. "He couldn't take anyone in. He told me, 'I'll say I adopted her for the press people.'"[30] That caused confusion for years, but Webb did have to sign on as her guardian when she was still under eighteen so that she could travel out of state with the band.

In early summer 1935, Fitzgerald started making her first trips with the band; some were one-nighters close to New York, and the band also went on short tours to Pennsylvania. These were the first times that Webb's band was on the road with a young female musician. Sally hardly ever traveled with the band at this time, and other spouses didn't either. The band didn't go out on really long tours yet.

"She was the only girl in the band, and everybody used to call her 'sis,'" Bardu Ali recalled. "Everybody was kind to her, and all of them admired her because she sang with such a perfect pitch. And she could read, you know, just give her the music and she can read. . . . Ella was very talented, just unbelievable. . . . From the very beginning, there's no two ways about it. She was just it! You can tune a band by her voice."[31]

12

Spinnin' the Webb

You can take a drum and transport people. I was taught by Chick
Webb that, if you're playing before an audience, you're supposed to
take them away from everyday life—wash away the dust of everyday
life. And that's all music is supposed to do.

—Art Blakey

When I got to the Savoy, he [Webb] was just climbing up the hill,
Ella was there, and they also played at the Apollo. Prior to that it was
just at the Savoy. It was such a joy as a young person dealing with
instruments, standing in front of that crowd. It was like being on the
subway at rush hour with that crowd, and the bass drum would just
go through your whole body. As a young drummer I was just infused
with that sound. You are conscious of the adrenalin, that ambience.
Anyone who heard Chick Webb would be influenced by him.

—Max Roach[1]

Chick Webb was incomparable as a modern jazz drummer, and ahead of
his time in several significant ways. He was the first jazz virtuoso on drums,
an exhilarating showman, and an expert technician able to tease a range of
sounds and colors from his instruments. Webb was the first big bandleader
who led the band from the drums. Added to that, said Kenny Washington, a
prominent contemporary drummer and bandleader:

Chick Webb really wrote the blueprint for big band drummers. The rest of
the guys—Papa Jo Jones, Buddy Rich, Gene Krupa, Art Blakey, Roy Haynes,
Ray McKinley, even Mel Lewis—all looked up to Chick because he wrote
the book, the blue print, in terms of big band drumming. That's really his
contribution. I've been told he couldn't read music but that he had fantastic
ears. At a rehearsal playing new music if Chick heard a wrong note, sure

enough when the band went over their parts, there was a wrong note in the saxes or trumpets. He was one of the first drummers that wanted musicians to be aware that a drummer isn't someone who is just sitting back there banging on the drums, he's got to know some music as well. Respect the drummer.

The Savoy Ballroom was not a concert hall or modern jazz club where the audience sat and listened. On the bandstand, Webb and his band emanated a power that made the dance floor bounce and the whole building rock. Other drummers, Black and white, came to the Savoy or caught him on tour and watched his every move. Webb "literally lifted the band," said Artie Shaw, a virtuoso himself on clarinet and Webb's peer as a bandleader. "When it cut loose he was behind every phrase like a charioteer driving horses."[2]

The sheer excitement that Webb projected from the bandstand comes through on a handful of the band's commercial 78-rpm recordings and rare recordings of the band's live broadcasts. His solos and performances on "Liza" and "Harlem Congo" and his band's covers of "One O'Clock Jump," "King Porter Stomp," and "Clap Hands, Here Come Charlie" are flawless and dramatic showstoppers. His playing is both aggressive and artistic, and he leads the band from the drums as precisely as a conductor does with a baton. His style and virtuosity would soon pave the way for Krupa's lengthy drum solos, something Webb himself rarely did on recordings, with "Liza" the fabulous exception. Krupa, Benny Goodman's super-extroverted drummer, repeatedly acknowledged Webb's mastery and influence. Both Webb and Krupa elevated drum solos in large and small ensemble settings that were then carried forward by bebop, post-bop, free jazz, jazz-rock, and rock 'n' roll drummers.

Webb's primacy as an innovator has been overshadowed by his tragic early death, and by the larger trove of recordings, radio broadcasts, feature films, and soundies by other prominent Swing Era drummers including Krupa, Sonny Greer, Jo Jones, Big Sid Catlett, Cozy Cole, Buddy Rich, and Jimmy Crawford. This historiographic problem—why didn't Webb feature himself more?—has bewildered jazz historians and critics to this day. Only two instances of Webb on film have surfaced: *After Seben* (1929) and a "March of Time" 1937 newsreel segment about Swing.[3] The newsreel footage was filmed at the Savoy Ballroom, and one can see Ella dancing on the side of the bandstand. Webb is just barely seen in the front row, nestled between his sax and brass sections. This was an unusual spot; most big band drummers sat behind the horns, central to the rhythm section. Max Roach vividly recalled: "He was the first drummer I've seen that sat in front of the band! He was introduced and sat right in front of the orchestra."

In big theater shows at the Apollo, the Paramount, or Lowes, Webb was usually on a platform with the rhythm section, behind the horns. Wherever he was positioned, Webb's fellow drummers, immediate successors, and present-day jazz drummers gave and still give full credit to Webb for putting the drums in the forefront of a band's sound and style.

When Webb began his career in the early 1920s, a drummer's main role was as timekeeper and showman. Throwing sticks in the air, "catching" dance steps, and comedians' pratfalls on cymbals were necessary skills for early jazz drummers' multiple roles in stage bands, vaudeville shows, revues, and pit bands. This was all part of the drummer's job. John Pearl Spears, an early twentieth-century drummer and drum teacher, wrote: "A drummer in a vaudeville house ... has to catch all the business on the stage such as falls, slides, summersaults.... There is no end to what a drummer is expected to do."[4]

For Webb personally, playing "tricks" on drums on the stages and bandstands of Baltimore was also a way that people could see beyond his spinal deformity and short stature. Renowned jazz pianist and educator Billy Taylor said Chick came up when "everybody had to hold his spot.... If you didn't get as much applause as the juggler, singer or shake dancer, then you lost the feature. Somebody else got it. It was a fight for survival. That's why drummers threw sticks and did all kinds of show biz things, while they tried to play in a marvelous musical manner.... Chick was in the forefront because he knew exactly how to deal with that situation."[5] As Webb's career advanced, he had to be an adept accompanist for comedians, chorus dancers, tap dance acts, eccentric dancers, acrobats, and singers at stage shows and revues at theaters like the Lafayette, Royal, Howard, and Apollo.

Cozy Cole, who played opposite Webb's band often as drummer for Willie Bryant in the mid-1930s, told stories of the difficulties he and other drummers faced backing up stage acts. Overcome by stage fright, he sometimes froze up and couldn't keep time. "The chorus girls, they were back there saying, 'Oh, get rid of that drummer, he's messing up our dancing!' ... I'd practice with a metronome, but up there, I would get excited, nervous." Cole was even fired from some of his first gigs in New York City. His first important jazz band job was with Blanche Calloway's Joy Boys from 1931 to 1933, which pushed his skills as an accompanist.

> Blanche would be in front of the band and if Ben [Webster] or one of the musicians had a solo, Blanche would still be out there dancing, selling the band.... Well, see, that's very unprofessional, with Ben Webster taking a solo, and you're up there trying to catch Blanche Calloway when she's kicking her legs up in the air on the cymbal! But it was Blanche's band. That's what she wanted.... She told Webster that if he "didn't like playing in her band, there were plenty of musicians on the corner waiting for the job."[6]

Webb didn't stay tethered to playing tricks. A developing musician when he got to Harlem, Webb knew that playing the drums involved perfecting technique and playing with feeling, as well as learning new dance rhythms and "catching" what the band and soloists were playing. Saxophonist/arranger Teddy McRae said:

> Chick Webb was a self-made drummer.... He'd tell his story where he used to beat on tin cans and things in Baltimore, but he could play anything, any style.... We'd go into places and we'd go into these tangos. We'd play the right tempo, we weren't just fooling with it! There is a right way to play a tango and a wrong way. It has to be authentic. You can't just get up there and play it because you're a colored band playing the tango. No! You play the music! This is what we used to do. We used to play waltzes. Chick used to say you're not a drummer if you can't play a slow and beautiful thing. He'd tell you, "Show me a guy that can play me a slow roll—like tissue paper. A slow roll—you're not a drummer unless you can do this."[7]

Art Blakey, master bebop and post-bop drummer, who absorbed Webb's records as a teenager, learned the "slow roll" lesson directly from him. In the late 1930s, Webb's band was playing in Pittsburgh, Blakey's hometown, and caught one of Blakey's club acts, in which he threw different colored drumsticks around. Webb encouraged him to concentrate on developing his technique and conception instead of the showy stuff. He told Blakey to come see him the next day. He made him practice playing rolls on a snare drum. "I want you to roll 'til you get to one hundred, and I don't want you to break that roll." Blakey showed up every day during Webb's visit and followed his instructions. "He was a disciplinarian," said Blakey. "I developed a press roll out of that."[8]

Ulysses Owens, Jr., another acclaimed contemporary drummer and bandleader, said that Webb must have put in a lot of time on the snare to build the kind of technical mastery he had.

> He must have spent a lot of time practicing rudiments. For someone like Webb, you see where things were and what they became in a very short time. Before him, drummers were just regarded as a necessary timekeeper. It's just what they did. . . . With Webb, you can see a genius in the imagination of that person. For drummers, Webb is also really special because our instrument is one that doesn't encourage your own voice. It is an instrument that really encourages you to serve other people, so the fact that Chick Webb was able to serve other people while simultaneously finding his own voice is really unique—and he was making it up as he went along.

On early jazz records, drummers were limited to just playing time on snare with brushes or on a woodblock; they couldn't use sticks or the bass drum, to avoid sound distortion. Owens explains:

> It wasn't 'til the late 1920s that guys like Zutty Singleton actually started doing embellishments. . . . Then you look and you've got this guy who has overcome sound limitations, he's being recorded, he's leading the band, he's deciding everything and he's soloing. So you are talking about a level of evolution in under twenty years of the drummer's role, from being in the background to being in the foreground musically. And because of Webb, we were open to an Art Blakey, we were open to a Buddy, we were open Max Roach, we were open to all these other drummers as bandleaders who would come, but he was the first model.[9]

Roach, raised in Brooklyn, painted a mustache on himself as a young teen so he could look old enough to get into the Savoy and hear Chick Webb.

> He [Webb] had the kind of precision—I use this word advisedly. The way Mr. Webb affected me when I say precision is different than a musician playing in a symphony. Louis Armstrong was a precision player, Mr. Webb was a precision player. He would make his instruments talk, so to speak. The instrument was a living entity—it became something else above and

Figure 1. Chick Webb and His Harlem Stompers, Savoy Ballroom, c. 1927. Center: Chick Webb; left of Webb: Johnny Hodges, Don Kirkpatrick (top), Elmer Williams. Courtesy of private collector.

Figure 2. Chick Webb and His Orchestra, Savoy Ballroom, c 1930.
Photograph by Berenice Abbott, courtesy of Hank O'Neal/Getty Images.

Figure 3. Beauty Contest at the Savoy Ballroom, c. 1928 w. Chick Webb and His Harlem Stompers.
Front row: Floyd G. Snelson; far right: Bill Robinson with his portrait; 2nd row: Ben Bernie, Editor of *Interstate Tattler*; 3rd row: Don Kirkpatrick (piano), Chick Webb (2nd right), unknown contestants. Schomburg Center for Research in Black Culture, New York Public Library.

Figure 4. Baltimore City Colored Park Band, Edward A. Prettyman, Conductor, 1941.
Photograph by Edward A. Prettyman. From the collection of Alfred E. Prettyman.

Figure 5. Chick Webb and His Orchestra in *After Seben*, 1929.
L to R: John Trueheart (banjo), Chick Webb, Bennie Morton (trombone), Ward Pinkett, Edwin Swayzee, (trumpet), Bobby Holmes (clarinet), Elmer Williams (tenor sax), Hilton Jefferson (alto sax). Courtesy of private collector.

Figure 6. Chick Webb and His Orchestra, c. 1929.
Bottom row, L to R: Elmer Williams (2nd from left, tenor sax), Johnny Hodges (alto sax), John Truehart (banjo), Don Kirkpatrick (piano), Chick Webb (cymbal). Courtesy of private collector.

Figure 7. Chick Webb and His Orchestra, 1931.
L to R: Louis Hunt, Louis Bacon (trumpet), Charlie Irvis (trombone), Shelton Hemphill (trumpet), Don Kirkpatrick (piano), Chick Webb, John Trueheart (guitar), Russell Procope (alto sax, clarinet), Elmer James (bass), Elmer Williams (tenor sax, clarinet), Hilton Jefferson (alto sax, clarinet). Courtesy of private collector.

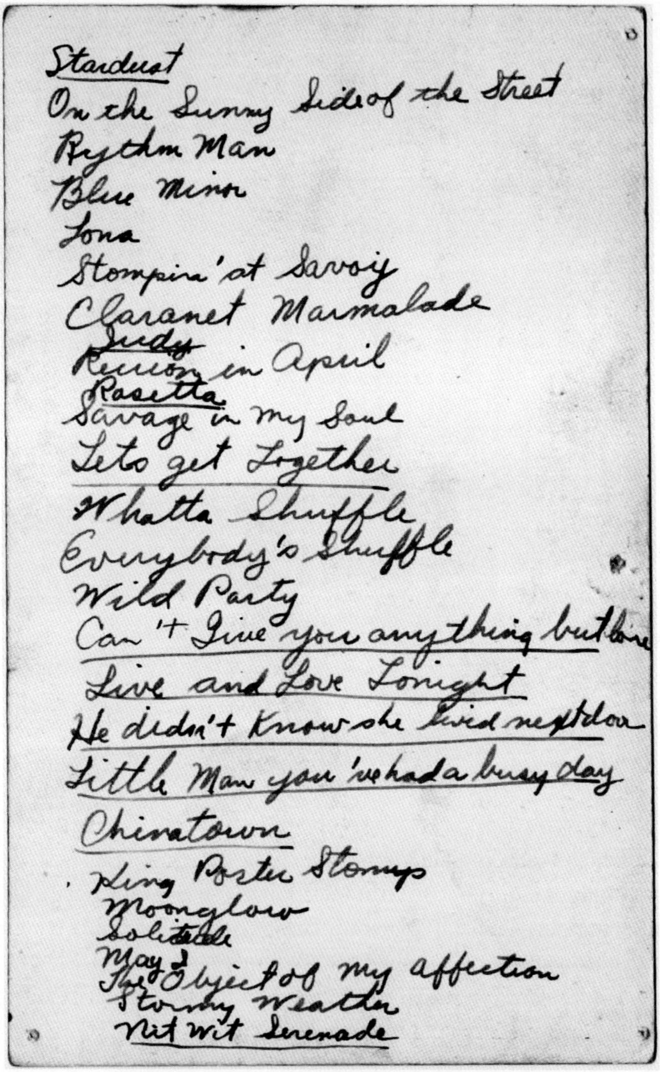

Stardust
On the Sunny Side of the Street
Rythm Man
Blue Minor
Lona
Stompin' at Savoy
Claranet Marmalade
Judy
Reunion in April
Rosetta
Savage in my Soul
Lets get Together
Whatta Shuffle
Everybody's Shuffle
Wild Party
Can't Give you anything but love
Live and Love Tonight
He didn't know she lived next door
Little Man you've had a busy day
Chinatown
King Porter Stomp
Moonglow
Solitude
May I
The Object of my affection
Stormy Weather
Nit Wit Serenade

Figure 8. Chick Webb's set list, back of souvenir photo, c. 1934. Courtesy of Philip J. Merrill, Nanny Jack & Co. Archives.

Figure 9. Chick Webb and His Orchestra, front of souvenir photo c. 1934.
L to R, bottom row: Sandy Williams (trombone), Reunald Jones, Taft Jordan,
Mario Bauza (trumpet), Pete Clark, Edgar Sampson (alto sax), Charles
Linton (vocalist, holding sax), Joe Steele (piano); top row: Chick Webb,
John Trueheart (guitar), John Kirby (bass). Courtesy of Philip J. Merrill,
Nanny Jack & Co. Archives.

Figure 10. Savoy Ballroom at Night c. 1950.
Photograph by Austin Hansen. Schomburg Center for Research in Black
Culture, New York Public Library. Courtesy Joyce Hansen/ Austin Hansen
Photo Collection.

Figures 11–12. Chick Webb and His Orchestra, Savoy Ballroom, c. 1937, both photos taken same night.
L to R: Bobby Stark, Taft Jordan (trumpet), Chick Webb, Sandy Williams (trombone). Photograph by Otto Hess. Otto F. Hess Photo Collection, New York Public Library for the Performing Arts.

Figure 12. Chick Webb and His Orchestra, Savoy Ballroom, 1937.
L to R: John Trueheart (probably, guitar), Bobby Stark, Taft Jordan (trumpet), Chick Webb. Photograph by Otto Hess. Otto F. Hess Photo Collection, Music Division, New York Public Library for the Performing Arts.

Figure 13. Publicity portrait (probably signed by Ella Fitzgerald).
Schomburg Center for Research in Black Culture, New York Public Library.

Figure 14. The Savoy Story, cover of the 25th Anniversary Commemorative
Booklet, 1951.
Schomburg Center for Research in Black Culture, New York Public Library.

Figure 15. Ella Fitzgerald and Chick Webb, c. 1938.
Courtesy of private collector.

Figure 16. Chick Webb–Benny Goodman "Battle of the Bands," Savoy
Ballroom, May 11, 1937.
L to R: Gladys Hampton, John Trueheart (probably, guitar), Ella Fitzgerald,
Hilton Jefferson (alto sax), Chick Webb. Photograph by Otto Hess. Otto
F. Hess Photo Collection, Music Division, New York Public Library for the
Performing Arts.

Figure 17. Chick Webb at home, c. 1937.
Courtesy of private collector.

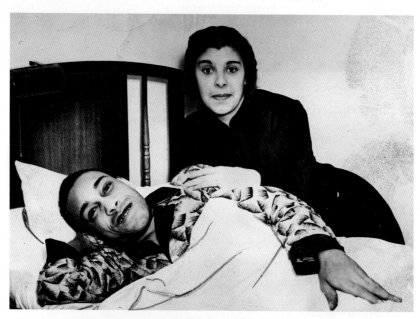

Figure 18. Chick and Sally Webb, June 18, 1938.
Baltimore Afro-American/Getty Images.

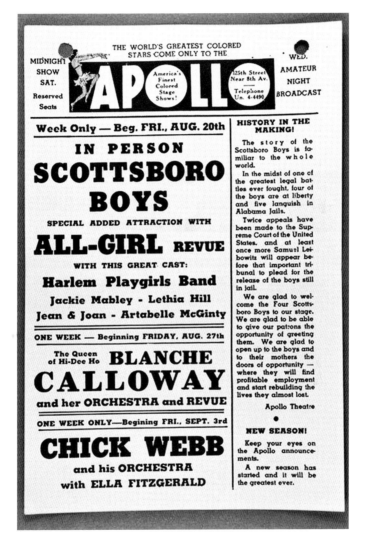

Figure 19. Apollo Theater Handbill, August 1937.
Courtesy of Apollo Theater Archives.

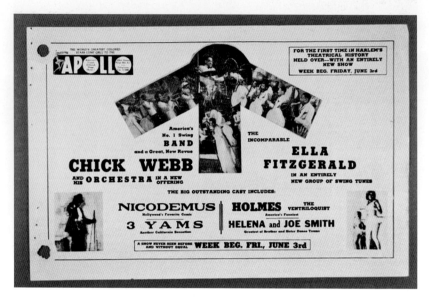

Figure 20. Apollo Theater Handbill, June 1938.
Courtesy of Apollo Theater Archives.

Figure 21. Chick Webb, Apollo Theater, 1937.
L to R: top row: Chick Webb, Bobby Johnson (guitar), Beverly Peer (bass);
bottom row: Pete Clark (flute), Louis Jordan (clarinet), Wayman Carver (flute),
Teddy Mcrae (clarinet). Courtesy of private collector.

Figure 22. Chick Webb and His Orchestra, Carnival of Swing, Randall's Island, NY, May 29, 1938.
Photograph by Otto Hess. Otto F. Hess Photo Collection, Music Division, New York Public Library for the Performing Arts.

Figure 23. NBC Studio, fan mail, 1937 (probably signed by Ella Fitzgerald). Courtesy of private collector.

Figure 24. Chick Webb and Ella Fitzgerald at the Paramount Theater, NYC, August 10–18, 1938.
Photograph by Popsie. Courtesy of William "Popsie" Randolph Collection © Michael Randolph.

Figure 25. Chick Webb and His Orchestra, Paramount Theater, NYC, August 10–18, 1938.
L to R: Bardu Ali, Hilton Jefferson (alto sax), Nat Story (trombone), Garvin Bushell (alto sax), Sandy Williams (trombone), Teddy McRae (tenor sax).
Photograph by Popsie. Courtesy of William "Popsie" Randolph Collection © Michael Randolph.

Figure 26. Savoy Lindy Hoppers, Paramount Theater, NYC, August 10–18, 1938. Photograph by Popsie. Courtesy of William "Popsie" Randolph Collection © Michael Randolph.

Figure 27. Mildred Bailey, Ella Fitzgerald, Helen Humes, Count Basie, Savoy Ballroom, 1940.
Photograph Otto Hess. Otto F. Hess Photo Collection, Music Division, New York Public Library for the Performing Arts.

Figure 28. Chick Webb, 1939.
Courtesy Archives of Fred Gretsch Enterprises, Ltd.

Figure 29. Chick Webb, Gretsch Company Catalog Cover #40, 1939.
Courtesy Archives of Fred Gretsch Enterprises, Ltd.

Figure 30. "The King" cartoon in Harlem World, 1939.
Courtesy of private collector.

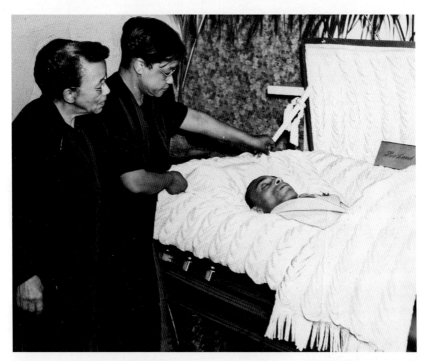

Figure 31. Chick Webb's Funeral, June 20, 1939. Waters African Methodist Episcopal Church, Baltimore.
Webb's grandmother, Mary Jones, and mother, Marie Webb. *Baltimore Afro-American*/Getty Images.

Figure 32. Chick Webb's Funeral, June 20, 1939. Waters African Methodist
Episcopal Church, Baltimore.

Figure 33. Portrait of Chick Webb by Anne Beadenkopf, 1948, for Chick Webb Memorial Recreation Center.
Courtesy of Philip J. Merrill, Nanny Jack & Co. Archives.

beyond that. Art Blakey got to that, so did Philly Joe Jones. The influence is more than just yes and no, who said what. You get something that comes out of the personality of that person—like Aretha Franklin.

His technical prowess—I don't think anybody can match that—it's like when you hear Art Tatum in person, it really does seem impossible. I would say that Webb was the Tatum of the drums. As a musician and instrumentalist, what he did was paramount. It took him above, he created a design and form. . . . Mr. Webb was here to show us a cornerstone, to be involved in what we are doing with jazz. If it hadn't been for him, there would be no me.[10]

On the bandstand at the Savoy Ballroom, people did not always notice Webb's unusual physique, stemming from his bout with spinal tuberculosis as a child: his four-foot height or the enlarged hump on his upper spine. Not one thing about his drumming—his force, power, and aggressive sense of swing—suggested that he was impaired.

Yet almost every news clipping about Webb brought up his spinal deformity, his height, or what is now considered his disability. He was called a midget, a crippled genius, a hunchback dwarf. Webb was afflicted with the chronic effects of disease and some forms of disability: an impaired spine, uneven gait, and sometimes severe pain. His childhood bout with spinal tuberculosis resulted in his shortened spinal column due to compressed vertebrae, as well as his hump. Webb himself never let on how much pain he endured until the late 1930s, when his health complications forced him off the bandstand and sent him to the hospital. His hospital stays were mentioned in the press, along with the band's more frequent tour dates.[11]

During Webb's childhood, having a chronic disease and/or visible disability was often a cause for shame, teasing, bullying, being ostracized, skipping school, or leaving school entirely. It was easier to be less visible, not more. But Webb, nurtured by his extended family and friends, was highly visible on East Baltimore streets, playing drums for parties and dances, and then on bandstands. People watched out for him and knew his comings and goings. Visibility—first as a newsboy, then as a performer—was Webb's path to normalcy, opportunity, and making a living in the status-heavy music scenes of Baltimore and Harlem. A toughened expert at trick drumming, Webb didn't perform as a freakish anomaly. As the first drummer-bandleader in jazz, he was non-diseased, differently-abled, decisive, and confident about his band's musical direction.

As Webb became more successful, Black and white entertainment reporters often composed tidy narratives of his triumph against all odds, including poverty and disability. A growing body of scholarship linking disability and musicology opens up different ways to think about these narratives (though some scholars feel compelled to re-present century-old articles claiming that jazz itself is a disease, a music of abnormality).[12] These feel-good narratives allow us to cheer our heroes on from a safe distance. We don't have to feel guilty about the social conditions—the system, the setup, the roadblocks, the obstacles—that Webb faced as a Black musician, compounded by his unusual body. If he could make it, anyone could! One can view Webb as exotic or exceptional: some reporters exaggerated his short stature to only "three feet tall." Only those who knew Webb intimately have what ethnomusicologist Terry Rowden considers a "realistic" approach. Eloquently pairing ethnomusicology and disability studies, Rowden writes that people's unease with viewing others' disabilities "inhibits us from doing the necessary work to understand the identities of these individuals and how their identities inform their cultural production."[13]

Webb's cultural production was music—jazz big band swing—*the* pop music of those years. He worked persistently to stand out as a musician, from the pre-swing years to swing, and emerged as an innovator in his approach to the drums in tandem with developing changes in the music. In spring 1935, he had an indirect link to radio star Connee Boswell of the Boswell Sisters, who was a formative influence on his new hire, the young Ella Fitzgerald. Boswell, afflicted with polio as a child, was the middle member of the close-harmony trio the Boswell Sisters, and was the group's arranger.[14] After the group split up in 1936, Connee came forward about her childhood disease and disability. In public appearances, Boswell accessorized her wheelchair with rhinestones and rolled onstage with grace and charm. No pity please.

Webb was not interested in pity either. Both musicians were incredibly adaptive people, totally committed to their work. Teddy McRae said self-pity was foreign to Webb. If anything, Webb was the opposite: outgoing, outspoken, feisty, persistent, and ambitious.

Chick was a self-made man. He knew where he wanted to go way before I joined him. When I used to hang out with him, he knew which direction he wanted to go. He'd spend his last money on something—this is what he was going to do! He was going to do this, he was going to be here by this time. "Next year I want to be here, and the next year I want to be there, and the next!" He told Charlie Buchanan, "Oh, you got a Caddy. I'm going to get one, too." Two years later, he had his Cadillac. This was one great part about this man. He was on his way.[15]

Webb had a special friendship with drummer Jo Jones, six years younger than him, who created the ineffable swinging groove for Count Basie's rhythm section. Jones, born in 1911, first met Webb in St. Louis in late 1936, and then got to know him better when the Basie band started spending more time in New York the following year. Jones said: "Mr. Webb had something else along with his leadership. He had to be a natural, a great natural. . . . It's impossible to write, to study, to do whatever—having the responsibility that he had, and not thinking so much about the economic, not thinking about the glory and what have you—and to be able to handle the group of men that was in his band."[16]

Webb had kept his band together through the worst years of the Depression and protracted recovery. Then, starting in 1936, his band's sound and style, especially with singer Ella Fitzgerald, finally caught on as swing big band music became the sound of America. Since Webb's debut as a bandleader ten years earlier, he had inspired loyalty and a unified spirit in his band, even as several sidemen came and went—a "farm" team. He projected leadership among musicians and other bandleaders and—as his radio, recording, and tour dates piled up—with a shifting cast of white executives and staffers in the expanding swing big band industry.

Webb had always shown his fierce competitive streak during the Savoy's frequent band battles, from 1927 on. Two of these have become the stuff of legend: with Benny Goodman's band in May 1937, and with Count Basie's in January 1938. But whomever Webb's band faced off against, trombonist Sandy Williams said that Webb was prepared. "We'd go into training like we were prizefighters. . . . We'd have special rehearsals. The brass was downstairs, the saxophones upstairs and the rhythm would get together somewhere else. We had the reputation of running any band that came to the Savoy."[17] Webb loved this kind of fight. Williams, who was one of Webb's most long-term musicians, said Webb was always focused on music.

Weekends at the Savoy were brutal. Saturday nights started at 4pm and go on until 4 am, Sunday matinees started at 3pm, and we'd end at 3am. There was no such thing that you had two days off out of the seven. And frankly speaking, Chick's whole life was music, nothing but music. To my knowledge he had no hobbies, no gambling or listening to ballgames or nothing—just music. He talked music from morning 'til night if you listened to him. That was just Webb—he would just stand on that corner and talk about different bands and different individuals in the bands. He was just wrapped in music, that's all.[18]

Webb could also be moody and quixotic. He was a complex person and sometimes got superstitious and turned on people. Webb let go of his great bassist John Kirby, who'd been with him for the most part from 1931 to 1934, when another band member convinced Webb that Kirby brought the band bad luck. Webb wasn't always the affable bandleader with a great sense of humor who befriended everyone. Dancer Norma Miller said: "He was testy. He wasn't a goody-goody sweet little guy. He was the great Chick Webb—I mean *the great* Chick Webb. You did everything but bow down in front of him. He had this habit of hitching up his pants like he would take on a giant. He was a 'Don't mess with me' character!"[19]

> Chick was built for the drums. You follow me? The way his body conformed to the drums—it was God's work, God's gift. Chick may not have had all the breaks in life. But the Lord has a way of evening things up.
>
> —Illinois Jacquet

> The greatest soloist I ever heard on drums was Chick Webb. In order to find out where drumming is at today, you must go back to the very beginning. And I think the greatest drummer that ever lived was Chick Webb. He was my favorite drummer. Not that I have too many favorite drummers: I'm not too easily impressed with people. But this man overcame all his difficulties; he was a dwarf, with a big hump on his back.
>
> He had a special set of drums made for him. Goose-neck cymbal holders, and everything was arranged so that he could reach it when he was up there. He had fantastic speed.
>
> —Buddy Rich[20]

Webb's strength and stamina—playing hours a night, often after playing four or five stage shows a day—was incredible, considering his health issues and the pain he often hid from bandmates, friends, and even his wife, Sally. Allen

Paley, one of the young drummers who crammed in front of the bandstand to watch Webb at the Savoy, described him in action:

> What he did was totally unbelievable. His huge 14" x 28" bass drum obscured him. The guy was so small and, in some ways, fragile looking. . . . I wondered how is he going to reach his cymbals, tom-toms and the bass drum? But it was no problem for him. He had strong wrists, long arms, huge hands, long fingers and legs. Only his torso was short and relatively undeveloped. Sitting up high, he'd lean over the set and hit or softly touch the various drums, cymbals, and other accessories almost without moving. Sometimes he'd stand up and play.
>
> Chick had great energy and power even though he was chronically ill. . . . [H]is illness and deformity didn't affect his playing. Fast, clean and flawless, he played like a machine gun, but with enormous feeling and understanding of what the band was trying to do. It was almost barbaric the way he drove that band. . . . He'd hold the sticks—7As, very thin—by the butt and use them just like whips. . . . None of us really knew what the hell he was doing because it was just too fast, the way he cut it.[21]

Webb's development as a drummer also went along with refinements in the drum set, drum hardware, and accessory instruments. Ken Kimery, drummer and director of the Smithsonian Jazz Masterworks Orchestra, noted how novel and inferior drum kits for dance and stage bands were in the 1920s. "Webb had to go through so many obstacles, and his own physical obstacles .... He was challenged in every aspect." The basic consolidated "trap" drum set—consisting of bass drum, snare drum, tom, and cymbals—started being used more widely in popular theaters starting in the early 1900s. This put the spotlight on a one-person percussion section but also benefited theater producers who only had to pay one person, not two or three, and freed up space in the orchestra pit or onstage. Early trap drummers had to devise their own foot pedals for the bass drum (usually clunky wooden devices), stands, and cymbals holders. At the time, drums had less precise metal parts and all wooden rims.

The Ludwig drum company patented the first metal bass drum pedal "to keep up with the ragtime tempos."[22] Drum and cymbal manufacturers kept improving their instruments throughout the 1920s, leveraging a growing market for drummers in dance bands, dance halls, and theaters. Top drum manufacturers like Leedy, Ludwig, and Gretsch (which produced premier banjos before developing its drums) published newsletters, advertised, and got musicians' endorsements. Though most of the drummers pictured in these early newsletters and ads were white, the March 1932 issue of the Leedy's newsletter, "The Exclusive Drummer's Paper," includes a small photo of Webb and his endorsement: " 'Have used all makes of drums. I find Leedy the best.' That is the tribute to Leedy by Chick Webb of Baltimore, MD. He has played drums for a period of ten years, having great success using Leedy Instruments. Without a doubt he will continue successfully."[23]

A publicity photo of Webb's band from 1934 shows Webb with his biggest arsenal of instruments and his biggest band to date. In addition to his Leedy drum set, he has a xylophone, tympani, tubular chimes, plus cowbell, woodblocks, and more.

In spring 1935, Webb got a new set of drums, custom-built by Frank Wolf, founder and owner of Frank Wolf Drummers Supplies, a drum shop that opened around 1910 with a small factory behind it on West 48th Street, a street lined with instrument stores nicknamed "Music Row." "Chick Webb has acquired one of the most elaborate and expensive set of drums in the profesh and looks like a million dollars when lined up in the whole outfit."[24]

Webb was a "gear freak," and Wolf's shop beckoned to drummers. Legendary drummer Billy Gladstone, Radio City's first percussionist and a patented inventor, often collaborated with Wolf on refining drum parts, tuning rods, lugs, and cymbal holders. According to drum historian Chet Falzerano, Webb and Gladstone struck up a friendship at the store, after Webb discovered the "Hand Sock" there, one of Gladstone's most popular inventions. A precursor to the hi-hat, the "Hand Sock" was a small pair of cymbals, mounted on a scissors-like device.

Webb's new bass drum was fourteen by twenty-eight inches—as big as they get—and Webb used timpani heads on the front and back of the drum to create a wide-open sound. His other drumheads were calf-skin, then the standard, and Webb spent a lot of time daily tuning his drums. This set had an emerald green sparkle finish and was mounted on a sliding console that Wolf imported from England. The console had metal arms on each side for Webb's suspended "gooseneck" cymbals. The cymbals were made by Zildjian, whose centuries-old metal-work traditions were passed down to Avedis Zildjian, who emigrated from Turkey to the US in 1929 and set up shop in Massachusetts. Webb also had four small temple blocks mounted on a rack over the bass drum.

None of Webb's drums or accessories were child size or made smaller. His cymbal holders were adjustable, and he used a taller throne seat with a back-rest to support his spine. If anything, Webb's set had to be adjusted to accommodate his strength and powerful attack. The console had additional locking spurs to keep it from moving around and a metal "eye" so he could bolt his bass drum through the front rim to a bandstand or stage.[25] In many photos at this set, Webb looks radiant and comfortable, his body embracing the drums.

A striking caricature of Webb's face, smiling, topped off with a rakish crown, was painted on the bass drum a couple of years later. This portrait was a copy of a drawing of Webb by Barend "Boy" ten Hove, a Dutch cartoonist and illustrator, who belonged to a circle of "hot jazz" lovers in Amsterdam in the 1930s. Ten Hove's stylized drawings of other top Black jazz musicians—Ellington, Fats Waller, Count Basie, Art Tatum, and, later on, Ella Fitzgerald—appeared in Dutch jazz journals and ended up on the walls of the Commodore Record Store, a hub in midtown Manhattan that attracted musicians and jazz lovers. Instrument shops, record stores, and other musical hangouts in midtown Manhattan were still rare oases of integration in the city, with its haphazard racial landscape.

The Gale Agency used ten Hove's images of Webb and Fitzgerald in print ads and posters for events at the Savoy and elsewhere. It's a striking image of Webb as a smiling, confident celebrity, and a rejoinder to racist cartoons of drums and drummers in the media, even in issues of *DownBeat*.[26]

In summer 1938, when Webb and Ella Fitzgerald scored the band's biggest hit record ever with "A-Tisket, A-Tasket," the Gretsch company sought out Webb's endorsement. The company had debuted its "Gretsch-Gladstone" snare in 1937. Gladstone came up with the idea for the new snare because, ever the inventor, he thought the older-style snare drums did not sound crisp enough on live radio and newly improved sound systems in theaters. The Gladstone-Gretsch snare also had a tuning and tension adjusting mechanism that drummers could use without lifting the drum off the stand. It was priced at a hundred dollars, much higher than other top snare drums at thirty-five dollars, and the company's ads appealed to "those artist-drummers everywhere whose high professional attainments entitle them to the finest of instrumental equipment, regardless of price."

Gretsch designed a new custom kit for Webb, the quintessential artist-drummer, which included the premier snare. Webb's new bass drum was emblazoned with a regal-looking crown and Webb's initials. Fred Gretsch, Jr.

(grandson of Fred Gretsch, Sr., the company's founder) said that Webb "was probably the first real drumming star to be promoted as a Gretsch artist." Gretsch-Gladstone drums quickly became the choice of the top Swing Era drummers, and the "paramount endorser among this group was Chick Webb." Webb's set was unique, even for the Gretsch company. "It was a combination of drums and 'traps'—four tuned temple blocks, wood blocks— mounted on a rolling console."[27] The rack over the bass drum was a precursor for the massive racks that contemporary drummers use. Webb's new set included two toms, one on each side of the console. The drums had a lustrous oriental pearl finish, inlayed with green sparkling "chicks" around the center of each drum. Visualize Webb's band at the peak of their success, rising up from the pit on an elevating stage at the Paramount Theater and other top theaters across the county, where they were often the first to break the color line. Audiences went wild as the band slowly came into sight with Webb at his drums, towering above his musicians, whose gleaming white music stands were stenciled with giant sparkling green chicks.

Webb was not only a virtuoso drummer and percussionist. He was an avant-garde modernist who used his instruments to advance technique and style for performing swing rhythms in a big band setting for dancers, still developing as an idiom. He was the first drummer who created a drum part for an entire arrangement, and the first drum soloist. He did so with his extremely melodic playing, his dramatic use of dynamics, and a swath of different sounds, never losing what drummers call "playing time."

Present-day large-ensemble jazz arrangers may include too much detail in notated drum parts, after studying transcribed parts for what Webb played. Jazz educator and drummer Justin DiCioccio explains:

Webb created a drum part, a perfect arrangement [of] what a modern jazz drummers would be given as notated drum part today.... He used all of the different parts of his drums. He played on the bass drum with a stick for effect. On some tunes he'd play the back-beat half on the rim, half on the snare head and use the shaft[butt] of the stick for a high-pitch sound.... He changed cymbal sounds for every soloist.... He was the first guy to do that.... But one of the most important things about his playing was that he listened and anticipated when to fill, when to play a hit and when *not* to play a hit. His listening skills were so great, so intuitive. And he'd do all this and play with dynamic contrast according to the music. Everything Webb played was new and innovative—no one had ever done it yet.[28]

In the early 1930s, Ludwig introduced the hi-hat, and Zildjian introduced a pair of cymbals, and Webb started keeping time on them rather than just on the snare. This was another way that he was a huge influence—to his peers, and to the bebop drummers coming right after him, Kenny Clarke, Art Blakey, and Max Roach. His playing on tunes like "Harlem Congo," "Undecided," "My Wild Irish Rose," and "By Heck" are terrific examples of this and show how Webb breaks up the time over several instruments and occasionally drops well-placed drum "bombs." Before 1938, drummers were either playing on a snare drum, "which is very much New Orleans-type rag-time and all that," said Ulysses Owens, Jr., "or they were using a China cymbal or a little splash cymbal, wood blocks."

> Drummers were still "marching" on a drum set, very snare drum-oriented, they had a regimented kind of sound. Then you get a guy like Chick Webb who goes from playing snare and bass drum, and starts playing all the instruments, and putting together solos. He is one of the first innovators of what is considered the drum solo. On "Harlem Congo," he's playing and catching all these hits, but he's also playing all these intricate rhythms.... He is on top of the band, and the drums are very prominent and that's a new sound.[29]

Jazz scholars often credit Kenny Clarke and Max Roach with making the ride cymbal the primary source for timekeeping instead of the hi-hat or snare. But Clarke, Roach, Art Blakey, and later drum artists like Philly Joe Jones trace that back to Webb, Jo Jones, and Sid Catlett. In 1938, Clarke sometimes played with Teddy Hill's band at the Savoy opposite Webb's band. "Chick was on the left bandstand and we were on the right. So whenever we finished, I would be sitting behind Chick. He always told me, 'Kid, you're making progress.... Keep it up. He would always encourage me.... I was so close to him, and why he liked me God only knows, but like I say, God has always been with me, my whole life."

When asked to elaborate on Webb's playing, Clarke said:

> Oh, Chick, I can't describe Chick. He was so fantastic because I knew that I would never be able to play like Chick—his conception, not his technique

and all. I could always copy his technique. But the way he played, I could never reach that stage—his conceptions, the way he would do things. All I could do was enjoy it and try to get as much out of it as I could. . . . Oh, my God I would stay behind him all day, all night. All night long, I was there. People would ask, "Hey, where's Kenny?" There I'd be, sitting behind Chick.[30]

Jo Jones spoke about his friendship with Webb and his influence in a lengthy, candid interview with another jazz master, bassist Milt Hinton. Jones recounts how he became a drummer, including his own history with a childhood disability. Trying to emulate an uncle lighting a cigar, Jones, then about five years old, lit a rolled-up newspaper, which caught fire. He suffered severe burns all over the right side of his body and didn't fully recover until he was teenager. Then, after picking up enough skills on piano, drums, and even tap dancing, performing was his opportunity, a way for him to earn money and discover the world. Jones spoke at length about the great drummers who preceded him and their styles, techniques, and influences. Just when you think he has omitted someone, Jones says:

Well, you know they always says the first should be last, the last should be first. Speaking about Chick Webb, I don't speak of Chick Webb the drummer, I speak of Chick Webb the epitome. Now, Mr. Chick Webb's sense of timing—he didn't settle for anything but the best. Mr. Chick Webb would get one arrangement, but he would also get two more arrangements. In other words, when he had one arrangement he had three arrangements, because he might play it this way at 9 o'clock, at 12 o'clock he'd play it another way; at 2 o'clock he'd play it another way, the same tune. He had music for all occasions. . . .

We developed a friendship and the man gave me some secrets that I could never divulge because I wouldn't know who to impart them to—even to my own son. This man was very musical. . . . Now you have to have all those two-pound weight sticks to bang, bang, bang. No, no, no no! He played the drums and he played them in tune. . . . When he found out I tuned my drums then he began to talk to me. He gave me some secrets.

This man saw what I was doing with the Basie band. He saw the material I had to work with. He would have loved to have had the material that I had to work with. But without this man's encouragement, without this man telling me what to do, you wouldn't have seen me sitting here today. I was ready to leave and go back. I would probably have taken up some scholastic career, gone back to Omaha, I didn't care. But he encouraged me and he told me of things to come.

There are things he told me I must do that I have never forgotten. He said, "It isn't a form of humility, it's just a form of 'don't lose your naturalness.'... You don't have to do this because somebody else is doing that. You just go and you develop what you develop, and pretty soon you'll have an understanding of Jo Jones, because you have a wealth and I'm looking at that." These are the kind of conversations I had with Mr. Webb. When everybody else was going to after-hours spots I would be with Mr. Webb. He would be talking and I would be listening. He showed me things, and he'd come out and check me out and see what I was doing.... [H]e'd stand around with his little wraparound coat on.[31]

Decades after Webb's death, Jones confided to Hinton: "This man was remarkable. Nobody that played with him appreciated him until after he died. They didn't know what a great man he was. I always wanted to do 'Jo Jones plays "Excerpts of Webb."' ... You have people going with Tommy Dorsey and the Benny Goodman story, and what have you. Why I can't do Mr. Chick Webb?"

Jo Jones never made a movie, but he recorded a brilliant "Excerpt of Webb" on his tribute to Webb and other formative innovator/drummers on his remarkable LP *The Drums*. Jones introduces each segment with his typically terse yet eloquent description, including his nicknames for some of the drummers. He called Sonny Greer "the Empire State Building" and Walter Johnson "Mr. Drums." He then re-creates their style perfectly, with every bass note, cymbal shimmy, and cymbal hit. When Jones gets to his rendition of Chick Webb's playing on "Harlem Congo," he says: "Now he plays a thing that nobody's gotten yet. It goes like this . . ."

"In later years since his death, I have had the pleasure of playing his records and asking some of the young great drummers to try to emulate him. I said, 'Let me hear you play this.' They'd say, 'He did all this?' And I said, "Yes. He did it with a pair of sticks that looked like pencils."[32]

13

Sing Me a Swing Song

This is the one place in New York where the twain does meet—and happily, too. . . . The porter who pulls a Georgia Buggy down Sixth Avenue in the day may be found pushing his boss's daughter here in the night. . . . [T]he dance is the thing. . . . A short frowsy white girl, with left-wing leanings looks up enraptured at a dark companion. . . . Perspiring couples melt into each other as Chick Webb's band wails the strains of some current hit. . . . This is the Home of the Lindy Hop. . . . Charles Buchanan, the manager, surveys the scene with esthetic satisfaction but with economic unhappiness—business is not so flourishing these days. But depression or no depression the boys must have their weekly thing. . . . The charm and patience the hostesses exhibit when carrying around a lumbering partner is something to marvel at. . . . Besides the bands, these girls are the super-saleswomen of the Savoy. . . . I sometimes wonder if these serenely lovely girls ever frown . . . but I guess they remember they are in the "Home of Happy Feet."

—Roi Ottley[1]

Savoy hostess Helen Clarke remembered every step:

You walked under the marquee and down a flight of stairs to the checkroom. Then you'd come back up to the lobby, and up one of two staircases on either side. At the top of the stairs was the entrance to the ballroom. You'd walk through a big door; on either side were potted plants. The dance floor itself ran the entire block, from 140th to 141st Street. Against the walls were booths, and there was beautiful carpeting and wicker lounge chairs with cushions. There was a one-room office stuck in a cubbyhole at the 140th Street side, and next to it was a soda counter. Later in the 1930s, beer came in, but never wine or hard drinks. But most of all, there was the

beautiful dance floor, with three chandeliers over it. It was the most fabulous dance floor in the city.[2]

Between 1933 and 1936, the Savoy Ballroom was ground zero for a cross-
country cultural wave: swing music and swing dance, fusing popular music
and dance moves. As powerful as pounding surf, Swing was foundational to
later popular music and dance moves, which rippled off in its wake starting
in the 1940s, with jump music, Rhythm & Blues, Rock and Roll, the Shag, the
Twist, soul line dancing, disco, and on to contemporary hip-hop, and house
party styles.

The Savoy was home base for Chick Webb's Orchestra and host to other
favorites including the orchestras of Fletcher Henderson, Cab Calloway,
Bennie Moten, and Duke Ellington; younger progressive Black dance bands
like Willie Bryant's and Teddy Hill's; top white bands such as the Casa Loma
Orchestra, Paul Whiteman's, and Guy Lombardo's; and many bands now long
forgotten. The Savoy was also homebase for the top teenage Lindy Hoppers
who lived in Harlem, including Frankie Manning, Norma Miller, Billy and
Willamae Ricker, Mildred Cruse, Leon James, Al Minns, and several others.
These dancers were the influencers of their time, with their intricate, fluid,
elegant, and acrobatic moves. No band was more identified with the Lindy
Hop and Savoy swing than Chick Webb's.

At the Savoy, several codes of behavior went on simultaneously. For one thing,
the Savoy hostesses were carefully supervised and protected. It was a status job,
glamorous and respectable. The hostesses—poised, beautiful, elegant, and alert
for any trouble—would escort single men to the dance floor, show them some
basic steps, and not get ruffled by the men's often clumsy attempts to stay afloat.
It was still a risky business, even in this safe space, and the ballroom's bouncers
were on alert for drunks, rudeness, and harassment and would kick offenders
out the door. These unwritten rules were in play as soon as a single man entered
the ballroom and went to the hostess station to buy dance tickets. Women did
not usually ask men to dance, except in the cordoned-off area (later known
as the "Cat's Corner"), where elite dancers showed off their latest moves. "If a
woman hadn't seen a guy dance," Norma Miller added, "she would check him
out first—she wouldn't just dance with anyone."[3]

The Savoy Ballroom, housed in its block-long edifice—dingy by day, sparkling at night—stood steady as a rock, grounded in the neighborhood and

the community, even as it proudly advertised itself as "World Famous." Moe Gale, Charles Buchanan, and the staff were vigilant—and had to be. By 1934, the ballroom attracted a larger white audience, especially on weekends. Integrated social spaces were still rare, and the city's vice squads were ready to pounce. The Savoy owners and staff ensured that the ballroom was welcoming, safe, and immaculate and took pride in every detail: the decor, the sparkling chandeliers, and, most of all, the Savoy's sprung maple dance floor, which was replaced every few years. Every day a staffer inspected the floor, cleaned it and waxed it down, and removed any chewing gum or other crud with a putty knife. Black communities elsewhere built large nightclubs (in Baltimore) and ballrooms (in Chicago and Pittsburgh) named "Savoy," but the original in Harlem was the biggest, most elaborate, and an international landmark and tourist destination.

Moe Gale's son Richard said that his father grew more confident as his and Buchanan's tactics kept the ballroom open during the Depression. Richard saw his father as "a modest self-effacing man, who always had a fascination for people who were the opposite, who had flamboyance, who were dashing. . . . I'm just speculating as to the psychological causes of my dad wanting to somehow break into the entertainment business. He was fascinated with the glamorous world. And it was quite the antithesis of what he was." At the same time, Moe Gale was a productive and creative businessman. "He was always in motion, he couldn't sit still for a moment. And I think he saw in the entertainment business the perfect outlet for his incredible amount of energy and excitement."

Richard Gale said that the ballroom "became his father's natural habitat," though Moe Gale continued to remain under the radar there. "He often took me along. When we would have a big night we would go up to take the money because we didn't want too much money to collect there. I remember carrying, you know—bags—out of the Savoy. He was very much at home there, and he loved the people. . . . Whoever it was, the doorman, the person taking tickets, my father would have a nice, personal thing to say to that individual. That impressed me—that he liked these people and took a real interest in them. And I think that's a very, very important factor in creating the kind of atmosphere the Savoy had."[4]

Muriel Petioni moved to Harlem from Trinidad with her family in 1919 and was an occasional visitor to the Savoy when she was young (she became a doctor and community health activist whom the *Amsterdam News* called "the mother of medicine in Harlem").[5] Many of her friends were Caribbean immigrants for whom job options were limited, even as the Depression was easing up. They got "live-in jobs" taking care of children, cleaning, and cooking, with days off every Thursday and every other Sunday. "So where do they go to have fun? The Savoy. They put on their nice little fancy dress and go Thursday nights and most of the day on Sunday. The music was going full blast and you could go and you meet people. The girls, maybe the girls didn't know anybody, maybe the boys didn't know anybody, but they'd go and dance. It was very respectful. And of course if they found somebody who was compatible with their style of dancing it was just heaven."[6]

It was heaven, most of the time. It is tempting to romanticize the Savoy as an equalizing space where race didn't matter and people always behaved well and had a great time. But conflicts played out in this public space as elsewhere: band members squabbled, Local 802 reps checked on traveling musicians' transfers, dancers and musicians had rivalries, and couples met and broke up there. Buchanan dealt with numbers runners in the back room, and staff members smuggled hard liquor to heavy-drinking musicians like Sandy Williams and Bobby Stark. Even so, as the 1930s went on, the Savoy generated an ever more diverse social scene. Prominent Black and white musicians and bandleaders, movie and stage stars, politicians and European royalty came to dance and be part of it. It was the place to see and be seen. The Savoy's attraction was its dense intimacy and participatory feeling. It had an inclusive reality, what American studies scholar Sherrie Tucker explores in *Dance Floor Democracy*, her social history of the Hollywood Canteen, another iconic dance space during World War II.[7]

Starting around 1936, when the swing era started to take off nationally, celebrities including Paul Robeson, Joe Louis, Cary Grant, Orson Wells, and Delores Del Rio came to the Savoy frequently. (Norma Miller vividly recalled Del Rio's fabulous hat and white fur stole.) "They knew they were not going to be bothered," said Frankie Manning.

> They came to see the dancers dance, and the dancers came there to dance—they didn't come there to ask people for autographs. . . . I remember seeing Marlene Dietrich with an entourage of maybe ten or fifteen people. And the reason I remember this is because I'd seen her in a movie where she has on this big hat. When she was there at the ballroom, she was dressed like that—with a big hat on. There were a lot of Black celebrities that came there, too. Ethel Waters used to come there frequently, so did Bill Robinson.[8]

It was a thrill to watch the dancers even if you weren't one, to be swooped up by this collective, dynamic life force and the music. In some photos, you see people sitting on the floor on the sidelines, their shoes lined up, watching the dancers go crazy.

Sigmund Galewski, Moe Gale's father, continued to handle the larger financial matters of the Savoy (the lease of the property, taxes, etc.) but hardly ever came to the ballroom except for special dances and events for the employees. According to his son Conrad, he knew the name of only one bandleader—Chick Webb—because Webb was such a fixture there for so many years. In his memoir, Duke Ellington described the mesmerizing way Webb egged on the dancers. "As a drummer, Chick had his own ideas about what he wanted to do. . . . Chick Webb was a dancer-drummer who painted pictures of dances with his drums. . . . The reason why Chick Webb had such control, such command of his audiences at the Savoy Ballroom, was because he was always in communication with the dancers and felt it the way they did. And that is probably the biggest reason why he could cut all the other bands that went in there."[9]

Webb's band, with its propulsive swing beat, and his dancing audience, set off waves that white bands like Benny Goodman's rode into the Swing Era. The dancers demanded it and Webb's band delivered.

The Lindy style was lower to the ground and more hip-centered than other ballroom dances of the time. The basic steps are syncopated and shaped by the eight-count rhythmic framework of the music. The longer phrases allow more time for the "breakaway," when the partners separated for a few more beats, which created room for improvisation. The rhythm didn't confine dancers like the stiffer two-step tempos of the late 1920s did.

At first, Lindy Hop dancers at the Savoy were viewed as disruptors—they took up a lot of physical space on the dance floor. Their movements were larger and freer; limbs went flying. In the late 1920s, the Savoy staff steered the Lindy dancers to a roped off area of the dance floor.

Chick Webb's music was perfect for the Lindy style and became the Savoy's soundtrack. Guitarist Lawrence Lucie, who performed with many bands at the Savoy, said that it was Webb who established the Savoy beat. When Webb's band started playing, "the whole house moved. They'd always win a battle of the bands, because as soon as they started, everybody would get on the floor. Their beat was exactly what the Lindy Hoppers wanted."[10]

Webb's records from 1933 to 1934—"Let's Get Together," "Blue Minor," "Blue Lou," and many others—exemplify the band's compelling sense of swing. As Webb's band solidified and expanded, bringing in a fourth sax and second trombone in 1934, their collective sound was powerful and unified. The spirit of the Chick Webb Orchestra was an outgrowth of Webb himself: happiness, lightness, joy, and dynamism. Richard Gale heard Webb's band as a young boy. "It lifted your spirit to listen to Chick Webb's band. . . . It swung very naturally effortlessly, nothing was forced. . . . [I]t was the perfect band for the Savoy for that era."[11]

Music and dance continued to evolve together. Shorty Snowden, Robert "Rabbit" Taylor, and Marion Edwards (who later married tap dancer Honi Coles) were a few of the Lindy's originators. Their successors—Frankie Manning, Leon James, Billy and Willamae Ricker, Ann Johnson, and Norma Miller—were kids who lived to dance and became a Savoy attraction themselves, with opportunities they'd never dreamed of.

Manning's family joined the Great Migration to Harlem in 1917. As a child, Manning moved to Harlem with his mother and aunt from Jacksonville, Florida. A friend of his mother worked on the luxury Cunard steamships and went back and forth from New York to Florida regularly. He got Manning and his mother free passage, though it meant staying in the segregated staff quarters. Manning's early memory of looking over the rail and watching the rhythmic play of light and shadow on the waves stuck with him all his life.

Manning's love of social dancing started when he was a preteen, watching his mother and her friends dance at parties. Walking home after church one Sunday, he noticed that the Alhambra Ballroom advertised dances for kids his age on Sunday afternoons with live bands. He and a couple of his friends started going, and a few months later they went to check out the Sunday dances at the Renaissance Ballroom, which had a slightly older crowd, thirteen- to eighteen-year-olds. That was where he first saw people dancing the Lindy Hop and "got into it. The Alhambra is like going to elementary school, the Renaissance is like going to high school. Then going to the Savoy is like going to college. Now you're up there in the big time."[12]

Manning and his friends first ventured to the Savoy before Webb's band played there regularly.

> I remember Fess Williams with his high hat and studded coat, and sequined jackets, people were doing the breakaway, the Charleston, the slow drag. . . . Everybody was afraid to go to the Savoy because we didn't think we could

dance well enough yet.... [T]he Savoy was an older crowd, teenagers and up. And we just felt we weren't ready for that. We also figured that if we went to the Savoy, we wouldn't get anybody to dance with! ... It was not the only ballroom in Harlem. There were so many other ballrooms. But the Savoy was *the* ballroom. They had the best bands and the best dancers, and they broadcast from the Savoy every night. It was also the best ballroom in the city! The first time we went, it seemed like everybody on the floor was doing the Lindy Hop, and the band was just swinging, and the people looked like they were just swaying with the rhythm of this band. This is what it's like to do the Lindy!

Soon, Manning and his friends went to the Savoy almost every Sunday nights, and brought the best girl dancers among their group. Manning recalled, "This is what we wanted to see, the guys dancing in the corner.... [I]t's not that people actually formed a circle to keep anybody out. People were standing around to give them room to dance in this circle. We watched these guys dance—and my eyes *popped*!"

Manning and his friends started competing in the Savoy's Lindy Hop contests on Saturday nights. These contests were instrumental in developing the dance, popularizing it, and making it a Savoy attraction. Though anyone could enter these contests, they were fiercely competitive. Again, Ralph Ellison's concept of "antagonistic cooperation" captures the spirit of these contests, which, like musicians' "cutting contests," drove the participants to push their skills and develop their art. Said Manning, "Dancers were friendly with each other until Saturday night when you went into the contest. Then you became enemies, and hit that floor swinging to beat each other."[13]

At the ballroom, Buchanan picked up on trends, and one thing led to another. Tuesday nights were for the 400 Club, a club for the top Lindy dancers, who received a special free ticket. Fewer people crowded the floor, and the dancers had more room to experiment with steps without kicking anybody. Dizzy Gillespie was a member. "I've always been a dancer myself.... Then, the Lindy Hop—I'm an expert at that. I was a member of the 400 Club at the Savoy ballroom. That was a club for dancers. I was the only musician that belonged to it. Members could get in the Savoy free. Tuesday night was exhibition night. I played one set with Teddy Hill's band and danced the next set with the Savoy Sultans."[14] On weekends, Buchanan started giving some of the best Lindy dancers a few dollars to excite the crowd or put on impromptu shows.

Herbert "Whitey" White, one of the Savoy's toughest bouncers, realized he could capitalize on the young dancers' mini-performances. A short, stocky, former pro-boxer and petty gangster, Whitey knew how to corral people into doing things for him.[15]

Initially, Whitey rounded up the top dancers at Buchanan's request. Then he started a side hustle: organizing them into small groups to perform at parties for a few dollars, most of which he would pocket. Soon his Lindy Hop groups were in shows at Harlem theaters, where they were the "new" novelty act. Whitey had no qualms about protecting what he considered his property and even beat up Lindy originators like Shorty Snowden, who performed at the Lafayette Theater. By 1934 all of Harlem was Whitey's turf—which meant all of New York City.

Frankie Manning and Norma Miller would become the most famous and long-lived of Whitey's dancers. A half a century later, a renewal of interest in the Lindy revived their careers as performers and teachers, along with Al Minns and a few others. Manning graduated from high school in 1933 and got a steady job through a friend with a furrier's company. He was making twelve dollars a week, big money in the Depression, and he liked the work. "At that period of time, I just did not think that dancing was going to be my career. I'm a furrier. That's what I wanted to be. I liked the business, I liked what I was doing there. I loved dancing, don't get me wrong. I danced as often as I could—we went to the Savoy all the time. But I didn't think I was a professional. I just thought that dancing was something I did in the ballroom, just dancing and enjoying it."

Norma Miller's family moved to Harlem from Barbados in 1919, before Norma was born, and lived around the block from the Savoy. An avid dancer as a child, she started dancing on the street outside the ballroom; "regulars" started sneaking her into the Savoy when she was a young teenager. She adored her role as a Savoy spokeswoman well into her nineties: "We were the people that were raised with Chick Webb and there was a whole lot of fighting about who was more important: who came to dance to your music, or who played the music?"

After she won a dance contest at the Apollo, Whitey asked her to join his group. She was one of the youngest dancers.

How could we kids turn him down? To us it was like getting selected by Ziegfeld. What were we going to say when the man said he was going to pay us to do what we ordinarily did for free? When we were going to get more money a week than our parents? . . . In those days we used to hang out in the Savoy all day long. We didn't hang out in the streets like most kids. We hung out in the Savoy, playing cards, rehearsing. . . . We were allowed to come to the ballroom everyday because this was the only way Whitey could control what was going on.[16]

At one Savoy contest, Manning and his partner Frieda Washington showed off their newest, most sensational move, in which one dancer threw and flipped their partner way up in the air: the air step. "That was a turning point in the development of the Lindy Hop and ensemble dancing," said Manning. "Before then, the Lindy Hop was considered to be amateur dancing. We'd do it in contests at the Savoy and the Apollo, and maybe at a benefit at a hotel or something. We never considered ourselves professional, and nobody else did either. But when we started doing ensemble dancing and air steps, the Lindy became so exciting that everybody wanted to see it. We started going onto the stage, into nightclubs and theaters, and so on. That's when we became professional."[17]

Not all of Whitey's dealings with his young dancers and teams were honorable; he was not entirely trustworthy and kept most of their earnings. His charges were young, broke, enthusiastic, and easy to take advantage of. But Whitey got them work. When Whitey's two top teams—Leon James and Edith Matthews, and Manning and his partner Maggie McMillan—won first and second place at the first Harvest Moon Ball on August 28, 1935, Whitey jumped right in it. He got them a deal to go to London and perform with Andy Kirk's Orchestra.

Manning told Whitey he did not want to go.

A couple of nights later, Whitey sat waiting for Manning on his stoop. Manning recalled:

Now Whitey is a stone con man. This cat can talk, he could talk blood out of a turnip. . . . But I think I had a little bit of stubborn streak in me. So he's telling me all the benefits of going and what a wonderful thing it is to see Europe, you know, at this age . . . and I'm going for free, they pay my way, and the all this. And I just listened to him talk, and I said, no. I just kept shaking my head. I'm not going, I'm not going.[18]

The third-place winners—Norma Miller and her partner Billy Hill—went to London instead of Frankie. It was Whitey's Lindy Hoppers' first trip abroad. But Whitey was just getting started. He would soon be sending Lindy Hoppers on more trips, getting them into Broadway shows and even into movies, as show-stopping Lindy Hop scenes became must-have acts in Swing Era films and theatrical productions.

"Radio Fans Call Chick Webb Best," reported the *Chicago Defender*. "NBC fans are unanimous in their description and appreciation of Chick Webb's music since his return to Radio City. The heavy fan mail, if boiled down to one word, would read: Wonderful."[19]

As a bandleader, Webb kept scrambling along the thorny pathway toward a wider audience. He'd witnessed the rise to national stardom of Duke Ellington, Cab Calloway, and Louis Armstrong; Ellington and Armstrong were now international stars, too. Webb was poised to expand his audience beyond Harlem. He knew that there was a growing appetite for swing music—categorically called "hot" music by the radio and record industry— among white audiences. Webb's Decca records were not at the top of the charts, or even on the charts—not yet. It didn't matter. The band finally had momentum and staying power. After his winter tours, Webb's NBC radio contract was renewed and he returned to his tri-weekly "live" shows from Radio City, giving him a huge lift in visibility and vistas.

Webb's NBC nationwide spots (on WJZ in New York) and the band's broadcasts from the Savoy kept their music on the air throughout the spring and summer of 1935 and gradually put a spotlight on their new vocalist Ella Fitzgerald. These broadcasts—or at least Webb's music—were well received. One review went: "Chick Webb's band getting plenty of deserved build-up three times a week on NBC studio sustaining.... The band itself is right there, but program is ruined by some smart-alecky white announcer who just doesn't know what it's all about ... more commercial showmanship pfui."[20]

Throughout 1935, Harlem benefits and fundraisers for a wider range of causes were frequent events. Activists, civic leaders, labor unions, leftist groups, and entertainers were among the sponsors and organizers, along with social clubs and church groups. The effects of the Depression in Harlem were systemically longer lasting, and FDR's New Deal did not reach deeply enough into Harlem's need for Black economic relief and development.[21]

On March 19, 1935, long-lasting tensions by Harlem residents erupted against white business owners on 125th Street, who had continued their unequal hiring policies and racial profiling of Black customers in spite of the boycotts of the previous year. White policemen jumped in and arrested a preteen reported for allegedly stealing a penknife in Kress's Department Store. The community exploded, reacting to rumors that the boy was beaten up and even killed, as scores of policemen rushed to the scene. Store windows and doors were smashed at Kress's and nearby businesses, and though the damage did not extend beyond 125th Street, the police responded even more violently. Over the next twenty-four hours, three Black people were killed and two hundred injured. Repercussions, anger, and tensions rippled throughout Harlem for weeks.[22]

Harlem had been home to Webb for almost ten years. He'd seen his neighbors, friends, and colleagues scuffling, celebrating, grieving, and dancing to his music. He was a central player in the community, culturally and socially. By the time of this riot, he and his band had performed frequently for a variety of benefits at the Savoy and in out Harlem.

Webb's and Willie Bryant's bands performed for the first Savoy benefit of the year on January 11, 1935, to support the completion of a monument to the abolitionist John Brown: "The Frederick Douglass chapter of the John Brown Memorial Association will present a benefit program at the Savoy.... Stars will include Buck and Bubbles, the Mills Brothers, Duke Ellington, Claude Hopkins, Tiny Bradshaw and Chick Webb."[23]

In February 1935, after his short winter tour, Webb was a featured guest at a benefit for the Hebrew Actors Union at the New York Coliseum. A small ad in the *New York Times* promised "a galaxy of Broadway and Yiddish stage, screen, night club and sport celebrities including Rudy Vallee, Aby Lyman, Milton Berle, Chick Webb, Ray Noble & others. Tickets $1 in advance/1.25 at door on sale at Leblangs and all Yiddish theaters."[24] Webb's appearance was probably Gale's doing. The Gale Agency's office was located at the RKO building in Radio City—a walk down the hall from top radio executives—giving Gale and Webb opportunities to meet radio stars such as Vallee and Berle. Even so, Webb's presence in this line-up was still unusual for show business.

A few weeks later, Webb participated in a bigger and even more unusual event downtown. On March 31, 1935, he and his rhythm section played at the New York Metropolitan Opera's annual fundraising gala, the first time that "a Negro organization had played from the Met's stage." The Metropolitan

Opera House was then located at 39th Street and Broadway. After the gala's intermission, "Chick Webb and His Orchestra" were part of a spoofed-up variety show entitled "Opera-tunities."[25] Webb and his musicians accompanied a trio of superstar sopranos—Lily Pons, Helen Jepson, and Gladys Swartout—as they clowned through two numbers, "Woodman, Spare That Tree," and "Minnie the Moocher," arranged and conducted by one of the Met's music directors. Were Webb and his musicians on stage and not in the pit due to New York's still largely segregated society and performance practices? Or were they on stage to make more of a sensation? International opera stars were welcome, but it wasn't until 1955 that the acclaimed African American contralto Marian Anderson made her debut with the Metropolitan Opera, paving the way for Leontyne Price and others.[26]

Chick Webb received his most widespread press coverage to date—for a benefit or for any performance. The news spread in the entertainment sections of prominent white and Black newspapers and their syndicates all over the country. The *New York Age* reported: "Chick's splash into grand opera at the Metropolitan Opera house last Sunday night is still the talk of New York." The *Los Angeles Times* picked up the story: "Photographers snapped the Harlemites right and left as Chick's band played 'Minnie the Moocher.'" The next morning the *Daily News* carried a two-page photo spread and the dignified *Herald Tribune* and *New York Times* linked Webb's name with Broadway celebrities. "Up in Harlem Chick was all the rage for blazing a new trail in this fast new company."[27]

Three weeks later, on April 24, Webb's orchestra was part of another celebrity event, a day-to-night roving tour of New York and Harlem ballrooms for a citywide benefit for unemployed members of Local 802. Other featured bands were those led by Paul Whiteman, Rudy Vallee, Guy Lombardo, Fred Waring, Don Redman, and Jimmie Lunceford. This racially mixed group of star bandleaders was a progressive signal for gradual desegregation among New York musicians—on bandstands, at recording sessions and at jam sessions. "The inclusion of Chick in this select company is the second distinct honor to come to the midget bandmaster in two weeks, he having appeared at the benefit of the Metropolitan Opera Co on March 31."[28] The Local 802 benefit started at Roseland and ended fittingly at the Savoy, and wrapped up with a surprise "battle of music" between Webb's band and the Casa Loma Orchestra.

The Casa Loma Orchestra, led by Glen Gray, was then one of the most popular jazz-oriented white big bands in the country, a model for emerging

West Coast bandleader/arranger Gil Evans, among others. In 1935–36, Casa Loma's well-arranged music, even with its stiff rhythms, was very popular with white college audiences.

By this time, Webb had engaged in many Savoy band battles, part of the Savoy's culture from the beginning, but this was his first "battle" with a white band. The *Norfolk Journal & Guide* reported:

> Chick tied up with none other than Casa Loma, Broadway headline organ-
> ization, and the contest was one to raise the hair on end. Chick, fresh from
> his excursion into grand opera less than a month ago, where he had been
> photographed many times by the tabloid newspapers ... sailed into the
> competition as though it was nothing at all. With three spots each week on
> WJZ under his belt and a recent new record at the Greystone Ballroom in
> Detroit, Chick gave Casa Loma and his musicians all he had, and Harlem
> gave him the biggest hand of his career. . . . Casa Loma knew he had been in
> a fight, and he knows Chick has *some* band.[29]

In June 1935 Yankee Stadium hosted an international sports event whose spectacular after-party took place at the Savoy: Joe Louis's boxing cham-pionship bout against Primo Carnera. The match, heavily publicized, had both political and racial overtones. Though Carnera had been living in America for several years, he was the favorite boxer of, and popularly asso-ciated with Benito Mussolini, Italy's prime minister and future dictator.[30] Joe Louis, Black and from Detroit, was nicknamed the Brown Bomber. He was instantly adopted by New York City and Harlem, and was en route to becoming the second Black world champion boxer, after Jack Johnson.

Months before the match, Buchanan had scheduled a huge party at the Savoy in Louis's honor. "Win, Lose or draw," the ad read, "Louis will re-ceive the warmest reception he has received since coming east." At Yankee Stadium, Louis knocked out Carnera in six rounds, though Carnera was five inches taller and sixty-five pounds heavier. All of Harlem celebrated—on the streets, in clubs and bars, and at the Savoy, which was packed for the event, and thousands of people outside surrounding the ballroom. Buchanan kept the ticket prices low—eighty-five cents—to make it pos-sible for "thousands of Harlemites to get a close-up of the new popular idol who brings with him to New York a reputation second to none."[31] Six bands were there to play in Louis's honor: Chick Webb's, Fletcher Henderson's, Teddy Hill's, the San Domingans, Willie Bryant's, and Fred Waring's. Webb met Joe Louis at the Savoy for the first time, and the two forged a lasting friendship.

The year 1935 was punctuated by landmark "firsts" for Webb and the band, and for his new hire, Ella Fitzgerald. On August 10, Webb's band and his vocalists were "the first colored musical outfit to play the Palisades Amusement Park at Fort Lee, New Jersey . . . where they 'swung out' at the big resort Sunday night. . . . The Palisades engagement is Chick's most unique since he played for a benefit at the Metropolitan Opera early last spring."[32] Webb's popularity on radio was key to these appearances and others. But the chart-topping band had yet to come out with a hit record. Still, Webb was heading toward what Mario Bauza called "jumping the fence"—crossing over to a bigger white audience.

Charles Blow, noted journalist and author, wrote about the significance of "firsts" for Black Americans in May 2021, following a year of racial strife, protests, and continued reckonings and challenges. "We celebrate firsts, as we should, I suppose. They reassure us of the notion of relentless American progress. . . . Although they are often also a reminder of how long people had been prohibited or denied. Those firsts carry with their honor a burden: the weight of representing the race. . . . They are simultaneously blazing trail and entering the crucible."[33]

Webb continued crashing through racial barriers as he became a bigger celebrity and media personality. He'd been bearing the "midget maestro" title for a while. He was determined to be celebrated for his band's music, the avant-garde of big band swing.

14

Chasin' the Blues Away

Ella was no great shakes when she started.

—Helen Clarke

Yes, I loved the music, and at the time, I loved the idea of people applauding for me. I don't think I really realized what was happening to me. When you're that young, it happens in such a way that you can't explain it. You don't believe it's happening to you!

—Ella Fitzgerald[1]

In 1935, when Ella Fitzgerald joined Chick Webb's orchestra, a handful of female jazz vocalists with big bands were making more of an impact: Ivie Anderson with Ellington; Mildred Bailey with Casa Loma, the Dorseys, and her husband Red Norvo's band; and Helen Ward with Benny Goodman's new orchestra. Billie Holiday had yet to sing with a big band, but was ascending as a star for her recordings with Teddy Wilson's small band: "I Wished on the Moon," and "What a Little Moonlight Can Do." A few years later, female singers were regular members of otherwise all-male big bands. But in Ella's first two years with Webb, as one of the first swing big-band singers, she had carte blanche developing her style and skills.

Dick Vance, one of Webb's chief arrangers for Ella and lead trumpet for Webb's band from fall 1938 to 1939, first heard Ella with Webb's band in 1935 when he was briefly with one of the alternate bands at the Savoy. "I had never heard anything like her in my life. She was a complete departure from ragtime singers or blues hollerers—they were still the thing that year. Sometimes I'd forget to come in on my own parts! At first, she was just a marvelous singer, and when I came into the band later she was even better. She was one of the most talented people musically I have ever seen."[2]

Vocal arrangements were a small portion of Webb's book when he first hired Ella Fitzgerald. Taft Jordan usually sang an Armstrong-style hit or two over the course of a night, and Charles Linton performed two or three "sweet" numbers during each set, which were still as crowd pleasing as the band's hot numbers, even at the Savoy. Other Black "sweet" male singers were on the scene, and this didn't seem like a passing fad. The *Chicago Defender* reported: "Harlem Chirpers Prove It's Sweet Singing Fans Prefer: Has the present trend of vocalizing turned to sweet singing? . . . No longer do the hoarse and husky voiced singers clutter the airwaves. . . . Today there are sweet, smooth and pleasant voiced singers accompanying our leading orchestras. There is Orlando Robeson, the smooth voiced young man with Claude Hopkins, Harlan Lattimore, the golden tenor with Don Redman, Chuck Richards, the sepia Bing Crosby with the Mills Blues Rhythm Band, Charles Linton, the lilting voiced chap with Chick Webb, and the newest member of the present crop, the high-pitched Herbie Jeffries with Ralph Cooper's Orchestra."[3]

At the same time, audiences at the Savoy really liked Ella Fitzgerald. Webb asked Edgar Sampson and his other arrangers to customize new charts to highlight her in light-hearted material that could swing. He didn't need her to sing slower ballads or torch songs—Linton fulfilled that role.

Ella's first months with Webb's band are as difficult to document as Webb's own early months as a bandleader. Judith Tick's biography of Fitzgerald, *Becoming Ella*, challenges the notion that Ella did not have agency—that she was shy, willing to sing anything, and awkward about finding her role in the band. To jump into this new existence, she had to be confident, single-minded, and as ambitious in her own way as Webb was. Her shyness may have been her cover to keep her own counsel amid waves of advice.

Varying points of view about Ella's introduction to Webb persist in a Rashomon-like kaleidoscope. Drummer Kaiser Marshall had also urged Webb to hire Ella—"You damn fool, you better take her"—along with Bardu Ali, Charles Linton, and Benny Carter, who'd already made their pitches. Once she was in the band, Webb's musicians accepted her and thought of her as a younger sister (they even called her "Sis"). Most of them quickly realized how gifted she was in this relatively new idiom—big band swing plus swing-style vocalist.

Ella Fitzgerald was lucky, after a risky year when she essentially lived on the streets. Moe Gale rented a room for her at the Braddock Hotel on 126th Street, right near the Apollo Theater. Sally Webb helped her find the right clothes and helped coach her about stage presence. She and the Savoy hostesses welcomed Ella into the Savoy "family."

Just as Fitzgerald entered Webb's world, Webb had plenty of airtime on nationwide radio and live Savoy broadcasts, and she was soon heard singing on the air. Radio was the best way that the Gale Agency promoted its Black artists. A Gale Agency press release picked up by several papers boasted: "Radio contacts of Gale, Inc., artists' representatives, have brought national popularity to more colored artists than any other single source." The release mentions that "the Four Ink Spots, Chick Webb and Willie Bryant are examples of performers under Gale's managerial wing who have risen to national fame."[4]

Willie Bryant had been a familiar stage presence in Harlem but had only recently become a bandleader. A handsome loose-limbed six-foot-tall dancer, comedian, and M.C. nicknamed "Long John," Bryant took over the leadership of Lucky Millinder's band after Millinder was asked to lead Mills Blue Rhythm, an Irving Mills ensemble. Bryant had a radio fan club with thousands of followers, the "Hoppin' John Club." The Ink Spots, an early model and forerunner of Black R&B vocal quartets, had some radio success in Indianapolis when they decided to come to New York to seek a recording contract. Moe Gale took great pride in discovering the group and kickstarting their career on national radio.

Gale's contacts in radio helped Gale advance his own career as an artists' manager "specializing" in Black artists. One has to give some credit to Gale for creating opportunities via radio, a career-launching medium, at the same time that he and his company, Gale Inc., perpetuated the "white gatekeeper" role in the entertainment business. The editor of the *Pittsburgh Courier* reported:

> It was at the Savoy that young Gale came in direct contact with colored bands and saw the opportunity for wider popularity than that achieved at the Harlem dance palace. . . . Gale has played his part in discovering new talent, also. He took the "Four Ink Spots" when they were unemployed and built them up to where they demanded $1750 a week, and at the same time filling a 3x a week sustaining program on NBC. . . . He watched Chick Webb grow from Harlem popularity at the Savoy to national fame. And Moe Gale believes there is an even greater future awaiting colored artists.[5]

In May 1935, Webb's band was booked in and out of New York, including dates in Washington, DC, where the band "will be heard by special arrangement of the National Broadcasting Company, on a nationwide hookup from

Washington on his regular Radio City broadcast, May 16. Chick and his Chicks will charm the ether waves from the capital from the regular NBC station there."[6] Although this hook-up was a technical matter—Webb was in the city—it's a testament to his on-air popularity that the network set it up. Webb, like other Black artists, could not get a national sponsor. But Webb's frequent airtime on sustaining programs, and the blizzard of attention from his appearance at the Metropolitan Opera gala, brought him widespread coverage in Black and white newspapers and trade magazines. Between 1935 and 1936, "Stompin' At the Savoy," was played on the air over 10,000 times.[7]

That spring, Webb and his orchestra went to New England—Ella's first trip with the band since she was hired—pinch-hitting for Willie Bryant's band, who left their own tour to perform at Detroit's Greystone Ballroom. On this trip to Boston, Providence, Rhode Island, and Portland, Maine, Webb's audience was mostly white. Ella Fitzgerald started getting her first press notices. The *Pittsburgh Courier* reported: "Not only did Chick's music go over, but the entertainment afforded by Charles Lynton, Ella Fitzgerald and Taft Jordan, members of his barnstorming crew, made the Easterners gape. . . . The people down East were greatly surprised on seeing Chick, but admired him all the more when they got a sample of his rhythm and saw him in action. Now famous as the 'midget' bandmaster, Chick's half-pint size usually sweeps the newcomers off their feet. But they are calmed down in a grand rush when Chick begins waving his baton."[8]

The band's live performances closed the disconnect between Webb, the invisible radio star, and Webb, the "half-pint midget bandmaster." It was surprising for audiences to see Webb in person after only hearing his band on the radio. This was Webb's gift and challenge as he made his way into national fame. One wonders if Webb actually kicked the band off with a baton or the press was exaggerating (not unusual). Webb didn't need to prove his conducting skills with a baton at the Savoy—he led from the drums.

Decca producer Jack Kapp scheduled the band's second recording date for June 12, 1935. Webb's radio fans were hungry for "more recordings of the popular tunes that dance fans have expressed the desire to have in record form so they can be played for small parties in the home whenever fancy dictates."[9]

Ella Fitzgerald made her first recordings at this session: "I'll Chase the Blues Away" and "Love and Kisses," songs she'd been singing at the Savoy, on air, and on the road in the previous weeks. This session also included Charles Linton's first recording for Decca, "Are You Here to Stay?" Though many of Webb's arrangers are not credited in various discographies, this song might have been arranged by Wayman Carver, woodwind player and arranger, who'd joined Webb the previous summer. The clue is the quasi-impressionistic introduction for flute, clarinet, and muted brass. Carver was an accomplished flutist and arranger who wrote several arrangements for Webb's band that included flute parts for himself. These may be the first instance of the use of flute in a jazz band setting. Linton's vibrato on this foxtrot is complemented by the soft backgrounds, and then the horns go all out on the last chorus, the rhythm section crisply swinging along to a Broadway show–style ending. Webb tops off the softer passages with bells, an example of how he likes "sweet" music to sound.

Linton's soft voice and stylized falsetto would soon sound dated compared to Ella Fitzgerald's fresh sound on "I'll Chase the Blues Away." Here is young Ella, her voice light and up in her chest, but singing with the buoyant vibe and bluesy inflections that would be her forte in this phase of her career. She both is in sync with Webb's forward-moving beat and relaxes behind it on some phrases. An Edgar Sampson arrangement, this song still has more of a two-step rhythm than full swing while Fitzgerald sings the verses. Then Taft Jordan plays a full-throated trumpet solo and Elmer Williams fluidly improvises on the bridge as the band kicks into a hard-swinging shout chorus and Webb takes it away. This recording had a choppy beginning and clear glitches, and the band recorded it again in October.[10] Fitzgerald sounds more assured in this second, smoother version, which was released a few weeks later.

Two more tunes were recorded on June 12, 1935, completing Webb's mix of sweet and hot. "Love and Kisses" was a medium swing number for Fitzgerald and a more syrupy offering than "I'll Chase the Blues Away." The second side was Wayman Carver's updated arrangement of "Down Home Rag," by Wilbur Sweatman, a tune first recorded by James Reese Europe's Society Orchestra in 1913. Webb's band takes it at a dizzying tempo, and Carver's arrangement again features the unusual combination of flute and two clarinets for the first reed statement, before the brass section wails out. Tenor saxophonist Elmer Williams plays a magnificent tenor solo on this record, presaging the playing of Ben Webster and others. Pianist Joe Steele breaks into a gorgeous two-fisted stride chorus, followed by clarinetist Pete Clark, as the band launches into a shout chorus. This side is an exciting demonstration of Webb's band transforming a ragtime tune to swing, perfect for the Lindy Hoppers—jazz development in action.

Starting in June 1935, Webb and his band—now a total of sixteen people— went out on a string of one-nighters and short tours. After the June Decca date, they returned to Boston and dates in New England, then west to a fra- ternity dance in Rochester, New York. They went on two- and three-day runs to Pennsylvania and New Jersey resorts, including Asbury Park, which was "sharpening up for the Harlem invasion" of people going on vacation and musicians crisscrossing with each other on the road. At the end of June, Webb's band had a Saturday night booking at the elegant Hershey Park Ballroom, in Hershey, Pennsylvania, a tourist destination even then for its amusement park, swimming pool, and fabulous creamery. The band played the weekend following Benny Goodman's band, on its very first tour, who'd been there midweek. Goodman's and Webb's band were among the first swing dance bands to perform at the Hershey Park Ballroom. Two years later, a constant parade of the top big bands played there.

That summer, Webb's band on stage was enhanced by Fitzgerald, and not just as a singer. Fitzgerald and Charles Linton worked out some banter and, in addition to Bardu Ali's on-stage clowning around, were "supporting humorists and funsters," who supplied "vocals and humorous interpolations."[11]

Percival Outram kept track of Webb's comings and goings that summer in his "Among the Musicians" column. Some of Webb's tour dates did not make much organizational sense. For one thing, Webb's band wasn't playing the Black circuit; the Gale office was trying to get Webb into more white venues, but because the band didn't have a breakout hit record, this strategy was not exactly successful. In late summer Outram reported that Webb and Willie Bryant would "sever booking relations with Gale, Inc." A couple of weeks later Outram wrote that Gale, Inc.'s booking operations were messed up. "Chick Webb is back in town after a short trip in the 'sticks.' . . . Chick and his orchestra left here with the expectation of making a long tour. This is not the only occasion trips of Chick and other bands have been likewise curtailed. What's the trouble with Gale, Inc., their bookers?"[12]

Back in New York, Webb could count on a big audience in Harlem. The band performed at the Savoy for a few nights and packed the Apollo for their debut week, starting July 19. For Webb and Fitzgerald, the Apollo stage would be as essential to their live performances as the Savoy Ballroom. Webb's first booking at the Apollo started a regular cycle there for the band and for Ella. The Harlem Opera House was now only showing movies, and the Apollo, co-managed by Sussman and Schiffman for the time being, was the premier stage-show theater in Harlem.

That July, Ella Fitzgerald's name appeared in the headline of a review for the first time, though it was misleading: "So-so show on Apollo's Stage: Pops and Louis . . . and singing of Fitzgerald Okay." Webb's portion of the show with Fitzgerald was the high point, while tap dance star Alice Whitman got panned, as did an act with live horses on treadmills: "Even Chick steps down from his drums to do a number . . . but it takes Ella Fitzgerald to send the audience into a vociferous display of enthusiasm. Her voice is seemingly tinged with honey and she sings with a rhythmic tempo that puts her over with a bang."[13]

In between trips that summer, Webb's health was reported in the press for the first time in the *New York Age*. Webb went to Johns Hopkins Hospital, Baltimore, for a few days in mid-August for rest and treatment, and "his friends flooded his New York headquarters." Webb's health issues, stemming from having spinal tuberculosis as a child, were not known publicly. It was surprising to his friends and colleagues to see their nonstop leader brought to a halt, even for a couple of days. Webb had not told them about his disease, and later on a couple of sidemen said that Webb told them his spinal deformity was caused by a fall when he was very young.

Webb was soon back on the road to Gary, Indiana, then back to Pittsburgh for Labor Day weekend. The band was returning to that city's active music scene in the Hill District and in nearby Homestead, a big steel town, six miles away. They stayed at the Bailey Hotel, one of Pittsburgh's best hotels for Black travelers; the *Pittsburgh Courier* listed the hotel's guests in its "Society" pages. That weekend, the hotel hosted members of Webb's band, some traveling with their wives, and Ella Fitzgerald, as well as Duke Ellington's former wife, Edna Thompson, and their son, Mercer, then fourteen years old. They were there to see Ellington, whose band was booked at Pittsburgh's Savoy Ballroom for an all-night dance on Labor Day. (Ellington et al. stayed in their Pullman cars at Pittsburgh's Pennsylvania Station.) In the local press, Webb's band generated as much buzz as Ellington's:

The whole town is talking about the coming of Chick Webb and his famous New York broadcasting orchestra. . . . This super attraction, with that personality boy, Chick Webb is sure to attract one of the largest crowds of the present dance season. . . . Not only has Chick Webb one of the best dance bands in the country with some of the nation's best known musicians on his payroll, the atmosphere and setting of the soft lights at Club Mirador provides an alluring spot for Pittsburgh dance lovers.[14]

Ella Fitzgerald's life as a new member of Webb's outfit included getting on a bus with Chick Webb and fifteen male musicians, heading for places she'd never been. Recalling her early time with the band, Fitzgerald said, "When I came up I didn't have anybody. . . . [W]e had to 'raise' my age for me to work at the Savoy. There were certain things I couldn't do, and certain places I couldn't go." At the Savoy, Fitzgerald got out on the dance floor in between numbers. "I used to like to ballroom dance, and they had Whitey's Lindy Hoppers out on the floor between songs, and when I wasn't singing, instead of being up on the bandstand, I'd be on the floor dancing."

She described herself as a tomboy. "The late Chick Webb's wife would do the picking of gowns for me, because that wasn't even on my mind." Arriving somewhere before a dance or a show, "they [Webb's sidemen] used to have to get after me. . . . When we'd get into town, instead of going to sleep, instead of resting like a young lady, I'd be out playing baseball, throwing balls!" When she had free time, "the only thing I had my mind on was playing ball or going to the movies or something like that." On the bandstand, on stage, and in rehearsals, she was a committed young professional. She didn't complain and went along with the crazy schedule: long days on the bus, long nights playing for dancers, and rehearsals and radio shows in between things.[15]

Vocalist Maxine Sullivan, whose light, buoyant style as a swing singer is often compared with Fitzgerald's, was from Homestead, Pennsylvania, where Sally Webb lived before she came to New York. Sullivan worked as a waitress and sang in some of Pittsburgh's popular small clubs. She wasn't quite ready to make the leap into performing professionally, though she got plenty of encouragement, and made her move to New York City in 1937 after connecting with Gladys Mosier, pianist in Ina Rae Hutton's all-female band. Sullivan had already heard Fitzgerald on the radio with Webb's band, due in town for

Labor Day weekend, 1935. She recalled: "I think there was a certain similarity between my style and hers. And of course, that's nothing to wonder about because we are all influenced by other singers. Ella had been a favorite of mine even back in Pittsburgh long before I ever thought I'd be coming to New York."

Sullivan belonged to a young women's social club called the Prosperity Club that sometimes promoted dances.

> It was their [Webb's band's] last night in Pittsburgh. . . . I don't know how we happened to get them, except for the fact that we had a very dynamic president who could get just about anything she wanted. . . . I was waiting tables during this affair. And all of a sudden I heard this voice and I knew it was Ella Fitzgerald. I didn't wait tables for the rest of the night. I went and sat right in front of the band. And I think that was one of the first tours that Ella was out on. This was right after she first got started. Ella was tops then, and she still is as far as I'm concerned.[16]

The popularity of swing music and dance expanded through 1935, then swept across America the following year, crisscrossing audiences, racially and economically. Hit radio broadcasts and swing records fed into this trend, and live swing dance bands started appearing in big cities and small towns, many for the first time. In tobacco barns and elaborate ballrooms, dancers wanted to swing out. More jobs opened up for musicians and singers in new venues. It was an astonishing melting-pot moment in America: young people all over the country started dancing to the same numbers, with regional variations. "Kids in Tennessee shagged to the same music as the 'sharpies' in the Bronx," said bandleader Joe Reichman.[17] Several dance events received national attention. These include the first "Harvest Moon Ball" dance competition at Madison Square Garden in August 1935, when Whitey's Lindy Hoppers swept the top prizes in the Lindy Hop contest, and the Benny Goodman Orchestra's triumphant performance at the Palomar Ballroom in Los Angeles that same month.[18] It was Swing's transformational moment in America, emerging from the harshest years of the Depression.

That moment, when a form of music and dance born in Black communities became America's music, unmasked ethical, racial, and professional issues, which were now visible as everyday examples of appropriation and cultural bias. Which was the most authentic Black band, which the best white band? What did "authentic" even mean? Who would arbitrate the Kingdom of

Swing? While big band swing and the music industry mushroomed, Black bandleaders and musicians had to compete alongside a growing army of newly formed white big bands and cope with shifting alliances among white managers, radio and recording executives, ballroom and theater owners, and music publishers. As Webb's and Ella's stock went up, Chick navigated through this tangle while keeping an eye on the separate unequal growth of the big band business.

Webb's next Decca session was on October 12, 1935. Unsurprisingly, producer Jack Kapp wanted to feature more vocals with greater "hit" potential. Furthermore, Kapp, Gale, and Webb himself were pursued by song publishers, the true engines of the music industry. Four of the five new issued sides were vocals. Fitzgerald's singing is far more assured on the new take of "I'll Chase the Blues Away," and she makes a mundane lyric sound good on "Rhythm and Romance." To contemporary ears, this entire session sounds antithetical to Webb's more forward-thinking instrumental recordings of just a year earlier, which were all jazz-oriented swing tunes. But the recording studio and the bandstand were different worlds for Webb. Like his bandleading peers, he was balancing popular trends—some driven by show and movie music—with jazz arrangements and room for soloists. Webb wanted a hit record as much as Jack Kapp did. "I May Be Wrong, but I Think You're Wonderful," which featured Taft Jordan's Armstrong-inspired singing and trumpet playing, was popular on the bandstand and on the band's live broadcasts, and Webb may have thought it would be a hit.

The other recordings from that session show a confusion of interests; even within one arrangement, the brass sounds choppy, then soars on solos. "Moonlight and Magnolias" sounds even more dated than Linton's first title on Decca from June 1935, "Are You Here to Stay?" But male crooners and "sweet music" didn't disappear with the emergence of swing. Charles Linton was a fixture in the band even as Ella Fitzgerald's growing skills and popularity would eclipse him (he left the band in 1937). Gordon Wright, pseudonym for George Simon, the swing reviewer for *Metronome* and one of Fitzgerald's first champions, offered his brief opinion: "Webb's brass bites terrifically! These sides show the boys are good on sweet, too. Everything right on the nose. Individual passages worth noting are Edgar Sampson's alto going into Ella Fitzgerald's good vocal in 'Rhythm.'"[19]

Two days after the session, Chick and the band went on their first tour south with Ella Fitzgerald. This trip was broken up in odd directions for one-nighters and occasional returns to New York. The band's first stops were familiar ground at the Royal and Strand Theaters in Baltimore, then the Howard in DC, where they were a huge success. Otherwise, they were headed to new cities, new stops, and new venues, some for all-white audiences, thanks to Webb's steady radio presence.

In Baltimore, Webb's band played a Battle of Music at the Strand Theater against his old friend, Bubby Johnson. Johnson had "inherited" Percy Glascoe's popular dance band after Glascoe died in 1932, and was Glascoe's successor as president of the Baltimore's "colored" musicians Local 543. That year Johnson's band also played at the Savoy Ballroom. Webb's band's next stops were Newport News, Virginia (Fitzgerald's birthplace), and then Atlanta, Georgia, where they performed at the Sunset Casino, a popular Black-owned dance pavilion. A local newspaper proudly noted that "Chick Webb Is Bringing Two Atlanta Boys Back to Town This Friday," Pete Clark and Wayman Carver. The Sunset was the "birthplace" of the Lindy for Atlantans, and the club brought in top Black bands like Webb's, which began to attract a young white audience. "Jim Crow laws didn't allow white patrons to enter the club under normal circumstances," wrote Nicole M. Baran. Southern venues devised numerous "White Nights" to accommodate the region's apartheid. A Black-run dance hall might open one night a week for white patrons at higher ticket prices or cordon off a section where they could watch and hear the music.[20] The following week Webb's band played in Nashville at the Nashville Cotton Club, in that city's Black entertainment district, where Ellington had played the previous year.

The Sunset Casino and the Nashville Cotton Club were two stops on the "Chitlin' Circuit," a string of safe harbors in the South for Black entertainers. Many Black musicians hated traveling in the South, with rough conditions for traveling and lodging. Gale did not arrange for Webb's band to have a Pullman car, as Irving Mills did for Ellington and Calloway. That made their travels not just safer and easier; it made quite an impression. Ellington wrote about this in his memoir: "In order to avoid problems, we used to charter two Pullman sleeping cars and a seventy-foot baggage car. Everywhere we went in the South we lived in them. This was our home away from home. Many observers would say, 'Why that's the way the President Travels!' It automatically gained us respect from the natives, and removed the threat of trouble."[21]

At this point in Webb's career his band didn't have an official road manager, and Gale chartered buses. Bardu Ali, so light-skinned that he could pass for white, took on the task of getting gas and sandwiches. According to Sandy Williams, some members of the band got guns for self-protection.

Black bands put up with these trips to the South because they got big audiences, especially when the Swing Era hit its zenith a couple years later. "Dances were packed," Garvin Bushell recalled, referring to southern tours he went on with Webb, Calloway, and others. "We used to play to audiences of 12,000 and 14,000 people." Bushell was with Calloway's band when they performed at a New Orleans racetrack for 11,000 people. "That's just to dance. Then one night in Atlanta with Chick Webb we had 4000 people. Many times we had 3000–4000 people at a dance. If it was a black dance, there would be white spectators who were not allowed to dance. If it was a white dance, then they didn't have black spectators."

Webb got plenty of press coverage during this tour. The *Philadelphia Tribune* reported that Webb's band "captivated" the South: "This diminutive, erudite Chick Webb has made an instant impression on the dance fans on his Dance Merry-go-round. Chick Webb has an exceptionally good band, far cleverer and far beyond musical score. Surprising to note, new appointments, in effects, have far excelled many whose attraction have been public prey. . . . The entertainment is supplied by Chas. Linton and Ella Fitzgerald."[22]

In early November 1935, Webb and the band played a string of one-nighters en route to Chicago, where they performed at Chicago's Savoy Ballroom, one of their last stops before heading back to New York. The event was a Battle of Music with Chicago jazz pioneer Jimmy Noone. An acclaimed New Orleans clarinetists who made his reputation in Chicago clubs in the 1920s, Noone made the transition to swing. As it happened, when Webb arrived in town, Benny Goodman's band was about to have its highly publicized debut at Chicago's Congress Hotel, capping off their successful performance at the Palomar Ballroom in Los Angeles. Over the previous months, Webb's and Goodman's orchestras crisscrossed a few times. During the next year, their intersections—musically and stylistically—would kick off the Swing Era.

15

Jumping the Fence

Here we are the toast of the country, playing exactly the same music we played a few years ago that nobody paid attention to. So there was a big promotion and a big commotion, and everybody's talking about "swing and swing." It's the same music we been playing all along!

—Mario Bauza

In those days, Negro bands were seldom able to break out of the promotional twilight that contained them. "Benny would make it, all right," Chick said. "You know it wouldn't be the same for us."

—Helen Oakley Dance[1]

Webb's band battle with Jimmy Noone at Chicago's Savoy Ballroom didn't get the usual interest from the Black entertainment press, and wasn't advertised much. The event did catch the attention of Helen Oakley, who wrote a lengthy column about Webb for *Tempo Magazine*'s December 1935 issue, under her gender-neutral pen name H. M. Oakley. It's unclear, though, if she made it to the ballroom herself.

"CHICK WEBB, ON WAY TO N.Y., HEARD HERE: It is a long time since there has been a good colored band in Chicago and Chick really made musicians realize how much they had been missing. He was in town one night a couple of weeks . . . and he played at the colored ballroom here, the Savoy on the South Side. Unfortunately, nothing was known about the date until almost the last minute and not many were able to get out, but those who were were very glad afterwards.

It's a splendid band, something on the type of band that Fletcher Henderson always had. They feature good arrangements and swing all the time. Any band could swing if Chick were playing drums. . . . Nearly any drummer that knows will say that it's hard to beat Chick. He has miraculous control over the band and is a great showman into the bargain.

Edgar Sampson, first alto, is exceptionally good and a brilliant arranger. Benny Goodman uses both his compositions and arrangements. Wayman Carver the flautist is one of the best in the business. . . . Brass is good. . . . Chick uses a lot of Fletcher's arrangements and several good ones by Benny Carter. The outstanding point about this band is the fact that they are able to play better commercial and pretty tunes than most white bands. Both Sampson and Carter arrange brilliantly in this manner. And the band is musicianly enough to play them well and with good intonation, but it is on the swing tunes that they sound best, and the supreme kick is Chick himself. This is one of the really better bands today, regardless of color.[2]

Oakley, born in 1913, was then a twenty-two-year-old female jazz critic who would be a jazz pioneer on several fronts, as jazz reviewer, record producer, and zealous promoter of musicians she championed. Adventurous, assertive, and creative, Oakley had been a "hot jazz" follower since she was a young teenager in Toronto; like John Hammond, she was raised in a wealthy privileged family. A bit of a rebel, but with some financial support from her family, she moved to Detroit in 1932 to become a singer, performed there briefly, then went to Chicago to work with a different band. Chicago was still a great city for hearing jazz, even though many of the famous South Side clubs had closed, and Oakley found her "tribe" among jazz musicians and other white "hot" jazz fans. In 1934 she asked the editor of the newly founded *DownBeat* magazine if she could write reviews of bands around town. For its initial issues, *DownBeat* was twelve pages, printed on newsprint, and primarily a networking newsletter for local white dance band musicians. Oakley's column was an asset for *DownBeat* and a terrific outlet for her as a young on-the-scene jazz critic, journalist, and advocate.

In the fall of 1935, Oakley convinced the Congress Hotel's stodgy manager to have a jazz concert/dance featuring Benny Goodman and His Orchestra in the Urban Room, the hotel's seven-hundred-seat auditorium. Goodman's band, glowing from their California triumph and boost in record sales, was already attracting nightly crowds to the Congress Hotel's ballroom. Oakley was an effective organizer, and thanks to her huge social circle, which included debutantes, jazz musicians, fans, and members of the press, the concert was sold out. "In as much as many of those present came to listen as well as to dance it was actually a concert as well as a dance. . . . Benny and his boys were naturally at their superlative best, and hearing them was a thrill that will never be forgotten by those present."[3]

This concert was a game changer for Goodman and his orchestra, and landed them a six-month residency at the Urban Room, though some critics described it as a "cold and dignified" setting for Goodman's music. Goodman's aim for his band was to excel at performing swing tunes and arrangements with plenty of room for virtuosic solos by himself and his musicians, inspired by the community of Black swing bands like Webb's and Fletcher Henderson's.

Webb's band was booked for the rest of 1935 mostly on a familiar circuit: to Club Mirador in Pittsburgh; the Apollo; the Pearl in Philadelphia; followed by Thanksgiving week at the Howard Theater in Washington, DC. The band would spend the holidays back in New York at the Savoy Ballroom, playing for several formal holiday dances and a New Year's Eve gala. The Goodman orchestra's sudden rise in popularity did not escape Webb or his sidemen's notice. Soon the swing craze and ensuing debates about the music were as ubiquitous in music circles as the inevitable commodification of hip-hop decades later.

Goodman, born in Chicago in 1909, was another fiercely ambitious band-leader, whose huge success starting in the mid-1930s eclipsed his and his family's struggles and migration history. His parents were Eastern European Jewish immigrants who married in Baltimore in 1894, then moved to Chicago, where they raised ten children in a string of tenement apartments, barely getting by. Free clarinet lessons set Goodman on his path to hanging out with other young musicians (the Austin High gang), all influenced by Chicago's Black hot jazz scene. In the late 1920s, he was settled in New York playing clarinet in Broadway shows and in radio studio bands, and was the main breadwinner for his mother and several siblings.

Goodman was prodigious, musically curious and had an abiding love of jazz, which in 1934 drove him to start his own jazz-oriented big band. New York contractors increasingly found him difficult to work with, and Goodman lost patience with "play for hire" studio dates. Starting in December 1934, his band's "hot" dance portion of the national hit radio show *Let's Dance* catalyzed his bandleading career.

Nobody questioned Goodman's choice to play hot swing with his own big band instead of earning excellent money playing "sweet" music in hotels, or as a studio and Broadway show musician—a career path still denied to Black musicians in New York City. Goodman now experienced the challenges of being a bandleader, but he had it easier than Webb. Goodman had a dedicated support team: manager/record producer/friend John Hammond, his new booking agent Willard Alexander, and reviewer and now concert promoter Helen Oakley. They were all as determined for his success as he was. There was no white burden of representation in the music business.

For his band, Goodman hired young studio and dance band and studio musicians who, like him, were meticulous players and loved jazz. One of his star attractions was drummer Gene Krupa.

Krupa was also from a large Jewish immigrant family and, like Goodman, was raised in the Midwest and started earning money as a teenage musician. After a couple of attempts, Hammond finally persuaded Krupa to join Goodman's band in early 1935. Hammond had an enormous influence on Goodman's career and an outsized role—career making and/or breaking—for other jazz bandleaders and musicians, Black and white. Without Krupa, Goodman's band would not have had the dynamic drive that gave the band its swinging joyful unity.

Webb and Goodman shared a problem: needing new arrangements for their radio shows on a weekly, sometimes daily, basis. Hammond helped Goodman hire top Black arrangers to develop a more authentic jazz sound—to be blunt, to sound more like a Black band. Goodman had another advantage. NBC gave him an arranging budget for eight new charts a week for the *Let's Dance* show. Webb had to pay for arrangements on his own.

Saxophonist/arranger Benny Carter started writing charts for Goodman shortly after Goodman's band started performing live on *Let's Dance*: "Benny Carter was discovered last week as the mystery man who makes intricate musical numbers for Goodman's band featured on the 'Let's Dance' program.... The genial Benny [Carter] has been with the aggregation more than four months. He divides his time now between arranging and recording. And he is doing well at both, he reports. His band is missed along Broadway and up Harlem Way."[4]

Edgar Sampson, still Webb's chief arranger, also wrote some charts for Goodman around this time. So did Fletcher Henderson and his younger brother Horace, and Jimmy Mundy, arranger for the orchestras of Claude Hopkins and Earl Hines. Goodman also had several white arrangers writing for him, including George Bassman, Gordon Jenkins, Dean Kincaide, and Spuds Murphy, all considered the best in the profession. But Hammond leaned on Goodman to use more of Fletcher Henderson's arrangements, convinced that these would make Goodman's band stand apart.

By now, Henderson's own band had broken up and Henderson himself had doubts about writing for Goodman. As Henderson biographer Jeff Magee explains, Henderson was "being asked to arrange for a band that he would not lead or perform with, and that featured much less improvising. These conditions—along with his reflexive resistance to highly structured, white-controlled milieu—undoubtedly intensified Henderson's well-known diffidence." For Goodman's *Let's Dance* portions and then his *Camel Caravan* radio show in 1936, Henderson was paid per arrangement—37.50 dollars per chart, as per Goodman's network allowance. Henderson's arrangements for Goodman resulted in some of the Goodman band's most inspired performances: "Blue Skies," "Sometimes I'm Happy," "King Porter Stomp," and "Christopher Columbus," a mix of popular songs and powerful swing "flag-wavers." For better or worse, Henderson's arrangements contributed to Goodman's being crowned the "King of Swing."[5]

A growing young white fan base loved Goodman and his attractive uniformed ensemble. Goodman was not oblivious to race issues and was aware that his band's new success was transformative: he was committed to playing music with a "jazz" orientation that swung and had its roots in Black musical culture. Further, Goodman would soon advance integration among jazz musicians on the bandstand and recording studio—incrementally, not wanting to rock the societal boat.[6] Goodman's workaround to get the sound and spirit he was after was to hire Black arrangers. As biographer and jazz historian Gary Giddins pointed out that Webb's recordings of Sampson's signature tunes for his band, like "Stompin' at the Savoy" and "Don't Be That Way," "caused small ripples, while cover versions by the Goodman orchestra caused tidal waves." The same would be true of Goodman's covers of Fletcher Henderson's "King Porter Stomp" and his band's showstopper "Sing, Sing, Sing." Said Oakley, "One thing about Benny Goodman: he didn't have any color bias. The only bias he had was a music bias."[7]

Webb and Goodman were both exemplars of musical racial fluidity in unexpected ways. Webb was after a particular sound too, one that was also a fusion of styles and mix of programming: of popular songs and hot swing arrangements by his arrangers—Sampson, Benny Carter, Charlie Dixon, and the Henderson brothers. Webb wanted to reach a broader audience and, like Goodman, held his musicians to really high standards. Many reviewers of the time commented on Webb's musicians' "great intonation," not a typical comment from entertainment reporters.

Webb and his musicians, though far from their starvation days, were still not making equal pay with the likes of Goodman. Webb had weathered a lot in his ten years as a bandleader. He'd lost several key musicians to Ellington and Henderson, or saw them launch their own bands. Some things were hard for him to take. Edgar Sampson, who'd helped Webb craft the band's sound, left Webb's band in the summer of 1936. Sampson had already been writing some charts for Goodman, who wanted more of them, and felt confident about going freelance. He also got assignments from the popular bandleader and contractor Dick Himber, the Dorseys, Red Norvo, and others as the Swing Era really started churning.

Tempo reported in September 1936: "Edgar Sampson, the Iron Man in Chick Webb's band, has slipped out of his seat in the reed section to freelance as an arranger, mostly for Dick Himber, although he had been doing some orchestration for Red Norvo, too. Webb, to fill the spot, has engaged the capable Hilton Jefferson on alto, and while he can fill the instrumental section admirably, there is no doubt but that Sampson's scoring will be missed. Webb anticipates to use Sampson on a freelance basis."[8]

Sampson still performed with the band through part of that fall, alternating with Jefferson on occasion. Webb wouldn't hold anyone back. He continued to use Sampson's charts on the bandstand and on broadcasts for years; he also turned two of Sampson's most popular instrumentals into vocal features for Ella: "Stompin' at the Savoy" and "Don't Be That Way." Both tunes became Swing Era anthems for Benny Goodman's Orchestra and other big bands to come, and Ella Fitzgerald sang these songs for decades.

Webb and his band kept up their intense pace, and in 1936 there were several personnel changes, including Sampson, who was also Webb's lead alto player, and tenor saxophonist Elmer Williams, one of his most inventive soloists. Over those months Webb hired Teddy McRae, Louis Jordan, and Al Feldman (later known as Van Alexander), all of whom helped push forward Webb's ever-increasing commercial appeal. McRae was an excellent all-around tenor player and composer/arranger with connections in music publishing; he became the band's music director later that year. Jordan filled out Webb's reed section on alto and baritone saxophone, and was also an excellent vocalist with soulful, forward-moving phrasing similar to Ella's. Feldman seemed the least likely to have a huge role in Webb's band. He was a white college student from Washington Heights with a musical background. He had been coming to the Savoy with his friends since high school and had hazy ambitions to become an arranger.

In early 1936, McRae was in New York City, playing with a group at a bar in Harlem. He'd been on the road with bandleader Lil Armstrong, who had decided to stop touring and stay in New York. McRae had been involved with other bands and played on a couple of notable recordings with pianist Teddy Wilson as leader, including sides with Billie Holiday ("Life Begins When You're in Love)" and with Ella Fitzgerald ("My Melancholy Baby" and "All My Life") before Ella had her own contract with Decca.[9]

McRae remembers Bardu Ali rushing into the bar where he was playing to tell him that Chick wanted to see him. Webb had told McRae earlier on that if Elmer Williams ever left the band, McRae was his next tenor player. "He always kept me in mind. . . . If Elmer leaves, you've got the job. I'd always say 'OK,' and laugh. That was during the lean years, when he still wasn't doing so good. We used to hang out together when he was doing these gigs, playing at the Alhambra. He hadn't moved into the Savoy yet."

Elmer Williams didn't want to go back on the road again, and McRae, knowing that tours were scheduled, told Webb that he'd need to speak with his wife. "I told my wife that Chick wanted to go on the road, then I talked to Chick. He said, 'Got any money?' I said, 'Yeah, I just came off the road with Lil Armstrong.' He said, 'Give me $36!' This was for joining Chick's band! Thirty-six dollars!"[10]

Webb told McRae that the band would only be out on tour for a month or two. As things turned out, the band toured for most of the summer and fall of 1936. Some trips were just for a few days, then back to New York; spouses joined Webb's entourage some weekends. McRae named some stops: "Baltimore, Washington, Virginia, on the beach there, at a school. We'd go on down to Atlanta, Charleston, all the way around. We played all the way down to Florida. Came back up through Cincinnati, Chicago. . . . Coming back to New York, we'd probably go to Detroit, Cleveland."[11]

Louis Jordan's hiring was typical of the "musical chairs" switches going on in all the top big bands. Webb mostly hired people he'd known or worked with previously, and now had a spot for, or musicians who had a good reputation. Jordan was all of that.

Jordan, a violinist and alto player, came from a small town in Arkansas and had studied music with his father, a music teacher and local band-leader. Jordan first worked in vaudeville and minstrel shows, then made his way to Philadelphia, where he joined Charlie Gaines's Philadelphia-based ensemble. Gaines had worked briefly with Louis Armstrong at the end of 1932 and made a few recordings on Victor that included Jordan.

Being around Louis Armstrong was a formative experience for Jordan and he learned a lot from Armstrong's musicianship and stagecraft. In the next few years Jordan worked with several groups, led by Leroy "Stuff" Smith, Clarence Williams, and others. Jordan sang on Williams's record, "I Can't Dance, I've Got Ants in My Pants," a surprise novelty hit that other bands covered, including Webb's.

In spring 1936 Jordan was with Smith's band when it stopped performing for a while. Ralph Cooper hired Jordan for the Apollo house band as a saxophonist when one of his musicians became ill. Meanwhile, a couple of other people in Webb's band came and went. Taft Jordan left briefly after a spat, and Hilton Jefferson, a key player with Webb in the early 1930s, rejoined Webb when Sampson left, then rejoined Fletcher Henderson, one of many top bands Jefferson worked with in the 1930s.

Webb heard about Louis Jordan from Ralph Cooper and hired him after Jordan finally got his Local 802 card. Jordan played the lead alto parts, but after a few weeks, McRae decided that Jordan was not a strong enough lead player. Clarinetist Peter Clark filled in on alto, and Jordan was switched to the baritone spot. Jordan was a bit of a ham, and audiences liked his jokey banter and clowning.

Jordan's first year with the band was mostly smooth sailing, and he was thrilled to be a member as Webb's popularity kept growing. As with Louis Armstrong, Jordan learned a lot as Webb moved into the top echelons of Black bandleaders. No one in Webb's band foresaw Jordan's own tremendous success as a bandleader with the Tympany Five, which he formed after leaving Webb in 1938. Nor did they foresee the problems that Jordan would cause in Webb's band before he left. Webb had taken a chance on Jordan, as he had with others. Ella was one of them. So was Al Feldman.

In April 1936, this item appeared in *Metronome*: "Al Feldman is making some swell arrangements for Chick Webb. Studies with Otto Cesana."[12] No one was more incredulous than Feldman himself when Webb hired him to write some arrangements. Feldman, then twenty-one, had idolized the drummer and his band's music since high school, when he and friends started going to the Savoy. His mother, a classical pianist, taught Feldman to play piano, "the beginning of my musical entrance into the world." Feldman (born in 1915, as Alexander Van Vliet Feldman) changed his name to Van Alexander—a less Jewish-sounding name—in 1939, a year after his arrangement for Ella Fitzgerald of "A-Tisket, A-Tasket" became a smash hit record, finally hurtling Webb, Ella, and Webb's band to stardom.

Van Alexander lived to be almost a hundred years old, and still thrilled when speaking of how he got his start with Webb. "I was interested in the great music of all the Black bands that played at the Savoy and would go as often as I could—three, four times a week. I'd stand on the side of one of the musicians and look at the music as he was playing it and, and say, 'Geez, look how those notes are written and how he interprets the rhythm. That was the fascinating thing for me. I couldn't understand how these fellows could read these orchestrations and arrangements."[13]

Alexander had fooled around arranging for a little band in high school, and when he heard the bands at the Savoy he wanted to try his hand at big band arranging. His mother insisted that he needed more formal training if he was serious, and he studied classical orchestration with Otto Cesana, who taught him about "strings and woodwinds and horns and everything."

> It was pretty competitive in those days. . . . Chick Webb was the mainstay at the Savoy. And I would stand in front of that band night after night. . . . After being there, you know, weeks at a time, I'd struck up sort of a nodding acquaintance with Chick. Like he'd say, "Hi, kid. Here again, huh?" And I'd say, "Yeah. I can't get enough." And we had this nodding and talking thing, and then during the break he'd come over to the table and we'd sit down and have a Coca-Cola or something together. I never saw him drink or smoke. . . . It was a great thing for me. . . . [W]ithout him, I don't know where I'd have been.

One night Alexander got more confident:

> "Chick, I have an arrangement at home that I think might fit your orchestra. Would you be interested in trying to rehearse it?" He says, "Sure, kid. Bring it, bring it back Friday night." . . . Well, I was bluffing, I didn't have any arrangement. So I went home and wrote an arrangement of "Keeping Out of Mischief Now." . . . [T]hat was my first arrangement for a band with a full five brass and four saxes and four rhythm. And so with a little fear and trepidation I put this thing together and I went down to the Savoy that following Friday.

Alexander didn't realize that Webb's rehearsals started at 1:30 or 2 a.m., after the band was done performing. He also didn't realize that Webb's top arrangers had their turns first: Edgar Sampson, Charlie Dixon, and Wayman Carver.

> I didn't get to hear my thing until about 4:00 in the morning. My mother was frantic. She called the police, and told them, "My son is in Harlem at the Savoy Ballroom. What can they be doing this time of the morning?" Anyhow they finally got to my arrangement, and the guys liked it and Chick liked it, and he says, "Wait a minute. I'm going to give you some money." ... So, he called Charlie Buchanan, the manager, over and said, "Give the kid $10." Well, I was on Cloud Nine. I'd sold my first arrangement and that was really the beginning of my career. Chick gave me a chance and I'll never forget him for it.

It was unusual in those days for a Black bandleader or musician to employ a white arranger. Increasingly, white bandleaders were hiring Black arrangers to write for them, largely due to Benny Goodman's hit records with arrangements by Edgar Sampson, Benny Carter, and Fletcher Henderson. Alexander said, "I wasn't the first white arranger that ever worked for a Black band but maybe the first successful one, I don't know."

Besides Webb's huge library of arrangements, Alexander thought Webb's brass section helped make the band unique. "He had five brass, three trumpets and two trombones. We called them The Five Horsemen. They had a great sound. They had a good lead trumpet player, Mario Bauza, and he had a good fat sound so that the brass section never sounded undernourished, so to speak. And the saxophones all doubled on clarinets and three of them played flute." Count Basie once said that Webb's band was so great because he had the arrangers writing for "flutes and toots and boots."

Starting in spring 1936, Webb assigned Alexander to concentrate on writing arrangements for Ella.

> I get a tingle because that was the beginning of my career and I guess it was all mapped out for me because one thing led to another.... I don't think she even had arrangements made at the time. She was singing, just winging it with the band.... But after I sold my first thing to Chick, he asked me to write her vocal arrangements for the recordings. I was thrilled. By that time I knew her voice and I knew her range and I knew what she could do. She always had something a little extra—a little variation. She was like

an instrument, you know, she improvised a lot, she started to scat sing. Goodness gracious, that was marvelous.

A couple of his best early arrangements for Fitzgerald were recorded on June 2, 1936: "Sing Me a Swing Song" and "A Little Bit Later On." Alexander remembers his first big hit for her was "Rock It for Me." "After that she had quite a few little hit records, 'Organ Grinder's Swing,' and 'Dipsy Doodle.' Moe Gale gave me a deal where I would do three arrangements a week for the band and he paid me $75. That would be $25 each arrangement but that included all the copying also. I was happy to do it and $75 a week in those days was pretty, pretty good money."[14]

> The only way you could make decent money was if you jumped the fence, like they used to say. You jump the fence and stop looking. So, he [Webb] had to make a transition after many setbacks. . . . He was entertaining properly with all these popular tunes and so forth. You play beautiful soft arrangements, now and then you throw in one of the jazz numbers and go back to the thing like a show. And that's how the band got to be national. Up 'til then it was strictly a Savoy band.
> —Mario Bauza[15]

Webb was ambitious; he'd always wanted to jump the fence. The fence was moveable, though; it meant different things at different times for different audiences. As arranger Dick Vance said, the key to a Black band's success was playing in a place with a radio wire or making a hit record. Those were the paths to jumping the fence, especially during a time when hosting dance parties at home was what a lot of people did. The popularity of Goodman's *Let's Dance* and *Camel Caravan* shows and Martin Block's *Make Believe Ballroom* show on WNEW attests to that.

The racial divide in radio was a fence too. Black bandleaders at that time could not get national sponsors. Advertising policies in southern states meant apartheid in the radio industry up north; national sponsors still feared losing white audiences in the South. Stations that aired sustaining programs did so à la carte. In the same way that Fletcher Henderson's band would never have been hired for the *Let's Dance* show, neither could Webb's band get a national sponsor, despite the popularity of his NBC sustaining broadcasts. Magee explained: "A regular, sponsored network show stood on an entirely different level of the music business than on-location broadcasts. In that context, no Black band could entertain the possibility of having a commercially sponsored radio network program. In the logic of institutional racism of the era, a Black band on such a program would signify the denial of white talent."[16]

Moe Gale had been successful at getting radio contracts for Webb on regular sustaining broadcasts on NBC at the Savoy and at Radio City a few times a week. In winter 1936, Gale leveraged his good relationships with the network into another sustaining show: a Black radio variety show called *Gems of Color*, which was renamed the *Good Time Society* in early 1937. The initial shows aired in New York from 10:00 to 10:30 p.m. and were picked up by stations in eastern and midwestern cities. "On April 18, 1936, Radio needed a real jam session to keep pace with the high-powered swing music. Heaven knows it has it now in that 'Gems of Color' show. Chick Webb's band, the Ink Spots, the Juanita Hall Choir plus Ella Fitzgerald (and she's dynamite) go to town with all the valves wide open."

The show got off to a rocky start and changed M.C.s and formats a couple of times. Juano Hernandez, Harlem actor and entertainer, was eventually chosen as the host, using a character he created, "John Henry," as M.C. and he wrote a weekly script that gave the cast a few speaking lines. Soon the show had a coast-to-coast hook-up. *Pittsburgh Courier* columnist Billy Rowe pronounced this version a success: "In the annals this present outfit for colored talent has reached a new milestone, for it is seldom, even in this town, that a brother of color is given such a chance. With the chance both Chick Webb and John Henry have done the race proud." Hernandez frequently used this introduction: "This is the Good Time Society, the imperial potentate speaking. We are calling on all the stations of the Good Time Society to tune in with us tonight. Stand by while we get station WEBB."

The *Good Time Society* had detractors, including Rowe's colleague Porter Roberts, who thought the show was a sham to please "ofays": "That 'Good Time Society' radio program has the same effect on intelligent colored people as 'Amos and Andy.' And boy, that's some letdown. . . . [T]hat's another way of saying the program is PUTRID."[17]

Roberts's columns were candid, often sarcastic. But many of them applauded the expanded popularity of bands like Webb's, Jimmie Lunceford's, and Ellington's, and praised their artistic integrity. At the same time Porter skewered the "illogic" of the racist divide and perpetual inequities in the entertainment business. His insightful critiques increased with the exploding popularity of swing.

Meanwhile, Teddy McRae helped Webb jump the fence. McRae was a terrific asset for Webb, not just as saxophonist but as a new music director he could trust. He was smart, sharp, and organized, and an aspiring song-writer and arranger. He knew the music publishing business and may have been more assertive with music publishers than Edgar Sampson earlier on (Sampson's nickname was "The Lamb"). McRae had become friendly with the big music publisher Jack Robbins, who proposed to give Webb songs for the band's live Saturday night broadcasts from the Savoy, and said he would pay for the arrangements.

They did a trial the following week, and after Robbins heard the broad-cast, he called McRae. "Everybody had a song for a picture on Paramount, United Artists, show tunes, big productions. Jack said, 'You have the best thing in the country. I'll give you a deal. We'll take care of all the arrangements, and all you got to do is broadcast. We're going to give you the hit songs that come out before anybody gets the hit songs, because we feel that Ella Fitzgerald is the hottest thing right now. We think she is really going to be tops.'"

"He was looking way ahead of what I'm thinking about," said McRae. "I'm just thinking, well, here is a guy that's going to give us some music. I told Chick Webb, 'Look, Jack wants to give us a deal. He's going to give us all the top songs, and whatever the arrangements cost they'll absorb it themselves.'" Robbins Music had song pluggers running around all over the country, and this was another way their songs could get plugged—the movies. Jack Robbins was on to this before anyone else. The company also rushed out hits as published sheet music, giving it several revenue streams.

McRae exulted: "He [Robbins] began to give us all the top songs. And we began to move Ella out of the other class of singing. We'd move her into pop." Webb was thrilled; this was one of the breaks he'd been hoping for. "We would rehearse an arrangement of a pop song. Chick would be sitting up there playing cards. Then he'd say, 'Okay, Ella, we're ready.' She'd come over and we'd hand her the sheet. She could sightread better than anybody, of all the singers. She was really fast. We'd be rehearsing the arrangement, she'd be listening. . . . She'd say, 'Okay, y'all ready for me?' 'Yeah!'"

By now, all the top publishers were giving Webb songs for Ella—Mills Music, Robbins, Shapiro-Bernstein. "Everybody was trying to get Ella to do the top hit songs. . . . Jack Robbins gave us this song 'Goodnight My Love.' He gave us that song for Ella before he gave it to anyone else. . . . And when Ella did this song, whoever came up behind her—they were just catching up."[18]

In the fall of 1936, Webb's interactions with Benny Goodman became more intertwined and conflicted, much of it due to that one song. Goodman was now paying close attention to Ella Fitzgerald, who was becoming a star attraction herself. Her 1936 recordings yielded the band's biggest hits so far: "Sing Me a Swing Song" and "You'll Have to Swing It (Mr. Paganini)." "Goodnight My Love," was a hit at the Savoy Ballroom, and on Webb's live radio broadcasts. In November 1936, Goodman's regular singer Helen Ward was on a short break while finalizing her divorce. He invited Ella to record "Goodnight My Love" and two other songs at his next RCA Victor session, and to sing with his band on his *Camel Caravan* show, at Radio City. These offers were thrilling and unexpected. "I nearly swooned," Fitzgerald said later. The result, Fitzgerald's biographer Judith Tick wrote, "plunged Fitzgerald into the middle of legal, professional and ethical disputes between two bandleaders and two record companies triggered by her improbable success with a song written for Shirley Temple." "Goodnight My Love" was written by Mack Gordon and Harry Revel for *Stowaway*, a movie featuring the child star as an orphaned stowaway, due for release at the end of December.[19]

Fitzgerald recorded it with Goodman on November 5, 1936, along with "Take Another Guess" (which she would record with Webb in January 1937) and "Did You Mean It?" RCA Victor released the latter title and "Goodnight My Love" on November 25.

According to Webb's contract with Decca, Fitzgerald could not record for another record label. Victor tried to skirt the legal issue by taking her name off the record (her name appears as "Helen Fitzgerald" on the session notes). "Goodnight My Love," minus Ella's name on the label, was soon a hit on the charts for "radio plugs and disk sales in regional record stores." The song's tie-in with *Stowaway* "helped Ella and Benny's version (minus her name and the only version being sold at that point) ascend to the top of the radio show, 'Your Hit Parade.' She could hope that most people realized she was the vocalist, and it seems likely that was the case—at least in the business." Tick explained.[20] The record was taken out of distribution and became a collector's item, until it was reissued by Victor in the 1960s on a Benny Goodman LP, with Ella Fitzgerald's correct attribution.

Things grew even more complicated for Fitzgerald after she performed on Goodman's *Camel Caravan* show on November 10, 1936. This was a huge coup for her, and Goodman loved how she sounded with his band. In December, Goodman attempted to buy out Fitzgerald's contract with Webb, reportedly for five thousand dollars. Webb, Webb's sidemen, and Gale were outraged, as were several outspoken Black journalists. Though Goodman had advanced the public breakdown of the color bar in music by hiring pianist Teddy Wilson and vibraphonist Lionel Hampton earlier in 1936, he did so hesitantly at first, and only performed with them on stage during "intermission." Goodman's interest in hiring Fitzgerald put her in an incredibly conflicted position—and in uncharted territory: for a young Black female singer to be featured with the most popular white swing band in the country, and to betray Webb, who'd hired her when no one else would. It was a flagrant example of how well-meaning "color-blind" hiring in the music industry reinforced a huge power imbalance.

Porter Roberts wrote:

Dear Readers: Did you ever hear of a boomerang? Get this: Benny Goodman went to Harlem to find a swing band to pattern his band after. He picked Chick Webb's band. And with the assistance of colored arrangers like Benny Carter and Edgar Sampson he developed a good "swing band" (not yet as good as Chick Webb's). . . . Still not enough! A few days ago he is said to have offered Chick Webb $5000 to release Ella Fitzgerald. . . . To this column, Ella Fitzgerald tops the women's division of swing singers. Uh, huh, that's why Benny wanted her as part of his band. I am really glad to see Teddy Wilson and Lionel Hampton working. They must eat, don't y' know. But what if other white bandleaders start raiding our bands for the best musicians in the world? . . . Picture the best colored bands becoming "farms or sandlots" with the big white bandleaders always stepping in to "buy" the best men! . . . Dear Reader, a Boomerang is a peculiar shaped little missile you can throw away with a smile. But it will return and knock a lump on your head if you don't watch it![21]

Under pressure and personally conflicted, Ella disappeared from public view for several days. When she returned she refused to answer questions about the episode. If there was any silver lining, it was that Jack Kapp woke up and took more notice of Webb's and Fitzgerald's increasing popularity on the airwaves. Decca extended its contract with Webb, and Ella Fitzgerald now had her own contract with the label.

A year later, in November of 1937, Fitzgerald was voted the Number One Female Vocalist in *DownBeat* and *Metronome* readers' polls. Chick was increasingly criticized for featuring Ella more prominently—by the press, and by some of his own musicians. Chick knew he was leading the band in a more commercial direction, but that's what he wanted: the band was finally achieving his dreams. Teddy McRae said, "Chick was a self-made man, and he knew where he wanted to go—next year, and the next year. He was on his way."[22]

16
Vote for Mr. Rhythm

In 1937, Webb, Ella, and the band kept hitting new strides, as Ella's voice, style, and buoyant swing phrasing grew more confident and unique. The band was booked constantly, and between trips and events they returned triumphantly to the Savoy Ballroom. Chick and Ella were getting eight radio slots a week, more than any other big band at the time: the March issue of *DownBeat* reported that "CHICK WEBB receives 5000 letters a Week." That spring the band's music was broadcast on a new BBC show in the UK, *America Dances—Swing Music No. 2.*[1]

For white jazz critics of that day and years after, "commercial" and "popular" were terms of opprobrium. Webb was increasingly criticized for going "commercial" from some of the same critics who'd previously raved about his band's music, particularly John Hammond and Leonard Feather. Now Webb was up against the "War of the Purists." For Hammond, a political activist and cultural voice of the Popular Front, swing music and jazz were not just entertainment but, as cultural historian John Gennari points out, "had deep cultural and historical significance that had to be understood and honored, and [it] was an important force for positive social change." White critics were dumbfounded that swing dancers at the Savoy and other ballrooms didn't treat the musicians as artists. "Why aren't they more interested in the music for its own sake?" Gennari imagines Hammond and Feather asking. Hammond in 1937 was ever more of a jazz "influencer," with an excellent track record as producer and manager for Benny Goodman and more recently Count Basie. He was highly opinionated, and his cultural capital counted a lot among his peers. But his published opinions could be excessive; he once called Duke Ellington "un-Negroid" for not connecting with the "troubles of his people." During the mid-1930s, writers like Hammond, Leonard Feather, Marshall Stearns, and Helen Oakley were arbiters of taste in predominately white jazz magazines such as *DownBeat, Metronome,* and *Tempo,* which, with few exceptions, didn't print feature articles or interviews with Black musicians until late 1936.[2]

After one conversation with Hammond about Webb's new records, Teddy McRae retorted, "John, if you're going to write anything about the band, if you can't write anything good, don't write anything at all, because right now we don't need bad publicity. . . . [W]e're going commercial." McRae knew that Chick felt strongly that the band was ready to keep going in this direction.

Hammond didn't listen. In a *DownBeat* review of November 1937, he took aim at Webb and Ella:

> As an ardent admirer of Chick Webb and his ability I would like to express the hope that he will make full use of the opportunity now facing him to become one of the more successful bands in the country. At least partly because of Ella Fitzgerald, the band is extremely popular these days, but I'm afraid its standard of musicianship is far below the standard Chick ought to set for himself. Instead of giving the public the swing it desires and the kind of stuff he can do best he bores them with the sweet genteel work of a saccharine male vocalist, elaborately badly written "white" arrangements, a "comedian" saxophonist, and an athletic director who jumps around but contributes not a whit to the musical proceedings. But Chick is such a swell performer and Fitzgerald so great a personality that crowds usually overlook such deficiencies. . . . In 1931 Chick had one of the great bands of its day and I think Chick would admit that it would give his present bunch a run for their money. All I hope is that Chick does some soul-searching and give to himself and the public a band that will conform to his own standards and one that makes no compromises for expediency's sake.[3]

Hammond wasn't the only one. In the January 28 issue of *Metronome*, George Simon, an enthusiastic admirer of Ella Fitzgerald all along, lodged similar advice: "Here's uttering a humble prayer that this truly great Chick Webb band, which can cut just about any swing outfit in the world, won't turn into one of those stiff, stagey aggregations, which measures glory in terms of quarts of grease paint and numbers of orchestra seats sold. The band is too great, both personally and musically, to allow itself to tumble into such listless doldrums!"[4]

Their opinions didn't matter in the long run. Webb was doing what he thought was best for the band and for Ella while dealing with increasing demands from radio executives, theater owners, song pluggers, and Decca producer Jack Kapp. He appeased them and kept up the band's momentum, though Gale was stingy, Buchanan rude to musicians, and Hammond overbearing. Webb was taking a chance, but everything he'd done in music involved taking chances. McRae was a terrific partner in this regard. Ella and the band were achieving his dreams, making it to the top levels of entertainment, and helping his band and Ella make more money. McRae knew this was an important juncture:

> 1937 was the beginning of Chick making his move, because we had some money from the one-nighters and college dates and things like that.... We had moved the band a step, a little bit more. Because when I came in, Chick wanted me to be the straw boss [band director], take over everything, ... take some of the worries off his shoulders. This began to move the band up because we got more things done. We began to pick music for Ella, and we were going into a different arrangement type of thing. We were doing all this stuff we got from Fletcher and different arrangers, Charlie Dixon was writing all these jazz things.... And Ella had really developed.[5]

Prominent Black entertainment and music reporters like Porter Roberts and Bille Rowe had no issue with Webb's musical trajectory. Roberts, an astute observer of Black musical culture who didn't dish out compliments, wrote: "Swing on, Chick Webb, you have the right idea! The way you balance your broadcasts deserves praise and your 'swingipation' rates tip-top.... Your new vocalist, Ella Fitzgerald, really knows how to put songs over with a bang! Continue to vary your broadcasts, Mr. Webb, with new arrangements and new songs and only the sky can limit your popularity." Later in the column, Porter also advises bandleaders on something that Webb had been doing all along—taking chances on people: "Dear famous artists: Fame is not everlasting. So I am suggesting that all of you give the new-comers in your field a 'break' whenever possible and help maintain the supremacy of colored people in the arts mentioned above (i.e. field of swing)."[6]

In December 1936, Ella Fitzgerald disappeared for a few days after the Goodman-Webb-Gale debacle about her work with Goodman. She never let on where she went or if she was ill (there were even rumors that she'd had an abortion). The young singer was upset by this kind of attention: the slurry of press articles saying Goodman wanted to "buy out her contract" with Webb, legal issues with Decca, loyalty issues to Webb, and her own ambitions.[7] Years later, in a conversation with Benny Carter about this period, Fitzgerald said that it was John Hammond who tried to "buy her out" of Chick Webb's band and join Goodman's.

In early 1937, Ella got opportunities that didn't have to be hidden. One was substituting (again) for Helen Ward as featured vocalist for violinist Stuff Smith on his sponsored radio show *Listenin' to Lucidin*. Ward had backed out, giving Fitzgerald what *DownBeat* called "the break of her lifetime." Smith's radio ensemble was a top-notch small group pulled from Webb's and Cab Calloway's bands. As thing panned out, Smith went on tour, and Webb took over the *Lucidin* show for a few weeks with Ella and a small group.[8]

Ella's confidence grew with her occasional work with Stuff Smith and some other top musicians. She recorded a softly swinging version of "Big Boy Blue," backed up by the Mills Brothers, a close-harmony male vocal quartet as popular as the Ink Spots (the Mills Brothers also had a Decca contract). Fitzgerald got irritable occasionally, with Webb and other musicians. Teddy McRae said that she sometimes got upset about repertoire choices, and about unexpected rehearsals when she had a date. She was now the band's star artist, and in photos of her on stage at this time she glows. Webb was concerned that her romantic involvements affected her professional life. There were rumors that Fitzgerald was dating saxophonist Vido Musso, who'd recently joined Benny Goodman's band. A few months later, she was romantically involved with drummer Jo Jones, when they were both living at the Woodside Hotel. Jones told jazz historian Phil Schaap that he'd been "snoring in her face since 1937."[9]

Ella's moment had come, along with Webb's. Gale and Jack Kapp seized that moment by recording Fitzgerald as a leader with her own Decca contract. Ella Fitzgerald and Her Savoy Eight, which included Webb on drums and other sidemen from Webb's band, recorded their first sides for Decca in November 1936. This group was created to feature Ella as a recording artist and for marketing purposes; they didn't perform as a stand-alone group. Among the best recordings by Ella's Savoy Eight is her rendition of the popular hit "Bei Mir Bist Du Schön," released in early 1938. Ella dives into her most extended scat yet on this tune, and the band's little bit of klezmer is irresistible.

In fall 1937, Decca also released four records by another breakout small group from Webb's orchestra, Chick Webb and His Little Chicks, a short-lived quintet. This ensemble was totally unusual at the time and featured virtuosic contrapuntal playing by Wayman Carver on flute and Chauncey Haughton on clarinet, with Webb's rhythm section players—Webb, Beverly

Peer on bass, and Tommy Fulford on piano, who all take solos. Along with the Benny Goodman Quartet, the Little Chicks predated other swing-based "chamber jazz" ensembles pulled from their leaders' big bands, such as Artie Shaw's Gramercy Five. Its musical significance is due to Carver, one of the first musicians to use the flute in a jazz setting. Carver's arrangements of "Sweet Sue" and "I Got Rhythm" show off the group's dizzying flair, as Carver and Haughton spin out long fluid lines at really brisk tempos. Webb performed with the Little Chicks during intermission at some theater venues, to give Ella and the band a break from their intense five-shows-a-day schedule.

Fitzgerald was now getting plenty of attention from entertainment reporters and the jazz press, Black and white. In November 1937, she was voted the Number One Female Vocalist in *DownBeat* and in *Metronome* readers' polls, having moved up from third place a few months earlier. This was unprecedented considering the racial divide of both magazines' readers' poll winners, going back to 1935. On mid- and up-tempo numbers, Ella started taking more liberties with lyrics, delving into them with more "spoken word" and scat passages. On "Rock It for Me" she mentions the need for help in a still-poor economy—"satisfy my dole with a rock and roll"—while rhythmically pointing toward a "rockin'" future. "Vote for Mr. Rhythm" is a tribute to Webb and a topical gem: "Now when I say vote for Mr. Rhythm, you all know I mean Chick Webb." Webb's drum breaks on this tune, "Squeeze Me" and other records from this period are clear, brilliant bursts of his melodic displays of fireworks, all within the space of four or eight bars. "Harlem Congo," an instrumental arrangement by Charlie Dixon, is one of the band's greatest recordings. It must have been thrilling to hear this tune live at the Savoy driving dancers into a frenzy. There is fantastic section work, and an inspired string of solos by Taft Jordan, Chauncey Haughton, and Sandy Williams. Webb drops well-placed bass drum "bombs" before he unleashes his magnificent twenty-four-bar solo, one of the most extended on his records. A good portion of Webb's recordings for Decca in 1937–38 are varied and swing powerfully, with terrific if brief solos by Taft Jordan, Sandy Williams, Webb, and others. It is difficult to figure out what Hammond et al. were fussing about.

In early winter of 1937, Webb and the band were not on the road much. Around this time, Webb met Helen Oakley, who would have a huge impact on his career for the next eighteen months. She had moved to New York the previous summer to do public relations work for Irving Mills, and to help Mills resolve contractual issues for his new record labels, Masters and Variety.[10]

Oakley, now twenty-four years old, settled into an apartment in Greenwich Village. She soon started going to the Savoy Ballroom and other clubs where she checked out Webb's band and other great Black swing bands that she had mostly previously heard on records or broadcasts. New York's jazz scene was much bigger than Chicago's. Plus, in Mills's office, she learned the inner workings of the entire music industry—music publishing, radio, recording deals. Mills's business was largely bankrolled by his profits from music publishing, and he wanted to leverage those profits into his artists' recordings of songs published by Mills Music for his own record label. Oakley learned from Mills's leave-no-stone-unturned business dealings. She developed into a bold, charming operator and created multiple career roles for herself in a field dominated by white men. She also saw herself as a talent developer. With the same logical zeal with which she'd convinced Goodman to hire pianist Teddy Wilson, she decided to give Chick Webb's band a boost.

In a 1963 profile of Webb that Oakley wrote for *Stereo Review* she explained: "In 1936 Chick was still fighting every inch of the way. He badly needed promotion, and to give it to him I left the Mills office, and added his band to the Bob Crosby and Mildred Bailey-Red Norvo accounts I then handled. I believed in him, but strangely enough the years that followed were more frustrating than rewarding."[11]

The word "frustrating" is a tipoff to Oakley's own attitudes about what was or was not "authentic" jazz. She started working with Webb in spring 1937 but did not officially leave Mills Artists until that summer. Before that she'd been promoted to record producer. In fall–winter 1936–37, she produced her first recordings for Mills's new Variety label. These included Ellington small band sessions led by his star soloists Johnny Hodges, Cootie Williams, and Barney Bigard. Oakley handled all the details for recording these brilliant cameos, while Ellington, who was in the studio with her for all the sessions, made musical suggestions. Busting through the gender-limited roles for women in the music industry, she earned the respect of Ellington and his sidemen-turned-leaders and from Variety's recording engineers and vendors. She took tremendous pride in putting various musicians together for these recordings, and overseeing every phase of production; musically, her role was largely supervisory.

Mills decided to celebrate the first batch of releases for both labels and asked Oakley to take charge. "This is typical Irving fashion—who wouldn't like a guy like this! He said to me, 'We'll throw a huge party and you be the hostess. You know everybody, ask everybody! . . . Get the drinks, the food, whatever you need." The party, on Sunday, March 14, 1937, was featured in a big photo spread in *Life* magazine, "Life Goes to a Party," and gave jazz a priceless image boost.

Over 500 people showed up including an array of prominent jazz musicians, Black and white, who jammed with each other throughout the day: Count Basie, Jo Jones, Lester Young, Frankie Newton, among them. "By this time I'd told everybody—like Chick Webb—that I was going to record them, and I loved them anyway. . . . And I had EVERYBODY, Chick and Artie Shaw and Gene Krupa, Duke and all the great Black drummers. . . . It turned into a big jam session. Benny's on clarinet, then Artie's on clarinet, Duke's at the piano, Chick's at the drums." The party ended with a trio jam by Webb, Rex Stewart, and Ellington, one of the day's highlights.[12]

Oakley's experience at Variety Records "was seventh heaven for me! All I really wanted to do in life was to be a record producer . . . with carte blanche, and with Duke to draw on. So it was wonderful."

Webb was on two dates for Oakley's Variety sessions, before and after the party. The first was March 3, 1937, with Jimmy Mundy and His Swing Club Seven, for two sides, "I Surrender Dear" and "Ain't Misbehavin'." The second was with the Gotham Stompers on March 25, reuniting Webb with his former Harlem Stompers: Cootie Williams, leader for this date, and Johnny Hodges. These four recordings feature a "dream" band with musicians from Webb's and Duke's current orchestras: Sandy Williams, Harry Carney, Barney Bigard, Tommy Fulford, and Ellington's vocalist Ivie Anderson. During that year, Oakley "just recorded everybody I could get my hands on as long as it lasted."[13]

Meanwhile, Webb was King at the Savoy. Eleven years since its founding, the Savoy was still presenting "Battles of Music," which were as great an attraction as ever, only now the bands were bigger—fifteen to seventeen pieces. Trombonist Sandy Williams said Webb pulled out his top arrangements for these situations and programmed every set strategically.

Webb's band rarely got defeated in informal audience polls. The real winners were the dancers and avid jazz fans. The Savoy's first band battles in the late 1920s mostly got attention from the Black press. That was still the case for two rare events in February and March 1937, when Webb's band "battled" the orchestras of Fletcher Henderson and Duke Ellington. *DownBeat* mentioned the Webb-Ellington event briefly before the fact: "Chick Webb with Ella Fitzgerald will play a double engagement opposite Duke Ellington with Ivie Anderson. . . . The Savoy Ballroom is the current musicians' hangout. . . . [T]he multiple Goodmans turn out en famille." Ellington's band traveled so much at that time that getting to hear his band back in Harlem was a rarity, and 3,100 people attended.[14] The Webb-Ellington battle, on March 7, 1937, was tough for Webb. Ellington's music—his ingenious compositions and his musicians' unique collective sound—was distinctly different from that of other top bands. Nothing about it was conventional, yet his band swung like crazy. At this time, Ellington's orchestra recorded for Mills's Masters label, updating "East St. Louis Toodle-Oo" and "Birmingham "Breakdown," recording new versions of "Caravan" and the impressionistic "Azure," while working on extended pieces such as "Diminuendo in Blue" and "Crescendo in Blue." Masters released its own recording of Ellington's "All God's Chillun Got Rhythm," a remake of Ivie Anderson's featured song in the Marx Brothers' hit comedy, *A Day at the Races*.[15]

Sandy Williams said that Ellington's orchestra was the only band that Webb's band "just could not take." In an interview with Stanley Dance decades later, Williams vividly remembered this night: "We opened and just about broke up the house. Then Duke started . . . and the whole room was just swinging right along with him. I looked over and saw Chick sneaking around the other side into the office. 'I can't take it,' he said. 'They out swung us, they out-everythinged us.'"[16]

Oakley probably went to the Savoy for the Webb-Ellington battle. She went to jazz events often and was usually escorted to the Savoy and nightclubs by Benny Goodman's younger brother Freddy. Having proved herself a successful promoter for Benny Goodman in Chicago the previous year, she thought that Goodman might like to play a battle of music at the Savoy, "the way the Black bands had always done for years. . . . And Chick was really the finest drummer of his time. . . . Gene Krupa thought the world of him, so there was no rivalry there. So I asked Benny, and he said, 'Sure, I'd love to.' So the word got out that in Harlem at the Savoy Ballroom, Benny would be coming."[17]

The Webb-Goodman "battle" took place at the Savoy Ballroom on May 11, 1937, and took on legendary status in "real time" as the atmosphere intensified. Christie Jay Wells lays out why this battle, among so many that

Webb participated in, became "a mythic event . . . a moment of central sym-
bolic importance in the history of swing music and . . . one of the Savoy
Ballroom's most unique spectacles." Wells points to two prior developments.
One was that ballrooms had become perfect spaces for events of "elevated
musical and rhetorical intensity" speaking to "broader social debates,"
thanks to continuous dancing and a huge participatory audience. The winner
was chosen by which band got the most applause. The second was that the
warfare rhetoric used to describe and advertise these events was now entrenched in popular culture. In this context, Wells continues, three elements
then converged to create this battle's "myth":

> Goodman's singular status as the white musician whose success most icon-
> ically represents "the swing era," an active and increasingly explicit debate
> over the racial ownership of jazz music, and the emergent significance of
> "Black champions" as politically significant cultural symbols.

Though racial "ownership" of jazz was one key element, this was not the
first interracial battle for either participant. Webb had previously "battled"
Tommy Dorsey and Glen Gray's Casa Loma Orchestra, and Goodman had
battled Walter Barnes's Royal Creolians and the Wildcats Orchestra in 1935
in an event sponsored by the *Chicago Defender*. But Goodman was especially suited for this particular battle: "Goodman could coherently symbolize
whiteness as the antithesis of Webb's blackness while simultaneously reading
as part of the white—and specifically Jewish—anti-racist jazz critical appa-
ratus standing in explicit solidarity with African Americans."[18]

> So with Benny Goodman there was a big promotion, a big com-
> motion, and people start talking about "swing and swing," and
> interviewed everybody. I said to myself that's a gimmick. It's a title.
> It's a gimmick—to elevate this newcomer Benny Goodman into
> King of Swing. It's the same music we've been playing all along.
> —Mario Bauza[19]

Helen Oakley set the stage for this event after getting to know Webb better,
going to hear his band at the Savoy and working with him for her Variety
record sessions. Years later, she was candid about wanting to "elevate" Webb's
band. "In those days, Webb was still fighting in every way," she wrote. "Black
bands were seldom able to break out of the twilight that contained them.

Chick badly needed promotion and I added his band to the accounts I handled. . . . I went with him because that little hunchback drummer had the
most wonderful band, and never got anywhere. I thought it's time that Webb
came into his own."[20]

In an interview with Oakley (later known as Helen Oakley Dance, wife of
British jazz writer Stanley Dance), jazz journalist and scholar Patricia Willard
asked Oakley about her early work in jazz, and about the Webb-Goodman
battle. During Oakley's career in the 1930s, she was just in her twenties and
didn't really think of herself as advancing racial justice by working in the
jazz field (she became actively involved in civil rights organizations in the
1950s). She saw herself as a smart, capable jazz advocate, promoter, and producer who lived for the music and knew what she wanted to hear. Willard
questioned Oakley about her "firsts."

> You mean first woman jazz journalist . . . and first woman jazz record pro-
> ducer . . . ? Yes. And also youngest? Yes. Run into adverse attitudes? No,
> I didn't. . . . I'm sure it was there: the same things everybody grumbles
> about. . . . I simply had such a narrow vision, I didn't let any other thoughts
> of any kind cross my mind, I just used all my energies and all my thoughts
> to try to accomplish what I thought could be accomplished. And the ter-
> rible thing is I really did it all for myself: everything! I just did what I wanted
> to hear . . . and that guided me. . . . I was young and single-tracked . . . and
> possibly I amused people.
>
> He [Webb] was a little hunchback who really was probably the greatest
> drummer that ever was . . . so I thought I'll try and make Chick Webb and
> the band [more successful]. It was always a wonderful band.

Oakley approached Webb—who called her "Oakley" or "kid"—and asked
him if she could become his publicist and arrange promotional events for
him. "He said, 'How am I going to pay you?' And I said, 'What about your office?' He said, 'They won't spend a dollar for anything.' And I said, 'Well they
might spend a dollar to get me out of Mills's office.'"

Oakley also had a few clients as a freelance publicist; she would have
worked for Webb for free but wanted to keep their relationship professional.
She asked what he could pay her. "He said, 'I'm only paying Ella Fitzgerald
$15 a week. . . . I'll take it out of my pocket and give you fifteen.' I said, 'That's
ok, Chick, you give me fifteen and I'll get something from Ol' Gale. And we'll
do that and we'll go to work.' . . . I didn't care!"

Oakley then approached the Gale Agency. "The first thing I did was I said to them, 'Let's have Benny Goodman come and play the Savoy Ballroom … which is Chick Webb's home, where he's King—and this will be news.' And, as you may have heard, they had the mounted police outside to control the crowds, and it was tremendous! And I knew that Chick had nothing to lose from that. People were crazy to hear Benny Goodman."[21]

Oakley knew this battle would generate a lot of publicity and press: Chick Webb, Harlem's own Savoy King, was going up against Benny Goodman, whom the white jazz press had crowned the King of Swing.

A few weeks beforehand, Goodman came up to the Savoy several times. Webb's musicians noticed. "If someone saw Benny in the house the band would change the tempo so he wouldn't know what tempo Webb's band would play on different numbers," McRae recalled.

> If it was fast, we would drop it down a little bit. . . . The night we were going to play it live, we'd pick it back up—sensational. We'd do things like that. We changed all the sets we were going to play. . . . [W]e would go back to the original tempos. . . . On the night of the battle, Benny asked us to change bandstands, so his band would be on the one Chick normally used. So, Chick said, "Ok, we'll change. You take our number one bandstand, we'll take the number two. It don't make no difference to us. Be our guest."[22]

Mario Bauza said that when the band members showed up at the ballroom that night, Chick told them, "Fellows, I don't have to tell you that this is the biggest thing that's going to happen to us. Tonight, we've got to make history. . . . I don't want any excuses. I don't want anybody drunk. I don't want anybody to miss a note. Anyone do any little thing wrong, don't look for me to give you notice. Just pack up and go home!"[23]

People started lining up to get into the Savoy at 5 p.m. When the doors opened at 8 p.m., four thousand dancers and listeners were lucky enough to get in and packed the place. There was hardly room to move, let alone dance. Several thousand more crowded around the block, hoping for a chance to get in. Outside police and mounted police tried to maintain crowd control. A few policemen were even stationed in front of the bandstands to keep crowds clear.

Webb's band played the first set, and one of his mentees on drums, Bill Beason, played most of it so that Webb could rest up for this long night. McRae continued:

The set included one of Chick's favorite little drum things. He liked to play "By Heck." It was written for Chick. So that night, we let this fella sit down to play the drums—really, tall fella, real wild, real crazy . . . and he broke up the Savoy Ballroom with his breaks. He was another fella that stayed around Chick Webb all the time, watching. He did all of Chick's breaks near as he could. And the place just went wild. Everyone thought that was the last number on that set.

Then Benny Goodman came over. He had to cross over our side of the bandstand to get to the other bandstand because it was so crowded. Chick came over just behind him, and when he heard his [Goodman's] band start "Come On and Hear," ["Alexander's Ragtime Band"] he sat down (at his drums). . . . We hadn't finished the set. Chick sat down behind the drums and said, "King Porter Stomp!" That was the opening of the battle—"King Porter Stomp!"[24]

Dancer Norma Miller remembered this battle as "the greatest night ever in the history of dance and music, the biggest night, and I was there! Chick wasn't going to let anybody run him off the bandstand, and he kicked ass, baby, he kicked ass." Roy Eldridge, then a rising star on trumpet, recalled: "Everybody was waiting to see what happened between Chick and Gene. Gene worked hard and played good; he even broke one of his drum heads. But he couldn't do anything with Chick. That little man was mean, baby. He was mean."[25]

By the night's end, the audience declared Webb's band the winner. Manning recalled: "I saw guys [in Goodman's band] just shake their heads." Goodman's sensational drummer Gene Krupa physically bowed down to Webb afterward. "I will never forget that night. Chick Webb cut me to ribbons," Krupa said. Helen Clarke, one of the Savoy's hostesses, who helped give the ballroom its aura of elegance and politeness, was near Chick when he came off the bandstand. She overheard him say, "I cut him a new asshole, didn't I?"[26]

John Hammond, in his review for *DownBeat,* felt that Goodman's band "was obviously flustered by the proceedings."

The noise level was so high that none but the brass soloists was even audible; the PA system went out from time to time. Consequently the band tried a bit too hard. . . . Although Chick's band indulged in much jive, they actually played better than I have heard them in ages, helped enormously by Ella Fitzgerald and Chick's spectacular drumming. . . . Chick placed himself and his drums right in front of his band, while poor Gene was buried in a back row, invisible because of the formidable cops who stood up in front of him.... The climax and thrill of the evening was provided by Chick Webb who in answer to requests, followed by playing Benny Goodman's own hit number "Jam Session" and blew the roof off the house with it.... The battle was considered to have the greatest drawing power of any similar event ever presented. Benny Goodman, who without a doubt is the supreme "King of Swing" among white bands, was forced in the instance to relinquish his title to Chick Webb who satisfactorily proved that in this, his very own field, he is absolutely unbeatable. Chick Webb may wear his success as a fitting crown for Harlem's true "King of Swing."[27]

Many reviews poured in, all reporting Webb's triumph, while still giving Goodman's band plenty of accolades for their great performance. This thrilling musical night was not recorded (neither was the Webb-Ellington "battle" two months earlier). But judging from some rare photos (see photo insert), a significant detail has been overlooked: that night the Benny Goodman Quartet with Teddy Wilson, Lionel Hampton, and Krupa played a few numbers during an intermission. From the look of these photos, the audience was spellbound, frozen in place. There wasn't an inch of open dance floor for the thousands of people who packed into the Savoy Ballroom to be part of this glorious night.

> You've got to remember—Chick Webb and Ella and the whole band, we're all one family. This is not just musicians just coming to work or something. This band is like one big family.
> —Teddy McRae[28]

Webb's personality as well as his music inspired loyalty, and he wanted the band to perform with power, spirit, and unity. But even Webb had conflicts. Webb, like Duke, didn't like to fire people. There were exceptions, but if a musician felt uncomfortable, that person usually resigned, or Webb hinted that he should. Webb's physical problems and uneven self-education may have contributed to his outsized, outspoken personality and competitiveness. A couple of sidemen said Webb was tense at times and would suddenly curse at someone; these moments were rare, but striking. Sandy Williams said that Chick occasionally gave him hell, though Williams admitted to having serious alcohol abuse issues in those years. Still, he knew Chick liked him. "There were a lot of guys in and out of the band.

When things got rough, they would quit. Once, when there was a question about money, Chick named those who had stuck with him when times were tough"[29]

Webb was also supportive about his players' musicianship. He gave them advice to get what he needed from them in terms of the band's arrangements, and so they would appreciate their own assets. Mario Bauza, Webb's lead trumpet player, said Webb told him early on not to be a copycat:

> He didn't want me to mess around with jazz like the other trumpet players. One day he said, "Never mind the stuff you want to play like Louie [Armstrong]. Never mind that. You've got to develop yourself into something else. See, every Negro trumpet player can outplay you on that kind of stuff, because that's their usual. . . . Do you hear those white trumpet players when they play jazz, like Red Nichols? They play around the melody. So that's what I want you to do—start simple, jazz around the melody. Don't try to do that hard stuff because you won't outdo them."[30]

Webb enjoyed his growing fame. Norma Miller said he wore custom-made suits, always looked sharp, and loved the attention and recognition he was now getting. Van Alexander recalled, "Chick was a big time bandleader, and had no trouble at all attracting young girls. They just wanted to be seen with Chick. I was privy to a lot of scenes with Chick and a couple of the dancing girls and, I thought to myself, 'Well, more power to you, Chick, go ahead.' He admired pretty girls, I know that. But his home life by contrast was pretty quiet."

Webb's relationship to Sally seemed happy and stable, and people remember them as a charming, intelligent, and outgoing couple who socialized during the band's breaks. Van Alexander said he visited them at their home many times, sat with Sally during rehearsals, and danced with her at the ballroom.

> Chick Webb's wife Sally would be at the Savoy almost every night, greeting publishers and talking with acquaintances. Their apartment was the ground floor of a brownstone building. . . . [I]t was pretty dark and wasn't expensively furnished, but they had their bedroom and the kitchen. . . . I had many, many cups of coffee and sandwiches there with them, and it wasn't opulent or extravagant. Mostly they talked about music. . . . She was a lovely looking lady, and certainly took care of Chick, to his every need.[31]

Sandy Williams said that Sally treated Webb "like a prince. She'd go to hell for him. That woman was crazy about him."[32] Their marriage elevated her social life around Harlem. She appeared in photos and items in the "Society" pages of the *Amsterdam News, Baltimore Afro,* and *Pittsburgh Courier,* and went on jaunts to Atlantic City and tennis tournaments at Lincoln University with other important Harlem women, including Bessie Buchanan, Charles's wife.

Webb was generous, as a person and as a musician. His long-time friend and guitarist John Trueheart got sick with tuberculosis in the spring of 1937. He left the band for almost two years to stay at a sanitarium in the Adirondacks, and Webb took care of his bills. Williams said that Trueheart was the person closest to Webb, "almost like a father. I have seen the time when Chick and John sat together beside the highway and split a loaf of bread and a can of beans together."[33]

After some of Van Alexander's charts became hits, Webb introduced him to other bandleaders, who gave him writing assignments. "He was very generous in introducing me around to get more arranging work. . . . [H]e didn't want to keep me all to himself. He wanted to further my career, which was the way Chick was, really. He was just outgoing. . . . Chick scuffled so, so long and hard to get what he achieved that he was always trying to help other people . . . and tried to further their careers."[34]

> If Webb's superior as a drummer exists, he must be hiding far out in the dark recesses of the hinterland. . . . Chick was born right here in Baltimore. He takes his place alongside Joe Gans, Cab Calloway and those other greats who have left this town and added their bit to the age-old bromide: "hometown boy makes good."
>
> "Swing, well, its easy to define," he said when questioned in his dressing room as to his version of the popular brand of music now sweeping the musical firmament. "It's nothing new. Simply a newer form of an old art—jazz. I've been familiar with this type of thing all my life. That's all I've ever played."
>
> —*Baltimore Afro*[35]

In summer and fall of 1937, Webb's band debuted at Lowe's State in Times Square, and was often on the road. They had several radio hits: "Rock It for Me," "If Ever I Should Leave You," and "Clap Hands, Here Comes Charlie," which Lunceford's arranger Sy Oliver brilliantly adapted for Webb. They toured the South, which they did again in 1938, the year that lynchings were covered for the first time in major newspapers. Once again, these trips had many back-to-back one-nighters, and travel was wearing, often demeaning, and sometimes dangerous.[36] They went to New Orleans; to Fort Worth and Dallas, Texas; on to stops in Oklahoma and Missouri; and then back south to Mississippi and Florida, before heading north. Webb's band was still the first "colored" band to perform at certain places: for "White Nights," sectioned-off Black or white audiences, or completely segregated audiences. Webb's date in Fort Worth on August 6 "drew the entire Paul Whiteman crew to the Negro Ballroom for a listen." On August 7, Webb's band gave back-to-back performances at the Pan-American Exposition in Dallas: a free concert for whites in the six-thousand-seat amphitheater, then at 10 p.m. at the Expo's Agricultural Hall for a Black dance, with a section for white spectators. "Ella Fitzgerald nearly wrung tears from the black and white crowd with her elegant styling of 'If You Ever Should Leave Me.' Grand trumpeting by Taft Jordan almost took the spectators with him, wherever he was (certainly not in this world)."[37]

Sandy Williams despised going on the southern tours:

> Tim [Gale] used to go out the road with us, for those damn one-nighters. That's what nearly killed me. You'd eat where you could eat. They used to send us down south in that mess, those road trips would last 2-3 months. Sitting on the side of the road and eat a can of beans, go to the bathroom out in the woods. It was nasty. These people would come hear you entertain and still call you "nigger." Them crackers were the boss anyway. Down there you could buy a gun just like you buy a pack a cigarettes. . . . I had that in my mind—to kill those crackers—they made you that way! But then they'd say Ella, "That nigger gal can really sing." Roy Eldridge almost had a breakdown. I hate like hell to even think about those days. Every time we went on the road, we'd buy guns.[38]

Still, as Garvin Bushell said, these dances in the South were attended by thousands and thousands of people. One can only presume the band's take was worth it as they racked up attendance records.

Back in New York, in fall 1938 Webb was endorsed by the New York-based drum maker Gretsch, when the company debuted its signature Gretsch-Gladstone drum set (see Chapter 12 for details). This set quickly became the top choice of the top drummers. Chick Webb was the "paramount endorser among this group," wrote Fred Gretsch, Jr., the fourth-generation company president. For most of Webb's performances from then on, Webb used this set. His new bass drum was adorned with a precisely cut, gem-pasted sparkling crown and his initials.

At Chicago's Palace Theatre, a pack of aspiring drummers went backstage to see Webb's new equipment: "an extra heavy batter head and a heavy clear snare head, a heavy tympani for the bass drum, all tuned exactly to his taste are Chick Webb's accessories. Everything else is mixed standard equipment."[39]

"Chick and His Orchestra Featuring Ella Fitzgerald" were Moe Gale's biggest-drawing clients, besides the Ink Spots. His other clients at various times included bandleaders Andy Kirk, Erskine Hawkins, Teddy Hill, and Lucky Millinder and blues singer Albert Hunter. Gale was one of a handful of white businessmen in the music industry who'd built their businesses by "developing" Black talent, within the framework of the systemically white-dominated music business. The other major players in the 1930s were Irving Mills (Ellington, Calloway, Mills Blue Rhythm), Joe Glaser (Louis Armstrong), and Harold Oxley (Jimmie Lunceford). Lunceford's musicians spoke kindly of Oxley ("he was the best of all of them"). Gale had a reputation for being a gentleman and a decent person, but even he got caught up being portrayed as the "Great White Father" of jazz. Sandy Williams said: "Moe Gale—he had control of the band, that's all. We had to do every damn thing they said. When it came down to vacation time coming around, you'd either get a suitcase or a watch, or something like that so you wouldn't be late for work. That was the cheapest man going. The only one of those Gale brothers I had any decent feelings for was Tim."[40]

Gale brought Helen Oakley on staff in August 1937. A press clip in *DownBeat* mentions that Oakley is "out of Mills Artists and now has her desk with Moe Gale, devoting her time to Chick Webb." The following month, *Metronome* ran a photo of Gale and Oakley smiling, poring over mountains of paperwork. The caption reads: "Spinning the web! Moe Gale, manager of Chick Webb's Chicks talking stuff with his new associate, Helen Oakley, former Benny Goodman war-time correspondent from the Chicago front."[41]

Oakley's projects at Variety Records were over. Except for the Ellington small band records, the releases she produced weren't making much money, and she knew she would no longer have so much autonomy. "That was it," she said. "I wasn't going to be told to do [record] the Three Musketeers or something. I was young, that was my life and I wasn't going to waste it. I was never in it for the money. And so I quit once I saw that I wasn't going to be able to go on making what I wanted to make."[42]

Oakley's major responsibility at Gale Agency, Inc. was promoting Chick Webb's band. A major issue for her was that she thought that Webb featured Ella Fitzgerald and pop material too much, in person and on their recordings. She thought that Webb wasn't showing off himself or his instrumental musicians enough. Oakley had what Gennari calls the "self-justifying sense of exceptionalism" that allowed her "exalted purpose" and freed her from the quagmire of a white critic or producer telling Black musicians what to do.[43]

This mini-culture jazz/pop music war was taking place as swing bands became an industry. Oakley recalled:

> But I loved Chick dearly and he loved me dearly, and we fought over the music constantly. He'd had the most marvelous band.... Fletcher Henderson came up, stole from him. Every band stole from him. Duke Ellington took Johnny Hodges, Cootie lived in Chick's apartment—they were all living on doughnuts.... He [Chick] was such a wonderful guy and so true blue. And now we had Ella, and it wasn't a first-class band, which killed me, and Louis Jordan was one of the stars, and I kept saying, "Get rid of that man!" And Chick used to say, "Oakley, I've got a chance to get somewhere!" He thought just as I did, but he wasn't going to do it. He at last had the chance to make the big time. I don't blame him. But I couldn't change myself either.

Webb resisted Oakley's strong opinions. She was a "gatekeeper" herself, running on her own "likes and dislikes"—which today one would call her white privilege. Oakley knew about Webb's continuous scramble to get to where he was as a bandleader. But she may have been insensitive about other things: what it took to keep his musicians employed and paid, the cyclical nature of popular music, and that Webb and his musicians would never be paid as much as Goodman's band, even if they outdid him at theater box offices. Webb had a longer view. Plus he was not entirely a healthy man, though he was on the move and never complained of pain or health issues in front of his band. He just kept going.

For Oakley, "It was both ironic and tragic that he took this stand precisely when the standard of musicianship he had represented for so long had finally come into its own. No one could ever convince him of the Swing Era's reality. He refused to believe that such popular acceptance could last."

That's when she schemed up a "shock treatment" for Webb—another pivotal band battle that she hoped would get Webb to change course back to a jazz orientation. This time, the band she had in mind was Count Basie's, whose reputation as a top swing band rose tremendously in the previous year, with the band's inimitable rhythm section and outstanding soloists. Oakley told Webb: "Now we're going to get Count Basie, we're going to have a battle with Count Basie," whom she had not consulted yet.

Chick's answer was typical: "'You don't scare me! I'll battle him, we'll battle him.'"[44]

17

Battling It Out in Swingtime

I remember what a beautiful engagement that was. The kids up there just loved her [Billie]. And it was a strange thing, Ella was on one stand with Chick, and we were on the other. It was a beautiful night.... Everybody loved it, it was so wonderful and Billie was so great there.... Oh, it was no battle or anything like that. It was very exciting to play opposite them.

I mean, I want you to know just this much—that you know with the First Lady of Swing up there, and Chick Webb and the band he had. You ever hear that band? Well, they were wild. If you had an orchestra, you didn't want to get mixed up with them—because he was a bad one, boy. He was a bad motorcycle, himself, and Billie and Ella were two very different singers.

—Count Basie[1]

The Webb-Basie band battle took place at the Savoy Ballroom on January 16, 1938, in the middle of Webb's already packed calendar. Webb's band started off 1938 with a New Year's dance in Charleston, West Virginia. It was a rare opporuntity in coal country for both Black and white miners, who drove long distances to attend dances like this one. Webb's date and other tours in West Virginia and Kentucky were set up by entrepreneurial Black promoter George Morton and local contacts who presented top bands like Webb's, Lunceford's, Basie's, Calloway's, and others in barn dances or small halls scattered in small cities and towns across the hills.[2] After West Virginia, the band made its way back to New York for a week at the Apollo starting Friday, January 7, doubling their schedule with dances at the Savoy. "You'd do four or five shows all day, then back up to the Savoy all night. The pace was brutal," said dancer Norma Miller.

Count Basie and His Orchestra had set the entire jazz-swing world in New York City on fire since fall 1936, when they made New York their base.

In addition to the band's great soloists, Herschel Evans and Lester Young on tenor saxophone, and Buck Clayton on trumpet, the Basie band had a fresh, loose approach to big band swing. Their rhythm section—Basie at piano, Eddie Durham on guitar, Walter Page on bass, and Jo Jones on drums—came to define the rhythm section as a unit in big bands that would become known as the "Great American Rhythm Section." The Basie band played with a more relaxed southwestern-style swing beat, which was powerful at medium or fast tempos. This was in contrast to Chick Webb, whose masterful playing—at any tempo, any dynamic—often overshadowed his gifted rhythm section players and other musicians. He could carry his band all by himself.

The scheduling of the Webb-Basie battle is still a mystery given that it took place the same night as another jazz benchmark, the Benny Goodman Orchestra's debut at Carnegie Hall. The Savoy "battle" didn't begin until after 10:30 p.m. Basie, Freddie Green, Walter Page, Lester Young, and Buck Clayton were at Carnegie Hall, playing the "jam session" portion of Goodman's concert, the first ever in this renowned concert hall. Goodman's concert was scheduled months in advance, and tickets were sold out for weeks beforehand. Hammond had a key role in planning and pushed to include the jam session. An all-star combo composed of Goodman, Krupa, Basie, Young, Clayton, and two of Ellington's great soloists, Harry Carney and Johnny Hodges, jammed on "Honeysuckle Rose" for over fifteen minutes.

Oakley was involved in the planning for both events. She had to coordinate with Gale and Buchanan to plan a date for the Webb-Basie battle, a scheduling challenge because both bands were constantly in demand. Additionally, she was friends with both Goodman and Hammond.

Goodman was anxious for weeks ahead of the Carnegie concert. "He rehearsed the band for three days beforehand and the band was nervous. And Benny asked me could I persuade Duke Ellington to let him present Ellington's three big stars, Johnny Hodges, Cootie Williams and Harry Carney." Goodman must have asked Hammond the same of Count Basie. Musically, it was a win-win situation—socially too. It was a progressive move for the jazz world, to present various mixed-race groups throughout the concert in different combos and segments. In addition to some numbers by the Benny Goodman Quartet, the jam session followed a "Twenty Years of Jazz" program that concluded with Carney, Hodges, Cootie Williams, and Goodman's rhythm section—Jess Stacy, piano; Harry Goodman, bass; and Gene Krupa, drums—performing "Blue Reverie," an extended impressionistic blues by Duke Ellington.

Carnegie Hall's printed program for the concert had extensive program notes by Irving Kolodin and included this invitation: "After the Concert attend the Battle of Swing between Chick Webb and his Orchestra with Ella Fitzgerald and Count Basie and His Orchestra with Billie Holiday TONIGHT. Savoy Ballroom, Lenox Ave and 140th Street."[3]

Double-booking Basie and his musicians that night seems exploitive and disrespectful to both Basie and Webb, who had their own big night ahead. Both bandleaders and their musicians were no strangers to all-night jam sessions and musical marathons—it was a necessary part of their lives as performers. But Oakley ramped up her efforts to publicize this particular battle, casting it as a gladiator-to-the-death contest instead of the fantastic musical event those who attended experienced. Decades later, she admitted that she had set up Webb: "I always felt so half-ashamed . . . that I pulled in Basie to defeat Webb. . . . This was something that I brought about. . . . I knew perfectly well that Basie would cut Chick. And I broadcast it on all the radio stations and made the biggest mess about it that I possibly could. . . . I knew it would be a terrible thing." Oakley defended her actions by saying that she had arranged the battle to teach Chick a lesson. "Chick was concentrating on Ella's share all the time on his sets. She was a wonderful singer, but he wasn't concentrating on the band. . . . And I kept thinking if we could sting them, then maybe they would decide they'd go for it themselves. . . . And of course it was a very touching moment . . . because you couldn't defeat Basie, you couldn't out-swing the Basie band."[4]

Webb didn't need the lesson. Ella Fitzgerald was now the "First Lady of Swing," and he and his band enjoyed intense loyalty and adulation from their Savoy followers. The Webb band was unequivocally one of the most popular in the country electrifying dancers with its hard-driving swing. Early that night, Webb heard a rumor that some of Whitey's Lindy Hoppers were taking sides, and that they thought the Basie band would run Webb's band off the bandstand. According to Norma Miller, Webb got mad and told Whitey: "I don't give a good goddamn what those raggedy Lindy Hoppers do or say. . . . As far as I'm concerned they can all go to hell."[5]

Oakley went to Goodman's Carnegie Hall concert first.

I didn't go backstage, I went out front. I wanted to sample the atmosphere. . . . [P]eople came in their evening gowns and cloaks . . . probably 40 percent of the people. And then the other 60 percent were all the people that were

determined to jam in and hear Benny. So everybody was looking at everybody else to see how they were behaving. . . . The band started and they were
all very nervous and it didn't come off awfully well. The programing was
reasonable, but it wasn't making it. . . . So for almost the first half of the program it was iffy. And so you just didn't know what to think. . . . And so then
Benny called "Sing, Sing, Sing," and that was it. . . . It turned the corner, for
the whole thing was a big success.[6]

Up at the Savoy, crowds started packing into the ballroom at 8 p.m. Jazz
royalty, press, and jazz music and dance lovers came out in force: Erskine
Hawkins, Roy Eldridge, Teddy Hill, Tommy Dorsey, Red Norvo, and many
others. Thousands of fans were turned away at the door. Bill Beason or another of Webb's other prodigious subs "warmed" up Webb's band during its
first set. Ellington, who'd rushed up from Carnegie Hall, where he'd been
listening from backstage, played a solo piano "intermission" while Basie and
his musicians were on their way uptown.

When the Carnegie Hall concert cleared out around 11 p.m., Goodman
and his musicians, Hammond, Oakley, other friends backstage, and many
audience members raced up to the Savoy in cabs.

Feelings ran high as each band played their hearts out. Billy Rowe
wrote: "Never in the history of the internationally known 'Home of Happy
Feet' has a more marvelous musical diversion ever been presented. From
door to door and from early evening to early dawn the spacious edifice of
gaiety was packed to the overflowing point. . . . Webb consistently stole the
show on the drums. But then one band kept outdoing the other, and the
crowds went wild. Towards the end, when Ella sang 'Loch Lomond,' the
whole crowd rocked with her."

The *Amsterdam News* reported that the fight "never let down in intensity
during the whole fray. Chick took the aggressive, with the Count playing
along easily, and on the whole more musically scientifically. Undismayed by
Chick's forceful drum-beating, which sent the audience into shouts of encouragement and appreciation and caused beads of perspiration to drop from
Chick's brow onto brass cymbals, the Count maintained an attitude of poise
and self-assurance." Afterward, about 20 percent of attendees filled out
ballots at the door. "Chick led Count Basie two to one and Ella polled three
times as many votes as Bille Holiday. . . . Ella Fitzgerald, unlike her boss,
played a confident defensive game. . . . Judge Public will not necessarily show
a superiority in ability since the two singers vary so differently, but a preference for singing style!"[7]

DownBeat's reviewer called it for Webb: "Webb Cuts Basie in Swing Battle":

> The affair drew a record attendance and hundreds were turned away. Applause for both bands was tremendous and it was difficult to determine which band was the most popular. . . . Feelings ran very high. . . . Both bands played magnificently, with Basie having a particular appeal for the dancers, and Webb consistently stealing the show on drums. Ella Fitzgerald caused a sensation with her rendition of "Loch Lomand," and Billie thrilled her fans with "My Man." When Ella sang, she had the whole crowd rocking with her. James Rushing had everybody shouting the blues, right along with him. . . . [T]he excitement was intense. . . . [T]here was good feeling all around, and it was decided that there would be a return battle in the near future.[8]

Oakley's attempt to "sting" Webb backfired. Webb knew Oakley had been manipulative; so did some of his musicians. So did Moe Gale. She recalled: "At the office, when they began to see what I was doing, they didn't like me. Not because I was a woman, but because I was working against them. What I believed in was not going to make money. It would have in the end—Benny made money, Duke made money. In the end my things will make money but not while you're building them."[9]

Oakley diminishes her own major accomplishments in this offhand remark—as a "first" female jazz record producer, journalist, and promoter of Black artists in white venues, and of prominent white musicians like Goodman. It is difficult to assess if her "causes" made money; that seems like a self-aggrandizing notion that obscures her real work. Her opinions, Hammond's, or their like-minded "jazz authenticity" peers could not stop the forward momentum of Webb's and Ella's growing mainstream popularity. Swing music made jazz and pop music synonymous. Webb and Ella now had legions of fans across the country, outside of New York City and far away from the insiders and influencers in the "industry of swing." Webb ignored the drumbeat of criticism—"the band sounds too white," "Ella's stealing time from the soloists," "they don't play real jazz anymore," etc.—that would increase over the next year and dribble into contemporary jazz criticism.[10] This corrosive criticism is part of the reason Webb and his band's music has been ignored for so long, even in jazz history programs.

Webb's sidemen felt the sting of the Webb-Basie battle too. "The band got together and called a band meeting, and they said to Chick, 'You gotta fire her. You've gotta fire her! She did it on purpose. You know she did. You

KNOW she did. She showed us up. We don't want anybody like that working for us," Oakley recalled. "No!"

She knew that Webb was too gracious to fire her. But Moe Gale knew the backstory, and what the sidemen thought. Oakley said:

> So after it was all over, the Webb band called a meeting and said, "She set us up, she exposed us." And I didn't care for the band anyway, and it wasn't a wonderful band, and naturally they didn't like me. And Chick, by that time was pretty ill, and he was frankly upset. And I said to him, "Chick, if the office wants to fire me, let them. I've done my job, I've put you where you're supposed to be and that's what they hired me for."[11]

Oakley continued to work for the Gale office for a few more weeks, working the press for his next appearances. Al Moses of the *Baltimore Afro* wrote: "I had the pleasure of meeting that highly efficient manager of Chick Webb, Miss Helen Oakley of Gale, Inc. Every detail of the organization, from making new Decca records, radio broadcasts, to personal appearance tours comes under the jurisdiction of a girl who might just as easily adorn magazine covers. . . . Miss Oakley is every inch the executive despite her unmistakable personal charm."[12]

Oakley's staging of the biggest of all big band battles—the Webb-Goodman battle of May 1937, and the Webb-Basie battle of January 1938—helped elevate Webb's and his band's visibility. This significant aspect of her work is hard to put a price tag on. She had no hand in Webb's recordings for Decca, though she may have helped promote them. She was never asked to supervise or advise on repertoire, as she had for Irving Mills's Variety label, though Webb's choice of material had been a main topic of her musical arguments with him. Repertoire choices were mainly up to Webb, with input from McRae and Ella—though producer Jack Kapp, Moe Gale, and music publishers and song pluggers had a big hand in this. Webb's radio audience also helped choose what ended up being recorded; Ella and the band performed many of their arrangements on live broadcasts and gauged listeners' preferences.

Webb's virtuosity was not always captured on his Decca recordings, except for his magnificent solo on "Harlem Congo" and his short but dramatic and incisive breaks on "Go Harlem," "Dipsy Doodle," "Rock It for Me," and others. Neither was that of his soloists, especially given the limits of 78s. At live performances Webb and his best soloists went all out in ways that were never caught on the Decca recordings. Sandy Williams spoke of this:

Of course, the arrangements of the get-off numbers were chopped down to fit the three-minute records. Some of those we played would last ten or fifteen minutes. I remember one Christmas at the Apollo Theater, we were playing a special Christmas benefit for the *Amsterdam News* fund for needy people. That night I counted the choruses I played on "King Porter Stomp." 23! Bobby Stark and I played as many choruses as we felt like, so long as each chorus was a little more exciting. This was our tune, Bobby's and mine.... But we were never allowed to let down. As long as you could keep it going Chick would let you go, but he had a special little beat to make you understand when to stop. He was a lot of fun![13]

A rare recording taken from a Savoy Ballroom broadcast in late December 1937 captures the band's and the audience's exuberance. Despite the rough recording quality, you can hear Fitzgerald's voice sound like an instrument, at one with the band on "Honeysuckle Rose." The band is precise, polished, and powerful on Edgar Sampson's up-tempo instrumental arrangement of "Don't Be That Way," with Webb hurling into one of his extended rolls, ending with a clatter of cymbal crashes.

In late January 1938, a couple of weeks after the Basie battle, Webb's band was back on the road for a week at the Howard Theater in DC, then the Strand in Baltimore, before heading to Boston. The band had a booking there that would be another "first," the Flamingo Room at Levaggi's, a whites-only nightclub in a city that still did not have much of a Black music scene. According to McRae, "It was the kind of place that was losing business with the white bands, so they decided to bring in the colored bands."

Oakley, still working in the Gale office, sent out press notices, something that club owner Jack Levaggi did not do, not even for a national radio star. Levaggi didn't place ads in the Boston papers either. George Frazier of *DownBeat* wrote that Levaggi was "heartily detested by every newspaperman in town. If it had not been for Helen Oakley, Chick's opening would have gone without anything save the most palpable of paid-for plugs.... Helen managed to wrangle invaluable plugs in all the columns. But now, unless Levaggi discards his snotty attitude, business stands to fall off sharply."[14]

Webb, Ella, and the band were a sensation at Levaggi's, thanks to Oakley's efforts and word of mouth. Two weeks after the opening, Webb's band was signed for another booking that helped break through the color line as performers, this time in his hometown of Baltimore. The management of Baltimore's Hippodrome hired him to "play the theater with a colored unit week of April 1st." This was a big surprise in musical circles, the "first time in many years that such has been the case.... From present indications Webb's demand performances rise with the times. Since opening at the exclusive Boston spot, theater managers learning of the huge business his swing style has created for Levaggi, are out to get him at all cost, putting him in the money class enjoyed by such attractions in past years."[15]

White jazz critics were still of two minds about Webb, depending on who and what they were writing for. George Frazier raved about Webb's band in *Tempo* magazine, attributing the band's confidence to coming through the Basie battle without being trounced.

> Chick's band sounds nothing short of superb these nights. It is loose and relaxed and its intonation is above reproach. Bobby Stark, Sandy Williams, Teddy McRae, Tommy Fulford and Chick himself are as exciting as hell. Ella is fine (although to me, not the artist Billie Holiday is). Her appeal to the public is an amazing thing. Every time she sings she stops things cold.... Boston night-club audiences are unbearably rude as a rule so the spectacle of a packed house in rapt attention while Chick's band went through a show must be regarded as something hitherto unheard of.

A month later in *DownBeat,* Frazier changed his tune, jabbing Webb, the band, and Ella with backhanded compliments, and congratulating club owner Jack Levaggi for hiring them. "With their accent on blare and almost total neglect of the band's substantial endowments, many of the arrangements leave me frigid, and Ella, popular as all hell though she may be, still impresses me as somewhat specious. Those, I admit, are rather carping objections, for the band has the stuff of thrills, both in its soloists and its intonation.... At Levaggi's the band has attracted capacity business—far and away the most astonishing business any Boston night club has been able to boast of in at least two years."[16]

Webb's success at Levaggi's was celebrated in the Black press, but not reviewed—probably because they couldn't get into the club. This was the case in other parts of the country as well.

Levaggi extended Webb's run from four weeks to twelve, through early May. Boston still had Sunday "blue laws"—no bars were open or liquor sold. Teddy McRae said Webb and the band returned to New York after each

Saturday night show. "Nobody stayed in Boston. All the musicians who were in Boston go back to New York over the weekend. The train would leave the main station and get to Back Bay at 12:05am. Everybody was rushing to get that train. Then we'd come back to Boston at 5 in the afternoon, just in time to get straightened out and go back to work on Monday night."

During Webb's run, clarinetist/bandleader Artie Shaw had a residency at Roseland in Boston. Shaw and his musicians went to hear Webb's band when they could, and Webb and his musicians reciprocated. The two bandleaders became friends.

Shaw, who had a reputation as hard to get along with, and someone who always had to be "right," admired Chick Webb. "Not only was Chick a great player and a gentle giving person," said Shaw, "he was ambitious for himself, his band and Black people in general." Shaw's band, which a few months later would rival Goodman's in popularity, was just coming together at that time. Shaw continued:

> During one of those rehearsals, he [Webb] sat very quietly in a dim corner, obviously deep in thought. When we got finished, he came over to me and said: "You know something, man? Someday I'm going to be walking up the street one way, and you're going to be coming the other way, and we're going to pass each other and say, 'Hello, best white bandleader in the world.' And you're going to say, 'Hello, best colored bandleader in the world.' You know that?" And he gravely shook hands with me on that statement, as if we were entering into a solemn pact, which I suppose we actually were.[17]

It was a pivotal time for Shaw's band, which had not had any significant hit records yet. That July, they recorded what would be their breakout hit, "Begin the Beguine." This was the B side of "Any Old Time," featuring Billie Holiday, her enduring hit recording with Shaw's band (Holiday then had her own recording contract with Columbia). Shaw hired Holiday that summer, still rare move for a white bandleader, but she only stayed with his band a couple of months. She told a *Downbeat* reporter that she was fed up by Shaw's and his manager's treatment of her.[18]

Shaw, like Goodman and other white bandleaders, was looking for a magic formula, by featuring singers like Fitzgerald or Holiday, or hiring a Black arranger like Fletcher Henderson or Jimmy Mundy, that could help craft his band's sound and swing more—to somehow sound more Black. Shaw asked Teddy McRae to write some charts for him. Like Webb, Shaw and his band were on coast-to-coast broadcasts several times a week and needed new material all the time. McRae remembered Shaw asking to "write me something like you all have. I need something to go off the air with." In late 1938, McRae wrote two pieces for Shaw that both became hits, "Back Bay Shuffle" and "Traffic Jam." "Traffic Jam" was inspired by the crazy traffic in Boston's Back Bay neighborhood where Roseland was located, right near Symphony Hall ("you couldn't even cross the street when a Boston Pops concert let out").[19]

The Webb band's time in Boston was also a creative time for Ella Fitzgerald. In her off-hours, she fooled around at the piano and came up with an idea for a song that she mentioned to arranger Van Alexander, still known as Al Feldman. Alexander came to Boston weekly to rehearse new material for the band's broadcasts. "One day Ella said to me, 'I've got a great idea for a song. Why don't you try to work up something on the old nursery rhyme, "A-Tisket, A-Tasket?'" She sang him a few bars. Feldman really liked the idea and told her he'd think about how to score it. Novelty swing songs were all over the airwaves, among them radio hits like "Jeepers Creepers" and "Music, Maestro, Please." On Alexander's next trip to Boston. Ella asked him if he'd done anything with it. "I said, 'Geez, Ella, I just didn't have time. Wait till next week.'"

Alexander was tied up with writing new arrangements for Webb's band two and three weeks in advance. "I didn't get to it," he recalled. "I didn't have the time to think about it. So by this time, she's gotten a little testy for a young girl. For the first time I saw that she was impatient."

He recalled her saying, "If you don't want to do it, I'm going to ask Edgar Sampson to do it." Feldman promised her he'd get to it that week.

He went back to New York and worked out the format. "As you know, the nursery rhyme is in public domain which meant anybody could write an arrangement of it and claim authorship." Alexander put it into a thirty-two-bar song form with a middle section "then with all the novelty things at the end— you know, 'Was it red? No, no, no, no. . . . Was it blue?'"

He took it to Boston and played it for Ella, who said it was wonderful but wanted to change a few words. Ella told him, "Don't say 'walking on down the avenue. Let's say she was truckin' on down the avenue.'" "'Truckin' was a big word in those days," said Feldman.

Fitzgerald changed a few other things too, and Webb and the band rehearsed it and liked it. So did the audience at Levaggi's, who requested the song several times a night. Alexander said that a song plugger for Robbins in Boston heard them perform it and got so excited that he called his boss and said, "Chick Webb and Ella Fitzgerald are doing a thing called 'A-Tisket, A-Tasket. You'd better take it off from the air tonight and see what you think about it.' Abe Alman, a vice president at Robbins, heard it and said, 'I think we got something here.'"

Three weeks later, Webb, Ella, and the band came to New York and recorded it at the Decca studio. Feldman said it was recorded—coincidentally— "on my birthday, May 2, 1938, and that summer that song just took off and it was Number 1 on the Lucky Strike Hit Parade for 19 weeks."[20]

Simultaneously corny and hip, "A-Tisket, A-Tasket" was above all catchy, with Webb playing an infectious rocking beat that the band excelled at, a harbinger of Rhythm & Blues. Alexander's arrangement is clever and full of surprising twists, "stop-times," and a call-and-response section with the band piping up vocally. Ella's blend of sassiness and innocence had universal appeal.

"At last," said McRae, "the band was a success all the way back, all the way to the coast and back. We broke record after record. People just lined the streets. . . . People brought their kids to the ballrooms, their little girls. Chick gave them prizes. . . . Everybody would bring their little girls, all dressed up and singing 'A-Tisket, A-Tasket.'"[21]

Moe Gale made out well financially with the Levaggi's engagement. The Ink Spots, Gale's other top artists, were booked for an extended run that spring at Levaggi's Grill Room right next door. Teddy Hill's band, also managed by Gale, subbed for Webb's band at the club when Webb's band went to Yale University for prom weekend March 11–12, 1938. Starting in May, Hill's band had their own long run at Levaggi's.

Webb's weekend at Yale that year was particularly special. His band was booked to play at the main prom and at fraternity events all weekend. The band was popular on the college circuit and played for proms at other Ivy League schools, including Princeton and Columbia. Being back on the Yale campus was a special return engagement for Ella, who'd had her "tryout" with Webb's band there just three years earlier. The weekend was topped off when Webb was given an "honorary" degree by fraternity students on Sunday, March 12:

Chick Webb Gets Yale University Degree. In the fraternity hall of Alpha Sigma at Yale university, Chick Webb, center, the drum king of swing, smiles happily as Palmer York, Jr., presents him with the "honorary degree" of D.M.S., as Walter Mennel looks on and sets Webb's student cap for the cameraman. Having played several Yale affairs, Webb, Ella Fitzgerald and his orchestra have become great favorites among the Yale students. This marks the first time that any orchestra leader, white or colored, has been so honored by this or any other university in the country. The new degree given the diminutive king of the drums knights him: "The Dark Master of Swing."[22]

The title of Webb's degree was a veiled way of alluding to Webb's race without appearing racist; they could have just honored him as the "True Master of Swing."

The band's pace was intense all spring, and Webb's health issues were worsening. He was often in pain, though he tried to hide it. The lingering effects from his childhood tuberculosis started to impact his kidneys and other organs. On April 4, 1938, Webb was admitted to Harlem View Hospital. "Webb Undergoes Minor Operation: Chick Webb, diminutive drumocating band leader who recently received a university degree in swing, is confined to the Hudson View Hospital here following a minor operation performed successfully last Thursday. Ella and the band are still holding forth at Levaggi's."

In another press item, the reporter wrote: "It took his [Webb's] wife to keep him away from his band."[23] Alexander, who'd visited the Webbs at their apartment many times, said Sally took excellent care of Webb in general, even before his health started declining: "She took care of his every need and watched him and so forth. She made sure his food was prepared properly. I don't remember seeing Chick drink any wine or liquor. I know he didn't smoke. I saw Sally just prepare his food at their apartment a couple of times and, and serve him and cater to him continually." Frankie Manning remembered Sally Webb as "a beautiful young lady and she was for Chick all the way."[24]

Another health issue of Webb's, which drummer Cliff Leeman referred to as the "drummer's curse," was chronic hemorrhoids, which could cause profuse bleeding. This painful condition was exacerbated by Webb's playing four to five theater shows a day, plus radio shows, plus dances at night, and added to that sitting in a bus or car on the road for long hours while on tour. It is impossible to imagine how Webb had withstood chronic pain for years yet pushed himself to keep going, hardly ever letting on to others about his condition. Oakley said that "he hated to confess that anything was wrong and never complained. . . . Many times after a show or set he would pass out . . . but game as anything, he would never quit."[25]

Webb was absent from Levaggi's for two weeks, but his band and Ella still packed the club every night. Webb's substitute on drums was Arnold "Scrippy" Boling, a New York drummer who was one of Webb's avid followers, like Beason, and could keep the band swinging and play many of Webb's special little breaks. Webb's musicians did not want to let the crowd down in their leader's absence, and put on a show. Louis Jordan's mugging and exuberant antics drove the audience wild. Beverly Peer recalled: "I've got a clear picture of us playing 'Alexander's Ragtime Band,' with Scrippy tapping his drumsticks on the wall, then we'd finish up by marching around the club." *DownBeat* reported: "Even with little Chick in the hospital the Chickadees have been outdrawing any attraction in town. The Four Ink Spots are the only boys to compare in popularity in this town."[26]

Levaggi managed to undermine the club's newfound success with swing fans and the college crowd, especially among Webb's fans. *Tempo* reported, "Jack Levaggi docked Chick Webb's salary while latter underwent serious operation. Much resentment by all who realize that Webb's band had built Levaggi's into city's most popular nitery."[27]

Webb was no stranger to stingy club owners and accepted other important engagements during the band's last few weeks at Levaggi's, though he was barely out of the hospital. In late April, Webb flew to New York City for a special appearance with Tommy Dorsey and His Orchestra at the Paramount Theater, inaugurating the theater's new series of guest appearances. Dorsey's honored guests were "Chick Webb, King of the Drums, and Duke Ellington, King of the Jungle Rhythm." That last description reflects the kind of lingering racist tropes attached to jazz music even for such top artists as Duke Ellington—a cruel residue that persists. Ellington's music had risen far beyond the Cotton Club.

Webb played the last two numbers with Dorsey's band. "The affair . . . reverted into the greatest jam session ever held on the stage of the Paramount . . . packed with jitterbugs, cats and ickies [non-dancers] from all sections of the city and all hues. . . . [W]hen his playing concluded he departed with that entire audience with him . . . and was not allowed to leave the stage."[28] This appearance helped Webb clinch a booking with Ella and his own orchestra at the Paramount a few months later, another milestone for Webb's and other top Black swing bands.

Webb, Ella, and the band bounced back and forth between Boston and New York for another few weeks: for the Decca sessions May 2 and 3, back to Boston for the band's closing night at Levaggi's, followed by a week at Boston's RKO Theater. The band had been based in Boston for almost three months and had time to do other things there, including play softball in the Boston Common, the idyllic fifty-acre park, complete with softball fields, in the city's center. "Webb's soft-ballers trounced Ben Bernie's in a softball game on Boston Common May 18. Webb's team met and defeated several local bands. . . . If the spectators were surprised to see some of the boys cavorting around the diamond in tuxedos, they were even more amazed at the brand of ball the musicians displayed on occasion." Ella Fitzgerald was a loyal "cheer-leader" at all Webb's baseball games and "enthusiastically cut out with vocals on behalf of the team."[29]

At the Decca sessions on May 2, the band recorded "A-Tisket, A-Tasket" and three other tunes. Ella's other standout recording that day was "I'm Just a Jitterbug," with Ella and the band swinging with a "who cares" vibe, in spite of the inane lyrics. On May 3, the band recorded two instrumentals, "Liza," and Wayman Carver's "Spinnin' the Webb." "Liza (All the Clouds'll Roll Away)," a Gershwin tune from the Ziegfeld musical *Show Girl*, was released as the B-side of "A-Tisket, A-Tasket." Jazz historian John McDonough points out that this was a "classic coupling of art and commerce," although no one at the time suspected "A-Tisket, A-Tasket" would become such a bestseller, and an iconic number for Fitzgerald. In fact, Jack Kapp was reluctant to record it, but Webb insisted. Beverly Peer said: "We almost didn't record it. Bob Stephens [recording engineer at Decca] didn't want to take it. Chick started to pack up his drums and forced the issue. If he hadn't bothered, there'd be no 'Tasket.' That was down to Chick."[30]

The arrangement of "Liza" by Al Feldman is a dazzling tour de force, showing off Webb's artistry and total command of the drums, especially on his twenty-four-bar solo, his lengthiest on a recording. He opens the tune with a breathtaking blur of notes going into a roll, and his dramatically building display of fireworks is precise and emphatic, every cowbell twang and rim shot aimed skyward. The score is so powerful and packed with flourishes that jazz scholars decades later insisted it could not have been written by Alexander, that it had to be by Benny Carter or Charlie Dixon. In subsequent years, Benny Carter confirmed it was Alexander's arrangement, putting this issue to rest. Gunther Schuller beautifully describes Webb's virtuosity: "He was an exceptional soloist with an . . . uncanny ability to articulate with total clarity every sound he produced. . . . In countless performances we can hear his inspirational swing feeling, determining, like some great maestro, the interpretation of the piece, urging the band to greater heights."[31]

On May 3, Decca recorded six tunes with Ella Fitzgerald and Her Savoy Eight, her second session as the nominal leader. All the songs from this session are similar in terms of their feel and mood. These midtempo love songs, including "We Can't Go on This Way" and "Saving Myself for You," fit a popular modality envisioned by song pluggers and Jack Kapp. None from this session became staples by Fitzgerald, as did "I Was Doing All Right," which she recorded in January 1938 with the Savoy Eight.

In the final two weeks of May, Webb's band was back at the Apollo Theater. Then on Sunday, May 29, 1938, they participated in yet another significant jazz event of the late 1930s, the "Carnival of Swing" at Randall's Island, the first outdoor day-long jazz festival. After the completion of the Triborough Bridge in 1936, Randall's Island, between Manhattan, the Bronx, and Queens, had been largely converted to parks and playing fields; it also had a stadium with a racetrack. The Carnival, a benefit for Local 802's Hospital Fund, attracted over twenty-three thousand swing fans and was emceed by Martin Block, host of WNEW's hit radio show *Make Believe Ballroom*.

The *Amsterdam News* reported:

Every swing band or unit of note was there (except Benny Goodman's) but the sepia boys soon made the crowd forget his absence. Those who thought that Duke Ellington was slipping from his throne were given the surprise of their lives when the Duke just took things in hand and laid it in the groove with "St. Louis Blues" and his latest, "I Let a Song Go out of My Heart," featuring Ivie Anderson. A near riot broke out when Duke and his band took the stage. . . . It did prove one thing, and that definitely— Duke Ellington is right out there in front as our ace delineator of swing, with Count Basie and Chick Webb following in close succession. . . . Maybe Goodman's absence was felt? So what![32]

A caravan of more than thirty swing bands and prominent jazz musicians, Black and white, played to ecstatic stadium crowds throughout the festival, which lasted over six hours. Among them were Bunny Berigan, Joe Marsala, W. C. Handy, jazz violinist Stuff Smith, and Slim and Slam. But it was the orchestras of Duke Ellington, Count Basie, and Chick Webb that drove everyone to stand up and dance in the bleachers. (Attempts to "swing out" on the fields and cinder tracks were squashed by officials, who didn't want the racetrack damaged.) Gene Krupa, now leading his own band, closed the festival with a swing favorite, "Don't Be That Way," which Edgar Sampson first wrote for Webb's band in 1934.

The entire day was documented by photographer Otto Hess, who immigrated to New York from Germany in 1930 and became an acclaimed photographer of jazz musicians, opera stars, dancers, and other cultural figures. Hess's hundreds of photos capture jazz artists in the moment—onstage and off—and the ecstatic crowd.[33] Among the most striking photos are those of Ellington, a silhouette of Stuff Smith, and of Webb. Hess zeros in on the drummer during his band's set. Webb and his drum kit are nestled between the edge of the piano and the trombone section, all in a row. Webb is half smiling, not really posing, poised between beats while the brass are playing something that doesn't require a lot of him in that moment. Other people are seen milling around behind the bandstand. But Webb doesn't look as healthy as in photos of him taken a few months earlier.[34]

In another feat of marathon musicianship, in the early hours of May 30, following the festival, Webb and Ella Fitzgerald joined another mixed-race array of theater stars, radio hosts, and Apollo favorites for the Apollo Theater's annual Monster Ball, a fundraiser for the Harlem Children's Center. Though the country had largely recovered from the worst years of the Depression, fundraising events in Harlem were an ever-present part of the community. Most likely Chick and Ella put in a short appearance, as did Ellington and Stuff Smith, who'd also spent the day at Randall's Island. Integrated fundraising events were now a normal part of New York's entertainment community. The Apollo show lasted until 5 a.m. and netted over three thousand dollars, enabling 240 children to attend camp that summer.[35]

A few days later, Webb received another honorary degree, this one from the senior class of New York University: "The jitterbugs have finally gained the recognition of the Academic side of the higher school of learning at an elaborate ceremony. . . . The Senior class of New York University conferred upon bandleader Chick Webb the honorary degree of M.D. Master of Drums [Yale's was Master of Swing]. Walter Winchell was awarded for outstanding newspaper columnist and commentator." Though Webb's honorary degrees were awarded to him by students from Yale and New York University, not by the universities, they were a different kind of symbol for Webb's hard-won, well-deserved recognition. People voted for Mr. Rhythm, even when institutions ignored him.

Webb got the biggest laugh at the ceremony by answering the question "How can a college kid get into the band business?" His reply was, "Well, first they have to get their union cards."[36]

18

The Last Grooves

"A-Tisket, A-Tasket" was an overflowing basket, the breakthrough hit that Webb had been yearning for and working toward for years. It was number one on the Hit Parade within a month of its release and stayed near the top for several more. The Gale agency got nonstop requests for gigs, theater and tour dates. Al Wilde, Oakley's replacement, now handled press and public relations for Webb. He was known to deliver baby chicks to some theaters along with press releases. His approach was more novelty driven than Oakley's; hers was strategic, tactically and musically.

Oakley easily found a new job in New York's jazz and big band scene, and still considered Webb a dear friend. In early April 1938, she started working for Joe Glaser, Louis Armstrong's long-time manager. Now the booking agencies were playing catch-up. *Billboard* reported: "Colored band booking field moves a step closer to big business category with MCA starting a detailed survey of that field in ork [orchestra] activity, and Joe Glaser adding Helen Oakley to his staff to head the promo work for his office. . . . Oakley ties with Glaser for further building of Armstrong, Andy Kirk, Willie Bryant and Hot Lips Page."[1]

Swing music reigned as the country's pop music, and some events, recording sessions, and radio broadcasts in New York and other cities were more racially inclusive, at least among some presenters, musicians, and bandleaders. Even so, these bursts of breaking through racial barriers took place in a saturated market for band bookings, and caused concern within the "big" business of swing and issues of appropriation.

In fall 1938, several articles by entertainment reporters reported that "Bookers and managers of Negro bands are becoming increasingly worried about evaporating time." Webb's success at Levaggi's and the Paramount and his band's theater attendance records were exceptional; other top bands like Andy Kirk's or Teddy Hill's never achieved the same huge attraction with white audiences. Additionally, many A-list bands like Kirk's and territory bands were now losing out on local theater dates: a "slow elimination of road stands and dance dates" was hurting them. "But the biggest slap came with the advent of white bands going into torrid Negro music—long ignored," wrote Frank Marshall Davis in the *Amsterdam News*, in a retort to an article in *Variety* about this subject. "Result finds white bands 'outheating' the originators of swing, and getting preference," making it ever more difficult for the Black bands to get engagements."

Davis's article continued:

> That whites have invaded the field of hot jazz, or swing . . . in large numbers is no secret, but as to the whites "outheating" the originators of swing I must take exception. . . .
>
> No critic who bases his judgment on performance rather than racial considerations can conscientiously class any white bands other than those of Goodman, [Bob] Crosby or T. Dorsey on the same level as the topnotch Colored orchestras . . . but even Benny must bow to such super-greats as Ellington and Basie. As for heat, who can get better than Armstrong, Lunceford, Webb et al, when they slip into the groove? . . . If the truth is wanted, then the old standard issue of race has caused this increasing freezing out of our bands.[2]

These issues grew more contentious with the Goodman band's unprecedented popularity and the industrialization of swing bands that ensued, especially in 1938–39. Other issues—what went into this music, not just "who invented swing"—were openly discussed by the Black entertainment press. The *Chicago Defender* reported:

> Owners and managers of name Race bands [Glaser, Gale, Oxley, Mills] sent out a plea this week asking that Benny Goodman and other big radio bands use another system of handling their song arrangements and not employ Race musicians as they have done in the past.
>
> The objection is based on the charge that so many of the arrangements being used are taken from other bands thus impairing their value during road tours. It is pointed out that many of the arrangers worked with large Race bands and that the style they take to the Goodmans, Krupas, Shaws and others in reality belong to the band they once played with. . . . Were the Race bands given the opportunity to appear on the air as commercials there would be no argument the managers point out. However the Race bands

are not given air commercials and they naturally suffer when they take a
number into a community that has been worn out over the air with iden-
tical arrangements.[3]

It is ironic and cruel to suggest that the same talented Black arrangers who
pioneered as swing band arrangers and then got hired by Goodman, Dorsey,
Artie Shaw, and others should now be denied the more lucrative work offered
by these bandleaders and their respective managers, booking agents, and
record labels. At the same time, the plea for a different system was justified—
especially to give Black bands equal opportunities and pay for national radio-
sponsored shows and tour dates. That would have helped to level the playing
field. Black arrangers in that era were asked to write arrangements that could
help mold a band's sound—a big chunk of its identity—to make it "sound"
more Black.

Meanwhile, Webb's band, then and now, was accused of sounding too
white. In the marketplace, though, whatever they were doing was working.
They were now the rock stars of their time. Teddy McRae was exultant about
the band's hard-won fame. "Songs like 'Love is Here' and 'Mr. Paganini.' No
colored girl was singing songs like that, man! We jumped out five years ahead
of everybody."[4]

Starting in mid-June 1938, Webb's band was on the road again almost constantly. The route was insane: to New England, all the way to Maine, then
west to Rochester, down through Ohio, then to Chicago and Detroit. After
a brief return to New York, the band headed south again on one-nighters to
dances in Black coal-mining towns in West Virginia, put together by Black
promoter George Morton, a West Virginian who masterminded many top
Black bands' visits there in the 1930s. Musicologist Chris Wilkinson's account of Morton's work documents his success in getting bands like Webb's
to venues in small towns and off-the-main-route places, and the granular
aspect of Morton's bookings: driving distances, advance ticket sales, etc. One
wishes that there were other Mortons, trustworthy entrepreneurs whose
local colleagues made these tour stops worth the trip, financially and socially. Morton's friendship with editors at the *Pittsburgh Courier* gave his
efforts visibility, and top bands on these stops were reviewed in the paper.[5]

For Webb's countless small-town one-nighters, it's difficult to know the
details, except by locating random scrapbooks or notebooks belonging

to a musician, fan, or long-ago connection. Who organized the Black so-rority dances outside of Tulsa, or similar one-nighters? Who were Gale's other foot soldiers? Did Gale consult Webb about small venues? The Gale Agency left no records or contracts to trace these trips. In September 1938, *DownBeat* reported on Webb's summer dates in the Midwest, but it only lists a couple of big ones. The band netted 1,600 dollars for five hours of playing at the Coliseum in St. Louis, Missouri, and 1,100 dollars for Fairyland Amusement Park in Kansas City, Missouri. Nothing is mentioned about the nameless dates in between at small ballrooms or city auditoriums. Webb's routes linking other one-nighters don't seem as logical as Morton's and his colleagues', though the Gale Agency continually followed up on booking agents' perceived demand for "hued" band attractions in Florida and other southern states. Mapping additional stops via newspaper ads and chance reviews are the only footprints Webb and Ella and the band left as they got on and off the bus.[6]

When Webb and the band returned to New York, it was to another break-through gig starting August 10. Their names were lit up on the biggest, brightest theater marquis of all, in front of the Paramount Theater in Times Square. These days, that notion—a variety stage show in the middle of New York City with a first-run movie, top-name swing band, and comedians and dance acts—seems quaint, another century's entertainment. In the late 1930s through mid-1940s, a booking at the Paramount was—literally—paramount. For swing big bands, "Bway's top variety house.... The Paramount is the Mecca of all concert bands of worth throughout the country. To be booked at the Paramount in America is better than a com-mand performance for the King and Queen of England.... For this booking Webb will headline an 'All-colored revue which is also a rarity in the house.'" The ad read: "'The Chick That Lays the Golden Eggs'—Chick Webb: The King of the Drums, Roosting at the New York Paramount Theater."[7]

Judging from other ads for the Paramount and notes kept by the theater's stage manager, the Swing Era didn't really "hit" the Paramount until 1937, though popular hotel bands like Art Shaw's (before he was known as "Artie"), Ozzie Nelson's, and other "sweet" big bands were there regularly. Benny Goodman's orchestra debuted at the theater in March 1937, followed by Louis Armstrong, and then the usual offerings. Starting in 1938, A-list big swing bands were booked almost every week and played to packed houses through the early 1940s. Webb's August 1938 engagement made him the first new Black bandleader to be hired there (Armstrong and Cab Calloway preceded him); his was among a handful of Black bands to perform at the Paramount during that entire period.

The stage manager's notes for the Paramount's shows from this time include run times and stage plots for most of them and are part of a small collection at the Performing Arts Library of Lincoln Center. The notes for Webb's debut week, in August 1938, are missing, but one can see his band's stage plot, which he signed, for the band's return engagement in March 1939. Since all photos from that period are black and white, handwritten notes on the stage plot provide new details: the stage setup row by row, Webb's elevated platform, which music stands to use, etc. The band would wear "powder blue suits" to match blue-and-white stage risers and cardboard "fronts" for the music stands. The typical program order was: newsreel, organ solo, cartoon, band, feature film, film short, and sports reel. Webb's sets ran fifty-five minutes, starting at 11 a.m., 1:30 p.m., 4:30 p.m., 8 p.m., and 11 p.m.—a brutal schedule.[8]

Webb, Ella, and the band were a sensation at the Paramount and broke attendance records. A few weeks later the *Afro* reported that Webb and the band received a bonus, and would return to the Paramount in 1939 with a thousand-dollar salary increase. "Chick and the Chickadees, with Ella Fitzgerald, now rate as the top sepia band in Paramount's lobby poll, with 5660 votes." The theater's exit contests for "Best Band" still segregated the contenders. "No sepia bands have cracked the top ten white bands, a contest now in its 5th month at the theater." Benny Goodman and Tommy Dorsey topped the Paramount's winners.[9]

Webb had to hire a few new musicians that summer and fall. Louis Jordan left in June, weeks before the big Paramount engagement. Jordan's biographer John Chilton wrote that it would be "fair to say that Chick Webb never really took to Louis Jordan." Chilton, Teddy McRae, and others suggested several reasons for Jordan's leaving. One was that Jordan, who was married, was having an affair with Ella Fitzgerald. This upset Webb, who knew that relationships within the band could be a distraction to all concerned. Mario Bauza thought highly of Ella and was protective of her. "Ella—she was never had luck with men. There was some guy who wanted to become her manager, then Louis Jordan. Louis Jordan was her boyfriend. I used to get so mad at them, 'You should be ashamed of yourselves.' I almost got into a fight—me and Louis, on account of Ella."[10]

Webb also got upset with Jordan about other things. Jordan was a comical extrovert as an entertainer; he occasionally stole the show, as a vocalist or fooling around. One night at Levaggi's when Webb was in the hospital, Jordan instigated a spontaneous parade around the club that brought down the house. Webb was furious when he found out about it. Jordan also complained to Bardu Ali that he should have been featured more on saxophone and as a singer. For all his complaints, Jordan learned a lot from Webb as a bandleader now in the top ranks of the profession.

Jordan's worst offense was that he started making plans to form his own group and approached Taft Jordan, Ella, and bassist Beverly Peer, none of whom would have left Webb at this point. Jordan's plans were vague, even though he was collecting arrangements and had some ideas. But he was still largely an unknown performer, with no guarantee of success. When Webb heard about these plans, he fired Jordan on the spot, while the band was at the RKO Theater in Boston in May 1938. Webb then gave Jordan a slight reprieve and let him work out his two-week notice.

Beverly Peer told Chilton:

> When Louis was planning to form his own band he may have thought it was a secret but to everyone else it was obvious. . . . He and Ella were pretty close at that time and he was definitely trying to corral her in his great plans. . . . Louis was always for Louis, he was aggressive and he was scheming. So when he asked me if I was interested in joining his band, I said, "There's no way I'm going to leave Chick to go with you." I don't think he ever forgave me.[11]

Another personnel issue came up during Webb's milestone week at the Paramount Theater. Webb gave Mario Bauza his notice, which, in this case, was heartbreaking. He'd taken a chance on Bauza early on, mentored him, and genuinely cared for him. Bauza had gone to speak with Charles Buchanan at the Savoy about getting better pay, for himself and the other sidemen. Bauza recalled:

> Chick's getting big, big. So naturally, I want to see some of that money, too. I know about who is already making money for that band, and they don't want to pay the guys, not so much. So I began to speak [to Buchanan]. That's Charlie Buchanan. He was partners with Moe Gale. . . . He said, "Oh, you're trying to create a revolution here. You're Latino, you're Franco, you're

a dictator." I said no, "I'm not a dictator. I think we deserve the money. *You* get money for the band!" . . . So the guy is so bad, he went to the Paramount Theater.

Bauza knew that this would be the end for him in Webb's band. Chick told him that Buchanan wanted him out. Bauza said, "So he gave me my two weeks notice. The day I'm supposed to leave he [Webb] comes into the dressing room. He starts crying, and says he doesn't want me to leave. I say, 'No, I'm a man of principal. I won't play another hour in this band. Not next month, or next year. . . . I got to leave. That's all there is to it.' "[12]

Webb's band, like other big bands, had "sliding scale" pay deals: star soloists like Taft Jordan and now Ella presumably were paid the most, as was Teddy McRae for taking on extra administrative tasks. Long-standing members such as Bauza and Sandy Williams also got a higher pay rate. John Chilton wrote that, except for Webb, rarely did anyone earn more than a hundred dollars a week, and Louis Jordan's share was often closer to seventy-five dollars. Since Moe Gale was taking so much off the top, Bauza and the other sidemen knew they were getting the short end of things, financially. It's unknown how much Webb's sidemen were actually paid on the southern tours, which made money. Gale and even Buchanan took a good chunk of the band's gross earnings. How much leverage did Webb have with Gale and Buchanan, known for being outrageously cheap with musicians? Why didn't Webb insist that his musicians get paid more when he could have? There was still an imbalance of power between Webb and Gale, despite Webb's celebrity status.

Bauza soon got another job, first with Don Redman's orchestra, then a couple of weeks later with Cab Calloway, which is where he met Dizzy Gillespie. Bauza's pathbreaking collaborations with Gillespie and their musical brainstorming leading to Afro-Cuban jazz fusion were several years in the future.

In fall 1938 Webb's band was back on the road for another southern tour. Even now, when the band was enjoying peak fame, Gale didn't pay for Pullman cars and the band was back on the bus, except for Webb, who rode with Bardu Ali in his Cadillac. Sally Webb didn't go with the band on long trips but sometimes drove with Webb to nearby cities such as Philadelphia or Baltimore to see Webb's family or DC. These tours had memorable moments, good and bad, echoing the experiences of other big bands on the road in those years.

McRae recalled:

When we got into Savannah, the bus went down and circled the main street of the colored neighborhood. And everybody was standing there with their little girls, waiting to meet Ella Fitzgerald. . . . Now we had been riding all day long. It was hot. And Ella wouldn't come out of the bus sometimes because her hair was all down. We had to keep her in the back. Then she got dressed, she'd come out—she had a welcome committee! . . . It was really rough on a girl traveling with the band, especially in the summer time. And here you've been riding half of the night and half of the morning in the heat, you don't have a chance to wash your hair and all. Chick would say, "Hey, wait a minute!" Everybody would get out of the bus, and Ella would go back on and fix herself up.

Gale's team didn't push to integrate venues, which Irving Mills insisted on for Ellington's and Cab's southern dates. Sandy Williams said repeatedly that these tours really got to him. He drank heavily in those years; he often tried to avoid doing so but sometimes couldn't resist. "Traveling by bus, sleeping in it, just getting a sandwich here and a sandwich there, you were naturally tired all the time. Then you say, 'To hell with it, I'm going to get a drink.'"

Williams said:

Most of the tours were in the South. Business was good there, and that's why the office sent us there. We might hit Chicago on a theatre date, but in the hot summer we always seemed to be in Texas. That was how Moe Gale booked us. . . . Oh, brother! Some parts of Texas were as bad as Mississippi. Going through states like Mississippi or Alabama, you wouldn't have any trouble in the big cities, but the highways were bad in those days. You might have to make a detour, get stuck in muddy roads, or make a stop at one of those dinky gas stations. With Chick, it was in a bus. We'd play some white dances in the South, and some Negro. Some had a rope stretched across the floor, so that whites danced on one side and the Negroes on the other. In others, the whites would be dancing and the blacks upstairs listening, and they all paid the same price. That used to burn me up and make me evil. And that was another reason to take a drink.[13]

Webb's road staff usually included Tim Gale; another white road manager known as "Frenchie"; and Joe Saunders. Saunders had started out as Webb's "band boy" and valet in the early 1930s and now helped with everything—packing and unpacking Webb's drums, assisting with stage management tasks, and taking care of Webb's communications. On the road in the South there was usually some incident involving racist affronts. For a dance near Houston, Texas, Bardu Ali drove into a parking lot near the dance hall in his expensive "$3000" car, and the attendant wouldn't let him park there. Ali was told, "Niggers are not allowed to park here unless they are driving for a white man."[14] Ali went to the local police department and lodged a complaint. The *Amsterdam News*'s next sentences could have been written today: "Charges of inefficiency, lack of intelligence and other charges have been filed. Recommendations for the establishment of a police school have been ignored by city officials."

When the band headed north to Baltimore, they helped break the color line in Webb's hometown, at least on stage. The band's booking at the Hippodrome, a three-thousand-seat first-run movie palace with live acts, big bands, and famous radio comedians, finally took place October 21–27, 1938. The only Black artists who'd performed there previously were Cab Calloway and Duke Ellington. When Webb's booking was first announced, the *Pittsburgh Courier* reported that it had been so long since another "colored unit" had appeared at the theater that "those young in the business can't remember the last time."[15]

In Webb's day, the Hippodrome did not allow Black customers to sit in the orchestra—or even get in. Webb's distant cousins Brad Rowe and Mary Williams recalled hearing Mary's mother talk about going with Sally Webb to go see Webb, Ella, and the band at the theater. Webb's mother and grandparents had to enter through the stage door and stand in the wings to hear the band play. Sally Webb wanted to give Helen, Mary's mother, a treat and sit out front in the audience.

> Now, I understand that Chick's wife was very fair skinned and she passed. When I say passed, I mean in those days black folks whose skin complexion could get them an upper hand, they could. So, she passed. Now, my cousin tells me that her mother and Chick's wife, Sally, went to the Hippodrome where Sally could get in and get a seat. But her mother couldn't because she was brown skin. . . . [T]hey didn't allow Blacks on the main floor in the Hippodrome. So, it must have been a disappointment. I mean, you know, to have one of the rock stars of the day, who's a member of your family, come

and you go to see him and can't sit close—first row or second row—because of the color of your skin.

Mary Williams remembered this was a huge slight to her mother and, in a different way, affected Sally. "Now, my mother said she went with Sally because Sally was fair skin, and thought she could probably get in, too, and they knew who she [Sally] was. But, because my mother was with her, they kind of like dispelled the myth, her myth anyway—of passing."[16]

Meanwhile, Webb's health issues were getting worse. After the Hippodrome engagement he was admitted to Johns Hopkins Hospital: "The midget maestro will enter Johns Hopkins Hospital for a thorough physical examination. Although ailing for several months, the dynamic leader has been loath to cancel his ever-increasing string of engagements."[17]

Webb stayed at Hopkins for a week for "treatment and observation." During his stay, he spoke with his long-time physician, Dr. Ralph J. Young. The two of them wanted to start a fund for a playground and recreation center for the children of East Baltimore. There was nothing of the kind in that part of the city, where Webb was raised. Webb wanted to bring the band to Baltimore for a series of concerts to kick off fundraising for this project but hadn't had time to organize the dates yet.

After Webb left Hopkins, he rejoined Ella and the band in Cleveland. Almost all the dates were one-nighters except for a week at the Regal Theater in Chicago. Their route took them to a sorority dance near Tulsa, Oklahoma; to Dallas; and then to Galveston, where the band got stiffed—this time by Black promoters—for a dance at the city auditorium. The two promoters were "alleged to have absconded with approximately $400 in advance ticket sales, leaving the Webb outfit unpaid for their performance. Charges of theft, a felony, were filed yesterday morning. Webb's manager said the men had signed a contract agreeing to pay the band $550 and that after the dance only $100 was in the box office. He said about $400 was from advance ticket sales."[18] But splitting $550 between Webb and the entire band, Bardu and Ella, the musicians would have earned $25 each for that night, if that.

Webb had been stiffed before. In some ways, the financial risks of playing one-nighters far from main hubs were high, considering the extra travel time. Gale and big booking agencies like MCA and Consolidated Radio Artists now had more leverage with large venues to hold the venues more accountable; the reverse was also true. Still, it's hard to know how much the band was actually paid for these trips.

Webb, Ella, and the band worked their way back to the East Coast with no further "gate" theft. The band played for a Black fraternity dance in upstate New York before starting the New Year of 1939 at the State Theater in Hartford, Connecticut. It was a wild ride for a drummer/bandleader who was getting increasingly frail and trying to hide it.

> And then the hard work began to tell on Chick. Because every time we closed a stage down, the valet had to go out and pick him up and bring him off stage. Because this was the beginning—that hump was beginning to tell on him, you know.
>
> —Teddy McRae

> Chick used to let me get by with so much stuff, but he thought the world of me and I thought the world of him. He used to tell me, "When I was broke I couldn't get a drink if I wanted one, now I got money and I can't drink." He had so much wrong with him it was pitiful, just pitiful.
>
> —Sandy Williams

In the winter and early spring of 1939, Webb and the band stayed in New York City. They were a triumph at the Apollo in mid-January, playing to standing-room-only houses for the entire week, and squeaking in a benefit for children at the Renaissance Ballroom. At the end of the month the band broke through another color barrier, this time in midtown Manhattan: they were booked for three weeks at the Cocoanut Grove, a rooftop nightclub at the Park Central Hotel across the street from Carnegie Hall. This was as rare a gig in New York City for a Black band as performing at the Hippodrome in Baltimore. Webb's band was the first "colored attraction since Noble Sissle's fling there several years ago. Tough assignment. Notwithstanding that the Park Central is one of the best known hotels in the country and one of the finest in New York, its nitery business has been far below par and no band has been able to make any sort of attendance records there in many years. The spot will make Webb the biggest attraction in the business with its four coast-to-coast broadcasts a week."[19]

The *Afro* reporter was more blunt:

> Funny thing about that Park Central job. The Park Central is a place where people of color are conspicuous by their absence. There are some

what-cha-may-call-ems going under the name of Porto Ricans, but no Harlem scenery among the employees. Added to that is the fact that ofay musicians who didn't like to see the browns taking the frosting off the cake did their bit by passing around a few digs in the back when Chick wasn't looking. But come hades or high tide, the Webb's boys got the job.[20]

One can hear a wide range of Webb's music during the band's last few months with their leader in early winter through May 1939. In addition to Webb's and Fitzgerald's Decca sessions, several reissue recordings of live radio broadcasts and transcriptions offer a wealth of rarely heard music.

Twelve instrumentals were recorded for radio transcriptions on January 9, 1939, by RCA Victor for NBC Thesaurus. Though they do not have terrific sound quality, musically they offer some of the best existing recordings of Chick Webb. Though Webb was getting progressively ill, he sounds strong and vigorous throughout—a crackling powerhouse. On "Tea for Two" and "Blue Skies," swing standards, the band is unified on the sectional playing with exciting solos by Taft Jordan, Bobby Stark, Sandy Williams, and Wayman Carver on flute on "Dinah." Pianist Tommy Fulford is on these titles; he's a versatile stylist, imaginatively breaking into stride at times, and swinging along with Webb. This is the third recorded version of Webb's showpiece "Liza." The first was the one Webb recorded with his orchestra for Decca in May 1938, and the second was in September 1938, live with the "Saturday Night Swing Club's" CBS studio band. These latter two are taken at even faster clips than the Decca recording and Webb is on fire, especially on the "Swing Club" broadcast, which also features Roy Eldridge soaring on trumpet. Both have ingenious touches on drums by Webb, who steams along. There are terrific ensemble passages leading up to Webb's fantastic drum roll finale.

Webb's Decca sessions of spring 1939 were split as previously with a few dates for the entire band and two sessions featuring Ella Fitzgerald and Her Savoy Eight. Kapp, Webb, and Fitzgerald wanted to capitalize on the success of "A-Tisket, A-Tasket." Some of the results from these sessions were genuinely awful novelty songs, like "Chew Chew Chew Chew, Your Bubble Gum." That Kapp et al. felt compelled to release this kind of follow-up seems ill-thought, compared to Fitzgerald's gems from these sessions, which were hits on the radio and live. One can imagine that romantic dance lovers would be swept into a reverie by Ella's "If Anything Happened to You" and "If You Ever Change Your Mind."

The best of the Decca records from spring 1939 are a couple of swing arrangements with the entire Webb outfit and Ella. On "Undecided," Webb playfully takes the time from a two-step and kicks it up to a fast 4/4. Like "Tasket," it's an undeniably hip number for Ella and the band. Ella's phrasing is relaxed and also moves subtly ahead of the beat in this clever Van Alexander arrangement, in which the brass and woodwinds break into a spirited call and response.

"T'aint What You Do," a cover of Sy Oliver's hit for Jimmie Lunceford's orchestra, is another standout from these Decca sessions. For years, other bandleaders performed and recorded their renditions of tunes and arrangements written for Webb by Edgar Sampson. It's a pleasure to hear Webb reciprocate on this number. After the ensemble builds intensity through the vamp, Ella finally enters and unleashes one of her most extended scat passages to date. No other vocalist could swing so hard and make this tune feel airborne.

Webb covers Count Basie's "One O' Clock Jump" on a broadcast recording from the Cocoanut Grove (from February 1939). Webb's band rocks on this hard-swinging favorite, a tribute to Basie and testament that Webb's band never lost its jazz feeling and orientation. By contrast, though many of Webb's Decca recordings are treasures, they do not convey the full power of the band in its performance contexts: at the Savoy, the Apollo, on the road, at the Paramount, and even at a posh New York hotel nightclub—swinging, everywhere they went.

On March 4, 1939, Webb and Ella Fitzgerald attended the groundbreaking ceremony for the Savoy Pavilion at the 1939 World's Fair, along with some of Whitey's Lindy Hoppers and twenty buses of dancers from Harlem, on a cold rainy day. The fair's opening was April 30; Webb's band was scheduled to perform that day, and a slate of other top-name big bands were scheduled to play at the Savoy Pavilion for the fair's duration. Moe Gale spent eighteen months negotiating with the city to construct the pavilion and about 130,000 dollars on its construction, utilities, promotion, and employees, including bands and dancers. It was a tall wedge-shaped structure, with an elegant exterior decorated with oversized images of the Savoy Ballroom's design logos—happy dancing feet and music notes. Along one outside wall was an elevated bandstand with room for a swing combo (not a full big band) and two of Whitey's

Lindy Hoppers. The musicians and dancers for this bandstand played and danced almost nonstop, seven days a week, from noon until closing time.

The Savoy Pavilion did not have a public dance area, but due to popular demand, weeks later the fair started holding dances for three thousand dancers in a different space. Inside the pavilion's interior was a bare seven-hundred-seat auditorium, a stark contrast to the exterior, where a twenty-minute dance exhibition was presented several times a day. Inside, starting at noon, and then every hour, a team of Whitey's Lindy Hoppers performed a "History of the Lindy Hop," beginning with African dance, on through the Cake Walk and Turkey Trot, on to the Lindy Hop, accompanied by a live band. Initially the Savoy Pavilion was "the only large concession featuring colored help and entertainment at the Fair" and was "the only spot considered as an outlet for race musicians." That was no longer the case when, during the last week of June, another attraction opened. "The Hot Mikado" starred tap dance legend Bill Robinson, with a second team of Whitey's dancers, all of whom started getting injuries from being overworked. The Savoy Pavilion closed at the end of July, a financial disaster for Gale despite the reams of publicity it generated for the ballroom, and for Harlem entertainment in general.[21]

As things turned out, Webb, Ella Fitzgerald, and the band only made a few special appearances at the World's Fair. Gale realized the band's intense schedule was impacting Webb's health. He hired Teddy Hill's band as the steady band during the Savoy Pavilion's first few weeks, and several other bands appeared later on.

Kenny Clarke was Hill's drummer at the time and played for the Lindy Hoppers at the Savoy Pavilion, "16 appearances a day." Clarke got to know Webb closely in 1938–39. Hill's band was frequently the alternate band at the Savoy Ballroom and the headliner when Webb's band as touring. Clarke was one of the younger drummers starting to perform in a more fluid style, headed toward bebop. Webb complimented Clarke on his playing and encouraged him whenever he heard him. "Chick was on the left bandstand and we were on the right," said Clarke.

> So every time, when we would finish, I would be sitting behind Chick. . . .
> He said, "What was that tune you just played?" I was so close to him, you
> know, and why he liked me, God only knows. . . . [M]usic was everything to
> him, that was his life. . . . He was so fantastic, because I knew that I would
> never be able to play like Chick—his conception. Not his technique and all,
> because I could always copy his technique. But the way he played, I could

never reach that stage—his conceptions, the way he would do things, throw himself in it. Project it. Oh, my God, I would stay behind him all day, all night. All night long I was there, "Hey, where's Kenny?" There I'd be, sitting behind Chick. That's where I was.[22]

Webb's band was back at the Paramount Theater the week of March 8, 1939. Webb's drumming was in no way diminished on stage, but offstage things were different. Sandy Williams said that Webb's valet Joe Saunders would have to pick him up off the bandstand. "He'd [Joe] come up on the bandstand at the Paramount after the curtain came down, and have to pick him up in his arms. Take his clothes off and wash him off, and dry him off. He had three or four tuxedos so they could dry out between shows. He could play his tail off."[23]

The band kept going. Decca sessions, radio broadcasts, short trips, and longer tours were coming up. Webb's biggest health issues—excruciating pain in his spine and kidney problems—were worsening, and the tubercular infection had spread to his kidneys. He was in and out of Johns Hopkins for treatment in April and May 1939 while the band started a long East Coast tour, from Boston to Florida. Webb had been at Hopkins so often that a room at the hospital's Halsted Clinic became known as Chick Webb's room. "Few of his admirers knew that every month or so in these late years he had to go to this hospital for treatment and rest."[24]

During these weeks, other drummers traveled with the band and substituted for whole nights, or played most of the sets when Webb still played a few numbers. "Big Sid" Catlett was one of them. Catlett worked with the top names in jazz—Louis Armstrong, Fletcher Henderson, Benny Carter, and many others—and had as big a reputation among swing drummers as Webb, though he now leaned toward playing with smaller combos heading in a boppish direction. Kaiser Marshall, Fletcher Henderson's long-time drummer, also helped Webb out during this time. Marshall had been working on his own, occasionally leading his own groups after Henderson's band finally broke up in 1936. Bill Beason, the younger drummer who often "warmed up" for Webb at the Savoy, worked with various bands but would try to drop anything to help Chick Webb.

Webb resisted sitting out his band's fantastic run. He was in a battle with his body until the end. At the end of March, the band went to DC for a week at the Howard Theater, and Webb went into Johns Hopkins, reportedly for a procedure to drain fluid from his spine that was causing intense pain. Kaiser Marshall took over for him, and Webb rejoined the band for at least part of their week at the Royal Theater, in Baltimore. Sally now traveled with Webb for all the trips that spring. The band returned to Philadelphia for a week's run, then a few days in New York, before going back to Boston for a three-week engagement, starting April 27, Thursdays to Mondays, at the Southland Cafe, a big venue downtown, right near the Boston Common.

The band had a fifteen-minute broadcast from Southland every night. A compilation of these broadcasts offers a thrilling experience of hearing the band from the dance floor during these last weeks of Webb's life. These performances are intense, raucous—far more alive and fiercely swinging than most of the band's recordings for Decca during the past three months.

The band's last broadcast from Southland was May 19, 1939. Webb's playing is stupendous. He is elegant on Ella's ballads, "I Never Knew Heaven Could Speak" and "If I Didn't Care," and magnificent on up-tempo numbers, pushing the beat, urging the band to its most exuberant playing. Both the audience and band members roar along with "Stars and Stripes Forever" as Webb keeps beating it out in a swinging tribute to American band music. "My Wild Irish Rose" is as much a masterpiece showcase for Webb as "Liza," as he follows a slow four-bar showtime vamp by the horns with impossibly fast four-bar breaks that get increasingly emphatic and wild. Soloists Garvin Bushell, Taft Jordan, and Sandy Williams rock out before Webb's lengthy solo, which builds with each beat. The band zings with unity at a whirling tempo.

On Sunday May 21, 1939, Webb and the band returned to the Savoy Ballroom for five nights, with Benny Carter's band playing the early sets, allowing Webb to rest up. Still, no one suspected that these would be his last nights at the ballroom, home of the Savoy King. The same was true when the band played at the Apollo, May 26–June 1, 1939. At one show, *Variety*'s reviewer reported that Webb didn't come on stage until the last fifteen minutes of the ninety-minute set; his sub—most likely Bill Beason—played from behind a screen. The Apollo's homegrown star Ella could hardly get off the stage; the crowd "didn't want to let her go."[25]

Chick Webb and Ella Fitzgerald were greeted with wild acclaim everywhere they went. On Monday, May 29, they were honored guests at a special swing concert sponsored by the National Swing Clubs of America at the Hippodrome Theater in New York. This was a huge event for the predominantly white parent organization, the United Hot Clubs of America, and Helen Oakley, Marshall Stearns, John Hammond, and their fellow club presidents, members, and VIPs attended. This concert featured a mixed-race jam session by its top award recipients, artist-bandleaders "picked for their outstanding ability in the world of swing, plus mastership of one or more instruments." Duke Ellington along with Paul Whiteman were selected to lead this aggregation, which included appearances by Chick Webb, Count Basie, the Dorsey Brothers, Benny Goodman, Louis Armstrong, Chu Berry, Cab Calloway, Roy Eldridge, Teddy Wilson, Charlie Barnett, and others. "Capturing the highest honor of the entire affair, Ella Fitzgerald has been selected to act as vocalist for the orchestra, advancing her, and rightfully so, as the top singer of popular songs in the country today. Each of them will receive a trophy for their part in the advancement of popular music." Jimmie Lunceford was selected as the bandleader who has added "the most originality. All the bandleaders were to share these honors with their bands.[26]

This concert and Webb's last nights at the Savoy and the Apollo were his last appearances in Harlem, New York City, his adopted hometown.

Webb, Ella, and the band returned to Washington, DC, for a couple of nights. Two engagements offer separate portraits of segregated entertainment in the nation's capitol. The first, Friday, June 2, was a dance at Suburban Gardens, a Black-owned and -managed amusement park, the only amusement park within city limits. Kaiser Marshall played for Webb the entire night. On June 3, the band played for a moonlight cruise on the SS *Potomac*; no Black patrons were admitted on the boat, which accommodated 2,500 people and had two sailings, one at 8:45 and the next at 11:45, a moonlight ride for forty cents. (Gene Krupa's band was booked for the following Saturday night.) Marshall played most of the night, until the boat headed back to the dock after the second show.

Bardu Ali vividly remembered this night:

The last dance he [Webb] played was on a boat on the Potomac River. . . . We carried Kaiser Marshall. I don't know if you remember, he was a great drummer . . . and he was a substitute drummer for Chick be cause Chick was hurting and he was in misery and everything. He couldn't play all night, so he would just play a few numbers. But this night, when we came back our theme song was "Let's Get Together," and boy, I'm telling you, Webb *played*. I can see it right now on that boat coming back to dock. He played so much drums that night, it was just unbelievable.

Helen Oakley never forgot this night, either. "The last dance he played was on a boat on the Potomac River . . . and the thing was that he went to Baltimore, and it broke my heart because I felt that he wanted me with him. And I should have been with him, and if he didn't have a bad office I would have been with him, no matter what, for anything. And I used to worry and worry about him, and he was progressively dying."

Oakley said the cruise was a "white" affair, and Webb gave her cues to speak with him behind the bandstand, but she didn't, worried about causing trouble by crossing the racial boundary in that setting. "Because I didn't want to get him in trouble either. I mean I could have also been in trouble, and I didn't want to get him in trouble, so I didn't. And it broke my heart because he was giving me that eye, that desperate eye, and I didn't." That was the last time Oakley saw him.[27]

Webb's devastating illness and pain were out in the open now, not only to Sally, but to McRae, Ella, and everyone. Other star drummers—Jo Jones, Cozy Cole, Jimmy Crawford, Gene Krupa, Davie Tough—all knew and were deeply worried about Webb. But Webb's spirit was huge. McRae said Webb would tell people, "Now, don't be down in the dumps, everything will be OK."

Jo Jones distinctly remembered watching a rehearsal of Webb's band with Kaiser Marshall during this period. Jones said he would carry this moment "with him for the rest of his life." Something about Kaiser's phrasing or accents bothered Webb.

> When everybody else was off someplace, we [Jones and Webb] were off to another place, and he must have known he was going to die, because I went down to Manhattan Center and Kaiser Marshall was playing the drums. We were backstage. . . . [H]e was listening to the band and he said, "No, Kaiser, not with my band."
>
> At that particular time I was tempted to leave Basie's band to join Chick Webb's band because of his kidney ailment, I was going to leave Basie's band and play with Mr. Chick Webb out of respect and out of love and at the same time I had a selfish motive. I realized that this man was dying and there were several drummers in New York that never took advantage of being around the man any longer than I had. But I figured if I could get any crumbs from the table having a direct contact with this man, I was going to tell Mr. Basie, "I'm going to join Chick Webb's band, and let Chick tell me." After that I followed the band to Washington, D.C.[28]

On Sunday, June 4, the night after the Potomac cruise, some of Webb's band members joined a local jam session. McRae stayed behind and had dinner with Webb and Sally at Keyes Restaurant near the Howard Theater, where many entertainers ate, before or after a show. Then they sat together in Webb's Cadillac, and Webb and McRae sat in the back talking for a long time. Sally was with them but didn't say anything. The band was due to get back on the bus the next morning and head south—Norfolk, Virginia; North Carolina; South Carolina; Atlanta, Georgia; on through to Alabama and Florida.

Webb told McRae that he would be going back into Hopkins for another surgery. McRae said, "He talked as long as he wanted. He said, 'What I want for you to do for me now, if you don't ever see me. . . . Look if this thing don't turn out right, do me a favor. Take care of the band, take care of Ella. Don't let the guys mess up, just take care of Ella.'"

McRae replied, "Ah man, come on, you're going to be all right. You know everything is going to be all right."

Webb said, "Nah. . . "

McRae waved goodbye and told Webb he'd see him in a few days in Florida. This time McRae had the feeling Webb would not bounce back.[29]

19

Have Mercy

On Monday, June 5, 1939, Chick Webb went back into Johns Hopkins Hospital, where he was treated by Dr. Young. From then on Sally barely left Chick's side, and Webb's mother Marie, sister Bessie, and grandparents soon joined her. That same morning, after their shows at the Howard Theatre were over, Webb's band boarded the bus for its scheduled southern tour, with Kaiser Marshall standing in for Webb on drums. Tim Gale, road manager, Joe Saunders, now the band's stage manager and main assistant, and Webb's valet Tommy Tompkins, who'd recently started working under Saunders's supervision, travelled with them.

Except for Webb's absence, the thirty-one-day route was routine, mostly one-nighters, with stops in Virginia, South Carolina, and Georgia, then on to Alabama and Florida. Once again it was a tour through Jim Crow restrictions: "white nights," ropes down the middle of the dance floor, etc. But as on the band's recent trips to South, nothing stopped the wildly enthusiastic reception that the band and Ella received everywhere they went.

This trip was the band's longest stretch without Webb. On June 14, nine days after they'd left Washington, DC, the band performed at City Auditorium in Atlanta, and the next night at Macon Auditorium in Macon, Georgia. Both were return engagements for their sell-out concerts/dances the previous September. One newspaper reported: "While more than 500 white enthusiasts looked on from the balcony, Negro couples in gay evening wear danced on the floor below."[1] Everywhere, fans clamored for Ella to sing "A-Tisket, A-Tasket" over and over.

The morning of June 16, this all changed. In Macon, Ella and the band got back on the bus and drove west, almost two hundred miles, to Montgomery, Alabama, a six- to seven-hour trip in those years. They arrived in Montgomery in time to find a place to eat, cool off, and clean up before their 8:00 p.m. dance at the "colored" Elk's Auditorium. Over eight hundred fans showed up, and the band's first set rocked the house. Then the crowd was suddenly silent. "What's wrong with these people out here?" asked Taft Jordan. "They don't like the band?"

The hall's manager called for an intermission. He pulled Jordan aside and told him that Chick Webb had died. The news was just then breaking on radio stations. Jordan then told the band members, who were all stunned. "We've been brothers," Jordan said. "Half of us couldn't play at all after intermission."

Teddy McRae said: "We hadn't heard.... We were traveling all day long. We came straight off the road, right into the ballroom. The manager knew it, everybody in town knew it.... But we didn't know it."

The next day the *Montgomery Adviser* reported:

The revelry had been in progress when the news came of Webb's death.... Though the spectators and members of the orchestra were unable to restrain real tears—the show went on—and Ella Fitzgerald kept on singing the "hot" numbers that made her famous despite the fact that she was choking with sobs. When the news was received of his death, the orchestra played first "Taps," and then "My Buddy."[2]

The hall's manager canceled the rest of the dance and people streamed out. Ella and all the musicians packed up, got back on the bus, and headed straight to Baltimore. Tim Gale, Joe Saunders, and Tommy Tompkins went with them. They arrived in Baltimore the next day and filled "every available room at the York and Penn Hotels."

Webb died at Johns Hopkins Hospital on June 16, 1939, his twelfth day there. His death certificate, signed by a Baltimore Department of Health official, states: "Immediate cause of death—Intestinal obstruction and uraemia [*sic*] (8 days?), due to Tuberculous peritonitis (8 days?), due to Tuberculosis of right kidney (?) Tuberculous cystitis (?). Other conditions—Tuberculosis of spine, old.... Major findings—of operations—Tuberculosis of rt ureter and kidney."[3] The certificate specifies the time of death as 7:35 p.m.

Sally and Webb's mother, sisters, and grandparents were devastated. The day after Chick's death, Clarence Jones began preparing for Chick's body to return home for the viewing, clearing out all the furniture from the small parlor and downstairs rooms at 1313 Ashland Avenue. The three-story rowhouse had been Webb's grandparents' home, and home to an extended family. On June 18, Webb's bier was set up in the parlor. Floral arrangements kept arriving by the hour, including a room-sized wreath from Webb's orchestra and huge wreaths from other bandleaders, including Count Basie and Jimmie Lunceford. Telegrams kept arriving from New York, from Moe Gale, Duke Ellington, Cab Calloway, and many friends and colleagues.

The family engaged an esteemed local funeral director from their church who made sure that every detail was perfect. The casket was draped in white satin and ruffled silk, and Webb was fitted out like royalty in a white dinner jacket. Hundreds of people of all ages from the neighborhood and all over Baltimore—school kids, cab drivers, truck drivers, school teachers—came to view the body at the family's Ashland Street house. McRae said that so many people streamed in that the family had "to open the back of the house, so people could walk through a narrow hallway to the kitchen, around the side and come out the back way."

The band members went to the house to pay their respects to Sally and the family, then were led upstairs to the third floor. Gene Krupa joined them, and McRae said that Krupa "sat there all day, sobbing." McRae also recalled that one of Chick's uncles joined them and told them jokes and stories and kept them laughing. That was probably what Webb would have wanted. McRae said, "Chick Webb wanted everybody to be happy. Like he would always take the burden, to keep everybody happy."

Webb's passing, inevitable after the cumulative effects of his disease, was still a sudden and unexpected loss. He'd been a steady strong light for them and for Ella Fitzgerald, whom he'd guided to this point in her career. Trumpet player and arranger Dick Vance said most of the band members were blindsided, despite the fact that they had often traveled with Bill Beason or Kaiser Marshall as substitutes. "I don't think any of us had any idea that he was that ill—none of us had any idea he was about to pass away. When Tim Gale broke the news—we were all surprised! He [Chick] would get up on the bandstand, he had to be helped up on the bandstand. But an outsider would never know it. We thought he'd bounce back, like he always did."[4]

Chick's mother Marie and the family felt strongly about giving Webb a proper funeral and "send-off" in Baltimore. Sally Webb, Moe Gale, and Charles Buchanan wanted it held in New York City, where Webb's fellow musicians, bandleaders, and entire musical community could pay tribute. Webb's family prevailed, and thousands of people came out to mourn Chick Webb.

The funeral, on June 20, 1939, was held at the Waters AME Church on Aisquith Street in East Baltimore, a few blocks from his grandparents' house.

Traffic was back-to-back all across the city. People swarmed the church, climbed trees, jammed the streets, and stood on cars and rooftops to try to get a glimpse of Ella Fitzgerald, Webb's musicians, and the other famous entertainers expected to attend.

Billy Rowe, the *Pittsburgh Courier* reporter who'd long been Webb's champion, wrote:

> Never in the history of this city or any city for that matter, has a man been given a more fitting funeral; by so many humans who were genuinely sorry in the face of death.... More than 20,000 people lined the streets and blocked traffic trying to get into the church which was already filled to the overflowing point.... No sadder funeral services have even been conducted.[5]

City officials tried to prepare for the crowds. There were Boy Scout troops, policemen, and firemen on hand to help keep the crowd orderly and assist family members, musicians, New York VIPs, and Baltimore's mayor and city officials maneuver their way into the church, which only held six hundred people. Webb's mother, sisters, and grandparents, Sally, and Ella Fitzgerald sat in the front rows, and the rest of the family, band members, and VIPs nearby. Uniformed nurses helped some family members who almost fainted from the heat or grief. Throughout the day, more and more people joined the throngs out on the streets near the church and nearby rooftops. This was the largest funeral in Baltimore's history, and it had the decorum of a state funeral.

Chick Webb's funeral became family lore for many Baltimoreans, among them historian Donna Hollie. Her mother, nineteen at the time, recounted her memories of that day for decades. She was among the crowd in front of the church trying to get in when her uncle spotted her and was able to get her through the crowds and seated in the balcony. He was a member of that church (AME Waters) and an undertaker, part of "a cohesive group that did everything they could to help each other. So for a huge funeral like Chick Webb's, every undertaker in town was serving and taking a limousine—I don't think any one undertaker had enough limousines to accommodate the crowd, especially the dignitaries." The same was true for the community's florists and wreath makers and their supply chains. They had never had so many simultaneous orders for wreaths and special arrangements, which were delivered steadily to the Ashland Street house, and then to the church.

"My mother said she got seated just in time to hear Ella Fitzgerald sing 'My Buddy.' She never got over that—this was a story that I heard over and over all of my life."[6]

Dick Vance spoke of another song Ella sang, "Have Mercy," which has been overlooked in the many accounts of the funeral. "I don't want to be maudlin, but Ella sang it at the funeral. Webb and Ella co-wrote it." The song is a beautiful romantic ballad that Vance had arranged and the band had recorded at their last Decca session on April 21, 1939. The song was never as well known as "My Buddy," so few people remember it.[7]

Moe Gale, Charles Buchanan, and their wives attended, as did all of Webb's band members, Conrad and Tim Gale, Joe Saunders, and Webb's Tommy Tompkins. Frank Schiffman and Ralph Cooper of the Apollo Theater and Ginger Young, one of Webb's first mentors when he moved to Harlem, came to Baltimore for the funeral, along with many friends and musicians from New York.

"From blocks away," McRae said, "people were just standing on the rooftops, looking down. You couldn't get near the church because of all the people in the street." Van Alexander and his wife drove down from New York City. He recalled:

> It was a sight to behold. There were just thousands of people around the church that wanted to get in, but couldn't. Traffic had to be stopped. People were sitting on top of trolley cars just to get a glimpse at some of the notable people that were attending.... So the people were just astounded at the amount of celebrities, and my wife and I had a tough time getting through the crowd.... I told one of the officers who I was and luckily he got us through. We got into the chapel, and it was a very warm, hot, humid day, no air-conditioning.
>
> The service started and it was just beautiful. Ella sang "My Buddy" and brought tears to everybody's eyes, and Teddy McRae played solo on the tenor sax, and there were many speeches and eulogies. Chick was given a sendoff like a president. It was a day to savor and remember, and I wanted to be there just to pay tribute to a great little man who had so much compassion and love and just didn't live long enough.[8]

When the service ended and people left the church, the family cortege drove slowly to Arbutus Memorial Park, ten miles away. Harlem bandleaders Claude Hopkins, Teddy Hill, Willie Bryant, and Ginger Young were among the pallbearers. Then a peculiar thing happened. McRae called it "[A] show of blessing."

> Right before the funeral started, even before they brought the body out, it rained like cats and dogs. The rain just came down. And just about two or three minutes before the funeral was over, it stopped. Nobody moved even though it was raining. People didn't move from the rooftops—they just stayed in the rain. I always said that was a shot of blessings from Heaven. All of a sudden this rainstorm came up, and passed over in a few minutes.

Webb's funeral was a state funeral for big America, the all-inclusive country, in which Chick Webb was a Baltimore hero for everyone—Black and white, in a city so deeply divided racially that even its cemeteries were segregated.

Chick Webb's death and chronic illness were as surrounded by confusion, errors, and mythology as his birthdate, and other aspects of his life. Inaccurate statements about the causes of his death were common at the time, and are now widespread thanks to the internet. Dr. Frederick J. Spencer, who examined Webb's medical history, cites numerous false or implausible claims about Webb's death and illness. "Aside from the indelicacy of describing him as 'Crippled' Chick Webb, a hunchback dwarf [as one website does], Webb did not die from 'Tuberculosis of the Spine.' He died from intestinal obstruction and uremia."

Spencer also calls out other myths:

> To write that Chick Webb died from "pneumonia and was too frail to treat" is not true. Nor can it be said that he died of "pneumonia at age 37." Pneumonia is not mentioned on Webb's death certificate. Some accounts attribute his death to unqualified "tuberculosis," which is correct, and others attribute it to "tuberculosis of the spine," "TB of the spine," "spinal tuberculosis," and "tuberculosis of the spine and liver," which are not correct. Tuberculosis of the spine did not kill him, and the liver is almost never the site of tuberculosis.... Chick Webb must first have had tuberculosis in a lung or the intestine. Blood-borne, it spread to his spine and led to a permanent deformity. Recurrence of a lung infection caused pleurisy. Further spread resulted in infection of his peritoneum and urinary tract.

Following a nephrectomy, bowel and renal failure led to intestinal obstruction, uremia, and death.[9]

After the funeral, Moe Gale canceled the rest of the tour and asked Ella and the musicians to return to New York. It was rough. Sandy Williams, who had been with Webb for eight years, shared many of his experiences with Webb and the band's ups and downs. "Chick's death was a terrible blow to me. Once, I remember as clearly as if it happened yesterday, Chick named those who had stuck by him when times were bad. They included Taft Jordan, Bobby Stark, myself and above all, the one who was closest to him—almost like a father, John Trueheart. . . . I stayed in the band another eight months after he died, but I lost interest in everything. Something was really missing."[10]

Days and weeks after Webb's death, scores of tributes, profiles, and obituaries were printed in newspapers across the country. Along with them were previously scheduled ads in trade magazines about bookings and tour dates for Chick Webb and His Orchestra, featuring the "First Lady of Swing," Ella Fitzgerald. The Gretsch Drum Company ran a big ad campaign in *Metronome, DownBeat, Popular Mechanics*, and other magazines showing a beaming Webb at his fabulous Gretsch-Gladstone drum kit, customized for the "King of the Drums."

Webb's death touched people all over the country. He was especially missed, not only in Baltimore, but also in his long-time adopted neighborhood, Harlem, where he was a familiar figure on the streets. The *Amsterdam News* printed a poem by a sixth-grade student from PS 90, a majestic beaux-arts-style school building in Harlem that still stands.

> The Departure
> It was a sad, sad day
> When Chick Webb went away;
> But God thought it best.
> That Chick Webb needed rest.
> Ella Fitzgerald was a friend—
> A true friend to the end.
> So let us all pray,
> For it was a sad, sad day.
> When God called our beloved Chick Webb away.
> —Dorothy Giles[11]

Epilogue

He'd tell his story where he used to beat on tin cans and things in Baltimore. He was a self-made man. And he knew where he wanted to go way before I joined him. When I used to hang out with him, he knew which direction he wanted to go. He'd spend his last money— this is what he was going to do. He was going to do this, he was going to be here by this time. Next year I want to be here and the next year I want to be there. But there was one thing Chick had a mind to do, to make Ella a star. I guess he had the foresight to see that something big was going to happen to him.

—Teddy McRae

After Webb's funeral, Ella Fitzgerald and Webb's band returned to New York, to rest and regroup. Rumors quickly emerged about the band: Who would be the leader, would they disband? Would Teddy McRae continue as music director? Would Benny Goodman finally "steal" Ella?

Nothing about this was easy. Some band members couldn't accept Webb's death; it still seemed sudden to them. They'd gotten used to seeing Joe Saunders or Tommy Tompkins carry Webb off the stage after a show. Webb had other drummers open up shows or at the Savoy for him for years, so that wasn't new. But during this past year, Webb couldn't play through the night more frequently, and drummers like Kaiser Marshall or Big Sid Catlett took over on tour. In spring 1939, there was talk that Webb would take more of a backseat role and not perform as much. That never happened. This time, Webb didn't bounce back. Webb truly loved Ella and his band, and literally worked himself to his death.

Moe Gale was saddened by Webb's death but did not want to cancel more dates. As it was, he canceled the rest of the southern tour, which would have lasted another two and a half weeks. Meanwhile, the show did have to go on. For Ella and the musicians, this band was their livelihood. For Gale, it was a business; the Chick Webb Orchestra with Ella Fitzgerald were his top clients, and Gale was also Fitzgerald's manager. In late June Gale announced to the press that Fitzgerald would be the band's leader. Out of tribute to Webb, the band was initially billed as "Ella Fitzgerald and the Famous Chick Webb Orchestra." Bassist Beverly Peer said: "Ella never skipped a beat and was back the next day. She was thinking about her future." Truthfully, there was no reason she shouldn't move forward, whatever people thought. Webb had shown her the way—to keep going, be persistent, keep working, ride the momentum they'd shared.

Gale hired drummer Bill Beason for the drummer's chair. Beason had been close to Webb, had filled in for him frequently the previous year, and the band members respected him. This was not an easy chair to fill. Teddy McRae said, "To follow a man like Chick is an incredible thing to do unless you could find someone in that class at that time."

Gale gave the band a few nights at the Savoy to "break in" Beason and pull themselves together. Teddy McRae and Dick Vance reset some of the band's instrumental arrangements that featured Chick's drum solos, cutting some of them and rebalancing the scores to feature other soloists or sections. They were scheduled for a Decca recording date on June 29, and a week at Loew's State Theater in Times Square soon after. The band then spent the rest of the summer at the Savoy, punctuated by one-nighters and short trips.

In their stage show programs, Ella and the band maintained their balancing act: a mix of Ella's pop material and the band's energetic swing instrumental numbers. In ballrooms, they played more to the dancers, just as Webb had. For their recordings, Ella herself, Moe Gale, and Jack Kapp still kept trying for a "Yellow Basket" follow-up, which resulted in some inane records, like "I Want the Waiter With the Water," "Coochi Coochi Coo," and "My Wubba Dolly."[1] The novelty numbers aside, Ella still charted several hits over the next two years, notably "Stairway to the Stars," "Five O'clock Whistle," and "Hallelujah, Come on Get Happy," and others that broke free of the nursery rhyme model.

Ella wasn't attempting new musical directions at this time. This was partly Gale's doing. He wasn't helping her advance as an artist; she was a big attraction as is. By the end of the summer the band was billed as "Ella Fitzgerald and Her Famous Orchestra." She picked up a baton and conducted sometimes, which audiences expected and adored. Like her mentor Chick Webb, she forged a direct connection with her fans. On stage she exuded warmth on ballads and spun out endearing jive talk and dance moves on swing tunes.

The day-to-day leadership was up to Gale and the succession of other music directors Gale or Buchanan appointed. This caused friction and confusion among Webb's sidemen, who had been so loyal to Webb. They did not like Gale's top-down decision-making and what they viewed as his interference in their usual routines. In fall 1939, Gale appointed Taft Jordan as music director, bypassing Teddy McRae, who'd been handling things for Webb for almost three years. Talented former sidemen such as Hilton Jefferson and Edgar Sampson were rehired and joined out of goodwill toward their lost leader, but Sampson left after a few weeks. He said: "Too many people were trying to lead Ella's band."

In fall 1940, Gale asked Benny Carter to take over as leader, but Carter didn't accept the job. Gale "rehired" McRae as music director just as the band was about to go on a tour of one-nighters through the South and Midwest.[2] No matter how popular Ella and the band were on the road, white jazz critics hated Ella's novelty numbers, among other gripes. One even wrote that Bill Beason "looked like the ghost of Chick Webb."

In May 1941, Fitzgerald and the band left for a coast-to-coast tour, packed with one-nighters, all by bus. Though the trip ended with a triumphant week at the Orpheum Theater in Los Angeles, drummer Bill Beason and Ella had a falling-out midway, when the band was in St. Louis, Missouri. Their next stop was Kansas City, where Gale's road manager told McRae that the office had already hired a new drummer to take over, a Kansas City local drum star and teacher named Jesse Price. McRae said that Price "saved" the band; the upcoming California dates were a first for them. "By the time we got to California, he was well rehearsed," recalled McRae. "We tried him out on a couple of things and he came through with flying colors. He was a carbon copy of Chick Webb—fast wrists, fast feet, fast everything. . . . He was just glued in there, he had in fact made an idol of Chick."[3]

Personnel changes had been ongoing since the previous spring. Back on the East Coast in Boston that fall, McRae had a falling-out with Gale over money, which had been an issue with the sidemen all along. McRae said, "The band was back where it was before Chick died. It was popular and the only thing that was missing was Chick. But they (Gale, et al) were making as much money or more because now that the thing had grown bigger, Ella had grown into her own." McRae pushed Gale for raises for the musicians and for himself as the leader behind Ella. Dizzy Gillespie came into the band briefly for the Boston engagement. Gillespie recalled: "Teddy McRae was the leader who took charge of everything. Ella just sang. It was Ella's band. But the money went to the Gale agency which paid Ella." Gale dismissed McRae as music director on the band's last night. He'd already hired saxophonist/ clarinetist Eddie Barefield to take over as leader. McRae stayed on in the sax section for a couple more months.[4] By spring 1942, almost all of Webb's long-term key sidemen—Garvin Bushell, Bobby Stark, John Trueheart, Sandy Williams, Nat Story, Hilton Jefferson—left the band. They felt that Gale was only using them as Ella's backup band with no regard for their musicianship.

Even so, there were many high points: a six-week residency at the Grand Terrace in Chicago in September 1939 and sold-out shows in New York at the Apollo Theater, at the Savoy, at Roseland, and in new territory—on Fifty-Second Street at the Famous Door, where changes in jazz styles, toward smaller bands and the emergence of bebop, were palpable. Ella was getting more recognition as a unique vocalist and engaging entertainer. She was also developing closer ties with other top bandleaders and jazz stars, and she socialized with them on stage and off. Still, there were nights when Webb's influences and style came through intensely. McRae recalled one night that "Ella really pulled everybody together. She started singing a medley of Webb's things and she had everybody in the ballroom in tears. That was one of those nights she was thinking about Chick. I guess something just hit her."[5]

In 1942, Gale started sending Ella out mainly with the Four Keys, another male vocal quartet with the Gale Agency, and with Barefield and small groups. Ella Fitzgerald's Famous Orchestra only got occasional bookings, and their last date together was at the Earle Theater in Philadelphia, July 30, 1942. This was her beginning as a solo artist and the formal end to the band that helped bring her to the world—Chick Webb and His Orchestra.

The band's dissolution was largely Moe Gale's doing, but conditions for big bands changed rapidly after the attack on Pearl Harbor on December 7, 1941, and the US entered World War II. Booking offices across the country were swamped with cancellations, and "dances promoted in spite of all else went waiting for audiences." Gale had new ideas, with plans to have his own radio locations and open a string of clubs to promote clients and attract new ones. In the early 1940s, the Gale Agency's artists included the orchestras of Benny Carter, Cootie Williams, Erskine Hawkins, and Lucky Millinder, whom Gale paired with his latest discovery, the brilliant guitarist and gospel-turned-R&B vocalist Sister Rosetta Tharpe. Gale also announced that he was opening an office in Hollywood, prompted by Ella's success in the movie *Ride*

'*Em Cowboy* and the Ink Spots in *The Great American Broadcast*. But Gale's ideas for expanding never became reality as the war's disruptions grew more widespread.

In January 1942, top Black bands including Ella Fitzgerald's, Erskine Hawkins's, Duke Ellington's, and Noble Sissle's signed on as "the first colored leaders to volunteer their bands to play during their off time ... in camps throughout the country." Travel restrictions impeded Fitzgerald's band, though her few USO performances were sensational.[6] Ella remained a top artist throughout the war years, but Gale's interest in managing her dwindled and he only handled her bookings. After the war, in the 1950s, Gale pivoted to music publishing and he handled bookings for a few opera singers, a startling turnabout for a man who advanced Black musical talent for so long.

The Savoy Ballroom remained a social center for Harlemites during the war, though thousands of families and lives were disrupted by the draft and by continuing inequities in economic development in the community. On April 22, 1943, a long looming threat to the Savoy by the city police and vice squad made Mayor LaGuardia padlock the ballroom's doors on framed charges that white servicemen had solicited the services of Black prostitutes there. Some members of New York's white establishment were as threatened by the Savoy's peacefully integrated social milieu as white politicians in the Deep South. Gale and Buchanan used a variety of strategies to get the city to reopen the ballroom. Their efforts were hampered by news of riots that summer in Black communities in Detroit and other cities in reaction to racial inequalities exacerbated by wartime conditions. Harlem was next. On August 1, 1943, a white policeman shot a Black serviceman near 125th Street. It turned out to be a superficial wound, but rumors flew that the serviceman had been killed. Within hours, the neighborhood erupted, provoking a predictable police crackdown.

Six months later, Gale and Buchanan were finally allowed to reopen the Savoy Ballroom. On October 22, 1943, they turned the occasion into an all-out Savoy gala. The centerpiece of an all-star eight-band line-up was Ella Fitzgerald, singing with the Cootie Williams Orchestra. Gale's interest in the Savoy had waned by now, and his focus was the Gale Agency. (Charles Buchanan bought out most of Moe Gale's financial interest in the Savoy around this time.)

During the 1950s, the Savoy was no longer a beacon for music and dance styles, and Buchanan refused to bring in R&B or Rock and Roll bands, counting on the ballroom's loyal swing dance following, accompanied by smaller bands with contemporary elements. No long lines around the block, no crowds of dancers waited to get in, no more big band battles that drew thousands of people.[7]

The Savoy Ballroom closed its doors forever on October 3, 1958, and the building and several adjacent blocks were razed to make way for a low- to mid-income housing complex. In 2002, a commemorative plaque was installed at the original site, with several notable speakers and dancers in attendance. The inscription reads: "Here once stood the legendary Savoy Ballroom. . . . During a time of racial segregation and strife, the Savoy was one of the most culturally and racially integrated institutions, and its fame was international. It was the heartbeat of Harlem's community and a testament to the indomitable spirit and creative impulse of African-Americans. It was a catalyst for innovation where dancers and musicians blended influences to forge new, widespread and long-lasting traditions in music and dance. . . . 'Home of Happy Feet,' 1926–1958."

Chick Webb's music in alliance with evolving dance styles at the Savoy was foundational to American popular music. Webb's legacy expanded with the musical and cultural richness added by Ella Fitzgerald and other musicians whom Webb took a chance on hiring. Mario Bauza was one of them. His tenure with Webb gave Bauza the experience, connections, and grounding in American jazz that prepared him for jobs with other top Harlem bandleaders in the late 1930s, including Cab Calloway's. A significant part of Bauza's own legacy was his collaboration with Dizzy Gillespie, whom Bauza helped get into Calloway's band. Cross-cultural musical adventurers, they experimented with fusing Afro-Cuban rhythms and jazz styles, which can be heard in the brilliant recordings of the Dizzy Gillespie Orchestra of the mid-1940s and in Bauza's groundbreaking Afro-Cuban Orchestra. Bauza's long residency at New York's Palladium in the 1950s made that space a crucible for Latin and Caribbean music and dance styles—the Savoy's counterpart—an enduring fusion of influences and rhythms in American pop music and dance.

Louis Jordan's groundbreaking group the Tympany Five, formed in 1939, did the same in a different direction, forging a pathway to jump music, R&B, and Rock and Roll. Jordan teamed up with Harlem arranger/bandleader Jess Stone and some of Stone's musicians for a job at a small club near the Savoy. Jordan and the group picked up a following quickly; his engaging and witty vocal style—rooted in southern blues and minstrel shows—was central to the group's crossover success.

Other musicians and colleagues left their own imprints. Edgar Sampson was active as an arranger for various bands and for TV until the mid-1960s. His biggest hits, "Stompin' at the Savoy" and "Don't Be That Way," were staples in Benny Goodman's and Ella Fitzgerald's repertoire for decades, and for countless modern swing bands and jazz vocalists in their wake. Clarinetist/ saxophonist Garvin Bushell enjoyed an extraordinary wide-ranging career, from his youth in early ragtime bands to swing bands, to playing with various reunion bands, as well as with modern jazz giants John Coltrane, Miles Davis, and Gil Evans. Wayman Carver and Dick Vance became jazz educators at Clark College in Atlanta and City College in New York, respectively.

Helen Oakley, Webb's former publicist and battle-stager, took a different turn during World War II, after the death of her older brother who died in the catastrophic Canadian raid at Dieppe. She enlisted in the Women's Army Corps, and was soon approached by the Office of Strategic Service (OSS, predecessor of the CIA), and carried out top-secret missions in North Africa and Europe. After the War, she reconnected with British jazz journalist and producer Stanley Dance, who she'd met on his first trip to New York ten years earlier. She recounted sitting at a bar at the time with Dance and Chick Webb, who took one look at Dance and told her, "Oakley, that boy's in love with you." They married, lived in the English countryside, and moved back to the States in the 1950s, encouraged by Ellington, who'd stayed with them while on tour in the United Kingdom. A storied couple in jazz circles as writers and producers, they travelled with Duke Ellington's entourage for years. Oakley Dance said they moved back to the States "to carry on with the Ellington story. It kept right on, it never did stop in all our lives."[8]

John Trueheart, Webb's steadfast friend and colleague, had accompanied Webb almost every step of the way, from small dance bands in Baltimore to Harlem to national fame. In his own way, Trueheart was also an innovator, setting a model as a dependable yet inventive early swing rhythm section guitarist who inspired Freddie Green, his peer in the Count Basie band.[9] Trueheart's long tenure with Webb was interrupted by his own bout with tuberculosis. He left the band in spring 1937 for a stay at a sanitarium in upstate New York, which Webb paid for. He got out in early winter 1939, resumed his spot in the band, and got to enjoy the last few months of Webb's life with him, in the spotlight. Trueheart continued on with Ella as bandleader but lived at the Harlem YMCA on 135th Street, no longer sharing rooms with other musicians. Due to his ill health, he did not serve in World War II, and he entered Sea View Hospital, a local sanitarium on Staten Island. He passed away there on October 7, 1943, not yet forty years old. The cause of death was "far advanced bilateral pulmonal tuberculosis." Trueheart, a quiet man, kept some things about his early years in Baltimore private. His death certificate states he was a widower, and his next of kin was his daughter in Baltimore, Dorothy Dorsey, then about twenty years old. Trueheart was buried at Arbutus Memorial Park, Baltimore, as was Chick Webb.

Webb and his "offspring" engendered this happy intersection of American pop: music and crowds of people dancing, a vibrant social force. For Ella, the best was yet to come, as she grew from the "First Lady of Swing" into the "First Lady of Song." Chick Webb's dreams for her had come true, in ways that he could not have foreseen.

> If it wasn't for me standing in front of Chick Webb's band, night after night, and Chick noticing me and nodding to me, saying, "Oh, hi, kid, you're here again … if it wasn't for that great moment, I don't think I would have half the success I had in my life because, that to me, was the jumpstart of my whole musical career—him just saying, "Hey kid, how are you? You're here again." And waving his drumsticks at me and, and acknowledging me. … I don't know whether it was fate, kismet or luck. Call it what you will.
>
> —Van Alexander

Van Alexander lived to be over a hundred years old. In countless interviews, he paid tribute to Webb, who inexplicably took a chance on him—Al Feldman, a white college kid, totally enamored by the power of Webb's band, who wanted to be an arranger. In the late 1930s, with the success of "A-Tisket, A-Tasket," he formally changed his name to Van Alexander from the name he was born with, Alexander Van Vliet Feldman. He did more freelance work and formed his own dance band in the early 1940s. After World War II, he moved to Hollywood and enjoyed a decades-long career as a film and television composer and arranger.

Alexander's band, an all-white ensemble, never attained the top-tier status of Webb's or other bandleaders for whom he'd written arrangements. Mainly they performed in hotels and small ballrooms on the East Coast. At one dance at a big hotel in central Pennsylvania, Alexander had a surprise encounter. He was standing in front of the bandstand when Sally Webb came over to greet him. She told him, "I'd like to introduce you to the gentleman I'm with, but don't say anything about the past." He agreed, and recalled that it was a strange moment. "She was with a white gentleman, and she evidently didn't want him to know anything about her past."

That was the last time Alexander saw her. He remembered Sally as a beautiful woman who was totally devoted to Chick. She made special meals for him and encouraged him to rest. "She was very light-skinned," he said. "Chick was light-skinned also, but she was more so. And, as they used to say, if she wanted to, she could pass."

Back in New York after Webb's funeral, Sally was faced with handling everything. Chick died without leaving a will. With Moe Gale's guidance, she hired his lawyers and successfully petitioned to be administrator of Webb's estate. A marriage certificate was not among the papers filed with the Surrogate Court in New York City which was unusual.

For a while, Sally continued to live at their apartment on 138th Street. She was involved with several tributes to Webb over the next year, notably the celebrity benefit for the Chick Webb Memorial Recreation Center, held in Baltimore in February 1940. A few months later, she was living in a brand-new building on West 26th Street, in Manhattan, married to a white man named Virgil Bowman, and used her given name, Martha. Virgil was a former vaudeville dancer who ran a small theatrical booking agency in upstate New York. It's hard to say just where they met. No marriage record was ever found for the Bowmans, or the Webbs.

Sally was indeed a woman of mystery, as were many newly independent young women who came to Harlem, hoping for a career in entertainment. When Dr. Ralph J. Young organized a follow-up benefit for the Chick Webb Recreation Center in March 1941, Sally wrote him that she could not attend. Around that time, estate documents signed by Sally Webb (not Martha Bowman) were notarized in Allentown, Pennsylvania. During that same period, Van Alexander's band played numerous times in Allentown and other small cities in Pennsylvania, where steel and metal plants would soon be commissioned for the war effort. The Bowmans worked in one of these plants, until Virgil shipped out with the US Navy, and Sally remained in Allentown.

In December 1941, when most of Chick Webb's estate matters were approved, Sally gave three thousand dollars to Webb's mother Marie and paid for the funeral expenses in Baltimore and other outstanding bills and debts. The estate's final accounting, including Chick Webb's music catalog and royalties, was settled in January 1942. Webb's total financial assets amounted to 19,049.96 dollars. Sally controlled 50 percent of Webb's interest in the catalog of his songs (the other 50 percent was held by Moe Gale), including some of the band's biggest titles: "Stompin' at the Savoy," "You Showed Me the Way," "Cryin' Mood," and novelty follow-ups to "A-Tisket, A-Tasket." She was also entitled to future copyright and mechanical royalties.[10]

The paper trail of copyright renewals from 1958 to 1966 confirms Sally's postwar identity as Mrs. Martha Bowman. Sally Webb, widow of one of the most popular bandleaders of all time, essentially vanished. She did not keep in touch with Gale, Ella Fitzgerald, or any of her Harlem friends. She lived her postwar life as Martha Bowman in Lehighton, Pennsylvania, a mother of two, devoted wife, and active in the VFW, local Democratic Party, Catholic Church (Virgil was a devoted Catholic), and other community organizations. One can see echoes of her younger beautiful face in photos of her with the Democratic Club in the mid-1950s. She died in April 1983.

As for Chick Webb's personal possessions, the most precious items listed in his estate's final accounting were his prized custom-made drum sets, valued at 150 dollars (approximately 2,800 dollars in 2019). Sally Webb may have given one set to Moe Gale. In spring 1940, Gale installed an exhibition hall in the basement of the Savoy Ballroom, which included a "photographic history of swing . . . the old Savoy Baby Grand, which has been pounded by many famous fingers, and the complete set of Chick Webb's trap drums." Admission was only a penny, and the proceeds were for the "Musicians' Sick Fund."[11] When the ballroom was torn down in the 1950s, most of the furnishings were auctioned off or given away. No one knows what happened to Webb's drums. Reportedly, a drum collector living in New Orleans salvaged a few parts, which were lost during Hurricane Katrina in 2005. Webb's striking bass drum painted with his smiling face and his special Gretsch-Gladstone kit, emblazoned with a sparkling crown, were never found.

Ella Fitzgerald kept leading her orchestra through spring of 1942, when American involvement in World War II was fully underway. The draft, gas rationing, and travel restrictions caused major disruptions for musicians, wherever they were. Life abruptly changed beneath America's feet, and the end of the big band era had been a foregone conclusion for months.

Ella, like Chick had, performed for many benefits with the band. She also brought the band together for several tributes to Webb. As mentioned earlier, one of the most significant was in February 1940, the first fundraiser for the construction of the Chick Webb Memorial Recreation Center, held at the Fifth Regiment Armory. The force behind this effort was Dr. Ralph J. Young, who treated Webb during his stays at Johns Hopkins and on his deathbed. Young had been thinking about founding such a center even before Webb's death and discussed it with him. Webb loved the idea.

Dr. Young followed up and contacted Joe Louis, Moe Gale, Ralph Cooper, and many others. It was a smashing success. Over 7,500 people paid 1.15 dollars a ticket for a star-studded night that was as notable as Webb's funeral for bringing together Black dignitaries and entertainers and white politicians and VIPs in a city and state that were still starkly segregated.

Journalist Lillian Johnson described the benefit, which started at 8 p.m. and ended around 3 a.m., in a page-long article for the *Afro*. Reportedly, Webb's last words to Dr. Young were: "Doc, if I live to ever leave this bed, I am going to do more with my life than I have done. I am going to get my friend Joe Louis to come to Baltimore and we will fill any house in the city. We will build a community center for the children of East Baltimore."

Dr. Young, wrote Johnson, is "himself an East Baltimore tradition, who is to the medical profession what Chick Webb is to the drums." At the benefit, Young told the audience: "I have never had a more ambitious, a more cheerful, and a more optimistic patient. . . . This, the carrying out of his [Webb's] idea, has been the happiest task of my life."

Joe Louis was the main attraction along with Ella Fitzgerald, but the parade of top-flight performers included the Nicholas Brothers, Jackie "Moms" Mabley, the Ink Spots, Peg Leg Bates, and on-stage greetings from Teddy Hill, Ralph Cooper, and many others. Bardu Ali and Billy Rowe, Harlem journalist/now media star, were the M.C.s. Baltimore was represented by Bubby Johnson's orchestra; the National Vocal Symphony, conducted by renowned music educator and music director W. Llewellyn Wilson; and Hughie Woolford, the society pianist who'd first invited Webb to visit him and Eubie Blake in Harlem in late 1924. Ella Fitzgerald and Her Orchestra closed the night and brought the crowd to its feet. Their final number was "St. Louis Blues." Lillian Johnson reported: "The band played the song in all its variations for 16 straight minutes," during which Clarence Jones, Chick Webb's grandfather, got on stage and "out jitterbugged the jitterbuggiest of them all." Johnson singles out Webb's long-term sidemen and John Trueheart, "who went with him [Chick] from Baltimore to New York in that trip that began the climb to fame."

Billy Rowe, one of Webb's long-term supporters, wrote that this event, which netted 8,500 dollars of seed money for the project, "surpassed anything in the history of white or colored show business ... to found a community center ... a lasting memorial for the man who brought greatness to himself and his people some twenty years after he first came out of the colored section of East Baltimore."[12]

Sally Webb, Chick's widow, was involved in the event's planning and was featured prominently in the slew of press photos that followed. She also was involved in a couple of other fundraising events for the center, including judging a fashion show. Plans were halted during World War II, but afterward Dr. Young didn't let the project go. The Chick Webb Memorial Recreation Center, a spacious two-story brick building near where Webb grew up, was dedicated on November 30, 1947. The ceremony included the unveiling of a portrait of Chick Webb, which hung in the director's office. In 1949, a swimming pool and full basketball court were added, housed in a two-story converted ice warehouse behind the center. The center quickly became central to the neighborhood: waiting in line to get into the pool was a social ritual. During its first few years, the center held an annual observance celebration for Chick Webb, to "keep Webb's ideas in the lives of youth today. In its scores of activities the center emulates the life of a game youth who attained his goal."[13]

For decades, "Chick Webb"—the neighborhood's name for the center—was everything Webb would have wanted. It had a full sports program, with swim lessons, award-winning synchronized swim and swim racing teams, basketball teams, and clubs and art classes for all age groups. Thanks to renewed community efforts, the building was designated a historic city landmark in 2017. Currently, there are plans to renovate the building and pool, and a modern housing development is under construction around the center. The neighborhood is in flux, with expansive plans in play by various developers. Some blocks where Chick grew up have disappeared, but the Waters AME Church still stands alone, with new apartments across the street. East Baltimore is still an economically challenged Black community, and the renovated center would provide welcoming multipurpose event spaces and a user-friendly recording studio. Renderings for large design panels featuring Webb, Ella Fitzgerald, and their peers are underway. The most striking sketch is for a huge mural on the outside walls, picturing Webb at his drum set with his sticks raised, and his wide, welcoming smile.

Notes

Chapter 1

1. Antero Pietila, *Not in My Neighborhood: How Bigotry Shaped a Great American City* (Chicago: Ivan R. Dee, 2010), 47–70.
2. William Webb, Sr., death certificate.
3. Mary and Robert Sanders had a son, Robert Sanders Jr., who lived with the family even after his father moved on. Webb had three aunts, three uncles, two sisters, and three first cousins.
4. Brad Rowe, interview with Jeff Kaufman for documentary *The Savoy King*, 2012. For relationships between Blacks and Jews see James McBride, *The Color of Water: A Black Man's Tribute to His White Mother* (New York: Penguin Publishing Group, 2006).
5. The Chick Webb Recreation Center opened in 1947, through the persistent efforts of Webb's physician, Dr. Ralph J. Young. See Epilogue.
6. Rowe, interview with Kaufman.
7. Rowe, interview with Kaufman.
8. Pietila, *Not in My Neighborhood*, 42, 54–72.
9. Jack Hement, "Souvenir of the Baltimore Fire, February 7, 8 and 9, 1904, as seen through a camera" (New York, published for the Illustrated Press Syndicate by the A. B. Benesch co. [c. 1904], http://hdl.handle.net/2027/loc.ark:/13960/t8gf1jc6n).
10. "WHAT WAS THE FIRE LOSS?: Many Baltimoreans Are Confused About Real . . . " *Baltimore Sun*, August 6, 1908, 12.
11. *Afro American Ledger,* February 20, 1904, 4. The *Afro American Ledger* dropped "Ledger" from its title at the end of 1915, and, known as the *Baltimore Afro-American* (the *Afro*), was one of the foremost Black newspapers in the country.
12. *Baltimore Sun*, February 20, 1904, 12.
13. Philip Merrill, interview with author, May 2019. Philip Jackson Merrill, *Images of America: Old West Baltimore* (Charleston, SC: Arcadia Publishing, 2020).
14. Antero Pietila, *The Ghosts of Johns Hopkins: The Life and Legacy That Shaped an American City* (Lanham, MD: Rowman & Littlefield Publishers, 2018), 122–23.
15. Frederick J. Spencer, *Jazz and Death: Medical Profiles of Jazz Greats* (Jackson: University Press of Mississippi, 2002), 235.
16. According to Brad Rowe: "I doubt if he even got paid for his services because they didn't have anything." Rowe, interview with Kaufman. It is unclear whether Dr. Young performed the surgery himself.
17. Rebecca Skloot, *The Immortal Life of Henrietta Lacks* (New York: Crown, 2010); Pietila, *The Ghosts of Johns Hopkins*.
18. Rowe, interview with Kaufman.

19. Brennan Jensen, "Drummin' Up the Story of Chick Webb," *Baltimore City Paper*, February 18, 1998, 17–19.
20. Rowe, interview with Kaufman.
21. University of Baltimore Special Collections and Archives, Baltimore Heritage Project, https://archivesspace.ubalt.edu/repositories/2/resources/38.
22. In the early 1930s Wilson was the first choral director of the Baltimore City Colored Chorus and the second music director of the Colored Symphony. He wrote a weekly music column, "Chords and Discords," for the *Afro* for over twenty years.
23. Brown starred in the world premiere of *Porgy and Bess* at the Colonial Theatre in Boston in 1935.
24. Alfred Prettyman, interview with author, January 2020. Prettyman's father, Edward, was a prominent Black municipal orchestra leader in Baltimore from the 1920s to the 1960s.
25. Jensen, "Drummin' Up the Story of Chick Webb," 17–19.

Chapter 2

1. *Baltimore Afro-American*, September 9, 1921, 4.
2. Garvin Bushell as told to Mark Tucker, *Jazz from the Beginning* (Ann Arbor: University of Michigan Press, 1988), 34.
3. See Linda J. Tomko, *Dancing Class: Gender, Ethnicity, and Social Divides in American Dance, 1890–1920* (Bloomington: Indiana University Press, 1999).
4. Reid Badger, *A Life in Ragtime: A Biography of James Reese Europe* (New York: Oxford University Press, 1995). Al Rose, *Eubie Blake* (New York: Schirmer and Sons, 1979), 70.
5. Badger, *Ragtime*, and Matt Brennan, *Kick It: A Social History of the Drum Kit* (New York: Oxford University Press, 2020), 61–64; James Reese Europe's Society Orchestra, *Castle Walk*, 1914.
6. Dixon was a central figure in Baltimore jazz circles for decades as bandleader, promoter, club owner, and producer. Maryland's Black chapters of the Masons, Pythians, Elks, and Galileans formed cooperatives to start their own banks and credit unions and to buy property. They also provided aid to families.
7. Coleman's directories also include profiles of community leaders, educators, clergymen, entrepreneurs, and statistics about Black populations in American major cities in the early twentieth century. Coleman's Colored Business Directories, Maryland State Archives, http://aomol.msa.maryland.gov/000001/000494/html/index.html. Philip Merrill, correspondence with author, 2019.
8. *Baltimore Afro-American*, October 6, 1917, 4.
9. Dan Burley, "From Newsboy to King: The Life of Chick Webb," *Amsterdam News*, July 1, 1939, 16.
10. Garvin Bushell, *Jazz from the Beginning* (Ann Arbor: University of Michigan Press, 1990), 11–13. Bushell's career ranged from working with Mamie Smith and Her Jazz

Hounds, to Chick Webb, Cab Calloway, and other bands in the Swing Era, to 1960s modern jazz giants, John Coltrane and Gil Evans.

11. Baltimore Local 543, the "colored branch" of the American Federation of Musicians (AFofM). Decades later, Local 543 combined with the Baltimore's white Local 40.

12. Reportedly, Brown was the first African American to lease a passenger and freight boat on the Maryland shore. "Marylanders Who Have Made Good: Captain George Brown," *Baltimore Afro-American*, May 20, 1921, 12.

13. *Baltimore Afro-American*, June 2, 1922, 1.

14. Thomas finally succeeded after Frederick Huber, Baltimore's director of municipal music, came to hear his band several times. *Baltimore Afro-American*, May 26, 1922, 11.

15. *Baltimore Afro-American*, March 25, 1921, 5.

16. Cy St. Clair, *Record Changer* 7, no. 5, May 1948.

17. *Baltimore Afro-American*, September 9, 1921, 4; "J. A. Jackson's Page: Baltimore's Contribution to Music," *Billboard*, September 24, 1921, 45.

18. *Baltimore Afro-American*, September 9, 1921, 4. A. Jack Thomas also founded two or three orchestras and choruses with which he produced huge pageants and parades. "Negroes to Parade Streets of City Singing . . . ," *Baltimore Sun*, August 28, 1925, 4. Also see "The Storm Is Passing Over: Celebrating the Musical Life of Maryland's African-American Community from Emancipation to Civil Rights," https://musiclibrary.peabody.jhu.edu/c.php?g=678315&p=4781386#s-lg-box-15004955.

19. *Baltimore Afro-American*, September 9, 1921, 4.

20. Eubie Blake and the Shuffle Along Orchestra, "Baltimore Buzz," 1921, audio recording, accessed January 22, 2022, https://www.loc.gov/item/jukebox-188961.

21. Daphne Brooks, "100 Years Ago, 'Crazy Blues' Sparked a Revolution for Black Women Fans," *New York Times*, August 10, 2020, 10.

22. "On Broadway," *Baltimore Afro-American*, May 30, 1925, 2. Glascoe returned to Baltimore c. 1926 and formed the Plantation Orchestra, one of Baltimore's top jazz bands of the late 1920s.

23. David Gilbert, *The Product of Our Souls: Ragtime, Race, and the Birth of the Manhattan Musical Marketplace* (Chapel Hill: University of North Carolina Press, 2016), 19–21. See Gilbert for importance of Black songwriters and publishers on Tin Pan Alley, and the neighborhood nearby that was a lively Black neighborhood the 1920s.

24. John Cowley, "West Indies Blues: An Historical Overview 1920s–1950s—Blues and Music from the English-speaking West Indies," in *Nobody Knows Where the Blues Came From: Lyrics and History*, ed. Robert Springer (Jackson: University Press of Mississippi, 2006), 187–263.

25. Bushell, *Jazz*, 34.

26. Sophie Tucker created a hit with one of Sissle and Blake's first songs, "It's All Your Fault." In 1918, Sissle went to France with Europe's 369th infantry band.

27. Caseem Gaines, *Footnotes: The Black Artists Who Rewrote the Rules of the Great White Way* (New York: Sourcebooks, 2021), 242.

28. Peter Calloway Brooks, interview with author, March 2020.

29. Billie Holiday got to know her father in Harlem in the early 1930s when he was playing with the orchestras of Fletcher Henderson, Don Redman, and other prominent bandleaders.
30. Andy Razaf, "Passing Years," *Negro History Bulletin*, January 22, 1959. Razaf ended his article bitterly with a quote from a Eubie Blake song, "We Are Americans, Too"; in Razaf's opinion, its lyrics were the "Voice of My People."

Chapter 3

1. The Goldfield Hotel's nightclub, which opened in 1907, was one of the first clubs in Baltimore that welcomed white and Black patrons.
2. President Franklin Roosevelt called Woolford his favorite pianist. Lillian Johnson, "7,500 Pay Homage to Death to Make Life More Abundant: Spirit of … ," *Afro-American*, February 17, 1940, 14.
3. *Baltimore Afro-American*, October 10, 1924, 8.
4. Lillian Johnson, "From Newsboy to King: The Story of Chick Webb Whose Genius Triumphed … ," *Baltimore Afro-American*, July 22, 1939, 11. It is unclear if Trueheart spent time in Harlem during that first trip.
5. Sonny Greer, interview with Stanley Crouch, January 1979, JOHP.
6. Russell Procope played with Chick Webb on and off in the late 1920s to early 1930s, and with various groups before starting his thirty-year tenure with the Duke Ellington Orchestra in 1946; Russell Procope, interview with Chris Albertson, March 1, 1979, JOHP. From the 1950s to the 1960s, construction of the Lincoln Center complex displaced thousands of Black and Hispanic residents.
7. Frank Byrd, "Rent Parties," in *A Renaissance in Harlem,* ed. Lionel C. Bascom (New York: Harper Collins, 1999), 60–61. The Federal Writers' Project was a Depression Era program, part of the Works Progress Administration (WPA).
8. Bardu Ali, interview with Steve Allen, 1974, BBC2, LAHM.
9. Bert Hall was manager of the Rhythm Club, a Local 802 delegate, and advocate for Harlem musicians. According to the 1930 census, Webb and Trueheart were lodgers in Ginger Young's apartment on St. Nicholas Avenue.
10. This estimate is based on Randy Sandke's estimates for similar jobs in New Orleans. Randy Sandke, *Where the Dark and the Light Folks Meet: Race and the Mythology, Politics, and Business of Jazz* (Lanham, MD: Rowman & Littlefield, 2010), 219–20.
11. Robert G. O'Meally, *Jazz, Collage, Fiction and the Shaping of African American Culture* (New York: Columbia University Press, 2022).
12. Danny Barker, *A Life in Jazz,* ed. Alyn Shipton (New York: Oxford University Press, 1986), 109.
13. Greer, interview with Crouch.
14. Greer, interview with Crouch.
15. Whitney Balliett, *American Musicians II* (New York: Oxford University Press, 1996), 127. Tommy Benford, interview with Phil Schaap, WKCR Chick Webb Festival, 1978.

16. Byrd, "Rent Parties," 62.

17. Greer, interview with Crouch. Hosts also called them "Social Party," "Parlor Social," etc.

18. Willie "the Lion" Smith, *Music on My Mind: The Memoirs of an American Pianist* (New York: Doubleday, 1964), 153–57.

19. Langston Hughes, "When the Negro Was in Vogue," in *The Big Sea: An Autobiography* (New York: Hill and Wang, 1940), 244–45.

20. Danielle Robinson, "'Oh, You Black Bottom!' Appropriation, Authenticity, and Opportunity in the Jazz Dance Teaching of 1920s New York," *Dance Research Journal* 38, no. 1/2 (Summer–Winter 2006): 19–40. Some dancing schools, downtown and uptown, had shady reputations and were venues for the commodification of Black female bodies and thinly disguised covers for prostitution. Danielle Robinson, *Modern Moves: Dancing Race During the Ragtime and Jazz Era* (New York: Oxford University Press, 2015), 124, 135–45.

21. Teddy McRae, interview with Ron Welburn, 1981, JOHP.

22. Procope, interview with Albertson.

23. Wallace Thurman, "A Negro's Life in New York's Harlem," in *The Collected Writings of Wallace Thurman: A Harlem Renaissance Reader*, ed. Amritjit Singh and Daniel M. Scott (New Brunswick, NJ: Rutgers University Press, 2003), 46–50.

24. Procope, interview with Albertson.

25. Frederic Ramsey Jr. and Charles Edward Smith, eds., *Jazzmen* (New York: Harcourt, Brace and Co., 1939), 279. The "Great White Way" then extended that far north, starting at Union Square and going all the way up Broadway.

26. Local 802 pay scale for dance halls in the late 1920s was thirty-three dollars a week.

27. Roseland had two bands for continuous music for the dancers; starting with Henderson's band, the ballroom typically hired one Black band and one white band.

28. David Suisman, *Selling Sounds: The Commercial Revolution in American Music* (Cambridge, MA: Harvard University Press, 2009), 216–18.

29. There is no archive of the Henderson Orchestra's contracts, payroll stubs, or other records. Henderson biographer Jeffrey Magee said that any financial records Henderson or his wife, Leora, kept were sketchy and typically discarded. Jeffrey Magee, interview with author, Spring 2019. Local 802's archives are piecemeal when it comes to contracts.

30. Barker, *A Life*, 13.

31. "Rise of a Crippled Genius," *DownBeat*, December 1937, 14, part 1 of 3. Several articles printed after Webb's death took information from this article, though some of it is unverifiable, and no author's byline appears.

Chapter 4

1. Sonny Greer, interview with Stanley Crouch, January 1979, JOHP.

2. John Gennari, *Blowin' Hot and Cool: Jazz and Its Critics* (Chicago: University of Chicago Press, 2006), 28.

3. Cary D. Wintz, *Harlem Speaks: A Living History of the Harlem Renaissance* (New York: Sourcebooks, 2007), 36–37.

4. Brenda Dixon Gottschild, *The Black Dancing Body* (New York: Palgrave Macmillan, 2003), 167.

5. Duke Ellington, *Music Is My Mistress* (New York: Da Capo, 1976), 99–100.

6. Helen Oakley Dance, "Drum Mad and Lightning Fast," *Stereo Review*, June 15, 1963, 52.

7. Rex Stewart, *Boy Meets Horn*, ed. Claire P. Gordon (Ann Arbor: University of Michigan Press, 1991). Stewart joined Ellington's band in 1934.

8. Harvey Cohen, *Duke Ellington's America* (Chicago: University of Chicago Press, 2011), offers a cogent explanation of Ellington's and Mills's business relationship, which lasted until 1939.

9. Stewart, *Horn*, 155.

10. Charlie Holmes, interview with Al Vollmer, October 9, 1982, JOHP.

11. Stewart, *Horn*, 208–9.

12. Con Chapman, *Rabbit's Blues: The Life and Music of Johnny Hodges* (New York: Oxford University Press, 2019).

13. "The Rise of a Crippled Genius," *DownBeat*, December 1937, 14. According to other anecdotal reporting, Moe Gale first heard Webb's band at the Paddock Club, but this was not documented by Gale or his associates.

14. *New York Age*, February 5, 1927, 11.

15. Fess Williams was married to Charles Mingus's aunt; Mingus stayed at their home in Queens when he first moved to New York City in 1961.

16. Steele was a key member of Webb's band from 1932 to 1934, after touring in the revue "Rhapsody in Black," starring Ethel Waters.

17. Holmes, interview with Vollmer.

18. Holmes, interview with Vollmer.

19. Holmes, interview with Vollmer.

20. Holmes, interview with Vollmer.

21. Christopher "Christi J" Wells, " 'Spinnin' the Webb': Representational Spaces, Mythic Narratives, and the 1937 Webb/Goodman Battle of Music," *Journal of the Society for American Music* 14, no. 2 (May 2020): 176–96. https://doi.org/10.1017/S175219632 0000061.

22. "'Battle of Jazz' Stirs Vast Crowd," *Amsterdam News*, May 18, 1927, 11.

23. "All Harlem Trots to Toots as 4 Bands Seek Jazzy Crown," *New York Herald Tribune*, May 16, 1927, 5.

24. *Baltimore Afro-American*, May 14, 1927, 8.

25. Local 802 was an integrated union from its beginnings, reaching back to 1860 when the Musician's Mutual Protective Union (MMPU) was founded in New York City. Its members were then the elite classical musicians of the city, and the membership exam was rigorous and wholly based on European music performance practices. In 1886, it admitted its first Black member, violinist and conductor Henry Craig, making it the first integrated musicians' union in the country; other Black classical musicians in New York City slowly followed Craig's lead.

26. Robert F. Wagner Labor Archives at New York University: Local 802 Archives.

27. Eva Jessye, "Around New York," *Baltimore Afro-American*, July 1927. Jessye was a pathbreaking composer, conductor, educator, and director of the Eva Jessye Choir. Her choir was chosen to perform in "Four Saints in Three Acts" by Virgil Thompson and Gertrude Stein, and in the original 1935 production of "Porgy and Bess," by George Gershwin.

28. "Society," *Baltimore Afro-American*, September 3, 1927.

29. Duke Ellington, "Jazz, As I Have Seen It, Part V," *Swing: The Guide to Modern Music*, Vol. 3 no. 1, July 1940, 10.

Chapter 5

1. Frankie Manning, interview with Robert P. Crease, February 22, 1990.

2. *Luggage and Leather Goods*, vols. 45–46, January 1, 1920, Business Journals Inc., 118.

3. "The Savoy Remembered," transcript, panel discussion sponsored by the New York Swing Dance Society, June 7, 1990, at Hudson Park Library, New York City.

4. "Ballroom for Negroes," *Variety*, February 25, 1925, 34.

5. Conrad Gale, interview by Robert P. Crease, February 24, 1989.

6. The engine numbers were obliterated, the cars were resold out of state, and insurance money was collected for them. "Net for Fake Auto Thieves Get Four," *New York Times*, February 8, 1922, 19. Russell Gold, "Guilty of Syncopation, Joy, and Animation: The Closing of Harlem's Savoy Ballroom," in *Of, by, and for the People: Dancing on the Left in the 1930s*, ed. Lynn Garafola (Madison, WI: Society of Dance History Scholars at A-R Editions, 1994, c. 1993).

7. Conrad Gale, interview with Crease.

8. "The Savoy Story," commemorative booklet, March 1, 1951, Crusader Democratic Club, Schomburg Center (Sc Ser.-M.C7636: 1951).

9. Gold, "Guilty of Syncopation."

10. The Savoy Ballroom was redecorated with new flooring installed several times. Note the difference in decor and bandstands in the mid-1920s and 1930s, https://www.welcometothesavoy.com/

11. Hank O'Neal, interview with author, September 2021. Only three other photos by Abbott using this camera have survived, two of James Joyce and one of the Fratellini Brothers, a circus family adored by the French intelligentsia.

12. Richard Gale and Frankie Manning, interviews with Jeff Kaufman, for documentary film *The Savoy King*, 2012.

13. Buck Clayton, *Buck Clayton's Jazz World* (New York: Continuum Publishing Group, 1995), 121.

14. *New York Age*, February 27, 1926, 3.

15. *New York Age*, March 13, 1926, 6. The mayor was an old friend of Faggen's; a few years earlier they met as aspiring songwriters and tried to sell songs to music publishers of Tin Pan Alley.

16. Shane White and Graham White, *Stylin': African American Expressive Culture from Its Beginnings to the Zoot Suit* (Ithaca, NY: Cornell University Press, 1998), 205, 218.

17. *New York Age*, February 27, 1926, 3.

18. *New York Age*, July 31, 1926, 6.

19. Duncan Mayer had been the Bearcats' nominal leader.

20. Helen Armstead Johnston Papers, Schomburg Center, Sc MG 599, Alphabetical Collections, B 15, Williams, Fess.

21. *New York Amsterdam News*, August 18, 1926, 13.

22. Jerome Bourke, "Not the First to Sign with Victor Company," *New York Amsterdam News*, August 25, 1926, 11.

23. *New York Age*, March 20, 1926, 8.

24. Audrey Elisa Kerr, "The Paper Bag Principle: Of the Myth and the Motion of Colorism," *Journal of American Folklore* 118, no. 469 (2005): 271–89, http://www.jstor.org/stable/4137914.

25. "Savoy Dance Hall Raises Employees' Pay," *New York Age*, April 24, 1926, 6.

26. *New York Age*, June 5, 1926, 6.

27. "Savoy Takes Over New Alhambra Ballroom," *Pittsburgh Courier*, September 14, 1929, 3.

28. "The Savoy Remembered," panel discussion.

29. David Evans, "High Water Everywhere: Blues and Gospel Commentary on the 1927 Mississippi River Flood," in *Nobody Knows Where the Blues Come From: Lyrics and History*, ed. Robert Springer (Jackson: University Press of Mississippi, 2006), 3–5. Bessie Smith's "Back Water Blues" and "Muddy Waters" were bestsellers, though Smith had recorded these songs months before the flood's worst impact.

30. Abel Green, "Night Club Reviews: Rose Danceland," *Variety*, December 21, 1927. The term "ultra-modern music" was associated with composer Arnold Schoenberg in the 1920s.

31. Fess Williams as told to Harrison Smith, "The Fess Williams Story," *Record Research* 3 (October/November 1957).

32. "The Savoy Remembered," panel discussion.

33. Mario Bauza, interview with John Storm Roberts, December 13, 1978, JOHP.

34. "Johnny Hyde Sets Duet of Turns for Loew's Dates," *Billboard*, December 24, 1927, 11.

35. "Listening In," *Baltimore Afro-American*, January 14, 1928, 9.

36. "Vaudeville: Webb's Band for Loew's," *Variety*, January 18, 1928, 34.

Chapter 6

1. *Pittsburgh Courier*, March 24, 1928, 14.

2. *Brown Skin Models* had its last run in 1954. See Lily Yuen Papers for theater programs, ads, and scrapbooks of Yuen performer in as a featured *Brown Skin Models*, and actress and dancer in Harlem during the Harlem Renaissance and later. Schomburg Center, MARB-Lily Yuen Papers (Sc MG 643).

3. Philip Merrill, interview with author, August 2019.

4. Lester Walton, influential and pioneering Black journalist and activist, took over the Lafayette's management in 1913 and instigated this action and others with help from the newly formed NAACP. The theater changed management several times in the 1920s. Ted Vincent, *Keep Cool: The Black Activists Who Built the Jazz Age* (London: Pluto Press, 1995), 40–43.

5. Schiffman had been working for Louis Brecher, a powerbroker in New York's "moving picture" theater business. After the first talking feature movie in 1927, theaters typically presented a hybrid format of stage shows and movies.

6. During the Depression the Lafayette Theater closed, then reopened in 1935 under the Federal Theater Project (a work program for theater artists funded by the WPA). Paul Robeson starred there in *Macbeth* in 1936, in a controversial interpretation by its director, twenty-year-old Orson Welles.

7. *New York Amsterdam News,* March 21, 1928, 8; *Interstate Tattler*, March 11, 1928, 8.

8. *New York Age,* March 31, 1928, 7.

9. Danny Barker, *A Life in Jazz* (New York: Oxford University Press, 1988), 112.

10. Barney Bigard, *With Louis and the Duke: The Autobiography of a Jazz Clarinetist* (New York: Macmillan, 1985), 61.

11. *New York Amsterdam News,* May 2, 1928, 7.

12. Fess Williams, as told to Harrison Smith, "The Fess Williams Story," *Record Research* 3 (October/November 1957).

13. Helen Armstead Johnston Papers, Schomburg Center, Sc MG 599, Alphabetical Collections, Box 15, Williams, Fess.

14. *Tattler*, July 6, 1928, 7.

15. *Baltimore Afro-American,* July 21, 1928, 9.

16. Max Jones, *Talking Jazz* (New York: W. W. Norton, 1987), 30–32.

17. Gunther Schuller described Ross's Syncopators as a sophisticated early jazz ensemble. Gunther Schuller, *The Swing Era: The Development of Jazz, 1930–1945* (New York: Oxford University Press, 1991), 775–76; Cootie Williams, interview with Helen Oakley Dance, May 1, 1976, JOHP.

18. Cootie Williams, interview with Oakley Dance.

19. Jones, *Talking*, 30–32.

20. Cootie Williams, interview with Oakley Dance.

21. Cootie Williams, interview with Oakley Dance.

22. Cootie Williams, interview with Oakley Dance.

23. Richard L. Black Jr., "Station NYLW Broadcasting New York Leagues Weekly Radio News," *New York Amsterdam News,* August 29, 1928, 8.

24. Lillian Johnson, "From Newsboy to King: The Story of Chick Webb," *Baltimore Afro-American*, July 29, 1939, 10.

25. Johnson, "From Newsboy to King," 14.

26. Floyd J. Calvin, "Savoy Doing Million Dollar Business," *Pittsburgh Courier*, February 25, 1928, 1.

27. Calvin, "Savoy," 1.

28. Charlie Holmes, interview with Al Vollmer, October 9, 1982, JOHP.

29. Percival Outram, "Activities among Union Musicians," *New York Age*, November 24, 1928, 7.
30. Outram, "Activities among Union Musicians," 7.
31. Cootie Williams, interview with Oakley Dance.

Chapter 7

1. *Baltimore Afro-American*, December 8, 1928, 16.
2. Cootie Williams, interview with Helen Oakley Dance, 1975, May 1, 1976, JOHP.
3. Dorothy Fields and Jimmy McHugh wrote many of the Cotton Club's hits shows in the late 1920s, and Ellington recorded several of their songs and his own compositions. "Brilliant 'Battle of Jazz' Stirs Vast New York Crowd," *Pittsburgh Courier*, December 29, 1928, C3.
4. "Hosts of Baltimoreans Greet Maryland Orchestra, No Decision Made in N.Y. 'Jazz War,' Six Bands in Contest," *Baltimore Afro-American*, December 22, 1928, 12.
5. Conrad Gale, interview with Robert P. Crease, February 24, 1989.
6. Conrad Gale, interview with Crease.
7. Marya Annette McQuirter, "Awkward Moves," in *Dancing Many Drums: Excavations in African American Dance*, ed. Thomas F. DeFrantz (Madison: University of Wisconsin Press, 2002), 97–99.
8. "New York," *Baltimore Afro-American*, November 2, 1929, 5. "Times Square: Chatter in New York," *Variety* 93 (October 24, 1928): 44.
9. *Asbury Park Press*, April 10, 1928, 14.
10. Shane White and Graham White, *Stylin': African American Expressive Culture from Its Beginnings to the Zoot Suit* (Ithaca, NY: Cornell University Press, 1998), 205, 218.
11. Fess Williams allegedly "cleaned up a thousand dollars a week making records while in New York, but since arriving here he has only canned one number for Vocalion. Then, Fess has never withdrawn his name from his New York Orchestra, and his return as their leader after Fess's phenomenal success here [in Chicago] would cause their stock to soar skyward." "Stage and Screen Gossip," *Baltimore Afro-American*, January 12, 1929, 7.
12. Stewart played with the Fletcher Henderson Orchestra often from the mid-1920s through the early 1930s, and also played with McKinney's Cotton Pickers, led his own band, and joined Duke Ellington in 1935. Rex Stewart, *Boy Meets Horn*, ed. Claire P. Gordon (Ann Arbor: University of Michigan Press, 1991), 93–94.
13. Cootie Williams, interview with Oakley Dance.
14. Duke Ellington, *Music Is My Mistress* (Boston: Da Capo, 1976), 119.
15. Barney Bigard, *With Louis and the Duke: The Autobiography of a Jazz Clarinetist* (New York: Macmillan, 1985), 73.
16. Cootie Williams, interview with Oakley Dance.
17. Cootie Williams, interview with Oakley Dance. Barry Ulanov, "Cootie Calls Chick Greatest Bandleader," *Metronome* 57, no. 7 (July 1941): 20, 21.

18. Maurice Dancer, "Harlem Show Talk," *Baltimore Afro-American*, March 23, 1929, 9.

19. *After Seben* is minstrel-style racialized slang for "After Seven." Barton was also an influence on Fred Astaire. Marshall Stearns and Jean Stearns, *Jazz Dance: The Story of American Vernacular Dance* (New York: Macmillan, 1968), 203.

20. Gabbard notes that King Oliver and Jelly Roll Morton started performing in minstrel shows, as did other jazz performers, including Louis Jordan, who would work with Webb in the 1930s before forming his own group, the Tympany Five.

21. Krin Gabbard, email correspondence with author, November 2021.

22. Chick Webb and His Orchestra (on camera): Edwin Swayzee, Ward Pinkett, trumpet; Benny Morton, trombone; tuba (unconfirmed); Elmer Williams, Bobby Holmes, Hilton Jefferson, reeds; John Trueheart, banjo; Don Kirkpatrick, piano; Chick Webb, drums. Dancer Shorty Snowden was an early innovator of the Lindy Hop.

23. Maurice Dancer, "Eastern Orchestra Gets Talkie Contract," *Pittsburgh Courier*, March 23, 1929, A3.

24. *Motion Picture News*, April–June 1929, 426, accessed January 2022, https://archive.org/details/motionpic39moti/page/n1257/mode/2up?q=James+Barton.

25. *Philadelphia Tribune,* April 18, 1929, 6.

26. Danielle Robinson, *Modern Moves: Dancing Race during the Ragtime and Jazz Eras* (New York: Oxford University Press, 2015), 134.

27. Cab Calloway and Bryant Rollins, *Of Minnie the Moocher and Me* (New York: Thomas Y. Crowell Company, 1976), 93.

28. Christi Jay Wells (aka Christopher J. Wells), *Go Harlem: Chick Webb and His Dancing Audience during the Great Depression* (Chapel Hill: University of North Carolina Press, 2014).

29. Most of "The Jungle Band" also appeared in the film *After Seben*, with Bennie Morton on trombone. Jan Evensmo, "Chick Webb," Jazz Archeology, http://www.jazzarcheology.com/chick-webb. Also see https://memory.loc.gov/diglib/ihas/loc.natlib.jots.200013054/default.html.

30. Webb's band covered at the Cotton Club for Duke Ellington's, while it was performing in *Ziegfeld Follies*. "Pittsburgh Theaters," *Baltimore Afro-American*, November 2, 1929, 9.

31. Jeffrey Magee, *The Uncrowned King of Swing: Fletcher Henderson and Big Band Jazz* (New York: Oxford University Press, 2004), 139.

Chapter 8

1. "At the Lafayette," *New York Amsterdam News*, September 18, 1929, 8.

2. Aubrey Brooks, "About Musicians," *Interstate Tattler*, September 27, 1929.

3. After his year with Fletcher Henderson, Armstrong returned to Chicago, where his famous "Hot Five and Seven" recordings launched his career. Peter Calloway Brooks, interview with author, May 2020.

4. "Kansas City Star Lauds Alabamians," *Chicago Defender*, July 20, 1929, 7.

5. Advertisement, *Amsterdam News*, September 18, 1929, 14.

6. *Philadelphia Tribune,* November 28, 1929, 6. In fall 1925, Blanche Calloway made her first 78 record with Louis Armstrong on cornet, "Lazy Woman's Blues" and "Lonesome Lovesick." Regarding Cab Calloway's early years in New York, see Alyn Shipton, *Hi-De-Ho: The Life of Cab Calloway* (New York: Oxford University Press, 2010). Jean Francois Pitet, http://www.thehidehoblog.com.

7. Peter Calloway Brooks, interview with author.

8. Russell Procope, interview with Chris Albertson, March 1, 1979, JOHP.

9. Teddy McRae, interview with Ron Welburn, 1981, JOHP.

10. "Savoy Takes Over New Alhambra Ballroom: 'World's Finest' Dance Palace," *Pittsburgh Courier*, September 14, 1929, A3.

11. "Alwyns Club Sponsors Dance: E. R. Eason Supervises Unique Decoration," *New York Amsterdam News*, April 30, 1930, 6.

12. Christi Jay Wells, "'And I Make My Own': Class Performance, Black Urban Identity, and Depression-Era Harlem's Physical Culture," in *Oxford Handbook of Dance and Ethnicity,* ed. Anthony Shay and Barbara Sellers-Young (New York: Oxford University Press, 2016), 27–29.

13. Jerry, "New York: The Social Whirl Sigmas Dance and SIP," *Baltimore Afro-American*, May 3, 1930, 7.

14. Jerry or Gerri Major was an editor, author, newscaster, and community leader. She had been a major in the Red Cross in World War I. She wrote columns for the *Pittsburgh Courier, New York Age, Interstate Tattler, Amsterdam News,* and the *Baltimore Afro*; later she wrote articles for *Ebony* and *Jet* magazines.

15. Jerry, "New York: Ellington Wins," *Afro-American*, April 19, 1930, 7.

16. Gerri [Jerry] Major with Doris E. Saunders, *Black Society* (Chicago: Johnson Publishing, 1976).

17. *Amsterdam News*, May 21, 1930, 9.

18. Shipton, *Hi-De-Ho,* 43.

19. *Pittsburgh Courier,* December 20, 1930, A9.

20. "Savoy in Full Holiday Program: Fletcher Henderson and Chick Webb to Carry On for Merrymaking," *New York Amsterdam News*, December 24, 1930, 8.

21. Calloway and the Missourians had a month-long tryout at the Cotton Club in fall 1930, when Ellington and his band were in Los Angeles filming the Amos 'n' Andy movie *Check and Double Check.* Elias E. Sugarman, "Vaudeville Reviews: The Palace, New York," *Billboard*, October 18, 1930, 18.

22. This caused friction and litigation with Moe Gale, who was still Calloway's booking agent. "Cab Calloway's Salary Check Is Withheld," *Philadelphia Tribune*, September 3, 1931, 7. "Music: Inside Stuff," *Variety*, October 13, 1931, 61. Shipton, *Hi-De-Ho,* 44–46.

23. Sandy Williams interview with Phil Schaap, Chick Webb Festival, WKCR, 1978.

24. Samuel Charters and Leonard Kunstadt, *Jazz: A History of the New York Scene* (Boston: Da Capo, 1981), 265.

25. Jeffrey Magee, *The Uncrowned King of Swing: Fletcher Henderson and Big Band Jazz* (New York: Oxford University Press, 2005), 141–45.

26. Harper hoped to get "Roseland Revels" on Broadway, but that didn't occur. *New York Age*, May 2, 1931, 6.

27. Russell Procope, interview with Phil Schaap, Chick Webb Festival, WKCR, 1978.

28. Percival Outram, "Activities among Urban Union Presidents," *New York Age*, April 11, 1931, 7. After 1929, Fletcher Henderson's Orchestra was no longer a permanent fixture at Roseland, and some of his musicians had lost confidence in him. Though personnel was in flux, Magee writes glowingly of Henderson's Connie's Inn Orchestra (1931). Magee, *The Uncrowned King of Swing*, 144–47.

29. Procope, interview with Schaap.

30. Trombonist Jimmy Harrison died of a stomach ulcer in July 1931, at only thirty years old.

31. Percival Outram, "Activities among Musicians," *New York Age*, November 21, 1931, 7.

32. In the early 1930s Bennie Moten's band included Hot Lips Page, trumpet; Bill [Count] Basie, piano; arranger/guitarist Eddie Durham; and singer Jimmy Rushing—the nucleus of the future Count Basie Orchestra.

33. Outram, "Activities Among Musicians," *New York Age*.

34. Linda Dahl, *Morning Glory* (Oakland: University of California Press, 2001). Blanche Calloway made her first recordings for Victor with what was essentially Andy Kirk's band with Mary Lou Williams on piano, from March to June of 1931.

35. *New York Amsterdam News*, October 7, 1931, 13; *Philadelphia Tribune*, October 15, 1931, 6.

36. "Blanche Calloway Making Record Is Premier Woman Band Leader," *Baltimore Afro-American*, October 10, 1931, 8.

37. "Battle of Music Coming to City," *Pittsburgh Courier*, October 3, 1931, 19.

38. Andy Anderson, "Depression Does Not Worry Orchestra Men," *Chicago Defender*, October 31, 1931, 5.

39. Anderson, "Depression," 5.

Chapter 9

1. Louis Armstrong, "Hobo, You Can't Ride this Train," lyrics (excerpt) transcribed by author.

2. Norma Miller, interview with author, 2017.

3. George S. Schuyler, "Views and Reviews," *Pittsburgh Courier*, January 30, 1932, 10.

4. Barney Bigard, *With Louis and the Duke: The Autobiography of a Jazz Clarinetist* (New York: Macmillan, 1985), 72. Jonathan Karp, interview with author, June 2020. Jonathan Karp, "Blacks, Jews, and the Business of Race Music, 1945–1955," in *The Jewish Encounter with American Capitalism*, ed. Rebecca Kobrin (New Brunswick, NJ: Rutgers University Press, 2012), 141–67, http://www.jstor.com/stable/j.ctt5hjf56.11.

5. "Jazz Outfits and Entertainers Slated to Tour Country," *Norfolk Journal and Guide*, December 12, 1931, 5.

6. Aileen Eckstine was singer Billy Eckstine's older sister. She was a columnist for the *Pittsburgh Courier* before her brother started singing professionally.

7. Percival Outram, "Among the Musicians," *New York Age*, June 25, 1932, 7.

8. Olivia Cunningham, "River Dance: There Was a Time When Harrisburg Tripped the Barge Fantastic," *The Burg*, April 29, 2016, accessed January 20, 2022, https://theb urgnews.com/in-the-burg/river-dance-there-was-a-time-when-harrisburg-tripped-the-barge-fantastic.

9. Garvin Bushell, *Jazz from the Beginning*, as told to Mark Tucker (Ann Arbor: University of Michigan Press, 1988), 100–101.

10. Advertisement, *New York Age*, October 1, 1932, 2.

11. "A History of Dominican Music in the US," CUNY Dominican Studies Institute, accessed January 20, 2022, http://dominicanmusicusa.com/narratives/1930s-dom inicans-and-the-first-latin-music-dance-craze/6.

12. "Depression Hits Cabarets of New York," *Chicago Defender*, August 20, 1932, 5. David Levering Lewis, *When Harlem Was in Vogue* (New York: Penguin Books, 1997), 243.

13. Percival Outram, "Among the Musicians."

14. Kenneth J. Bindas, *The New Deal and American Society, 1933–1941* (Oxfordshire, UK: Routledge, 2021).

15. Armstrong's record sales were phenomenal, considering the industry's decline in the early 1930s.

16. The recordings were made before Okeh was acquired by Brunswick/Columbia.

17. Thomas Brothers, *Louis Armstrong, Master of Modernism* (New York: Norton, 2014), 408–9. Ricky Riccardi, *Heart Full of Rhythm* (New York: Oxford University Press, 2020), 103–5. Both authors sum up the legal wrangling that led to court depositions in 1931 to decide whether or not Armstrong was an irreplaceable entertainer.

18. Riccardi, *Heart Full*, 129–30.

19. Gunther Schuller, *The Swing Era: The Development of Jazz 1930–1945* (New York: Oxford University Press, 1989), 181.

20. Irving Kolodin, "All God's Chillun' Got Rhythm," *Americana Magazine*, February 1933.

21. "Whiteway: The Sideliner," *Baltimore Afro-American*, December 24, 1932, 9.

22. In 1932 Oberstein started RCA Victor's budget Bluebird label, a prudent Depression-era strategy. These 78 records were sold thirty-five cents for one, and three for a dollar.

23. Mezz Mezzrow and Bernard Wolfe, *Really the Blues* (New York: NYRB Classics, 2016), 271.

24. Walter Winchell, "On Broadway," *Akron Beacon Journal*, January 24, 1933.

25. "13 Year Anniversary, That's My Home, Heart Full of Rhythm (and Other Dispatches from a Pandemic)," July 13, 2020, accessed September 2020, https://dippermouth. blogspot.com/2020/07/dispatches-from-pandemic.html.

26. Armstrong recorded two medleys of his hits with Gaines's band, including Louis Jordan, for the December 21, 1932, session. Riccardi, *Heart Full*, 131. Riccardi notes that Armstrong does "one of his finest renditions" of "Sleepy Time Down South," replacing the lyric with the words "When It's Slavery Time Down South."

27. Riccardi, *Heart Full*, 131. *Pittsburgh Courier*, December 24, 1932, 16.

28. "'Heil Hitler' Roars Out at Nazi Rally," *Baltimore Sun*, May 19, 1935, 22. Various clubs used Lehman Hall, including the Baltimore chapter of the Friends of New Germany, who hosted a Nazi rally there in 1935. "Five swastikas, emblem of Hitler Germany, were among the flags dedicated, the first time the Baltimore branch has had the official right to fly the banners of their parent organization."

29. Riccardi, *Heart Full*, 131; Mezzrow, *Really*, 275. Mezzrow was a great raconteur, and many episodes in his memoir were exaggerated.

Chapter 10

1. Richard Gale, interview with Jeff Kaufman, for documentary *The Savoy King*, 2012.

2. Chappy Gardner, "A Bandleader's Rise," *Pittsburgh Courier*, March 18, 1933, A7.

3. *New York Age,* February 4, 1933, 6.

4. For Webb's total fees of $800 or $900, his musicians were paid between $65 and $75 per week, for six nights a week, five or six shows a day. Information from Frank Schiffman's ledgers, courtesy of Brad San Martin, Digital Archivist, Apollo Theater. Correspondence with author October 2020.

5. Margo Jefferson, interview with author, August 2020.

6. "Valaida Snow Heads Revue," *Amsterdam News*, June 21, 1933, 7A.

7. Roy Eldridge, interview with Dan Morgenstern, June 1982, JOHP.

8. Ted Yates, "Around Town, New York," *Pittsburgh Courier*, January 14, 1933, 17.

9. Ted Yates, "Around Town, New York," *Pittsburgh Courier*, February 4, 1933, 16.

10. Benny Carter then went out on his own as leader. See Chapter 8 for Carter's recordings with Webb.

11. Gary Giddins, *Visions of Jazz: The First Century* (New York: Oxford University Press, 1998), 141.

12. Gunther Schuller, *The Swing Era The Development of Jazz 1930–1945* (New York: Oxford University Press, 1989), 295.

13. Mark Tucker, *Ellington: The Early Years* (Urbana: University of Illinois Press, 1991), 136. In the mid-1920s, various saxophonists "had stints with him [Ellington] . . . Sampson, Benny Carter and Don Redman, joining Otto Hardwick and Perry Robinson to form a three-piece reed team." Benny Carter said some early Ellington club dates called for ten pieces, not just six.

14. Rex Stewart, *Boy Meets Horn*, ed. Claire P. Gordon (Ann Arbor: University of Michigan Press, 1991), 111. Bobby Stark was also a heavy drinker, whose "supreme combination of irresponsibility and talent got him fired and hired at least twice a season."

15. Horace Henderson, interview with Tom McCluskey, April 9, 1975, Denver, Colorado, JOHP. Horace was also a talented pianist and arranger, and left New York to join Don Redman's McKinney's Cotton Pickers, led his own band briefly, and returned to New York in the early 1930s.

16. Quentin Jackson, interview with Milt Hinton, June 1976, JOHP.

17. Jo Jones, interview with Milt Hinton, May 15, 1973, New York City, JOHP.

18. Mario Bauza, interview with John Storm Roberts, December 13, 1978, New York City, JOHP.

19. Schuller, *The Swing Era*, 295.

20. *Atlanta Daily World*, August 29, 1934, 2.

21. Ellington's band recorded for Victor and other labels previously under several names, such as the Harlem Footwarmers, the Jungle Band, etc.

22. John McDonough, liner notes for *The Complete Chick Webb and Ella Fitzgerald Decca Sessions (1934–1941)*, Mosaic Records, 2013.

23. "Harlem Raves Over the Music of Chick Webb," *Chicago Defender*, November 3, 1934, 9. The reviewer incorrectly wrote that "Free Love" was one of Webb's discs. It was a Benny Carter tune and arrangement that Webb may have performed live.

24. John Storm Roberts, *The Latin Tinge: The Impact of Latin American Music on the United States* (New York: Oxford University Press, 1979, 1999).

25. Bobby Sanabria, interview with author, August 2019. Many Latin musicians settled in East Harlem, between Lenox and Lexington Avenues from 110th to 118th Street, before the neighborhood was known as El Barrio (Spanish Harlem). Musicians frequented La Moderna, a bakery owned by Simón Jou, from Cuba. Jou was then the only contact in New York able to get authentic conga drums and other percussion instruments from Cuba.

26. Sanabria, interview with author. By this time, Bauza had moved in with one of the San Domingans.

27. Teddy McRae, interview with Ron Welburn, 1981, JOHP.

28. Bauza, interview with Roberts.

29. Ted Yates, "New York after Dark," *New Journal and Guide*, July 14, 1934.

30. "Bardu Ali a New York Sensation," *Chicago Defender*, March 31, 1934, 9.

31. Vivek Bald, *Bengali Harlem and the Lost Histories of South Asian America* (Cambridge, MA: Harvard University Press, 2013).

32. "Bardu Ali Is Home after a Stay Abroad," *Chicago Defender*, January 19, 1935, 8.

33. *New York Age*, June 23, 1934, 5. *New York Age*, May 19, 1934, 5.

34. Maurice Dancer, "Harlem Night by Night," *Pittsburgh Courier*, March 25, 1933, 9.

35. *New York Age*, March 18, 1933, 2.

36. Frankie Manning and Cynthia Millman, *Frankie Manning: Ambassador of Lindy Hop* (Philadelphia: Temple University Press, 2007), 67.

37. Jervis Anderson, *This Was Harlem: A Cultural Portrait, 1900–1950* (New York: Farrar Straus Giroux, 1982), 313.

38. Richard Gale, interview with Kaufman.

39. Christi Jay Wells (aka Christopher J. Wells), "Thriving in Crisis: The Chick Webb Orchestra and the Great Depression," Virtual Seminar for the Frankie Manning Foundation, May 30, 2020. Christi Jay Wells, *Go Harlem: Chick Webb and His Dancing Audience during the Great Depression* (Chapel Hill: University of North Carolina, 2014).

40. Bert Hall's death in 1933 was a huge blow to the Harlem musicians' community and the Rhythm Club.

41. "Harlem Raves Over the Music of Chick Webb," *Chicago Defender*, November 3, 1934, 9.

Chapter 11

1. Happy Caldwell, interview with Stanley Dance, 1976, JOHP.
2. In the early 1940s, Bradshaw was in the vanguard of Boogie Woogie and R&B styles with hits such as "Shout, Sister, Shout."
3. The Boswell sisters were raised in New Orleans, then moved to Los Angeles and New York, where their radio career took off. Connee Boswell wrote the group's vocal arrangements, and her own influences included prominent Black artists such as Louis Armstrong and Ethel Waters.
4. Schiffman was also manager of the Lafayette Theater.
5. Bessye Bearden was the mother of renowned Harlem artist Romare Bearden. Many of Bearden's collages and paintings depict musicians (including Chick Webb), performers, and dancers at the Savoy, the Lafayette, and the Apollo.
6. Vincent Ted, *Keep Cool: The Activists Who Built the Jazz Age* (London: Pluto Press, 1995), 189–92. The Lafayette Theater stopped having stage shows in 1933 and became the home for the Negro Theater Guild under the Works Progress Administration (WPA) in 1936.
7. Frankie Manning interview with Robert P. Crease, New York City, February 22, 1990.
8. *New York Amsterdam News,* June 23, 1934, 6.
9. "Harlem Amateur Night Is Winning Radio Plaudits: Wednesday Midnight … ," *Pittsburgh Courier*, December 1, 1934, A8.
10. The Harlem Opera House was built by Oscar Hammerstein, Sr. in 1889, as a thousand-seat opera house. In the early 1930s it was a movies-only theater, then introduced stage shows.
11. Sidney S. Cohen was a pioneer in creating early movie house chains. The feud was "over" in May 1935, but problems between the co-managers drove Sussman out of the Apollo by 1936.
12. Ralph Cooper, *Amateur Night at the Apollo: Ralph Cooper Presents Five Decades of Great Entertainment* (New York: HarperCollins Publishers, 1990), chaps. 4 and 5.
13. According to Schiffman's ledgers, the fee for Webb's band at the Harlem Opera House was 700 dollars for the week of August 1934; 950 dollars for the week of November 2, 1934; and 950 dollars for the week of March 1, 1935. His son Jack said that Webb's fee stayed the same for the next couple of years, and other bands received far more money. Jack Schiffman, *Uptown* (New York: Cowles Books, 1971), 152.
14. Schiffman ran the Apollo for over forty years, then handed it over to his sons, Robert and Jack.
15. "War Declared by Gangsters: Attempt Reported to Have Been Made to Keep … ," *Amsterdam News*, January 3, 1934, 7.
16. *Pittsburgh Courier*, October 6, 1934, 19.
17. Pittsburgh's Savoy Ballroom, in the Hill district, was a smaller version (1,500 capacity) of its Harlem namesake and opened in 1933.
18. "Snow Stops Trip of Chick Webb," *Atlanta Daily World*, February 18, 1935, 2.

19. Census records from 1920 and 1930 list Margaret Loretta Ferguson's parents as white; it's possible she was mixed race or was adopted. Her Social Security application states she was born on June 15, 1913.

20. The material about Sally Webb was found through the author's research with assistance by Chris McKay, and has never been published previously.

21. Ella Fitzgerald, interview with Steve Allen for BBC2, 1974, LAHM.

22. Caldwell, interview with Dance.

23. Judith Tick, interview with author. Nina Bernstein, "Ward of the State: The Gap in Ella Fitzgerald's Life," *New York Times*, June 23, 1996, Section 4, p. 4. Alison Cornyn, interview with author, founder of Incorrigibles Project, https://incorrigibles.org.

24. Fitzgerald, interview with Allen.

25. Bardu Ali, interview with Steve Allen, BBC2, 1975, LAHM.

26. Stuart Nicholson, *Ella Fitzgerald: A Biography of the First Lady of Jazz* (London: Orion Books, reissued 2001, c. 1993, 1996), 34–37.

27. Margo Jefferson, "Ella in Wonderland," *New York Times*, December 29, 1996, Section 6, p. 41.

28. Ali, interview with Allen. Carolyn Wyman, *Ella Fitzgerald: Jazz Singer Supreme* (New York: F. Watts, 1993), 30.

29. Ella Fitzgerald, interview, *Ella on Ella: A Personal Portrait*, Essence, the Television Program, 1986, Schomburg Center: MIRS (Sc Visual VRA-33).

30. Nicholson, *Ella Fitzgerald*, 36.

31. Ali, interview with Allen.

Chapter 12

1. Rick Mattingly, "PAS (Percussive Arts Society) Hall of Fame: Art Blakey," https://www.pas.org/about/hall-of-fame/art-blakey. Max Roach, interview with Phil Schaap, Chick Webb Festival, WKCR, 1978.

2. Burt Korall, *Drummin' Men: The Heartbeat of Jazz—The Swing Years* (New York: Schirmer Books, 1990), 19.

3. The March of Time Newsreel "Swing," January 1, 1937. The same footage of Webb's band was used in a second March of Time newsreel in 1939, which included a short clip about the Savoy Ballroom.

4. Matt Brennan, *Kick It: A Social History of the Drum Kit* (New York: Oxford University Press, 2020), 29.

5. Korall, *Drummin' Men*, 21.

6. Cozy Cole, interview with Bill Kirchner, April 1980, JOHP.

7. Teddy McRae, interview with Ron Welburn, 1981, JOHP.

8. Mattingly, "PAS Hall of Fame: Art Blakey." A press roll is formed by playing a very fast series of double strokes with drumsticks on the drum head (usually snare drum), almost bouncing the sticks off the head, producing a sustained vibrating sound. Press rolls are often used to end a phrase or add drama.

9. Ulysses Owens, Jr., interview with author, February 10, 2021.

10. Roach, interview with Schaap. Also, Rick Mattingly, "PAS (Percussive Arts Society) Hall of Fame: Max Roach," https://www.pas.org/about/hall-of-fame/max-roach.

11. "Chick Webb Took a Trip to John Hopkins Hospital in Baltimore for Rest and Treatment. His Friends Flooded His New York Headquarters," *New York Age*, August 24, 1935, 4.

12. Laurie Stras, "Sing-a-Song-of-Difference: Connie [Connee] Boswell and a Discourse of Disability in Jazz," *Popular Music* 28, no. 3 (2009): 297–322. George McKay, "Jazz and Disability," in *The Routledge Companion to Jazz Studies*, ed. Nicholas Gebhardt, Nicole Rustin-Paschal, and Tony Whyton (London: Routledge, 2019), 173–84. Neither Stras nor McKay mentions Webb.

13. Terry Bowden, *The Songs of Blind Folk: African American Musicians and the Cultures of Blindness* (Ann Arbor: University of Michigan Press, 2009), 3–12.

14. Judith Tick, conversation with author. See Chapter 11 for more about Connee Boswell and her influence on Fitzgerald.

15. McRae, interview with Welburn.

16. Jo Jones, interview with Milt Hinton, New York City, May 15, 1973, JOHP.

17. Sandy Williams, interview with Stanley Dance, *The World of Swing: An Oral History of Big Band Jazz* (New York: Da Capo Press, 2001), 71.

18. Sandy Williams, interview with Phil Schaap, Chick Webb Festival, WKCR, 1978.

19. Norma Miller, phone interview with author, September 2018.

20. Korall, *Drummin' Men,* 34. Les Tompkins, "Buddy Rich: Interview 1," January 1, 1980, https://nationaljazzarchive.org.uk/explore/interviews/1621492-buddy-rich-interview-1?q=Buddy%20Rich.

21. Korall, *Drummin' Men*, 15–16.

22. Billy Gladstone patented over forty inventions, including the "Hand Sock Cymbal." Radio City opened December 27, 1932.

23. *Leedy Drum Publications*, March 1932, Elkhart, Indiana.

24. *Metronome*, April 1935, 45.

25. Chet Falzerano, *Chick Webb—Spinnin' the Webb: The Little Giant* (Anaheim Hills, CA: Centerstream Publishing, 2014), 29. Falzerano, correspondence with author. Webb used the Hand Sock on many recordings. Frank Wolf's drum shop produced a unique "two-to-one" snare drum, which improved regulating tension on the snares.

26. Steven Cerra, "Barend Boy ten Hove - Jazz Caricatures," *Jazz Profiles*, March 7, 2019, accessed January 21, 2022, https://jazzprofiles.blogspot.com/2019/03/barend-boy-ten-hove-jazz-caricatures.html. Danny, "For Musicians Only," *DownBeat*, December 1937, 12.

27. *Metronome*, September 1937. Fred W. Gretsch, "Chick Webb: The Little Giant," February 6, 2015, accessed January 21, 2022, https://www.gretsch.com/tag/the-savoy-king/. Fred W. Gretsch, phone interview with author, June 2021.

28. Justin DiCioccio, interview with author, New York City, April 2019.

29. Ulysses Owens, interview with author. Anthony Brown, "Modern Jazz Drumset Artistry," *Black Perspective in Music* 18, no. 1/2 (1990): 39–58, https://doi.org/10.2307/1214857.

30. Kenny Clarke, interview with Helen Oakley Dance, September 1, 1977, JOHP.
31. Jones, interview with Hinton.
32. Jo Jones, quote from *The Drums* (Jazz Odyssey JO-0001-2 LP, release c. 1973). Jones, interview with Hinton.

Chapter 13

1. Roi Ottley, "This Hectic Harlem: Savoy Ballroom: 'Home of Happy Feet,'" *Amsterdam News*, December 1, 1934.
2. "The Savoy Ballroom Remembered," panel discussion sponsored by the New York Swing Dance Society, June 7, 1990, Hudson Park Library, New York City. Participants included Savoy hostess Helen Clarke, vocalist Charles Linton, musicians Panama Francis and Lawrence Lucie, dancers Frank Manning and Norma Miller, and Conrad Gale, moderated by Robert P. Crease.
3. "The Savoy Remembered," panel.
4. Richard Gale, interview with Jeff Kaufman, for documentary *The Savoy King*, 2012.
5. Paul Vitello, "Muriel Petioni, 97, Prominent Harlem Physician, Dies," December 10, 2011, https://www.nytimes.com/2011/12/10/nyregion/muriel-petioni-prominent-harlem-physician-dies-at-97.html?searchResultPosition=1.
6. Muriel Petioni, interview with Jeff Kaufman, for documentary *The Savoy King*, 2012.
7. Sherrie Tucker, *Dance Floor Democracy: The Social Geography of Memory at the Hollywood Canteen* (Durham, NC: Duke University Press, 2014).
8. Frankie Manning, interview with Robert P. Crease, "The Swing Era," Smithsonian Jazz Oral History Project, New York City, July 22–23, 1992.
9. Duke Ellington, *Music Is My Mistress* (New York: Da Capo Press reprint of 1973 ed. by Doubleday), 100.
10. "The Savoy Remembered," panel.
11. Richard Gale, interview with Kaufman.
12. Manning, interview with Robert P. Crease.
13. Manning, interview with Robert P. Crease. Fess Williams returned to the Savoy briefly in the early 1930s. The Savoy Ballroom's Lindy Hop contests started in 1932.
14. Les Tompkins, "Dizzy Gillespie Tells His Story," *Crescendo*, September 1973, 21, https://nationaljazzarchive.org.uk/explore/journals/crescendo/crescendo-1973-september/1274241.
15. Whitey was a former professional boxer and "dancing waiter" at Barron Wilkins's Club in the 1920s.
16. Manning, interview with Robert P. Crease. Norma Miller, interview with author, October 2018.
17. Manning, interview with Robert P. Crease.
18. For more details about Harvest Moon Balls, see Christi Jay Wells, *Between Beats: The Jazz Tradition and Black Vernacular Dance* (New York: Oxford University Press, 2021), 85–96.

19. *Chicago Defender*, April 27, 1935, 10.
20. *Metronome* 51, no. 6 (June 1935): 21.
21. Cheryl Greenberg, *Or Does It Explode? Black Harlem in the Great Depression* (New York: Oxford University Press, 1991), 4–6, 85–89. On church, self-help organizations, Harlem activism: see 104–6.
22. Greenberg, *Or Does It Explode?*, 4–6, 85–89. Mayor La Guardia appointed a biracial Commission on Conditions in Harlem. The commission's report recommended anti-discrimination measures in city housing, relief agencies, and hiring practices for municipal jobs and special training for the police department.
23. Alexander C. Flick, "John Brown Memorial Statue," *New York History* 16, no. 3 (1935): 329–32, http://www.jstor.org/stable/23135025.
24. Display ad, *New York Times*, February 20, 1935, 22.
25. H. Howard Taubman, "Opera's High Jinks Convulse a Throng," *New York Times*, April 1, 1935, 16. The event netted $14,000 for the Metropolitan Opera Maintenance Fund. The *Daily News* printed the most photos of this event; it appears that Webb was there with just his rhythm section.
26. Pons was one of the first "cross-over" classical pop stars.
27. *New York Age*, April 13, 1935, 4.
28. *New York Age*, April 20, 1935, 4.
29. The Casa Loma Orchestra helped paved the way for the popularity of big band swing, and played for college audiences at Yale, Dartmouth, and other Ivy League schools. *Norfolk Journal & Guide*, May 4, 1935, 15.
30. Mussolini acted on his neo-colonialist ambitions by sending troops to Eritrea and preparing to invade Ethiopia.
31. "Joe Louis Will Be at the Savoy Ballroom: Win, Lose or Draw," *Amsterdam News*, June 22, 1935, 11.
32. "Chick Webb Shines in New Spot," *Chicago Defender*, August 10, 1935, 7. Webb's band was not the first Black band to perform at Palisades Park. Tim Brymn, conductor/songwriter, led one of his revues at Palisades Park in the early 1920s.
33. Charles Blow, "Freed in Their Blackness," *New York Times*, May 10, 2021.

Chapter 14

1. Ella Fitzgerald, interview with Steve Allen, 1974, BBC.
2. Dick Vance, interview with Phil Schaap, Chick Webb Festival, WKCR, 1978.
3. "Harlem Chirpers Prove It's Sweet Singing Fans Prefer," *Chicago Defender*, May 18, 1935, 7. Vocalist Chuck Richards, from Baltimore, appeared with Webb's band in late 1933 to spring 1934 and recorded "Imagination" with Webb's Savoy Orchestra for Columbia, May 9, 1934. He was the vocalist with Mills Blue Rhythm for most of the mid-1930s.
4. *Pittsburgh Courier*, June 8, 1935, 22.
5. "Gale Has Contacts in Radio: Success of Four Ink Spots," *Pittsburgh Courier*, June 8, 1935, 22.

6. "Chick Webb Booked in D.C. Hookup," *Pittsburgh Courier*, May 18, 1935, A8.

7. "Music: Played Over 10,000 Times in 1936," *Variety*, January 26, 1938, 44.

8. *Pittsburgh Courier*, June 1, 1935, 18.

9. *Pittsburgh Courier*, June 15, 1935, 23.

10. The first recording of "I'll Chase the Blues Away" was released by British Brunswick in 1940.

11. "Chick Webb Is Back in Old Harlem," *Chicago Defender*, July 20, 1935, 6. "Chick Webb and Band in Boston Run," *Chicago Defender*, June 22, 1935, 7.

12. *New York Age*, August 24, 1935, 4. *New York Age*, September 4, 1935, 4.

13. *New York Age*, July 27, 1935. Alice Whitman, now a solo act, was the youngest of the Whitman Sisters, a family of Black female entertainers who produced their own vaudeville shows and revues from 1900 to 1943, and were stars on the Black theater circuit.

14. *Pittsburgh Courier*, August 24, 1935, 17.

15. Fitzgerald, interview with Allen.

16. Maxine Sullivan, interview with Phil Hughes, July 1980, JOHP.

17. Lewis Erenberg, *Swingin' the Dream: Big Band Jazz and the Rebirth of American Culture* (Chicago: University of Chicago Press, 1998), 38.

18. The Goodman band's first cross-country tour in 1935 did not generate much attention until they played at the Palomar. Ross Firestone, *Swing, Swing, Swing: The Life & Times of Benny Goodman* (New York: Norton, 1994), 148–53.

19. Gordon Wright, "DISCussions," *Metronome* 51, no. 12 (December 1935): 29.

20. Nicole M. Baran, "Jitterbuggin' with Jim Crow," *Atlanta Constitution*, October 20, 1935, 12, https://bittersoutherner.com/jitterbugging-with-jim-crow-lindy-hop-swing-music.

21. Duke Ellington, *Music Is My Mistress* (New York: Da Capo Press reprint of 1973, ed. by Doubleday), 86.

22. "Chick Webb Scores on Southern Tour," *Philadelphia Tribune*, October 31, 1935, 10.

Chapter 15

1. Mario Bauza, interview with John Storm Roberts, December 13, 1978, JOHP. Helen Oakley Dance, "Drum Mad and Fast and Lightning Fast," *Stereo Review*, September 1963, 53–54.

2. H. M. Oakley, "Chick Webb on Way to New York, Heard Here," *Tempo* 3, no. 6 (December 1935): 6.

3. *DownBeat* 3, no. 1 (December 1935–January 1936): 9.

4. Benny Carter, like Webb, did not have steady work for his own band from 1932 to 1934, and wrote arrangements for others, including Paul Whiteman, Claude Hopkins, and Benny Goodman. Morris Berger, Edward Berger, and James Patrick, *Benny Carter: A Life in American Music* (Lanham, MD: Rowman & Littlefield, 2002, Second Ed.), 131. "Benny Carter Now on Let's Dance Program," *Pittsburgh Courier*, March 9, 1935, A8.

5. Jeffrey Magee, *The Uncrowned King of Swing: Fletcher Henderson and Big Band Jazz* (New York: Oxford University Press, 2005), 190–93.

6. Several jazz writers consider Goodman's work with pianist Teddy Wilson and vibraphonist Lionel Hampton starting in 1936 as the start of a "chamber jazz" trend.

7. Gary Giddins, *Visions of Jazz: The First Century* (New York: Oxford University Press, 1998), 141. Helen Oakley Dance, undated interview with Patricia Willard, Stanley Dance and Helen Oakley Dance Papers, MSS 62, Box 18, Yale Music Library.

8. *Tempo* 4, no. 3 (September 1936): 8. *DownBeat* 3, no. 9 (September 1936): 3.

9. Teddy Wilson's Brunswick sessions, January and March 1936, also include Webb's guitarist John Trueheart.

10. Teddy McRae, interview with Ron Welburn, 1981, JOHP.

11. *DownBeat* 3, no. 9 (September 1936): 3.

12. *Metronome,* April 1936, 47.

13. Van Alexander, interview with Jeff Kaufman for 2012 documentary, *The Savoy King*. This book mainly refers to Al Feldman by his familiar professional name, Van Alexander.

14. Alexander, interview with Kaufman.

15. Bauza, interview with Roberts.

16. Magee, *The Uncrowned King of Swing*, 193.

17. Billy Rowe, "Chick Webb Is 'Tops' on Big NY Broadcast," *Pittsburgh Courier*, March 21, 1936, 17. Edgar T. Rouzeau, "How Radio Stations Conduct Broadcasts: Juano Hernandez Directs Program with Ella, Chick," *Pittsburgh Courier*, March 6, 1937, 18. Porter Roberts, "Praise and Criticism," *Pittsburgh Courier*, August 21, 1937, 21.

18. McRae, interview with Welburn.

19. Shirley Temple plays an orphaned Chinese girl in a movie whose implausible characters and plot were typical of Depression-era movies. The song was a lullaby.

20. Judith Tick, email communication with author.

21. Porter Roberts, "Praise and Criticism," *Pittsburgh Courier*, December 19, 1936, 7.

22. McRae, interview with Welburn.

Chapter 16

1. "Chick Webb Receives 5000 Letters a Week," *DownBeat* 4, no. 3 (March 1937): 14.

2. John Gennari, *Blowin' Hot and Cool: Jazz and Its Critics* (Chicago: University of Chicago Press, 2006). *DownBeat* and *Metronome* did not print ads with Black musicians as instrument endorsers until late 1936.

3. *DownBeat* 4, no. 11 (November 1937): 15.

4. George Simon, *Metronome* 54, no. 1 (January 1938): 20.

5. Teddy McRae, interview with Ron Welburn, 1981, JOHP.

6. *Pittsburgh Courier,* May 9, 1936, 17.

7. Judith Tick, conversation with author.

8. *DownBeat* 4, no. 2 (February 1937): 6, 25.

9. Judith Tick, correspondence with author, November 2020. Stuart Nicholson, *Ella Fitzgerald: A Biography of the First Lady of Jazz* (London: Orion Books, reissued 2001, c. 1993, 1996), 50. Jo Jones, interview with Phil Schaap, Chick Webb Festival, WKCR, 1978.

10. Mills met Oakley in March 1936, when she set up a concert for Duke Ellington's Orchestra at the Urban Room, Congress Hotel in Chicago.

11. Helen Oakley Dance, "Drum Mad and Lightening Fast," *Stereo Review*, June 15, 1963, 53–54.

12. Jim Prohaska, "Irving Mills—Record Producer: The Master and Variety Record Labels," https://www.yumpu.com/en/document/read/29078926/the-master-and-variety-record-labels-the-iajrc. Helen Oakley Dance, undated interview with Patricia Willard, Stanley Dance and Helen Oakley Dance Papers, MSS 62, Box 18, Yale Music Library.

13. Oakley Dance, undated interview with Willard. The Gotham Stompers were so named to elude the musicians' contracts with other record labels. "They'd all call themselves 'Jack Johnson' or some name to be able to sign up with me." She referred to her role at Variety as an "A&R Man" ("Artists & Repertoire" directors at record companies helped choose what material artists recorded, etc.).

14. *DownBeat* 4, no. 3 (March 1937): 14. Benny Goodman's brothers, Harry was also Goodman's bassist; Freddy, the youngest, played trumpet. They sometimes went out together to hear jazz.

15. After the Masters label folded, Ellington recorded for Columbia/Brunswick and was re-signed by RCA Victor in 1940. Ivie Anderson sang "All God's Children" with Ellington's orchestra and the Crinoline Choir in *A Day at the Races*, which includes a segment with Whitey's Lindy Hoppers.

16. Stanley Dance, *The World of Swing* (New York: Da Capo Press reprint, 2001), 71. "The Duke Is Honored by Dance Fans," *Chicago Defender*, March 20, 1937, 20.

17. Helen Oakley Dance, interview with Oren Jacoby, March 10, 1993, for the documentary *Benny Goodman: Adventures in the Kingdom of Swing*, PBS American Masterworks.

18. Christi Jay Wells (aka Christopher J. Wells), "'Spinning the Webb': Representational Spaces, Mythic Narratives, and the 1937 Webb/Goodman Battle of Music," *Journal of the Society for American Music* 14, no. 2 (May 2020): 176. https://doi.org/10.1017/S1752196320000061.

19. Mario Bauza, interview with John Storm Roberts, December 13, 1978, JOHP.

20. Oakley Dance, "Drum Mad and Lightning Fast."

21. Oakley Dance, interview with Willard.

22. McRae, interview with Welburn.

23. Bauza, interview with Roberts.

24. McRae, interview with Welburn.

25. Norma Miller, interview with author, 2018. Burt Korall, *Drummin' Men: Heartbeat of Jazz—the Swing Years* (New York: Schirmer, 1990), 34.

26. "The Savoy Remembered," Helen Clarke to Robert P. Crease, panel discussion, Hudson Park Library, New York City, June 10, 1990.

27. *DownBeat* 4, no. 6 (June 1937): 3.

28. McRae, interview with Welburn.

29. Sandy Williams, interview with Dance, *The World of Swing*, 72.

30. Bauza, interview with Roberts.

31. Van Alexander, interview with Jeff Kaufman for the 2012 documentary *The Savoy King*.

32. Sandy Williams, interview with Delilah Jackson, Delilah Jackson Papers, Manuscript Collection 923, Series 8, AV8, Rose Manuscript, Archives & Rare Book Library, Emory University.

33. "Sandy Williams, a Portrait by John Simmen," *Storyville* 116 (December 1984–January 1985), 54, https://nationaljazzarchive.org.uk/explore/journals/storyville/storyville-116/1267964.

34. Van Alexander, interview with Kaufman.

35. Leon Hardwick, "Swing Is Newer Form of Old Art," *Afro-American*, October 16, 1937, 10.

36. In Miami, the Ku Klux Klan wrecked a nightclub, then "ordered it to stay closed." The owner reopened it a few months later, and the Ku Klux Klan beat the entertainers and waitresses, wrecked the club's interior and furniture, and pilfered cash and guns from the owners' office: *DownBeat* 4, no. 12 (December 1937): 1.

37. *Metronome* 53, no. 9 (September 1937): 64.

38. Williams, interview with Jackson.

39. *Metronome* 53, no. 12 (December 1937): 32.

40. Williams, interview with Jackson.

41. *DownBeat* 4, no. 8 (August 1937): 24. *Metronome* 53, no. 9 (September 1937): 28.

42. Oakley Dance, interview with Willard.

43. Gennari, *Blowin' Hot and Cool,* 23.

44. Oakley Dance, "Drum Mad and Lighting Fast." Oakley Dance, interview Willard.

Chapter 17

1. Count Basie, interview with Linda Kuehl, November 1, 1978, JOHP.

2. Chris Wilkerson, *Big Band Jazz in Black West Virginia, 1930–1942* (Jackson: University Press of Mississippi, March 2014).

3. James Reese Europe's 1912–14 concerts with his Clef Club Orchestra are considered to be the "first" jazz concerts at Carnegie Hall, though the era was "prejazz," and the program included several genres. Reid Badger, *A Life in Ragtime: A Biography of James Reese Europe* (New York: Oxford University Press, 1995). Catherine Tackley, *Benny Goodman's Famous 1938 Carnegie Hall Jazz Concert* (New York: Oxford University Press, 2012).

4. Helen Oakley Dance, interview with Patricia Willard, Stanley Dance and Oakley Dance Papers, MSS 62, Box 18, Yale Music Library. Helen Oakley Dance, interview with Oren Jacoby, March 10, 1993, for the documentary *Benny Goodman: Adventures in the Kingdom of Swing*, PBS American Masterworks.

5. Norma Miller, *Swingin' at the Savoy: The Memoir of a Jazz Dancer* (Philadelphia: Temple University Press, 1996), 104.

6. Oakley Dance, interview with Jacoby.

7. "Chick, Basie Battle It Out in Swingtime: Savoy Is Scene of Tune War . . . ," *Amsterdam News*, January 22, 1938,16.

8. *DownBeat* 5, no. 2 (February 1938): 2.

9. Oakley Dance, interview with Willard.

10. Leroi Jones/Amira Baraka, "Jazz and the White Critic," *DownBeat* 30, no. 23 (August 15, 1963): reprinted in *Black Music* (New York: William Morrow & Co., 1968). Baraka wrote that white critics' concepts about authenticity pushed "jazz music into that junk pile of admirable objects and data the West knows as culture."

11. Oakley Dance, interview with Jacoby. Oakley Dance, interview with Monk Rowe, San Diego, California, February 12, 1998, Milton and Nelma Fillius Jazz Archive, Hamilton College.

12. Al Moses, "Backstage with Chick and the Boys," *Afro-American*, January 22, 1938, 10.

13. "Sandy Williams: A Portrait by Johnny Simmen," *Storyville*, December 1984–January 1985, 52–54, https://nationaljazzarchive.org.uk/explore/journals/storyville/storyvi lle-116.

14. *DownBeat* 5, no. 4 (April 1938): 14, 16.

15. "Chick Webb Booked to Play at Hippodrome in Baltimore with Colored. . .," *Pittsburgh Courier*, February 26, 1938, 20. *Tempo* 5, no. 9 (March 1938): 6. Webb's appearance there was delayed until October 1938 due to Webb's health issues and packed schedule.

16. *DownBeat* 5, no. 4 (April 1938): 14, 16.

17. Burt Korall, *Drumming Men: Heartbeat of Jazz—The Swing Years* (New York: Schirmer, 1990), 17–18.

18. Holiday had equal billing with Shaw's band but was treated horribly on tour with the band, and by Shaw back in New York. "When I wasn't singing, I had to stay backstage. Artie wouldn't let me sit out front with the band. . . . [A]t the Lincoln Hotel, the hotel management told me I had to use the back door. That was all right. But I had to ride up and down in the freight elevators, and every night Artie made me stay upstairs in a little room without a radio or anything all the time." Dave Dexter, "Billie Holiday for the First Time Tells Why She Left Shaw & Basie: 'Too Many Bad Kicks,'" *DownBeat*, November 1, 1939, https://downbeat.com/archives/detail/billie-holi day-for-the-first-time-tells-why-she-left-shaw-basie-too-many.

19. Teddy McRae, interview with Ron Welburn, 1981, JOHP.

20. Van Alexander, interview with Jeff Kaufman.

21. McRae, interview with Welburn.

22. *DownBeat* 5, no. 4 (April 1938): 2. *Chicago Defender*, March 26, 1938, 18. That year, Yale University gave an honorary Doctor of Music degree to Serge Koussevitzky, Russian composer and conductor of the Boston Symphony Orchestra, 1924–49.

23. *Pittsburgh Courier*, April 9, 1938, 20. *Chicago Defender*, April 9, 1938, 18.

24. Alexander, interview with Kaufman. Frankie Manning, interview with Jeff Kaufman.

25. Cliff Leeman, interview with Milt Hinton, June 1979, JOHP. Helen Oakley Dance, "Drum Mad and Lightning Fast," *Stereo Review* (September 1963): 53–54.

26. Beverly Peer, interview with John Chilton, *Let the Good Times Roll: The Story of Louis Jordan and His Music* (Ann Arbor: University of Michigan Press, 1997), 57. *DownBeat* 5 (May 1938): 20.

27. *Tempo* 5, no. 12 (June 1938).

28. Isadora Smith, "Chick Webb and Duke Ellington Guests of Tommy Dorsey at the Broadway Paramount Theatre," *Pittsburgh Courier*, April 30, 1938, 13.

29. *Metronome* 55, no. 6 (June 1939): 8.

30. Beverly Peer interview with Loren Schoenberg and Stuart Nicholson, *Ella Fitzgerald: A Biography of the First Lady of Jazz* (London: Orion Books, reissued 2001, c. 1993, 1996), 54.

31. Gunther Schuller, *The Swing Era* (New York: Oxford, 1989), 299–300.

32. "Jitterbugs Jam Randall Island Swing Carnival," *Amsterdam News*, June 4, 1938, 17.

33. Jessica Wood, "Carnival of Swing: Uncovering an Historic Jazz Concert at Randall's Island Stadium, 1938," New York Public Library for the Performing Arts, September 25, 2018, https://www.nypl.org/blog/2018/09/25/carnival-swing-jazz-randalls-island-stadium-photos-1938. Otto F. Hess Photographs, New York Public Library for the Performing Arts, call number JPB 17–12.

34. Hess's photos are the most accessible visual documentation of that special day. A brief clip of the Count Basie Orchestra's performance was broadcast on a newsreel (though it lacked audio), and parts of the concert were broadcast on WNEW, but to date these items have not surfaced in archives.

35. Dan Burley, "240 Kids to Go to Camp This Summer; Benefit Successful: Harlem . . . ," *Amsterdam News*, June 4, 1938, 20. Billy Rowe, *Pittsburgh Courier,* June 18, 1938, 21.

36. *DownBeat* 5, no. 7 (July 1938): 2. Musicians who have received honorary doctorates include Taylor Swift, New York University, 2022; Herbie Hancock, Juilliard, 2019; Joao Gilberto, Columbia University, 2017; Aretha Franklin, Harvard University, 2014; and Stevie Wonder, Rutgers University, 1999: https://www.billboard.com/photos/musicians-with-honorary-degrees/13-billy-joel/.

Chapter 18

1. "Music: Colored Band Biz Becoming Big Biz," *Billboard*, April 2, 1938, 50, 14, 13.

2. Frank M. Davis, "Bands Are Worrying: Writer Tells of Things That Militate Unfavorably," *Amsterdam News*, September 10, 1938, B6. Frank Marshall Davis, a prominent Black journalist and editor, was also an acclaimed poet.

3. "Bands Complain of Loss of Arrangers to White Outfits," *Chicago Defender*, August 26, 1939, 21.

4. Teddy McRae, interview with Ron Welburn, 1981, JOHP.

5. Chris Wilkerson, *Big Band Jazz in Black West Virginia, 1930–1942* (Jackson: University Press of Mississippi, March 2014).

6. "Webb to Invade Florida," *Pittsburgh Courier*, July 2, 1938, 20.

7. "Chick Webb First Colored Orchestra in over 5 years to Play Paramount," *Pittsburgh Courier*, July 30, 1938, 21.

8. Paramount Theatre Stage Manager's Records, 1936–1956, T-Mss 1989-015, Box 1, New York Public Library for the Performing Arts, Billy Rose Theatre Division.

9. "$1,000 Increase to Chick," *Afro-American*, September 10, 1938, 10.

10. Mario Bauza, interview with John Storm Roberts, December 13, 1978, JOHP.

11. John Chilton, *Let the Good Times Roll* (Ann Arbor: University of Michigan Press, 1997), 52–59.

12. Bauza, interview with Roberts.

13. Teddy McRae, interview with Ron Welburn, JOHP. Sandy Williams, interview with Stanley Dance, *The World of Swing* (New York: DaCapo Press, reprint 2001), 73.

14. "Chick Webb's Band in Texas Learns South: Dixie Whites Resent $3,000 . . . ," *New York Amsterdam News*, August 14, 1937, 7.

15. *Pittsburgh Courier,* February 26, 1938, 20.

16. Brad Rowe and Mary Williams, interview with Jeff Kaufman for the 2012 documentary *The Savoy King*.

17. *Pittsburgh Courier*, October 22, 1938, 21.

18. "Negro Orchestra Loses Pay as Promoters Skip," *Galveston Daily News*, December 16, 1938.

19. *Pittsburgh Courier,* November 12, 1938, 21.

20. "Spotlight on Bands," *Afro-American*, April 15, 1939.

21. Billy Rowe, "Top Colored Bands Set for World's Fair Spots: Lunceford, Webb . . . ," *Pittsburgh Courier*, April 29, 1939, 21. Harry Heinilä, "An Endeavor by Harlem Dancers to Achieve Equality: The Recognition of the Harlem-Based African-American Jazz Dance between 1921 and 1943," University of Helsinki, January 16, 2016, 241–247. Alexandre Abdoulaev, "Reassessing the Role of the "World's Finest Ballroom" in Music and Culture, 1926–1958," Boston University, 2014, 256–62. The Savoy Pavilion was very popular, despite a lot of sniping between Gale and city and World Fair officials.

22. Kenny Clarke, interview with Helen Oakley Dance, September 1, 1977, JOHP.

23. Sandy Williams, interview with Delilah Jackson, Delilah Jackson Papers, Manuscript Collection 923, Series 8, AV8. Rose Manuscript, Archives & Rare Book Library, Emory University.

24. *Afro-American*, June 24, 1939, 14.

25. Ron Fritts and Ken Vail, *Ella Fitzgerald: The Chick Webb Years and Beyond* (Lanham, MD: Scarecrow Press/The Rowman and Littlefield Publishing Group, Inc., 2003), 42. The Apollo's weekly attendance records showed a significant drop from the band's appearance there in January 1939, from 42,907 to 32,227.

26. "Artists Will Be Honored by National Swing Club: Lunceford Acclaimed . . . ," *Pittsburgh Courier*, June 3, 1939, 18.

27. Bardu Ali, interview with Steve Allen for BBC2, 1974, LAHM. Helen Oakley Dance, interview with Monk Rowe, San Diego, California, February 12, 1998, The Milton and Nelma Fillius Jazz Archive, Hamilton College.

28. Jo Jones, interview with Milt Hinton, May 15, 1973, New York City, JOHP.

29. McRae, interview with Welburn.

Chapter 19

1. Ron Fritts and Ken Vail, *Ella Fitzgerald: The Chick Webb Years & Beyond* (Lanham, MD: Scarecrow Press, 2003), 32.
2. *Montgomery Advertiser*, June 18, 1939, 2.
3. Frederick J. Spencer, *Jazz and Death: Medical Profiles of Jazz Greats* (Jackson: University Press of Mississippi, 2002), 235.
4. Dick Vance, interview with Phil Schaap, Chick Webb Festival, WKCR, New York, 1978.
5. Billy Rowe, "Tragic Death of Chick Webb in Baltimore Stuns Music World: Had Risen . . . ," *Pittsburgh Courier*, June 24, 1939, 1. Billy Rowe, "Why Chick Webb Was Not Given N.Y. Funeral," *Pittsburgh Courier*, July 1, 1929, 20. "10,000 at Chick Webb Rites," *Washington Afro American*, June 24, 1939, 1.
6. Donna Hollie, interview with author, September 2020.
7. Dick Vance, interview with Phil Schaap, Chick Webb Festival, WQXR, 1978.
8. Van Alexander, interview with Jeff Kaufman for the 2012 documentary *The Savoy King*.
9. Spencer was associate dean emeritus of the School of Medicine in the Medical College of Virginia at Virginia Commonwealth University. Spencer, *Jazz and Death*, 233, 236.
10. "Sandy Williams: A Portrait by Johnny Simmen," *Storyville*, December 1984–January 1985, 52–54, https://nationaljazzarchive.org.uk/explore/journals/storyville/storyville-116.
11. Dorothy Giles, "The Departure," *Amsterdam News*, July 1, 1939, 10.

Epilogue

1. All three titles were recorded after Webb's death.
2. Bardu Ali was let go after the Loew's engagement. Benny Carter didn't accept Gale's offer because he wanted the band billed under his name: the Benny Carter Orchestra featuring Ella Fitzgerald.
3. Teddy McRae, interview with Ron Welburn, 1981, JOHP. On this trip, Ella made her Hollywood movie debut in *Ride 'Em Cowboy*, an Abbott and Costello comedy; in her big scene, she sings "A-Tisket, A-Tasket" on a tour bus.
4. Dizzy Gillespie, with Al Frazer, *Dizzy: To Be or Not to Bop* (London: Quartet Books, 1979), 133. Drummer Kenny Clarke also played with Fitzgerald briefly at this time.
5. McRae, interview with Welburn.
6. Isadora Smith, "Gale, Glasser See Sharp Upturn in Band Business," *Pittsburgh Courier*, January 3, 1942, 19.
7. Alfred A. Duckett, "Vice Raid Closes N.Y. Savoy Ballroom," *Chicago Defender*, May 1, 1943, 1. Russell Gold, "Guilty of Syncopation, Joy, And Animation: The Closing of Harlem's Savoy Ballroom," *Of, by, and for the People: Dancing on the Left in the 1930s*, ed. Lynn Garafola (Madison, WI: Society of Dance History Scholars at A-R Editions, 1994, c. 1993), 57–62.

8. Helen Oakley Dance, undated interview with Patricia Willard, Stanley Dance and Helen Oakley Dance Papers MSS 62, Box 18, Yale Music Library.

9. Nick Rossi, "The Captivating Harlem Swing Rhythms of Freddie Green, John Trueheart, Bernard Addison, Morris White, and Al Casey," *Acoustic Guitar*, June 9, 2021, https://acousticguitar.com/string-kings-of-harlem-swing-the-captivating-rhythms-of-freddie-green-john-trueheart-bernard-addison-morris-white-and-al-casey/.

10. Chick Webb claimed copyright interest on some titles, though he was not the composer or lyricist. This was a common practice at the time since bandleaders were entitled to a small percentage of mechanical royalties. For example. Benny Goodman also claimed a percentage of copyright claims for "Stompin' at the Savoy," which was written by Edgar Sampson.

11. "Swing Museum," *Billboard*, March 30, 1940, 10.

12. Lillian Johnson, "The King of the Drums Returns Again," *Baltimore Afro-American*, February 17, 1940, 14. Billy Rowe, "10,000 Attend Webb Memorial in Baltimore: Racial Prejudices Forgotten . . . ," *Pittsburgh Courier*, February 24, 1940, 21.

13. Lloyd Taylor, " How Jazz Built a Monument . . . ," *Pittsburgh Courier*, August 28, 1954, SM8. Baltimore Mayor Thomas J. D'Alesandro Jr. appropriated over 120,000 dollars for the Chick Webb Center.

Sources

Historical Newspapers and Magazines, including: *Baltimore Afro-American (Baltimore Afro), Baltimore Sun, Billboard, Brooklyn Eagle, Chicago Defender, Daily Worker, DownBeat, Interstate-Tattler, Jazz Hot, Jazz Record, Melody Maker, Metronome, New York Age, New York Amsterdam News, New York Clipper, New York Daily News, New York Times, Norfolk New Journal and Guide, Philadelphia Inquirer, Pittsburgh Courier, Swing, Variety.*

Abbreviations

IJS—Institute of Jazz Studies, Rutgers University, Newark, New Jersey

JOHP—Jazz Oral History Project, initiated in 1972 by the Jazz Advisory Panel of the Music Program of the National Endowment for the Arts. Administration and archiving of JOHP was turned over to the Institute of Jazz Studies in 1979.

LoC—Library of Congress

LPA—New York Public Library for the Performing Arts (NYPL research library)

NYPL—New York Public Library

SCHOMB—Schomburg Center for Research in Black Culture, NYPL research library

Archives and Special Collections

Eubie Blake National Jazz Institute and Cultural Center, Baltimore

Gilmore Music Library, Yale University Music Library: The Papers of Stanley Dance and Helen Oakley Dance, MSS 62

Hamilton College, Milton and Nelma Fillius Jazz Archive, Hamilton College, https://www.hamilton.edu/campuslife/arts-at-hamilton/jazz archive/interviews

Institute of Jazz Studies (IJS), Rutgers University, Newark, New Jersey:

Jazz Oral History Project (JOHP), initiated in 1972 by the National Endowment for the Arts. Many interviews digitized: https://ijsresea rch.libraries.rutgers.edu/jazz-oral-history-project

Library of Congress: loc.gov

Louis Armstrong House Museum (Digital Collections): https://collecti ons.louisarmstronghouse.org/

Maryland Center for History and Culture, Baltimore, Maryland (many collections now digitized)

Moorland-Spingarn Research Center, Howard University, Washington, DC

National Jazz Archive (UK), https://nationaljazzarchive.org.uk/

New York Library for the Performing Arts, Lincoln Center, NYPL.org

Reginald F. Lewis Museum, Baltimore, Maryland

RIPM-Jazz (Retrospective Index to Music Periodicals), ripmjazz.org

Robert F. Wagner Labor Archives at New York University: Local 802 Archives

Rose Manuscript, Archives & Rare Book Library, Emory University: Delilah Jackson Papers, Manuscript Collection 923

Schomburg Center for Research in Black Culture, New York Public Library, New York, NYPL.org

Smithsonian National Museum of American History:
    Smithsonian Jazz, https://americanhistory.si.edu/smithsonian-jazz
    Smithsonian Online Virtual Archives, nova.si.edu

Bibliography

Alexandre, Abdoulaev. "Reassessing the Role of the 'World's Finest Ballroom' in Music and Culture, 1926–1958." PhD diss., Boston University, 2014.

Anderson, Jervis. *Harlem: The Great Black Way.* London: Orbis Publishing, 1982.

Badger, Reid. *A Life in Ragtime: A Biography of James Reese Europe.* New York: Oxford University Press, 1995.

Bald, Vivek. *Bengali Harlem and the Lost Histories of South Asian America.* Cambridge: Harvard University Press, 2013.

Balliett, Whitney. *American Musicians, II: Seventy-One Portraits in Jazz.* New York: Oxford University Press, 1996.

Barker, Danny. *A Life in Jazz.* Edited by Alyn Shipton. New York: Oxford University Press, 1986.

Barlow, William, *Voice Over: The Making of Black Radio.* Philadelphia: Temple University Press, 1999.

Bascomb, Lionel C., ed. *A Renaissance in Harlem: Lost Essays of the WPA,* by *Ralph Ellison, Dorothy West, and Other Voices of a Generation.* New York: Amistad, 2001.

Berger, Edward, Morrow Berger, and James Patrick. *Benny Carter: A Life in American Music.* Lanham, MD, and London: Institute of Jazz Studies and Rutgers, 2002.

Bigard, Barney. *With Louis and the Duke: The Autobiography of a Jazz Clarinetist.* New York: Oxford University Press, 1986 ed.

Brennan, Matt. *Kick It: A Social History of the Drum Kit.* New York: Oxford University Press, 2020.

Brooks, Daphne. *Liner Notes for the Revolution: The Intellectual Life of Black Feminist Sound.* Cambridge, MA: Belknap Press of Harvard University Press, 2021.

Brooks, Tim. *Lost Sounds: Blacks and the Birth of the Recording Industry, 1890–1919.* Urbana, Chicago, and Springfield: University of Illinois Press, 2004.

Brothers, Thomas. *Louis Armstrong, Master of Modernism.* New York: Norton, 2014.

Brown, Anthony. "Modern Jazz Drumset Artistry." *Black Perspective in Music* 18, no. 1/2 (1990): 39–58. https://www.jstor.org/stable/1214857 JSTOR.

Brown, Jayna. *Babylon Girls: Black Women Performers and the Shaping of the Modern.* Durham, NC: Duke University Press, 2008.

Bushell, Garvin, as told to Mark Tucker. *Jazz from the Beginning.* Ann Arbor: University of Michigan Press, 1988.

Calloway, Cab, and Bryant Rollins. *Of Minnie the Moocher and Me.* New York: Thomas Y. Crowell Company, 1976.

Chapman, Con. *Rabbit's Blues: The Life and Music of Johnny Hodges.* New York: Oxford University Press, 2019.

Chapman, Erin D. *Prove It on Me: New Negroes, Sex, and Popular Culture in the 1920s.* New York: Oxford University Press, 2012.

Charters, Samuel, and Leonard Kunstadt. *Jazz: A History of the New York Scene.* Boston: Da Capo, 1981.

Chilton, John. *Let the Good Times Roll: The Story of Louis Jordan and His Music*. Ann Arbor: University of Michigan, 1997.

Clayton, Buck. *Buck Clayton's Jazz World*. New York: Continuum Publishing Group, 1995.

Cohen, Harvey G. *Duke Ellington's America*. Chicago: University of Chicago Press, 2010.

Cooper, Ralph. *Amateur Night at the Apollo: Ralph Cooper Presents Five Decades of Great Entertainment*. New York: Harper Collins Publishers, 1990.

Cowley, John. "West Indies Blues: An Historical Overview 1920s–1950s—Blues and Music from the English-Speaking West Indies." In *Nobody Knows Where the Blues Came From: Lyrics and History*, edited by Robert Springer. Jackson: University Press of Mississippi, 2006, 187–263.

Dahl, Linda. *Morning Glory: A Biography of Mary Lou Williams*. New York: Pantheon, 1999.

Dance, Stanley. *The World of Duke Ellington*. New York: C. Scribner's Sons, 1970.

Dance, Stanley. *The World of Swing*. New York: Da Capo Press, 2001.

Dixon Gottschild, Brenda. *The Black Dancing Body*. New York: Palgrave Macmillan, 2003.

Dixon Gottschild, Brenda. *Digging the Africanist presence in American performance: Dance and Other Contexts*. Westport, CT: Greenwood Press, 1996.

Dixon Gottschild, Brenda. *Waltzing in the Dark: African American Vaudeville and Race Politics in the Swing Era*. New York: St. Martin's Press, 2000.

Doerksen, Clifford J. *American Babel: Rogue Radio Broadcasters of the Jazz Age*. Philadelphia: University of Pennsylvania Press, c. 2005.

Downe, Kathleen. *Spirits of Defiance: National Prohibition and Jazz Age Literature, 1920–1933*. Columbus, OH: Ohio State University Press, 2005. Project MUSE. muse.jhu.edu/book/28267.

Edwards, Brent Hayes. "Armstrong and the Syntax of Scat." *Critical Inquiry* 28, no. 3 (Spring 2002): 618–49. https://www.jstor.org/stable/10.1086/343233 JSTOR.

Ellington, Duke Ellington. *Music Is My Mistress*. New York: Da Capo, 1976.

Ellison, Ralph. *Living with Music*. Edited by Robert G. O'Meally. New York: Modern Library, 2001.

Engelbrecht, Barbara. "Swinging at the Savoy." *Dance Research Journal* 15, no. 2 (Spring 1983): 3–10. https://www.jstor.org/stable/1478672.

Erenberg, Lewis A. *Steppin' Out: New York Nightlife and the Transformation of American Culture, 1890–1930*. Chicago: University of Chicago Press, 1981.

Erenberg, Lewis A. *Swingin' the Dream: Big Band Jazz and the Rebirth of American Culture*. Chicago: University of Chicago Press, 1998.

Evans, David. "High Water Everywhere: Blues and Gospel Commentary on the 1927 Mississippi River Flood." In *Nobody Knows Where the Blues Come From: Lyrics and History*, edited by Robert Springer. Jackson: University Press of Mississippi, 2006, 3–75.

Falzerano, Chet. *Chick Webb—Spinnin' the Webb: The Little Giant*. Anaheim Hills, CA: Centerstream Publishing, 2014.

Firestone, Ross. *Swing, Swing, Swing: The Life & Times of Benny Goodman*. New York: Norton, 1993.

Floyd, Samuel A., ed. *Black Music in the Harlem Renaissance*. Knoxville: University of Tennessee Press, 1993.

Free, F. Corine Anderson. "The Baltimore City Colored Orchestra and the City Colored Chorus." DMA diss. University of Alabama, 1994.

Fritts, Ron, and Ken Vail. *Ella Fitzgerald: The Chick Webb Years & Beyond*. Lanham, MD: Scarecrow Press, 2003.

Gabbard, Krin. *Representing Jazz*. Durham, NC: Duke University Press, 1995.

Gaines, Caseem. *Footnotes: The Black Artists Who Rewrote the Rules of the Great White Way.* New York: Sourcebooks, 2021.

Garrod, Charles. *Chick Webb and His Orchestra, Including Ella Fitzgerald and Her Orchestra.* Zephyrhills, FL: Joyce Record Club Publication, 1993.

Gennari, John. *Blowin' Hot and Cool: Jazz and Its Critics.* Chicago: University of Chicago Press, 2006.

Giddins, Gary. *Visions of Jazz: The First Century.* New York: Oxford University Press, 1998.

Gilbert, David. *The Product of Our Souls: Ragtime, Race, and the Birth of the Manhattan Musical Marketplace.* Chapel Hill: University of North Carolina Press, 2016.

Gillespie, Dizzy, with Al Fraser. *To Be or Not to Bop.* Garden City, NY: Doubleday, 1979.

Gold, Russell. "Guilty of Syncopation, Joy, and Animation: The Closing of Harlem's Savoy Ballroom." In *Of, by, and for the People: Dancing on the Left in the 1930s*, edited by Lynn Garafola. Madison, WI: Society of Dance History Scholars at A-R Editions, c. 1994, 50–64.

Goldberg, Jacob C. *Swingin' the Color Line.* Amherst, MA, c. 2008.

Gourse, Leslie, ed. *The Ella Fitzgerald Companion: Seven Decades of Commentary.* New York: Schirmer Books, 1998.

Granlund, Nils T., with Sid Feder and Ralph Hancock. *Blondes, Brunettes and Bullets.* New York: David McKay, 1957.

Greenberg, Cheryl Lynn. *Or Does It Explode?: Black Harlem in the Great Depression.* New York: Oxford University Press, 1997.

Harker, Brian. "Louis Armstrong, Eccentric Dance, and the Evolution of Jazz on the Eve of Swing." *Journal of the American Musicological Society* 61, no. 1 (Spring 2008): 67–121.

Harris, LaShawn. *Sex Workers, Psychics and Numbers Runners: Black Women in New York City's Underground Economy.* Urbana, Chicago, and Springfield: University of Illinois Press, 2016.

Hartman, Saidiya V. *Wayward Lives, Beautiful Experiments: Intimate Histories of Social Upheaval.* New York: W. W. Norton & Company, 2019.

Hawkins, Alfonso. "Broadway: The Harlem Showcase Toward a Definition." *Studies in Popular Culture* 23, no. 2 (October 2000): 37–54. https://www.jstor.org/stable/23414543.

Heinilä, Harry. "An Endeavor by Harlem Dancers to Achieve Equality: The Recognition of the Harlem-Based African-American Jazz Dance between 1921 and 1943." PhD diss. University of Helsinki, 2016.

Hildebrand, David K., and Elizabeth M. Schaaf. *Musical Maryland: A History of Song and Performance from the Colonial Period to the Age of Radio.* Baltimore: Johns Hopkins University Press, 2017.

Hughes, Langston. *The Big Sea: An Autobiography.* New York: Hill and Wang, 1940.

Hurston, Zorah Neale. *Hitting a Straight Lick with a Crooked Stick: Stories from the Harlem Renaissance.* New York: Amistad, 2020.

Johnson, Aaron J. "A Date with the Duke: Ellington on Radio." *Musical Quarterly* 96, no. 3/4 (Fall–Winter 2013): 369–405. https://www.jstor.org/stable/43865494.

Johnson, Wilfred J. *Ella Fitzgerald: An Annotated Discography: Including a Complete Discography of Chick Webb.* Jefferson, NC: McFarland, 2001.

Jonah, Jonathan. "Selected Observations from the Harlem Jazz Scene." MA thesis. Rutgers University, 2015.

Jones, James Nathan, Franklin F. Johnson, and Robert B. Cochrane. "Alfred Jack Thomas: Performer, Composer, Educator." *Black Perspective in Music* 11, no. 1 (Spring, 1983): 62–75. https://www.jstor.org/stable/1215143.

Jones, LeRoi [Baraka, Amira]. *Black Music*. New York: William Morrow & Co., 1968.

Jones, Max. *Talking Jazz*. New York: W. W. Norton, 1987.

Karp, Jonathan. "Blacks, Jews, and the Business of Race Music, 1945–1955." In *Chosen Capital: The Jewish Encounter with American Capitalism*, edited by Rebecca Kobrin. (New Brunswick, NJ: Rutgers University Press, 2012), 6: 141–67. http://www.jstor.com/stable/j.ctt5hjf56.11.

Karp, Jonathan. Foreword to *There Was a Fire: Jews, Music and the American Dream*, by Ben Sidran (Madison, WI: Nardis Press, 2015).

Karp, Jonathan. "The Roots of Jewish Concentration in the American Popular Music Business, 1890–1945." In *Doing Business in America: A Jewish History*, edited by Hasia Diner. Purdue University Press, 2019, 5: 123–44.

Kenney, William Howland III. "The Influence of Black Vaudeville on Early Jazz." *Black Perspective in Music* 14, no. 3 (Autumn 1986): 233–48. https://www.jstor.org/stable/1215064.

Korall, Burt. *Drummin Men': The Heartbeat of Jazz—The Swing Years*. New York: Schirmer Books, 1990.

Lewis, David Levering. *When Harlem Was in Vogue*. New York: Oxford University Press, 1979.

Magee, Jeffrey. "Before Louis: When Fletcher Henderson Was the 'Paul Whiteman of the Race.'" *American Music* 18, no. 4 (Winter 2000): 391–425. https://www.jstor.org/stable/3052583.

Magee, Jeffrey. *The Uncrowned King of Swing: Fletcher Henderson and Big Band Jazz*. New York: Oxford University Press, 2005.

Major, Gerri [Jerry], with Doris E. Saunders. *Black Society*. Chicago: Johnson Publishing, 1976.

Manning, Frankie, with Cynthia Millman. *Frankie Manning: Ambassador of Lindy Hop*. Philadelphia: Temple University Press, 2007.

McDonagh, John. Liner notes to *The Compete Chick Webb & Ella Fitzgerald Decca Sessions (1934–1941)*. Stamford, CT: Mosaic Records, 2013.

McQuirter, Marya Annette. "Awkward Moves." In *Dancing Many Drums: Excavations in African American Dance*, edited by Thomas F. DeFrantz. Madison: University of Wisconsin Press, 2002, 3: 81–103.

Melton, Mandy. "Anne Arundel County's Historic Beach Destinations (Late 19th to Early 20th Century)." Report for the Learn S'Mores History Project: A Heritage Research and Public Outreach Initiative, focusing on Anne Arundel County's Early Twentieth-Century Beach Resorts and Communities. Submitted to the Anne Arundel County Trust for Preservation, Inc., June 2017.

Mezzrow, Mezz, and Bernard Wolfe. *Really the Blues*. New York: NYRB Classics, 2016.

Miller, Norma, with Evette Jensen. *Swinging at the Savoy: The Memoir of a Jazz Dancer*. Philadelphia: Temple University Press, 1996.

Murray, Albert. *Stomping the Blues*. New York: Da Capo Press, 1978.

Nicholson, Stuart. *Ella Fitzgerald: A Biography of the First Lady of Jazz*. London: Orion Books, reissued 2001, c. 1993, 1996.

Ogren, Kathy. J. *The Jazz Revolution: Twenties America and the Meaning of Jazz*. New York: Oxford, 1989.

O'Meally, Robert G. *Antagonistic Cooperation: Jazz, Collage, Fiction, and the Shaping of African American Culture.* New York: Columbia University Press, 2021.

O'Meally, Robert G., ed. *The Jazz Cadence of American Culture.* New York: Columbia University Press, 1998.

O'Neal, Hank. *The Ghosts of Harlem: Sessions with Jazz Legends.* Nashville: Vanderbilt University Press, c. 2009.

Pietila, Antero. *The Ghosts of Johns Hopkins: The Life and Legacy That Shaped an American City.* Lanham, MD: Rowman and Littlefield, 2018.

Pietila, Antero. *Not in My Neighborhood: How Bigotry Shaped a Great American City.* Chicago: Ivan R. Dee, 2010.

Prohaska, Jim. "Irving Mills - Record Producer: The Master and Variety Record Labels." *IAJRC Journal* 30 (Spring 1997): 1–9. iajrc.org/irivng_mills_variety.prf.

Ramsey, Frederic Jr., and Charles Edward Smith, eds. *Jazzmen.* New York: Harcourt, Brace and Co., 1939.

Razaf, Andy. "Passing Years." *Negro History Bulletin.* January 22, 1959.

Reed, Ishmael. "Who Are the Jazz Martyrs?" *Black Renaissance* 14, no. 1 (Spring 2014): 42–48.

Riccardi, Ricky. *Heartful of Rhythm.* New York: Oxford University Press, 2020.

Roach, Max. "What 'Jazz' Means to Me." *Black Scholar* 3, no. 10 (Summer 1972): 2–6. https://www.jstor.org/stable/41206834.

Robinson, Danielle. *Modern Moves: Dancing Race during the Ragtime and Jazz Eras.* New York: Oxford, 2015.

Robinson, Danielle. "'Oh, You Black Bottom!' Appropriation, Authenticity, and Opportunity in the Jazz Dance Teaching of 1920s New York." *Dance Research Journal* 38, no. 1/2 (Summer–Winter, 2006): 19–42. https://www.jstor.org/stable/20444657.

Sandke, Randy. *Where the Dark and the Light Folks Meet: Race and the Mythology, Politics, and Business of Jazz.* Lanham, MD: Rowman & Littlefield, 2014.

Schuller, Gunther. *Early Jazz, Its Roots and Development.* New York: Oxford University Press, 1968.

Schuller, Gunther. *The Swing Era: The Development of Jazz, 1930–1945.* New York: Oxford University Press, 1991.

Shipton, Alyn. *Groovin' High: The Life of Dizzy Gillespie.* New York: Oxford University Press, 1999.

Shipton, Alyn. *Hi-De-Ho: The Life of Cab Calloway.* New York, Oxford University Press, 2010.

Simon, George. *The Big Bands.* 4th ed. New York: Schirmer, 1981.

Skloot, Rebecca. *The Immortal Life of Henrietta Lacks.* New York: Crown, 2010.

Sloan, Naten. "Constructing Cab Calloway: Publicity, Race, and Performance in 1930s Harlem Jazz." *Journal of Musicology* 36, no. 3 (Summer 2019): 370–400. https://doi.org/10.1525/jm.2019.36.3.370.

Smith, Peter Dunbaugh. "Ashley Street Blues: Racial Uplift and the Commodification of Vernacular Performance in Lavilla, Florida, 1896–1916." PhD diss. Florida State University, 2006.

Smith, Willie "The Lion." *Music on My Mind: The Memoirs of an American Pianist.* New York: Doubleday, 1964.

Spencer, Frederick J. *Jazz and Death: Medical Profiles of Jazz Greats.* Jackson: University Press of Mississippi, 2002.

Stearns, Marshall, and Jean Stearns. *Jazz Dance: The Story of American Vernacular Dance.* New York: Da Capo, 1994.

Stewart, Rex. *Boy Meets Horn.* Edited by Claire P. Gordon. Ann Arbor: University of Michigan Press, 1991.

Stowe, David W. *Swing Changes: Big Band Jazz in New Deal America.* Cambridge, MA: Harvard University Press, 1994.

Suisman, David. *Selling Sounds: The Commercial Revolution in American Music.* Cambridge, MA: Harvard University Press, 2009.

Tackley, Catherine. *Benny Goodman's Famous 1938 Carnegie Hall Jazz Concert.* New York: Oxford University Press, 2012.

Teachout, Terry. *Duke: A Life of Duke Ellington.* New York: Gotham Books, 2013.

Thomas, Sarah. "A Message of Inclusion. A History of Exclusion: Racial Injustice at the Peabody Institute." Submitted to the Johns Hopkins University in fulfillment of the Hugh Hawkins Research Fellowship for the Study of Hopkins History. Baltimore, MD, 2019.

Thurman, Wallace. *The Collected Writings of Wallace Thurman: A Harlem Renaissance Reader.* Edited by Amritjit Singh and Daniel M. Scott. New Brunswick, NJ: Rutgers University Press, 2003.

Tick, Judith. *Becoming Ella: The Jazz Singer Who Transformed American Song.* New York: W.W. Norton, 2023.

Tomko, Linda J. *Dancing Class: Gender, Ethnicity, and Social Divides in American Dance, 1890–1920.* Bloomington: Indiana University Press, 1999.

Tucker, Mark, ed. *The Duke Ellington Reader.* New York: Oxford University Press, 1993.

Tucker, Mark. *Ellington: The Early Years.* Urbana and Chicago: University of Illinois Press, 1991.

Vincent, Ted. *Keep Cool: The Black Activists Who Built the Jazz Age.* London: Pluto Press, 1995.

Welburn, Ron. "James Reese Europe and the Infancy of Jazz Criticism." *Black Music Research Journal* 7 (1987): 35–44. https://www.jstor.org/stable/779447.

Welburn, Ron. "Jazz Magazines of the 1930s: An Overview of Their Provocative Journalism." *American Music* 5, no. 3 (Autumn 1987): 255–70. http://www.jstor.com/stable/3051735.

Wells, Christi Jay (aka Wells, Christopher J.). "'Ace of His Race': Paul Whiteman's Early Critical Reception in the Black Press." *Jazz & Culture* 1 (2018): 77–103. https://www.jstor.org/stable/10.5406/jazzculture.1.2018.0077.

Wells, Christi Jay." "'And I Make My Own': Class Performance, Black Urban Identity, and Depression-Era Harlem's Physical Culture." In *Oxford Handbook of Dance and Ethnicity,* edited by Anthony Shay and Barbara Sellers-Young. New York: Oxford University Press, 2016, 1: 17–40.

Wells, Christi Jay. *Between Beats: The Jazz Tradition and Black Vernacular Dance.* New York: Oxford University Press, 2021.

Wells, Christi Jay. *Go Harlem: Chick Webb and His Dancing Audience during the Great Depression.* Chapel Hill: University of North Carolina, 2014.

Wells, Christi Jay. "'Spinnin' the Webb': Representational Spaces, Mythic Narratives, and the 1937 Webb/Goodman Battle of Music." *Journal of the Society for American Music* 14, no. 2 (May 2020): 176–96. https://doi.org/10.1017/S1752196320000061.

Wells, Christi Jay. "Thriving in Crisis: The Chick Webb Orchestra and the Great Depression." Virtual Seminar for the Frankie Manning Foundation. May 30, 2020.

White, Graham, and Shane White. *Stylin': African American Expressive Culture from Its Beginnings to the Zoot Suit*. Ithaca, NY: Cornell University Press, 1998.

Wilkerson, Christopher. *Big Band Jazz in Black West Virginia, 1930–1942*. Jackson: University Press of Mississippi, 2014.

Wilson, James F. *Bulldaggers, Pansies, and Chocolate Babies: Performance, Race, and Sexuality in the Harlem Renaissance*. Ann Arbor: University of Michigan Press, c. 2010.

Wintz, Cary D. *Harlem Speaks: A Living History of the Harlem Renaissance*. New York: Sourcebooks, 2007.

Selected Discography

For detailed discographies see:

The Complete Chick Webb and Ella Fitzgerald Decca Sessions (1934–1941), Mosaic Records, 2013

The Drums of William Chick Webb, Solographer: Jan Evensmo, http://www.jazzarcheol ogy.com/chick-webb/

Johnson, J. Wilfred. *Ella Fitzgerald: An Annotated Discography: Including a Complete Discography of Chick Webb*. Jefferson, NC: McFarland & Company, Inc., 2001.

Tom Lord, *The Jazz Discography,* https://www.lordisco.com

K. B. Rau, *The Harlem Fuss: Investigating Jazz Recordings of the Harlem Era and their Musicians*, http://www.harlem-fuss.com/index.html

CHICK WEBB'S HARLEM STOMPERS, New York, August 25, 1927
Bobby Stark (tp), William R. Paris, Johnny Hodges (as), Elmer Williams (ts), Don Kirkpatrick (p), Benny James (bj), Leon England (tu), Chick Webb (d)
Low levee - high water (unissued - Vocalion - master no longer exists)

CHICK WEBB AND HIS ORCHESTRA, New York, March 1929
Ward Pinkett, Edwin "King" Swayzee (tp), Bennie Morton (tb), Bobby Holmes (cl), Hilton Jefferson (as), Elmer "Tone" Williams (ts), Don Kirkpatrick (p), John Truehart (g), prob. Elmer James or Leon England (tu), Chick Webb (dm)
Film soundtrack for *After Seben* (Paramount, released May 18, 1929)
Sweet Sue; Tiger Rag; I Ain't Got Nobody

THE JUNGLE BAND, New York, June 14, 1929
Ward Pinkett (tp, vo), Edwin Swayzee (tp), Robert Horton (tb), Hilton Jefferson, Joe Garland (as), Elmer Williams (ts), Don Kirkpatrick (p), John Trueheart (bjo), Elmer James (tu), Chick Webb (dm). For Brunswick: Dog Bottom (WP, vo)
New York, June 27, 1929: Same personnel with reeds doubling on (cl), John Trueheart (g)
Jungle Mamma

CHICK WEBB AND HIS ORCHESTRA, New York, March 30, 1931
Shelton Hemphill, Louis Hunt (tp), Louis Bacon (tp, vo), Jimmy Harrison (tb), Benny Carter (cl, as, arr), Hilton Jefferson (cl, as), Elmer Williams (cl, ts), Don Kirkpatrick (p), John Trueheart (g), Elmer James (b, tu), Chick Webb (dm, cel, bells)
For Vocalion: Heebie Jeebies; Blues in My Heart (LB, vo); Soft and Sweet

LOUIS ARMSTRONG AND HIS ORCHESTRA, Camden, NJ, December 8, 1932
Louis Armstrong (tp, vo), Louis Bacon, Louis Hunt, Billy Hicks (tp), Charlie Green (tb), Pete Clark (cl, as), Edgar Sampson (as, vln), Elmer Williams (ts), Don Kirkpatrick (p), John Trueheart (g), Elmer James (b, tu), Chick Webb (dm), Mezz Mezzrow (bells)

For Victor: That's My Home; Hobo, You Can't Ride This Train; I Hate to Leave You Now; You'll Wish You'd Never Been Born

CHICK WEBB'S SAVOY ORCHESTRA, New York, December 20, 1933
Mario Bauza, Reunald Jones (tp), Taft Jordan (tp), Sandy Williams (tb), Pete Clark (as), Edgar Sampson (as, arr), Elmer Williams (ts), Joe Steele (p), John Trueheart (bjo, g), John Kirby (b), Chick Webb (dm)
For Columbia: On the Sunny Side of the Street (TJ, vo)
New York, January 15, 1934, same personnel: If Dreams Come True; Let's Get Together

CHICK WEBB'S SAVOY ORCHESTRA, New York, May 9, 1934
New York, May 18, 1934, Same personnel as December 20, 1933
For Columbia: I Can't Dance (TJ, vo); Stomping at the Savoy
July 6, 1934, Same personnel as December 20, 1933, except Bobby Stark (tp) replaces R. Jones; Fernando Arbello (tb), Wayman Carver (ts, fl), Charles Linton (vo) added.
For Okeh: Blue Minor; True (TJ, vo); Lonesome Moments; If It Ain't Love (CL, vo)

CHICK WEBB AND HIS ORCHESTRA, New York, September 10, 1934
Mario Bauza, Bobby Stark (tp), Taft Jordan (tp, vo), Sandy Williams, Claude Jones (tb), Pete Clark (cl, as), Edgar Sampson (as, arr), Wayman Carver (fl, ts), Elmer Williams (ts), Joe Steele (p), John Trueheart (g), John Kirby (b, tu), Chick Webb (dm)
For Decca: Rhythm Man (TJ, vo); Lona; Blue Minor
New York, November 19, 1934: Same personnel: Don't Be That Way; What a Shuffle; Blue Lou

CHICK WEBB AND HIS ORCHESTRA, New York, June 12, 1935
Mario Bauza, Bobby Stark (tp), Taft Jordan (tp, vo), Claude Jones, Sandy Williams (tb), Pete Clark (as), Edgar Sampson (as, arr), Wayman Carver (fl, ts, arr), Elmer Williams (ts), Joe Steele (p), John Trueheart (g), John Kirby (b), Chick Webb (dm), Ella Fitzgerald (vo), Charles Linton (vo)
For Decca: I'll Chase the Blues Away (EF, vo); Down Home Rag (WC, arr.); Are You Here to Stay? (CL, vo); Love and Kisses (EF, vo)
New York, October 12, 1935
For Decca: Personnel as June 12, 1935, except Bill Thomas (b) replaces John Kirby
Rhythm and Romance (EF, vo); I'll Chase the Blues Away (EF, vo); Facts and Figures

CHICK WEBB AND HIS ORCHESTRA, New York, February 19, 1936
Chick Webb (dm, dir), Mario Bauza, Bobby Stark, Taft Jordan (tp), Sandy Williams, Claude Jones (tb), Pete Clark (cl, as), Edgar Sampson (as, arr), Ted McRae (cl, ts), Wayman Carver (fl, ts), Don Kirkpatrick (p), John Trueheart (g), Bill Thomas (b), Ella Fitzgerald (vo), Charles Linton (vo)
Twelve titles recorded for World Transcriptions, including Go Harlem; Keepin' Out of Mischief Now; King Porter Stomp; Stompin' at the Savoy; Big John Special; Don't Be That Way

CHICK WEBB AND HIS ORCHESTRA, New York, April 7, 1936, Same personnel as February 1936, add Van Alexander, arranger.

For Decca: Crying My Heart Out for You (EF, vo, VA,arr); When I Get Low I Get High (EF, vo, VA, arr)
New York, June 2, 1936, Same personnel as February 1936, except Nat Story (tb) replaces Claude Jones
Go Harlem (ES, arr); Sing Me a Swing Song (EF, vo, VA, arr); A Little Bit Later On (EF, vo, VA)
CHICK WEBB AND HIS ORCHESTRA, New York, October 29, 1936
Mario Bauza, Bobby Stark, Taft Jordan (tp), Sandy Williams, Nat Story (tb), Pete Clark (cl, as, bar), Wayman Carver (fl, ts), Ted McRae (ts), Tommy Fulford (p), John Trueheart (g), Beverly Peer (b), Chick Webb (dm), Ella Fitzgerald (vo), Van Alexander (arr)
For Decca: (Mr. Paganini) You'll Have to Swing It (EF, vo, VA, arr); Swinging on the Reservation (EF, vo, VA, arr); Vote for Mr. Rhythm (EF, vo, VA, arr)

JIMMY MUNDY'S SWING CLUB SEVEN, New York, March 3, 1937
Walter Fuller (tp, vo), Trummy Young (tb), Omer Simeon (cl, as), Jimmy Mundy (ts, arr), Billy Kyle (p), Dick Palmer (g), Quinn Wilson (b), Chick Webb (dm).
For Variety: I Surrender Dear; Ain't Misbehavin'

CHICK WEBB AND HIS ORCHESTRA, New York, March 24, 1937
Mario Bauza, Bobby Stark, Taft Jordan (tp), Sandy Williams, Nat Story (tb), Pete Clark (cl, as, bar), Louis Jordan (as), Wayman Carver (fl, ts), Ted McRae (ts), Tommy Fulford (p), John Trueheart (g), Beverly Peer (b), Chick Webb (dm), Ella Fitzgerald (vo), Van Alexander, Charlie Dixon, Edgar Sampson (arr)
For Decca: Rusty Hinge (LJ, vo, VA, arr); You Showed Me the Way (EF, vo, VA, arr); Clap Hands! Here Comes Charlie! (ES, arr); Cryin' Mood (EF, vo, VA, arr)

THE GOTHAM STOMPERS, New York, March 25, 1937
Cootie Williams (tp), Sandy Williams (tb), Barney Bigard (cl, ts), Johnny Hodges (as), Harry Carney (bar), Tommy Fulford (p), Bernard Addison (g), Billy Taylor (b), Chick Webb (dm), Wayman Carver (arr), Ivie Anderson (vo)
For Variety: My Honey's Lovin' Arms (IA, vo); Did Anyone Ever Tell You? (IA, vo); Alabamy Home; Where Are You? (IA, vo)

CHICK WEBB & HIS LITTLE CHICKS, New York, September 21, 1937
Chauncey Haughton (cl), Wayman Carver (fl, arr.), Tommy Fulford (p), Beverly Peer (b), Chick Webb (dm)
For Decca: In a Little Spanish Town; I Got Rhythm; I Ain't Got Nobody

CHICK WEBB AND HIS ORCHESTRA, New York, October 27, 1937
Personnel as October 29, 1936, except Chauncey Haughton (cl, as), Bobby Johnson (g) replace Clark and Trueheart. Ella Fitzgerald (vo).
For Decca: I Got a Guy (EF, vo, VA, arr); Strictly Jive; Holiday in Harlem (EF, vo)

CHICK WEBB AND HIS ORCHESTRA, November 1, 1937: Personnel as October 27, 1937, add Charlie Dixon, arranger
Rock It for Me (EF, vo, VA, arr); Squeeze Me (CD, arr); Harlem Congo (CD, arr)

CHICK WEBB AND HIS LITTLE CHICKS
Sweet Sue, Just You (WC, arr)

CHICK WEBB AND HIS ORCHESTRA, New York, December 10, 1937. Personnel as
    October 27, 1937, except Garvin Bushell (cl, as) replaces Haughton
Broadcast from the Savoy Ballroom: Bronzeville Stomp; Honeysuckle Rose

CHICK WEBB AND HIS ORCHESTRA, New York, December 17, 1937, same personnel
For Decca: I Want to Be Happy (EF, vo, VA, arr); The Dipsy Doodle (EF, vo, VA, arr);
    Hallelujah! (EF, vo, VA, arr)

ELLA FITZGERALD AND HER SAVOY EIGHT, New York, December 21, 1937
Taft Jordan (tp), Sandy Williams (tb), Louis Jordan (as), Ted McRae (ts, bar), Tommy
    Fulford (p), Bobby Johnson (g), Beverley Peer (b), Chick Webb (dm), Ella Fitzgerald
    (vo), Van Alexander (arr)
For Decca: Bei Mir Bist Do Schön; It's My Turn Now
New York, January 25, 1938: It's Wonderful; I Was Doing All Right

ELLA FITZGERALD AND HER SAVOY EIGHT, New York, May 3, 1938, Personnel as
    December 21, 1937
For Decca: This Time It's Real; What Do You Know About Love?; You Can't Be Mine;
    Saving Myself from You

CHICK WEBB AND HIS ORCHESTRA, New York, May 2 and 3, 1938:
Mario Bauza, Bobby Stark, Taft Jordan (tp), George Matthews, Sandy Williams, Nat Story
    (tb), Pete Clark (cl, as, bar), Garvin Bushell (cl, as), Louis Jordan (as), Ted McRae (ts),
    Wayman Carver (ts), Tommy Fulford (p), Bobby Johnson (g), Beverly Peer (b), Chick
    Webb (dm), Ella Fitzgerald (vo-all)
For Decca: A-Tisket, A-Tasket (EF, vo, VA, arr); I'm Just a Jitterbug (EF, vo, VA, arr);
    Azure; Spinnin' the Webb (WC, arr); Liza (VA, arr)

CHICK WEBB AND HIS ORCHESTRA, New York, June 9, 1938
Personnel as May 2, 1938, except Hilton Jefferson (as) replaces Louis Jordan
For Decca: Pack Up Your Sins and Go to the Devil (EF, vo, VA. arr); Everybody Step (EF,
    vo, VA, arr); Ella (EF, TJ, vo, VA, arr)

SATURDAY NIGHT SWING CLUB ORCHESTRA, New York, August 13, 1938
Big band personnel (from a CBS studio orchestra directed by Leith Stevens) with Roy
    Eldridge (tp—"Liza"), Chick Webb (dm), Ella Fitzgerald (vo—"A-Tisket, A-Tasket").
    Broadcast "Saturday Night Swing Club" from CBS Studios

CHICK WEBB AND HIS ORCHESTRA, New York, August 17/18, 1938, Same personnel
    as June 9, 1938
For Decca: I Can't Stop Lovin' You (EF, vo, VA, arr); Who Ya Hunchin'?; I Let a Tear Fall in
    the River (EF, vo, VA, arr)

ELLA FITZGERALD AND HER SAVOY EIGHT, New York, August 18, 1938
Personnel as May 24, 1937, except Hilton Jefferson (as) replaces Jordan.
For Decca: Woe Is Me (EF, vo)

CHICK WEBB AND HIS ORCHESTRA, New York, October 6, 1938
Personnel as June 9, 1938, except Dick Vance (tp) replaces Bauza. Ella Fitzgerald (vo-all)
For Decca: F. D. R. Jones (DV, arr); I Love Each Move You Make (VA, arr); It's Foxy (WC, arr); I Found My Yellow Basket (VA, arr)

CHICK WEBB AND HIS ORCHESTRA, New York, January 9, 1939, Personnel same/ similar to above
Twelve titles recorded by RCA Victor for NBC Thesaurus transcriptions:
Tea For Two; How Am I to Know?; One O'Clock Jump; Blue Room; Crazy Rhythm; Sugar Foot Stomp; Grand Terrace Rhythm; By Heck; Blue Skies; Dinah; Who Ya' Hunchin'?; Liza

CHICK WEBB AND HIS ORCHESTRA, New York, February 10, 1939, Personnel same as October 6, 1938
NBC broadcast from the Cocoanut Grove at the Hotel Park Central
Let's Get Together (Theme); Blue Room; Deep in a Dream (EF, vo); One O'Clock Jump; That Was My Heart (EF, vo); Everybody Step

CHICK WEBB AND HIS ORCHESTRA, New York, February 17, 1939, Same personnel (EF, vo, VA, arr, on all). For Decca: Undecided; 'Tain't What You Do; One Side of Me
New York, March 2, 1939
Same, except John Trueheart (g) replaces Bobby Johnson. Ella Fitzgerald (vo-all)
Sugar Pie; It's Slumbertime along the Swanee; I'm Up a Tree; Chew Chew Chew Chew

ELLA FITZGERALD AND HER SAVOY EIGHT, New York, March 2, 1939
Personnel as August 18, 1938, except John Trueheart (g) replaces Bobby Johnson.
For Decca: I Had to Live and Learn
New York, April 21, 1939. Same personnel: Don't Worry 'Bout Me; If Anything Happened to You; If You Ever Change Your Mind

CHICK WEBB AND HIS ORCHESTRA, New York, April 21, 1939
Personnel as March 2, 1939. Ella Fitzgerald (vo—all)
Have Mercy (DV, arr); Little White Lies; That Was My Heart

CHICK WEBB AND HIS ORCHESTRA, Boston, May 4, 1939. Personnel same or similar to above. Broadcast from the Southland Cafe
Let's Get Together (Theme); Poor Little Rich Girl; A New Moon and an Old Serenade (EF, vo); Breakin' 'Em Down; If I Didn't Care (EF, vo); The Stars and Stripes Forever; I Never Knew Heaven Could Speak (EF, vo); My Wild Irish Rose

SELECT FILMS
After Seben, Directed by S. Jay Kaufman (Paramount, 1929)
Ella Fitzgerald: Something to Live For, directed by Charlotte Zwerin (for PBS American Masters, 1999). For unedited interviews: https://www.pbs.org/wnet/americanmasters/archive/interviews/505
Ella Fitzgerald: Just One of Those Things, directed by Leslie Woodhead (Eagle Rock Productions, 2019)

Benny Goodman: Adventures in the Kingdom of Swing, directed by Oren Jacoby for PBS American Masters, 1993. For unedited interviews: https://www.pbs.org/wnet/americanmasters/archive/interviews/407

The Savoy King: Chick Webb and the Music That Changed America, directed by Jeff Kaufman (Floating World Pictures, 2012)

Index

For the benefit of digital users, indexed terms that span two pages (e.g., 52–53) may, on occasion, appear on only one of those pages.